A History of Ireland's School Inspectorate, 1831–2008

A History of Ireland's School Inspectorate, 1831–2008

John Coolahan
with Patrick F. O'Donovan

FOUR COURTS PRESS

Set in 10.5 on 12.5 point Ehrhardt for
FOUR COURTS PRESS LTD
7 Malpas Street, Dublin 8, Ireland
e-mail: info@fourcourtspress.ie
http://www.fourcourtspress.ie
and in North America for
FOUR COURTS PRESS
c/o ISBS, 920 N.E. 58th Street, Suite 300, Portland, OR 97213.

A catalogue record for this title
is available from the British Library.

ISBN 978-1-84682-211-7

Printed in England
by MPG Books, Bodmin, Cornwall.

*For the many who served education
and cherished the children
in Ireland*

Contents

5

Tables

Abbreviations

ANCO	An Ceardchomhairle Oiliúna
ASTI	Association of Secondary Teachers of Ireland
BEd	Bachelor of Education
CDVEC	City of Dublin Vocational Educational Committee
CEB	Curriculum and Examinations Board
CNEI	Commissioners of National Education in Ireland
DATI	Department of Agriculture and Technical Instruction
DEIS	Delivering Equality of Opportunity in Schools
DIT	Dublin Institute of Technology
ESLI	Early School Leavers' Initiative
ESRU	Evaluation Support and Research Unit
EUA	European Universities Association
FETAC	Further Education and Training Awards Council
HEA	Higher Education Authority
HETAC	Higher Education and Training Awards Council
ICDU	In-career Development Unit
INTO	Irish National Teachers' Organisation
ISCIP	Integrated Science Curriculum Innovatory Project
ITEA	Irish Technical Education Association
IVEA	Irish Vocational Education Association
LCA	Leaving Certificate Applied
LCVP	Leaving Certificate Vocational Programme
MAC	Management Advisory Committee
NA	National Archives
NCCA	National Council for Curriculum and Assessment
NCEA	National Council for Educational Awards
NCGE	National Council for Guidance in Education
NCSE	National Council for Special Education
NCTE	National Council for Technology in Education
NCVA	National Council for Vocational Awards
NEPS	National Educational Psychological Service
NEWB	National Education Welfare Board
NIHEL	National Institute of Higher Education Limerick
PCSP	Primary Curriculum Support Programme
PIPE	Programme for the Integrated Provision of Education

PMDS	Performance Management Development System
PPDS	Primary Professional Development Service
RTC	Regional Technical College
SDPI	School Development Planning Initiative
SDPS	School Development Planning Service
SEC	State Examinations Commission
SESP	Social and Environmental Studies Programme
SESS	Special Education Support Service
SICI	Standing International Conference of Inspectors
SLSS	Second Level Support Service
SMG	Senior Management Group
SPIRAL	Shannon Project of Interventions for Relevant Adolescent Learning
TIB	Technical Instruction Branch
TMG	Top Management Group
TUI	Teachers Union of Ireland
VEC	Vocational Education Committee
VPTP	Vocational Preparation and Training Programme
WSE	Whole School Evaluation
WSI	Whole School Inspection

A NOTE ON TERMINOLOGY

While the term 'national' was the official designation of the state-supported primary school system, in the interests of clarity the terms 'national' and 'primary' are used interchangeably in this book.

Acknowledgments

The authors wish to express their grateful thanks to those who assisted them in the preparation of this study. A work such as this incurs a debt of gratitude to the many people who have contributed in various ways to the formulation of this history of the inspectorate of the Department of Education and Science. It may be borne in mind that the nature of the study allowed inquiry of just some of those who gave service in the inspectorate or in the Department in recent decades while documentary records are the only source material for the earlier periods.

In particular, we wish to thank the following people who were generous with their time in providing interviews: Pat Burke, John Byrne, John Dennehy, Dennis Healy, Martin Hanevy, Gabriel Harrison, Noel Lindsay, Seán MacCárthaigh, Seán MacGleannáin, Brigid McManus, Jack O'Brien, Dr Fionnbarr Ó Ceallacháin, Gearóid Ó Conluain, Torlach O'Connor, Dr Carl Ó Dálaigh, Seán Ó Donnabháin, Paddy O'Dwyer, Tony Gorman, Dr Liam Ó Maolcatha, Ian Murphy, Pádraig Ó Nualláin, Eamon Stack and Dr Don Thornhill.

Interviews were also given by the following former inspectors all of whom have now passed away but whose insights were of particular value for this work: Dónal Ó Coileáin, Tomás A. Ó Cuilleanáin, Tomás Ó Domhnalláin, Aodán Ó Donnchadha, Con Ó Súilleabháin and Michael Sheridan.

We wish to thank a number of people who provided source documentation and advice helpful for the research: Declan Cahalane, Jim Cooke, Tony Gorman, Michael Kelleher, John McGinty, Dr Carl Ó Dálaigh, Seán Ó Floinn, Liam Ó hÉigearta, Mícheál A. Ó Loingsigh, Dr Liam Ó Maolcatha, Dr Eoghan Ó Súilleabháin (nach maireann) and Dr Barney O'Reilly. Dr Harold Hislop has been of major assistance to the project both in supplying source documentation and in organising the publication process.

We are also grateful to Professor Áine Hyland, Dr Séamus McGuinness and Dr John Nolan who read and commented on a draft of the text.

A Note on Authorship

Very little has hitherto been published on the Irish inspectorate despite its long existence and extensive involvement with the development of the education system. In 2005, I was contacted and asked to design and write a history which would encompass the three branches of the inspectorate. The purpose was to produce an independent, academic study based, as much as possible, on original source material and what other research might be available. In this context, there was an outstanding piece of academic research which has been conducted by Patrick O'Donovan as a PhD student, under my supervision. This dealt with the development of the national school inspectorate from circa 1860 to 1960. I considered it appropriate to invite Dr O'Donovan to contribute material from his research to this study. The assistance was readily given and the general text also benefited from discussions we had on various aspects of the work. While gratefully acknowledging this assistance, as overall author I take full responsibility for the academic independence and accuracy of the study.

JOHN COOLAHAN

Preface

In view of the significant role played by the school inspectorate in the development of the Irish education system, it is surprising that no history of its contribution has hitherto been published. Apart from Eustás Ó Héideáin's monograph (1967) on the early years of the primary inspectorate very little scholarly research on the work of the inspectorate is available, although a few autobiographies of inspectors do exist. Pre-dating the establishment of inspectorates in England and Scotland, the Irish school inspectorate has had a long and intimate involvement with the school system. This book which focuses on the main stages of development of the three branches of the inspectorate for Irish schools – national (primary), vocational and secondary, aims to fill this significant gap in the history of Irish education.

The three branches are now unified as a single inspectorate, which has been significantly restructured in recent years. However, they originated and developed in quite different ways. By far the oldest is the national school inspectorate, with its origins in the Stanley letter of 1831, the year that the national school system was established. Many generations of Irish people obtained all their formal education within the national system, in the development of which, the inspectorate played a major part. The inspectors fulfilled many roles within the system and were key link persons between the central educational authority and the individual schools. The technical inspection branch emerged at the turn of the twentieth century, following the establishment of the Department of Agriculture and Technical Instruction (DATI) in 1900. When the Vocational Education Act of 1930 was passed the role of this branch of the inspectorate became more extensive. In later decades their work also related to the tertiary education sector. The secondary school inspectorate was established on a permanent basis in 1909. It carried out inspection duties in the voluntary secondary school sector, and assumed major responsibilities for the State Examinations, instituted following political independence in 1922. Up to 1922 the inspectorate related to all the schools on the island. Following independence, new political and educational priorities had a big influence on the culture of the inspectors as they engaged with the school system of the Irish Free State (later Republic of Ireland).

A study of the work of the inspectorate provides illuminating insights into school conditions, pedagogical approaches, curricular implementation, assessment issues and the general progress of the schooling enterprise. As a notable public service agency, part of the civil service, which operated according to distinctive regulations and conventions and established its own traditions and sub-cultures, the inspectorate merits in-depth examination and appraisal. Through such examination of the training, roles, mode of operation and career pattern of the inspectorate much can be revealed about emerging concepts of education, of ideas on teaching and of evaluation of standards of pupil learning, all of which enrich our knowledge of the developing Irish school system. The work and functioning of the inspectorate also provide important insights to the administrative history of the education system and of the social history of Ireland. The research involved has also thrown new light on aspects of educational policy formulation. The living, working and travelling conditions of many inspectors were frequently demanding as they sought to improve educational provision in schools scattered throughout the country. In general, their work ethic was strong and accountability tended to be rigorous. They benefited from good social status and emoluments, but the work was arduous and, in the case of the national school inspectorate, frequently conducted in considerable professional isolation.

This book locates the work of the inspectorate within the changing political, social, economic, educational and administrative contexts of Irish society at the different stages of its development. The impact of all major reports and policy landmarks on the inspectorate is analysed. As an administrative history, it eschews much of the anecdotal material, whose inclusion would have made the book unwieldy. While throwing light on the work of the administrative agencies to which inspectors reported pre-1922, and of the Department of Education, following its establishment in 1924, there are many aspects of the work of such bodies which are not encompassed by this study, and which merit further research. The contributions of the schools' inspectorate are embedded in the concepts of their role, their conditions of work, regulations, spread of activities, career framework, professional inputs, and so on. The role of the inspectorate became very diversified for a period and its personnel, which became depleted over the years, were challenged to fulfil the extensive expectations placed upon them. Now that a re-structured, unified inspectorate is at the early stages in a new era of educational change, it is timely for the self-understanding of the inspectorate profession that a study be made available of the key stages of its past development.

As the history of the national school inspectorate is the oldest of the three branches, and has had the most extensive engagement with the greatest number of schools, its component of the overall inspectorate story looms largest. The traditions of the two post-primary branches evolved very differently from each other and the contrasting subcultures are quite fascinating. Up until the mid-sixties their staff numbers were small, but they established their own *esprit de corps*, which did not favour integration. This study draws heavily on original documentary sources. However, Irish educational archive material is less well preserved than historians would wish. Accordingly, it was a privilege and a pleasure for the authors to interview a large number of inspectors, many of them enjoying long lives in retirement. We consider that their 'memoire collective' greatly enriches the source data on the culture of the Irish school inspectorate.

A list of all those who served in Ireland's school inspectorate, in so far as the names can be established, is included in the Appendices.

Foundation and Early Decades of the Inspectorate

The story of the Irish school inspectorate is an interesting and complex one, with its roots deep in the early nineteenth century. The Irish national school system, which is now the primary school provision for over 95% of the age group was, on its establishment in 1831, an innovative and experimental initiative in the socio-economic, religious and political circumstances of the Ireland of that time.[1] As early as 1832, a state school inspectorate system was inaugurated. This built on the precedent of school inspection instituted in 1818 by the state supported voluntary education agency, the Society for the Promotion of the Education of the Poor of Ireland (Kildare Place Society).

The Society's inspectors performed their extensive duties according to a formal set of regulations drawn up by the Inspection Sub-Committee of the Society.[2] It is noteworthy that the Benthamite concept of human motivation being driven by hope of reward or fear of punishment underlay the inspection plan as it was considered necessary to check on masters 'whose exertions will be found to relax when not upheld by a sense of duty, a dread of reprehension or by hope of reward.'[3] It is also interesting to note that, from the first, the conception of the inspectors' status was that of 'gentlemen of education and character', so as to fulfil their multifaceted roles. Their salaries were pitched at levels about ten times more than teachers' remuneration. From the beginning, inspectors were expected to provide detailed reports, on printed forms, on their visitations to schools, and to make observations on associated responsibilities.

While the Kildare Place Society had aimed at supporting school provision that would be open to all denominations, its requirement that the scriptures be read in schools 'without note or comment' proved to be unacceptable to Catholics. This, allied to evidence that the Society gave funds to schools that also received grants from overtly proselytising agencies, increasingly undermined Catholic confidence in this approach. From the early 1820s, Catholic

1 Donald H. Akenson, *The Irish Education Experiment: The National System of Education in Nineteenth Century Ireland* (London: Routledge and Kegan Paul, 1970). 2 H. Kingsmill Moore, *An Unwritten Chapter in the History of Education (Kildare Place Society), 1811–1831* (London: Macmillan, 1904), pp 306–36. 3 Quoted in Eustas Ó Heideáin, *National School Inspection in Ireland. The Beginnings* (Dublin: Scepter, 1967), p. 14.

authorities pressed the government to adopt a new method of state support for primary education, other than subventing the Kildare Place Society. A Commission of Inquiry was set up in 1824 which issued nine reports.

This was followed by a Parliamentary Committee set up in March 1828 to review the sequence of reports which had been prepared on Irish education and to point a way forward. It produced its short, well-focussed report in May 1828.[4] The Committee urged the setting up of a new government board which would support and supervise a new system of multi-denominational education in Ireland on the principle of non-interference with the specific denominational beliefs of participants. Children would be together for combined literary and moral instruction, with separate provision for specific denominational instruction, under the exclusive superintendence of the clergy of the respective denominations. The achievement of Catholic Emancipation in 1829 was a landmark in the development of Catholic rights as citizens. Furthermore, the formation of a Whig cabinet in 1830 changed the political climate. Following much pressure from Irish MPs such as Thomas Spring-Rice and Thomas Wyse, Lord Stanley, chief secretary for Ireland, took the initiative in parliament in September 1831 of indicating a change in government policy. This change was developed in the so-called Stanley letter of October 1831, which became the foundation document of the new Irish national school system. This involved the establishment of a new government-appointed, mixed denominational board to superintend a system of national education.

Despite difficult political and religious circumstances of the time, the Commissioners of National Education of Ireland (CNEI) got to work efficiently and effectively in establishing the national school system.[5] The CNEI held their first meeting on 1 December 1831, and appointed Thomas F. Kelly to be secretary to the Board. Shortly after, one of the Commissioners, Revd. James Carlile was appointed as Resident Commissioner, a fulltime roll. These two men headed up the administrative staff of the National Board. The Board's first offices were in Merrion Street but, in 1834, Tyrone House in Marlborough Street, with four adjacent acres, was purchased and, from 1836, became the Board's headquarters. The Board got regulations and application forms for aid drawn up very quickly, in December 1831, and roll books and other school desiderata were designed. The Board quickly got to work in publishing school textbooks, school slates, blackboards, maps, stationery and such requisites. Three model schools – male, female and infants – were set up on the Marlborough Street site, as well as a male training college. In 1838 a model farm was established in Glasnevin, and in 1842 a training college for women was set up, linked to the Marlborough site and facing Talbot Street.

4 *Report from the Select Committee to which the Reports on the Subject of Education were referred* (HC 1828 (341), iv).   5 John Coolahan, 'The Daring First Decade of the National Board', *The Irish Journal of Education*, 1983, xviii, 1, pp 35–54.

The Board issued its first annual report in 1834, a practice continued until the Board's abolition in 1922. The work of the administrative staff grew as the system rapidly expanded. When inspectors were appointed, they were viewed mainly as 'field staff' who would relate to the national schools throughout the country, although senior inspectors came to exercise an administrative role.

The Board adopted the principle of the 1828 report of a combined literary and a separate religious education for pupils. Among its many directions for the operation of the system, the letter stated: 'They (board members) will at various times, either by themselves or by their inspectors, visit and examine into the state of each school, and report their observations to the board.'[6] Thus, from the outset, an inspection process was envisaged to ensure the implementation of regulations. It was the accepted wisdom of the day that a state supported education system should include a formal inspectorial dimension to ensure that regulations were fulfilled and that teachers were accountable for their performance. In the context of the religious sensitivities in the Ireland of that time, the inspectors would help to uphold the foundation principle of the new system and act as guarantors against proselytism in the schools.

The Commissioners of National Education held their first meeting on 1 December 1831. At their meeting, the following April, the issue of organising an inspectorate was raised and it was agreed that a copy of the Kildare Place Society's instructions to inspectors should be sought. A comparative analysis of the Board's 'General Principles of the System of Education to be Attended to by the Inspectors',[7] with the Kildare Place Society code of instructions for inspectors clearly establishes that the Board relied very heavily on the Society's model, both in content and vocabulary. The only relevant differences were that, unlike the Society's instructions, the Commissioners ordered inspectors not to give advance notice of their visits, 'but rather endeavour to arrive with each (school) when he is not expected.' Furthermore, when in Dublin, national school inspectors were expected to attend the model school, or any other school that may be pointed out to them and were expected, 'unless other duties prevent them, to call at the office every day', whereas, the Society's inspectors were less restricted in this regard.

The National Board's instructions to inspectors reflected a comprehensive concept of their role. These instructions were first issued in 1836, four years before such instructions were issued in England. Inspectors were allocated a list of schools by the Board, to be visited 'in such order as may seem most convenient'. They were to investigate whether grants provided by the Board had been properly applied. They were expected to have communication with the conductors or patrons of the schools visited. Each inspector was to make

6 Text of Stanley Letter in Áine Hyland and Kenneth Milne (eds), *Irish Educational Documents*, vol. 1 (Dublin: CICE, 1987), pp 98–103.   7 Ibid., pp 114–18.

inquiry respecting the general state of education in every neighbourhood that he visited. Inspectors were to avoid being drawn into political or theological discussions. During every circuit they were to inform the Board's secretary of the progress of their itinerary and were to call at every post-office on their route for letters.

To equip themselves for the work, inspectors were to make themselves masters of the system of education being promoted by the Board 'in its fundamental principles'. In the actual conduct of in-school inspection, inspectors were required to introduce themselves to the teachers and examine whether the regulations of the Board were being complied with. The mode of teaching was to be observed, and appropriate suggestions made for improvement, where necessary. Very strikingly, inspectors were to relate courteously to teachers in the following manner:

> In all his intercourse with teachers, he will treat them with the most perfect kindness and respect appraising them privately of what he may see defective, and noting it to be reported to the Board, but by no means addressing them authoritatively or animadverting on their conduct in the hearing of their scholars.[8]

Inspectors were to ascertain the educational proficiency of pupils, with a special emphasis on the 3Rs. They were also to scrutinise the roll and register of pupil attendance and use the most effective means for establishing the number of children 'really in attendance at the school'. As well as their academic performance, inspectors were also expected to observe the behaviour of pupils, as well as their general appearance and cleanliness. The two guiding principles of order, which were to have a long life with the national system, were iterated: 'A place for everything and everything in its place and a time for everything and everything in its time.'

At the close of each tour of inspection, the inspector was to send a general report to the Board's secretary on the state of education in the districts visited, suggesting whatever improvements he wished to make. Thus, it is quite clear that the inspector was envisaged as filling a crucial role between the central Board and the local management and its school. He was the eyes and ears of the Board, promoting its objectives, evaluating progress, gathering information, ensuring implementation of regulations and reporting back on a regular basis. However, inspectors were specifically alerted to the fact that as the Commissioners did not directly control any school, other than a model school, 'inspectors will therefore, not give direct orders, as on the part of the Board, respecting any necessary regulations, but point out such regulations to the conductors of the school, that they may give the requisite orders.'[9]

8 Ibid., p. 117.

The instructions to inspectors were re-formulated in 1842, as thirteen statements which differ in tone from the 1836 formulation and which were more specific in their demands on the inspectors. They were now expected to inspect each school 'at least three times in each year'. They were to examine the Visitors' Book and send a report on every significant observation made therein to the Commissioners. Each inspector was to record the date of his visit and the precise time his visit commenced and ended. He was to report on the result of each visit following an examination of all the classes, 'in their different branches of study'. The inspector was to examine the class rolls, register and daily report book. He was to receive a monthly report from the teacher of each school, and to submit a quarterly report to the Commissioners, in addition to his ordinary report after each school visit.[10] Thus, a more intense investigatory and more detailed reportage role emerged, without a great deal of trust implied on the data recorded by teachers. This formulation of the instructions for inspection was not re-issued until 1855, when it was re-cast again in an even more detailed format. However, by then, other developments in the system led to a more extensive work-load on the inspectorate.

STAFFING AND ORGANISATION OF THE EARLY INSPECTORATE

The National Board at its meeting on 5 May 1832 decided to appoint four inspectors, at a yearly salary of £250 each, this sum to include 'all charges and travelling expenses'. Applications were sought and fourteen candidates were short-listed for interview from thirty-eight submissions. It is noteworthy of the serious approach taken by the Commissioners at that time, that they interviewed the candidates individually. The four candidates selected were Messers Sullivan, Murray, Hamill and Robertson – two Catholics and two Protestants. Each was assigned the schools of a province – Sullivan in Ulster; Murray in Leinster, Hamill in Munster and Robertson in Connaught.[11]

The two Catholic inspectors did not remain long on the inspection staff. Murray was dismissed in February 1834 for infringing the Board's rules by publishing a political pamphlet on Repeal, while Hamill resigned in September 1834. Robertson continued in the service of the Board until he retired as a head inspector in 1847. Sullivan left the inspectorate in 1839 to become one of the professors in the Teacher Training College, established in 1838 by the Commissioners. It became quickly apparent that the four first inspectors of the National School system faced a daunting task, as applications for affiliation with the National Board expanded rapidly. In August 1833, four 'temporary' inspectors were added. At that time, each inspector had about

9 Ibid., p. 115   10 *Ninth Report of the Commissioners of National Education in Ireland* (CNEI) *for 1842*, Appendix 4.   11 Minutes of the CNEI, 14 June 1832.

100 schools to report on, as well as investigating applications for financial assistance from the Board by other schools.

As early as 1834, the Commissioners had presented the Irish government with a proposal to divide the country into school districts, each under an inspector. In their report for 1837 they envisaged the establishment of twenty-five school districts, each with an inspector.[12] This plan was implemented in 1838, with the inspectors being given the new name of 'superintendents', which was changed back to 'inspectors' after a few years. Salaries were re-structured in relation to the new system. Since 1833, an inspector received £300 per year. This was now changed to £125 per year, with a lodging allowance of £30 and 5 shillings per day if obliged to travel more than twenty miles from the centre. In 1840, this was again altered to £200 per year, with no allowances. That the posts were highly attractive is evidenced by the fact that there were 600 applicants for the new positions created in 1838.[13] Perhaps, because of the workload involved, inspectors appointed after 1838 were appointed on the basis of quality of the application and testimonials and were not subject to interview or examination. Retired head inspector Kavanagh, in *The Catholic Case Stated* (1859), maintained that this process gave rise to undesirable appointment by patronage, with some inspectors being unqualified and unsuited to the job. Some were recruited from occupations in which they had no connection with education.[14] In 1860, the mode of appointment of inspectors was altered after the Civil Service Commission came into being and competitive examinations were deemed necessary for appointment to public positions. The Board drew up an examination framework for candidates for the inspectorate. It is interesting to note the range of subjects and the marks allocated to each. The compulsory subjects were: English (2000 marks); elementary mathematics (1,700) geography (500); political science (600); logic (300); political economy (300); book-keeping (200). The optional subjects comprised the language, literature and history of France, or Germany, or Italy (400); advanced logic (400); history and philosophy of education (400); advanced political economy (400); higher mathematics (600); and natural science (1,300). In view of the nature of the position it is noteworthy that 'the history and philosophy of education' was only an optional subject, attracting the relatively low level of 400 marks. Applicants had to be in the age range 23–38, and to be of good health and character. Those successful at the examination were required to be vetted at the Board's inspection office and at the schools in Marlborough Street where, through their conduct and performance on tests, an evaluation would be made of their suitability for the position. This more rigorous approach to selection for the inspectorate is likely to have improved the calibre of those appointed.

12 *Fourth Report of the CNEI for 1837*, pp 3–4.   13 A Catholic Layman (James Kavanagh), *Mixed Education: The Catholic Case Stated* (Dublin: Mullany, 1859), p. 322.   14 Ibid., pp 322–27.

Bearing in mind the denominational balance of the population with the great majority being Catholic, it is revealing that through the early decades those adhering to Protestant religions formed a majority within the inspectorate. According to Kavanagh in 1859 of a total of 70 inspectors, 37 were Protestants and 33 were Catholic, with Presbyterians the largest category among the Protestants. At that time, Catholic pupils numbered 486,426, while Protestant pupils only amounted to 80,888. Kavanagh also held that non-Catholics were more favoured for the senior positions and were allocated more favourable districts.[15]

As the national school system expanded, the number of inspectors also increased, but the ratio of schools under the jurisdiction of each inspector remained fairly consistent at about 100 schools per inspector. The deployment of inspectors through the various districts tended towards occupational isolation as the inspector strove to fulfil his duties regarding the schools and associated matters. As well as the ordinary national schools, the Board had responsibilities regarding other categories of school which were established. These included model schools, agriculture schools, workhouse schools, industrial schools, and schools associated with prisons. The careful planning of inspectorial routes and itineraries was subject to disruption due to such occurrences as very bad weather, sickness epidemics, and travel difficulties. The inspector was advised not to omit visiting a school on hearing reports that it was closed; he was to proceed and check it out for himself. While the railway system was initiated in Ireland in 1834, it took many years for a national rail-network to become established. Even then, inspectors were instructed not to travel third class, as being beneath their status. In any case, the rural location of many small national schools meant that travel by rail was not possible for much of the work. While not forbidden to arrive on foot, it was regarded as more becoming to an inspector to arrive on horseback, by horse and trap, or by Bianconi car. Inspectors usually had to maintain a horse or have ready access to one. There were three categories of inspectorial visits – special, ordinary, and incidental; the ordinary and incidental being the most common. It is on record that some inspectors displayed considerable ingenuity in fulfilling the Board's admonition of arriving at schools unexpectedly. Securing satisfactory accommodation when on inspectorate duties also posed problems on occasion. Despite difficulties, the foundations for a national school inspection system were being well laid. As well as receiving their written reports, the Commissioners decided to call all their inspectors to Dublin at the end of 1838 and 1839 for individual oral reports on progress:

> We called our several inspectors to Dublin in December last, and examined them, not only as to the efficiency of the national schools

---

15 Ibid.

in their respective districts, but also as to the feelings of the people towards them; and the accounts they gave us as to both were highly satisfactory.[16]

As the number of schools expanded adjustments were made in the deployment of inspectors. The number of school districts was raised to 32 in 1844, and to 34 in 1846.

In July 1845, Thomas J. Robertson was appointed as the first head inspector, with three others promoted to this position in 1846. The head inspectors were charged with over-seeing the administration of the inspectorial service, examining special cases or complaints, and advising upon all aspects of the developing national school system. They operated 'out on the field', and were not located at headquarters. Each had about eight or nine district inspectors under his supervision. In 1847, a category known as subinspectors was introduced, initially as assistants to inspectors, at a lower salary and usually drawn from teachers who had distinguished themselves. The Board now referred to 'a chain of promotion', with three categories: subinspectors, district inspectors and head inspectors.

Soon after the establishment of the Board of National Education, it was found necessary to appoint one commissioner, the Revd James Carlile, as Resident Commissioner to be effectively the executive head of the national school system. He was succeeded in 1839 by Alexander Macdonnell who occupied the position until 1871. As time went by the Commissioners employed a staff of clerks to carry out the various duties associated with the administration of the system. In time, the most senior officers of the Board were the Secretaries two of whom were maintained, one Catholic and one Protestant, with a view to preserving a denominational balance in the affairs of the administration. Though the national school system was not given a statutory basis, Royal Charters of Incorporation were granted by Queen Victoria in 1845 and 1861. The later charter set the number of commissioners at twenty with the understanding that ten would be Catholic and ten Protestant. A similar denominational balance was set for the appointment of inspectors and throughout the years under the National Board, all the appointments and promotions of inspectors had to preserve the dual arrangement.

EXPANDED WORKLOAD OF THE INSPECTORATE

New policy initiatives regarding teachers also meant an extension of the role of the inspectorate. In 1846, the Commissioners expanded the scheme of paid monitors from model schools whereby bright pupils from national schools, aged between fourteen and sixteen, could compete for monitorships. Acting

16 *Eight Report of the CNEI for 1841*, p. 4.

as apprentice teachers and taking a sequence of monitors' examinations they could qualify as teachers. The aspirant monitors were to be selected by examinations conducted by the district inspectors. The Board laid out the elements for the examination of candidates and also, the 'Programme of Examination and Course of Study for Paid Monitors' for each year of a four-year programme. The examinations involved the mastery of designated course content and also the demonstration by the monitors of practical teaching skills, on a graded level of difficulty from first to fourth year.[17]

Work also expanded in the forms of reportage to be submitted by the inspectors on a range of issues. Some of this related to reports on the work of schools, others to applications for aid towards buildings, or for teachers' salary. Originally these queries were sent to the personnel involved seeking the aid at local level but 'having found it difficult to get full and satisfactory answers to the queries' from this source, the Commissioners put the onus on the inspectors to inquire and report on the applications. The forms were extensive requiring, in the case of applications for building aid, answers to 27 queries, and, in the form for teachers' salaries, a total of 46 queries.[18]

A number of other formal report forms relate to the more direct work of the inspectors, such as District Inspector's report on Ordinary National Schools, Head Inspector's Report on Ordinary National Schools, District Inspector's Report on District Model Schools. The District Inspector's Report form for Ordinary National Schools was a remarkably detailed document inquiring about every aspect of the school and its operation. The introductory part sought a lot of specific factual data on the location of the school, attendance of pupils at all the sub-sets of the curriculum, the arrangements for religious instruction, and so on. The main part of the report comprised 21 sections, with about 75 questions to be answered. The remarkable detail of these documents was a tribute to the thoroughness of the bureaucratic mind, but it could also be regarded as undermining their usefulness in terms of over-reporting on schools the number of which had expanded to 5,408 by 1858. The distillation and utilisation of this mass of data were daunting tasks for the central office.

Another development which caused a major amount of work to inspectors was the new mode of classifying teachers which became operative in 1848. In 1839, teachers were organised into three categories, 1st, 2nd and 3rd for males and females separately; 1st class male teachers were allocated £20 salary; 2nd class £15 and 3rd class £12. The corresponding scales for females were £15, £12 and £10. The Commissioners declared:

> Examinations will be held from time to time by Superintendents (Inspectors), with a view of raising meritorious teachers to a higher class, or of depressing others who may have conducted themselves

17 *Fifteenth Report of the CNEI for 1848*, pp 208–10.   18 *Ninth Report of the CNEI for 1842*, pp 37–41.

improperly, or whose schools have declined in consequence of their inattention.[19]

However, no specific detail was given on the nature of these 'examinations'. This greatly changed in 1848. A new classification scheme was devised as in Table 1.1:

Table 1.1: Salary structure for national teachers, 1848			
		Males	*Females*
First Class	1st Division	£30	£24
	2nd Division	£25	£20
	3rd Division	£22	£18
Second Class	1st Division	£20	£15
	2nd Division	£18	£14
Third Class	1st Division	£16	£13
	2nd Division	£14	£12

Source: 15th Report of the CNEI for 1848, Appendix xxvi, p. 58.

This classification also reflects the bureaucratic mind in its gradations and small variations of award within the grades. Teachers were now to be classified following detailed oral and written examination. In 1848, all male teachers in the country were so examined and classified, except for the absentees who did not appear for the examinations. Female teachers were examined in 1849. The examinations were conducted by the four head inspectors, with the assistance of the district inspectors in their region. Each of the four head inspectors provided detailed accounts of the process. There is a good deal of commonality in their reports and they are revealing of the systematised approach taken. The time taken up by three of the head inspectors stretched, roughly, from early March to late October in 1848. A variety of district localities in each province was selected in the interests of not imposing undue travel demands on attending teachers. Teachers attended at these centres for two full days of examination, at their own expense. The first day was devoted to written papers in the following subjects – grammar; geography; money matters; arithmetic and algebra; geometry and mensuration, and natural philosophy. The second day was devoted to oral examination. Detailed reportage was recorded for each teacher in both written and oral examinations. These marks were considered in association with the gradings by the district inspectors of the teachers' schools in terms of methods of teaching; discipline;

19 *Seventh Report of the CNEI for 1840*, p. 6.

cleanliness; extent of instruction; proficiency of junior classes; and proficiency of senior classes. The questions for the written examinations were devised by the head inspectors, and an analysis of them indicates that they were of a demanding standard.[20] The inspectorate carried out the herculean task of examining the written scripts, and calculating the oral marks for each of the 2,284 teachers involved within a short period. Arising from the examinations adjustments were made in the teacher classifications which involved lowering as well as improving the existing gradings. About 90 teachers were dismissed following the process, many of whom were probationary teachers.

A NOTABLE INSPECTOR

One of the personalities who emerged in the 1850s to play a remarkable role in the inspectorate, and in nineteenth-century Irish education, was Patrick J. Keenan, and it is informative to outline the nature of his influence, which is evident also in subsequent chapters. The career of Patrick Joseph Keenan is of particular importance in gaining insight into the affairs of national education in nineteenth-century Ireland. Pre-eminent among the inspectors of the period, Keenan was a figure of considerable power and influence and one who had profound effects on education in the Ireland of his time.

Born in County Meath, Keenan attended Ratoath National School. Having served as a monitor and an assistant teacher for a period, he was appointed, in 1845, as headmaster of the Central Male Model School in Marlborough Street. In 1848, he became a district inspector but, within a few months, he was reappointed to the Central Model School. A few years later, he was acting as assistant to the professors in the training college in Marlborough Street. His service under the National Board was given prominent recognition by his elevation, in 1855, to the position of head inspector when only twenty-nine years of age. His rapid rise to prominence may be accounted for by the contribution he made to a scheme for organising schools. First mooted in the early 1850s, this was an attempt to organise the teaching in new schools and improve the arrangements of schools already established and was directed mainly towards the enhancement of work within the schools. Keenan gave a preparatory course of instruction and practical training to organisers, described by P.W. Joyce as

> a series of lectures on the science and practice of school management, including, among a variety of subjects, a detailed description of the systems of organisations best suited to the National schools of Ireland.[21]

Joyce attended Keenan's lectures as an organiser and later became a professor in the training college and a distinguished scholar. He wrote that his

20 *Fifteenth Report of the CNEI for 1848*, pp 117–81. 21 P.W. Joyce, *A Handbook of School Management and Methods of Teaching* (Dublin: Gill, 1892 ed.), preface to first edition, 1863.

Handbook on School Management originated in the course given by Keenan in 1856. Joyce's manual was a compendium of teaching methods and school arrangements with detailed instructions covering all aspects of furnishings, apparatus, timetables, lessons and guides for successful teaching. Many editions of this manual were published and for a long time it was the major sourcebook for teachers under the national system.

Keenan's annual reports of the later 1850s mark him off from his fellow inspectors and reveal him to been a man of considered views and a capable official in the service of the Commissioners. He thought deeply about effective teaching and he was assiduously attentive to the details of school administration. Despite his limited formal education, Keenan was clearly possessed of exceptional self-confidence in dealing with the affairs of national education. Not alone did his growing up coincide with the growth of the national system but he, more than most, was thoroughly acquainted with the practical business of classroom practice. He evinced great interest in the details of effective classroom work and was notably precocious in advancing suggestions for improvements in the system. He seems to have had an almost uncanny sense of timing with regard to what was needed to bring about useful change. For example, in his report for 1855, Keenan strongly recommended that the Commissioners have a headline printed in each page of their copybooks so that teachers would be saved trouble and so that 'one uniform style of good writing' would be achieved. In this, he prefigured the development of the celebrated Vere Foster copybooks, a feature of the schools for decades.

Keenan was fortunate enough to emerge unscathed from the 'round robin' incident of 1856 when the head inspectors protested against the actions of Mr McCreedy as Chief of Inspection. Keenan was himself appointed as a second Chief in April 1859. This ensured that he was to play an important role in the affairs of national education throughout the 1860s. There is reason to believe that Alexander Macdonnell, the ageing and long-time Resident Commissioner, relied heavily on Keenan's comprehensive knowledge of the school system for the transaction of the administration business of the Commissioners. In December 1871, Keenan was nominated by the government to be Macdonnell's successor as Resident Commissioner. Fortune smiled on Keenan in this appointment, as in his appointment as Chief of Inspection, since he happened to be ideally placed at the moment when circumstances ordained that the government should appoint a Catholic to the most senior position in Marlborough Street.

A BACKWARD LOOK

Reflecting back on the early decades of the National Board a number of striking features emerge. The establishment of the national school system involved a significant intrusion into the prevailing socio-economic ideology of laissez-faire capitalism. At one level, the system could be viewed as having a 'bottom-up' dimension in that the initiative for establishing schools, or seeking the Board's aid for existing schools, was a local one. Yet, the rules and regulations devised by the Board were such that, under the lord lieutenant and parliament, it exercised a strong central control, which was not achieved in England until 1870 or in France until 1881. The powers exercised by the Board gave a very 'top-down' character to the system, as it evolved. Bearing in mind that members of the Board were unpaid, and all of them had important other duties, and that the denominational and political context in which they operated was fraught with animosities, the speed and efficiency with which they established the system was remarkable. One of their members, the Revd James Carlile was given the full-time post of Resident Commissioner. The Board quickly acquired impressive premises in Marlborough Street, set up administrative arrangements, drew up forms for applications for aid, established a central model school and training colleges for teachers, acquired the Glasnevin Model Farm and Garden, published an impressive range of textbooks and school requisites and arranged for their dissemination. They also drew up a radical ten-year plan for development in 1835, not all of which was fulfilled. The early Commissioners gave evidence of both vision and practical efficiency.

Yet, apart from the training colleges and the model schools, which were established by them and under their direct management, the Commissioners operated at a remove from the ordinary national schools, which were only supported, not owned or managed by them. The mode of exercising a controlling influence was by means of rules and regulations, which became more detailed over the years. The key agency to see that the regulations were implemented at local level was the inspectorate. However, school inspection in the sense of evaluating the education work in the schools was but a part of the many-sided role the inspectors fulfilled. They were the key liaison personnel between the Board and the managers and patrons of schools. In particular, they were charged with investigating whether the rules on religious teaching were observed. On the detailed forms, discussed above, they were to inquire into many features of the applications for aid, and teacher gratuities. They also needed to check on buildings and facilities which were aided by the Board. Furthermore, they were expected to inform themselves on the general character of education and of the attitudes of the population towards it in their districts. They had to investigate complaints and, sometimes, carry out special inquiries on behalf of the Board. They became responsible for the conduct of the individual examinations of monitors and teachers.

The inspectorate exercised significant influence on the gratuities being paid to teachers and on their promotion, demotion, or dismissal in the classification grade. This gave them intimate power over the teachers. When this was coupled with the strong policing and investigating role regarding pupil attendance, school roll records, days of school holidays and so on, a pattern of relationship evolved whereby the inspector tended to be dreaded by many teachers because of the authoritative role with which he was empowered. Inspectors were discouraged from being familiar with teachers, and the gap in social status also emphasised this.

However, this strong, top-down, regulatory, investigatory system fostered by the Board also had an invidious impact on the inspectors. The extent of the reportage they were required to undertake was an enormous burden, which must have been particularly irksome when they realised some of it went unread. The head inspectors had strong investigative powers over the district inspectors, and were expected to check their entries in school observation books. All inspectors had heavy workloads and they had to account in detail for how they spent their time. The early decades had witnessed a striking growth in the national school system and the successful implementation of many administrative and procedural matters. The inspectorate played a huge role in helping to lay the foundations of the system. However, the character and atmosphere of the system which evolved could be characterised as rigid and over-bureaucratic, with little or no emphasis on the joy and satisfaction which pupils, teachers and inspectors should draw from a teaching-learning process.

2

The Development of the Inspectorate, 1855–72

RESTRUCTURING OF THE INSPECTORATE

Irish inspectors resented the fact that the salaries of school inspectors in England were higher than what they obtained, though they considered that their conditions of work were more arduous. It is interesting to note the different tradition of inspection at the time in England and Scotland to that which had evolved in Ireland. The framework and internal dynamics of education in Britain prior to the legislative action of the 1870s determined that inspection there had quite a different genealogy. The emphasis on limited but benevolent state action in aid of local and voluntary effort ensured that inspection in both England and Scotland developed along divergent lines and with traditions dissimilar to Ireland.

The most remarkable difference in the conception of school inspection in England is evident in the instructions prepared by Sir James Kay-Shuttleworth and issued in 1840 by the Committee of the Privy Council on Education. These instructions established the pattern followed by the English inspectorate at least until the Revised Code of 1862, and in some respects, until a much later date.[1] The keynote of the instructions is found in Kay's enlightened explanatory letter to inspectors:

> it is of the utmost consequence you should bear in mind that this inspection is not intended as a means of exercising control, but of affording assistance; that it is not to be regarded as operating for the restraint of local efforts, but for their encouragement; and that its chief objects will not be attained without the co-operation of the school committees; – the Inspector having no power to interfere, and not being instructed to offer any advice or information excepting where it is invited.[2]

In sharp contrast to the strong central control exercised in Irish education, the Committee of Council aspiration was in close accord with the prevailing ideology of free enterprise and laissez faire. This fundamental canon was very

1 N. Ball, *Her Majesty's Inspectorate, 1839–49* (London: Oliver & Boyd, 1963), p. 6.   2 Ibid., p. 67.

influential in determining the nature of school inspection throughout Britain. In the words of one commentator:

> The inspectorate was, in short, to be a safeguard, not a straitjacket.[3]

Inspectors in England and Scotland, appointed by the sovereign in council, thereby entitled to the prefix H.M., enjoyed a measure of independence quite different to their longer-established counterparts in Ireland. Denominationally organised for a generation, the British inspectors collected information, reported to the Committee of Council and generally promoted educational endeavour by conciliating the support and assistance of the gentry and the clergy. Her Majesty's Inspectors were sometimes notable clergymen, most had distinguished academic honours from Oxford and Cambridge, and almost all were the sons of the gentry, the clergy, civil and military officials, and professional men.[4] The prestige and influence of the inspectorate in Britain derived from the high calibre of its personnel, its considerable contacts with the establishment and most of all from the very nature of the Committee of Council's limited intervention in education.

Quite clearly the approach to inspection, the workload of Irish inspectors, and their conditions of work were very different to the English model. The Irish inspectors, led by Inspector McCreedy presented cases to the Lords Committee of Inquiry into the system, in 1854, for an increase in the number of inspectors and for higher salaries to attract the best people to the position. They met with a favourable response. Salaries were increased in 1855, with head inspectors getting an increase of 33%, from £300 to £400 per annum, exclusive of allowances. District inspectors were now classified as first class and second class. The first class now had a beginning salary of £320 rising to £370 per annum. The scale for second class went from £275 to £305, while the sub-inspectors' scale went from £200 to £250 per annum. The total number of district inspectors was raised to fifty.[5]

By 1859, the total number of inspectors had increased to sixty-six, all of whom were male. Table 2.1 sets out the pattern of increase in the inspectorate staff in relation to the expanding number of national schools coming under the jurisdiction of the Commissioners.

The overall career structure of the inspectorate corps was pyramidical in shape. At the lowest tier were the fifty-eight district inspectors, territorially organised and based in centres throughout Ireland. The middle layer was the group of six head inspectors, chosen from the best of the district inspectors, strategically placed in cities, overseeing the work in their several districts and carrying out special duties when asked. Only in exceptional circumstances

3 A.S. Bishop, *The Rise of a Central Authority for English Education* (CUP, 1971), p. 34.   4 J. Hurt, *Education in Evolution* (London: Paladin, 1972), pp 173–77.   5 *Twenty-first Report of the CNEI for 1854*, p. 19.

Table 2.1: Expansion of the inspectorial staff for national schools, 1832–59

Year	1832	1833	1838	1844	1846	1849	1853	1854	1859
No. of Inspectors	4	8	25	30	36	40	50	60	66
No. of Schools	–	789	1384	3153	3637	4321	5023	5178	5408

Source: Eustás Ó hÉideáin, *National School Inspection*, p. 50.

were they at the Office in Dublin. The duties of head inspectors included supervision of the work of district inspectors, reporting on the model schools, carrying out special inquiries and conducting the examinations of teachers for classification purposes. At the top of the pyramid were the two Chiefs of Inspection, former head inspectors with considerable experience of national education, joint heads of the major administrative unit within the central establishment in Tyrone House and among the most senior and distinguished officers in the service of the Commissioners of National Education.

TROUBLE AT THE OFFICE

As was predictable with the mass of documentation being made available to the central office in the 1850s, it became clear that sufficient resources did not exist to handle it, and a huge amount of reports went unread, the office staff being unable to cope with the large volume of material. In January 1855, the head inspectors were summoned to headquarters and given the task of sorting out the problems. They were asked to give their opinions in written reports on thirty-nine special matters referred to them. They read, examined and reported on 11,000 reports by district inspectors, and worked off about a year's arrears of business which had accumulated in the central office. They framed and lithographed various circulars and skeleton forms of official letters. They re-formulated the code of instructions for inspectors. Five of the head inspectors returned to their regions in April 1855, but their colleague, Mr McCreedy, was invited to stay on 'in temporary charge of the direction of the inspection office'. This organisational work was in advance of an investigation visit from a Treasury monitoring group, which recommended that a 'General Inspection and Statistical Branch' be set up. Following from this, McCreedy was appointed to the new post of Chief of the Inspection and Statistical Department.

However, following their return to their regions, the other five head inspectors became very aggrieved at what they perceived as new policies which emerged from the central office. On 31 May 1856, they took the unprecedented step of sending a Joint Letter of Remonstrance to the Commissioners against the direction being taken by the Inspection Department. In it they objected to lack of consultation with them on inspectorial matters, to the 'tone, spirit and terms' of letters addressed to the inspectors, to changes in the style of correspondence to school managers, to new forms issued to the inspectors, and to punishments inflicted on teachers. The head inspectors had been refused permission to attend their planned annual conference in Dublin, in 1856, where they hoped they could privately raise their concerns with the Commissioners. The head inspectors concluded their submission by stating: 'We unanimously feel, that it merely requires such an evil to be made known to the Commissioners, and its correction, so far as possible, will speedily follow.'[6]

In this belief, the head inspectors were gravely mistaken. On 6 June, the Commissioners issued a strong condemnation of the letter which they received 'with the utmost surprise and disapprobation; they consider it to be marked, throughout, with an amount of indecorum, indiscretion, and insubordination never before exhibited by any persons engaged in their service'. The head inspectors were told if they were dissatisfied with their position 'their proper course will be to withdraw from the service, and that the Commissioners are prepared, at once, to accept their resignation.' If they did not resign, they were warned under pain of 'instant dismissal' to refrain from all such action in the future and to exhibit 'the most cheerful obedience to their [the Commissioners'] will'.[7] This was a remarkable manifestation of the authority exercised by the Commissioners and an unambiguous effort to put their senior professional officers in their place as subservient to the Commissioners' will, without any questioning by them. No doubt, the incident affected the morale of the inspectorate and was probably seen by their subordinates as a loss of face for the head inspectors. Nevertheless, no further confrontation occurred and the system continued to operate. The fact that one of the signatories, P.J. Keenan, a Catholic, was promoted as a second Chief of Inspection shortly afterwards, in 1859, would suggest that no grudges were retained from this robust clash of attitude. However, another author of the Joint Letter, James W. Kavanagh, ran foul of the Commissioners again in 1857 by reading a paper before the British Association on the subject of education, the paper being regarded as offensive by the Commissioners as well as being unsanctioned by them. The Commissioners viewed Kavanagh's defence of his action as being discourteous and penalised him by depressing him to the rank of first class inspector, from his status as a head inspector. Kavanagh resigned from the service in February 1858. However, the Commissioners were to find in Kavanagh a redoubtable foe and his voluminous publication in March 1858, *Mixed Education: The Catholic Case Stated*, was a major critique of the national school system. It alleged that there was a consistent anti-Catholic bias in the operation of the system. His criticism had a significant

6 Text of letter in Appendix O of *Mixed Education: The Catholic Case Stated* (op. cit.), pp 424–27.   7 Text of letter in Appendix P, *Mixed Education: The Catholic Case Stated*, p. 428.

impact on the public and on the Catholic hierarchy in particular. Kavanagh also made strong criticisms of aspects of the inspectorate, of which he had been a member since 1846.

Following a sequence of representations including letters to Chief Secretary Cardwell, and pastoral letters by bishops, in December 1859 the government agreed to change the composition of the national board to include ten Catholics and ten Protestants. Under the leadership of Cardinal Cullen the Catholic Church continued to raise objections to aspects of the national school system through the 1860s. This might have happened without Kavanagh's action, but his attacks certainly provided ammunition against the Commissioners, who had adopted such an authoritarian attitude to Kavanagh and his colleagues in 1856.

GOVERNANCE BY RULES: THE SIGNIFICANCE OF THE 1855 INSTRUCTIONS FOR INSPECTORS

The role of inspection in the national schools of Ireland was determined first and foremost by the fact that the Commissioners were charged with overseeing a vast network of primary schools and ensuring that the Board's wishes were complied with. The *Rules and Regulations of the Commissioners*, published regularly, became the touchstone of the national education system and the concise manifestation of the Board's requirements. Since most eventualities were covered by some rule, the weekly business of the Board was greatly simplified because the administrative staff of the Office could process a large number of cases by applying the regulations.

The rules were well disseminated and were familiar to teachers and school managers. Less well known but of enormous importance was the system of precedent. This was the accretion over the years of a set of practices and procedures established by decisions of the Commissioners in respect of particular cases or points of difficulty, and was known to, and understood by the senior officers in the service of the Board. Almost always enshrined in 'Board Orders', precedents were of great significance and provided ready guidelines for action, frequently in respect of disciplinary matters. This is not surprising considering that the Commissioners had to have recourse to sanctions to enforce their rules and to be seen to do so systematically. A school 'struck off' or salary withdrawn from a teacher, could be relied upon to act as a warning to others that flouting the regulations did not in the final analysis pay. That punitive action or the threat of it so frequently followed swiftly the visit of an inspector, did little to endear inspection to the various parties involved.

The role of inspection and the conduct of national education generally is neatly encapsulated in the frank statement of Sir Patrick Keenan, speaking in 1884:

> Externally the inspectors, and internally the Board and the Office
> in Dublin, control all the operations and fortunes of the system.[8]

Essentially, the role of inspection in Ireland was to assist the Board to maintain control over the national school system, and the rules were a central element in defining the parameters of that control.

The re-drafting of the code of instructions for inspectors by the head inspectors in 1855 was of major importance and had long-lasting effects. Described as *Instructions for the Guidance of District and Sub-inspectors*, this was for a long period the official code for inspectors.[9] Although various circulars subsequently modified certain features of inspectors' work, the 1855 code was not comprehensively updated at any later time. Comprising some eighty-five detailed instructions and covering all aspects of inspectors' business, the 1855 code was a key element underlying inspectorial practice in the national system from then on.

The inspector was required to visit and report on every school in his district three times each year. At least four to five hours each day, exclusive of time travelling to and from schools, was to be spent in the actual inspection of schools. Irrespective of all other work and vacation periods, forty-two weeks per year were to be devoted to the inspection of schools. As many incidental visits as possible were to be made to schools with the specific objective of preventing or correcting what were termed 'abuses' and 'evils', and also for checking up on suggestions previously made. The inspector was to make a point of visiting such schools as were convenient when *en route* to distant schools. If two schools shared the same building or were immediately contiguous, the inspector was to 'pass rapidly from the one to the other' before returning to the one to be examined first. The inspector was enjoined 'to take care to visit schools as unexpectedly as possible' and to vary his routine to maintain the element of surprise in the visitation of schools. In the case of applicant schools already in operation, the inspector was to furnish a report on the site, premises, furniture and attendance of the school along with an account of the teaching given. The inspector was to interview the manager of the school after his inspection.

Having entered a school and introduced himself to the teacher, the inspector was to check at once whether the fundamental regulations of the Board were complied with, whether the movable tablet denoting 'Religious' or 'Secular' instruction was correctly displayed, whether a copy of the Commissioners' rules was suspended for the perusal of visitors, and whether the time-table was being observed. The inspector was to ascertain if the 'General Lesson' or a lesson of similar import was used at the time of com-

8 *Report of the Select Committee on Education, Science and Art (Administration of Votes) and minutes of evidence* (312), HC 1884, xiii, p. 52.   9 *The Report of the Royal Commission into Primary Education in Ireland* (Powis Commission), vol. vii, returns of the National Board, pp 179–85.

bined ordinary instruction. He was to examine the rolls, registers and report book, using effective means to discover any deliberate 'falsification'. All 'business of this preliminary nature' completed, the inspector was then to commence 'the more important part of his duty' which was the examination of the school 'as to its educational condition'. The inspector was to have careful regard for the school programme and the degree of proficiency attained in the various classes, taking into account also the teacher's methods and preparation, and having regard for the tone and spirit pervading the school. He was to record his opinions and remarks in the school's Observation Book and also enter the time and date of his visit along with the number of pupils present.

The inspector was to bear in mind that he was not 'an administrator or authoritative director of the National system' but simply and essentially an inspector of its schools, whose chief duty was to forward 'clear, faithful, and comprehensive reports' so that the Commissioners might act as necessity required. The inspector was forbidden to give direct orders in a school but could make such suggestions to the patron and teachers as he thought proper for the correction of faults or the improvement of the organisation and management of the schools. The inspector was enjoined to treat teachers 'with the most perfect kindness and respect', to counsel them privately on any faults and not to animadvert on their conduct in the hearing of their pupils who were in turn to be treated considerately and courteously. He was also expected to keep himself informed about the general character of the teachers, how they were regarded by the people of their locality and about their conduct as members of society.

Thus, it can be seen that the code of 1855 involved a development and extension of that issued in 1842. Strange as it may seem, no significant revision of the instructions was undertaken subsequently so that the code of 1855 remained in force and endured for a considerable number of years. Instead of a comprehensive revision of the instructions, the practice was adopted of issuing circulars as circumstances required so that over the decades, inspection was governed by the code of 1855 and the accumulation of circulars and conventions added on with the passage of time. For a system the great rule of regularity and order of which was 'a time and a place for every thing', it was in many ways quite extraordinary that neither time nor place was found to recodify properly the instructions to inspectors.

The instructions to inspectors of 1855 were the bedrock of inspection in the national school system and they had a profoundly important shaping influence on inspection for many decades.

Apart from the work in schools, the 1855 instructions to inspectors contained an abundance of ordinances governing the official life of inspectors. An inspector was not to leave his district except on the authorised business of the Board or else having previously obtained permission from the Office. Except in the case of illness or 'some other unavoidable calamity', the inspector was to forward to the Office his Diary or daily journal for the previous week, along with his reports on schools, so as to reach Dublin not later than each successive Monday morning. If away on duty from his allotted centre for one or two days, the inspector was expected to arrange to have official letters forwarded to him. He was to keep a notebook of the kind supplied by the Board and in this, he was to enter full details of his visits to schools so that such notings could be taken as a faithful record on which subsequent reports were based. The inspector was also obliged to keep up to date his District Book in which information about schools was recorded. The inspector was expected to preserve in a 'guard-book' all official letters and circulars, and all such documentation was to be available for examination by the head inspector should he request it. In all his correspondence with the Office, the inspector was to express himself with clearness, propriety and precision, and to habituate himself to a style of penmanship 'at once neat, well defined, and entirely legible'. While there was no rule forbidding an inspector from walking to the schools, it was thought 'more becoming and more economical of the public time' that he should drive to and from schools, and therefore he was expected to provide himself with a horse.

The instructions of 1855 directed inspectors to become thoroughly acquainted with the fundamental principles of the national system of education, the rules of the Board, and the general history and progress of its administration. Inspectors were expected also to enlarge their knowledge of literature, philosophy and science, to be familiar with the state of popular education at home and abroad, and to keep in touch with the writings of the eminent educationists of the time. All polemical discussions of a religious or political nature were to be avoided, and in his public capacity, the inspector was to discharge his duty impartially and conscientiously with a courteous and conciliatory demeanour towards all persons. In his private life, the inspector was required to 'support in a modest but becoming manner, the bearing, character, and standing of a gentleman', doing nothing to lessen the respectability of his position or detract from the influence of his office.

As is clear from the foregoing, inspectors were governed by an extremely detailed code of instructions. It seems clear that the Board had very high expectations of its inspectors. The concepts of duty and of public service were prominent features while compliance with bureaucratic routine was also a notable emphasis.

TOWARDS CLASSIFICATION OF INDIVIDUAL PUPILS' ACHIEVEMENT

Undoubtedly, the furnishing of three major reports each year on each school, apart altogether from special and incidental reports, imposed a severe burden of work on the inspection staff. Alexander Macdonnell outlined in 1868 the three kinds of report that were required.[10] A primary report, giving a state-ment of the premises and the state of education therein, and two different types of secondary report were expected. One of the secondary reports, which was to be done when attendance was largest, necessitated the individual examination of every child and its classification under the main heads of the national school programme. It is apparent that this very detailed examination into the proficiency of the pupils commenced in the late 1850s and was extended considerably in the early 1860s. A circular to inspectors, originally issued in May 1858 but reissued in a modified and enlarged format in February 1862,[11] contained detailed guidelines on the assessment of pupils. This circular drew attention to enormous differences in the returns of the inspectors 'wholly inexplicable by any imaginable diversity of circumstances in the schools' which could only be accounted for by the belief

> that the Inspectors as a body are practically without any uniform standard of judgment in these matters, and that few of them have a common understanding one with the other or even with the Head Inspectors, as to the *criteria* by which the general character of the instruction imparted under our system, whether as regards pupils or schools, is to be determined.[12]

It is clear that uniformity of judgment among inspectors had become an issue of concern at about the same time that the Revised Code was introduced in England. It became the practice in Ireland that the annual reports of the Commissioners included tabulated accounts of the proficiency of pupils. These tables were based on the examination of proficiency carried out by inspectors and forwarded to the Office on the secondary report forms. For example, in the year 1870, inspectors examined individually some 293,909 pupils which was 81.8% of the average daily attendance for that year.[13] It seems apparent that this type of examination of pupils was a heavy burden of work for inspectors on top of their other duties.

This remarkable feature of inspection in Ireland – prior to the introduc-tion of payment by results and obviously influenced by the Revised Code – requires further elaboration. The classification of pupils by individual exam-ination entailed hearing children read, seeing their writing, testing their answering in grammar, geography and arithmetic, and deciding whether or not the children met the requirements specified in the 1862 circular. To be included under the head 'able to read the Second Book correctly', the inspec-tor had to be satisfied that the pupil could read readily at sight without naming letters or spelling syllables, with correct pronunciation, in the more advanced sections of the book. To rank under the head 'able to work cor-

10 Ibid., vol. iii, *Minutes of Evidence*, p. 20.   11 Ibid., vol. vii, *Returns of the National Board*, pp 187–88.   12 Ibid., p. 188.   13 *Report of the CNEI, for 1870*, Appendix, p. 171.

rectly and readily a sum in subtraction', the pupil had to know the meanings of the terms used in addition and subtraction and be able to work and prove a test question. To be returned under the head 'acquainted with the map of Europe or Ireland', the pupil had to demonstrate factual knowledge on such matters as area, population, rivers, towns, cities and so forth. Inspectors were enjoined to classify pupils' writing from dictation in two categories. If the writing was executed with only three or four mistakes and these not 'very gross', the pupil could be returned under 'tolerable accuracy'. The pupil with no error or one or two 'excusable' mistakes could be rated in the column denoting writing 'with ease and correctness'.

In addition to the classification of pupils, the 1862 circular gave specific guidelines to inspectors to determine the character of a school in its overall success in reading and penmanship. Thus, in order to be pronounced 'quite satisfactory', the following convoluted formula had to be met:

1 All the fifth and fourth class children, and three-fourths (or thereabouts) of the third class should read the earlier lessons of their respective class-books with ease and intelligence.

2 The remainder of the third class, the Sequel classes, and one-half (or hereabouts) of the second class, should read the Second Book correctly.

3 The remainder of the second class, and at least _one third_ of the first class children should read the First Book fairly (that is, with correct pronunciation of the words).[14]

Terms such as 'fair', 'good', 'middling', and 'quite satisfactory', became common parlance in inspectorial work, though it is difficult to believe that formulas such as the above were always rigorously obeyed in arriving at estimates of the quality of work done in schools.

In the context of a broad move for greater accountability for the expenditure of public funds for educational purposes and the influence of utilitarian ideology a system of payment by results was introduced in England, under the Revised Code of 1862.[15] In a letter of 19 June 1866 Chief Secretary Fortescue stated to the Commissioners of National Education:

I am directed by His Excellency to inform you that Her Majesty's Government are desirous of drawing attention of the Commissioners to the important principle upon which the remuneration of teachers, supported by the State, has with such marked success been recently

14 _Powis Commission_, vol. vii, _Returns of the National Board_, p. 188.   15 John Coolahan, 'The Ideological Framework of the Payment by Results Policy in Nineteenth Century Education', _Proceedings of the ESAI Conference_ (Cork, 1977), pp 166–71.

regulated in England and Scotland; I refer to the principle of State payments apportioned to the ascertained results of education.[16]

He went on to urge that the Commissioners should consider the introduction of such a scheme, 'not necessarily in the precise form which it has assumed in England', but on line with 'the wants and circumstances of Ireland'.

In a reply of 30 June, the Commissioners stated, 'they beg to express their general approbation of these proposals, without binding themselves to the adoption of any particular procedures.'[17] Thus, the Board was giving its approval to the principle of a payment by results system.

In a speech to parliament on 5 August 1867, Lord Naas, the current chief secretary, announced that he intended to set up a Royal Commission to inquire into the whole system of education in Ireland. In outlining points of inquiry for such a commission he stated:

> It would be of the greatest advantage to the national system of education in Ireland if some system of payment by results could be introduced.[18]

At the time, teachers were very dissatisfied with their rates of remuneration and both in 1866 and 1867 presented memorials to the Commissioners of National Education seeking redress of their grievances. Contemporary remarks from inspectors' reports bear witness to the impoverishment of teachers, as in the following:

> The majority of teachers are very poor, and find it hard to keep up a respectable exterior, such as becomes their profession ... The wonder is not that teachers are not more respectably dressed, but that they are able to appear at their work with anything like becoming decency at all.[19]

It was in this context that the Irish National Teachers' Association (later Organisation) was founded in 1868 to promote better salaries and conditions of work for teachers.

THE POWIS COMMISSION, 1870

The Royal Commission of Inquiry into Primary Education (Powis Commission), set up on 14 January 1868, had a membership consisting of seven

16 Mayo Papers, MS 11217, National Library of Ireland (NLI). Text also included in Minutes of CNEI, MS 5549, NLI, pp 479–84. 17 Minutes of CNEI, MS 5549, 30 June 1866, p. 486. 18 *The Times*, 6 August, 1867. 19 Quoted in Mary McNeill, *Vere Foster: Irish Benefactor* (Newton Abbey: David and Charles, 1971), p. 153.

Catholics and seven Protestants, under the chairmanship of Lord Powis. The Commission had extensive terms of reference and engaged in a large-scale survey of the Irish primary education system. It produced nine large volumes of a report and evidence in 1870. It was a landmark event in the history of Irish education.

Though the Powis Commission did not examine the inspection system in depth, inspectors were to be very much affected by the recommendations of the Commission, particularly the proposal to introduce in Ireland a system of payment by results. The Commission had sat for over two years and gathered a large amount of evidence and information about the provision for primary education in Ireland, delving deeply into many aspects of the national system. The Commission was concerned with all the major issues of the time including the quality of instruction, school-buildings and sites, books, local and government funding for education, denominational questions, teacher training, school attendance and many other matters. In all, the Commission made 129 recommendations based on its findings and some of these had very important implications for inspection. The Commission concluded that the progress of the children in the national schools, and indeed in other schools, was 'very much less than it ought to be' and it recommended that in order to secure a better return for public money, teachers should receive in addition to the fixed class-salaries, payments dependent on individual examination of pupils by inspectors.[20] Inspectors were to be the determiners of satisfactory progress on the part of the children based on individual examination. Thus, in accordance with the expectations of many observers of the period, payment by results was recommended as a means of effecting improvement in the proficiency of pupils.

This was perhaps the most outstanding feature of the report and it was also the one which was most swiftly acted upon. It is clear that payment by results was anticipated by virtually all the inspectors, many of whom gave evidence to the Commission. Few inspectors expressed reservations about introducing payment by results to the national schools. In fact, many inspectors favoured its introduction, none more prominently than P.J. Keenan, one of the Chiefs of Inspection at the time of the Powis Commission's work.

As early as the 1850s, Keenan had been a devotee of individual examination of children by inspectors. This is very evident from this extract from Keenan's annual report for 1858 when he comments on substantial numbers of children not present at primary inspections:

> The only remedy for this defect is to have one thorough and scruti-
> nising examination annually *of every child undergoing the continuous
> process of education*; and this examination, I would suggest, should be

held in the most formal manner possible. I would call it, as heretofore, the primary inspection, and I would make it, under forfeit of a
continuance of the grant or of some other advantage or privilege,
obligatory upon managers and teachers to cause all the pupils of the
school to be in attendance at such an inspection.[21]

Not surprisingly, this was brought prominently into view at the Powis
Commission.[22] It may be surmised that Keenan as a Chief of Inspection was
influential in bringing about the formalised individual examination of pupils
in the national school system. Further, it seems likely that Keenan at this
early stage was moving inexorably towards the kind of thinking that was
coming to the fore in England from the appointment of the Newcastle
Commission until the appearance of the Revised Code of 1862. It is apparent
that payment by results found in P.J. Keenan a supporter of unremitting
ardour and enormous influence for a very considerable period in the national
schools of Ireland.

Other preparatory work undertaken about this time included a detailed
investigation of the pattern of school attendance carried out by the inspectors.
This involved 'an immensity of labour' and gave a 'complete exposition of the
quality of the attendance' said Keenan, and was done in connection 'with the
plan of paying chiefly for ascertained results.'[23] There is little doubt but that
Keenan was one of the main driving forces in the campaign to introduce payment by results to the national schools. Keenan's memorandum on a results
system to suit Ireland was entirely his own creation as he had not shown it to
his joint-Chief, W.A. Hunter, nor indeed consulted him about it. One of the
Secretaries, W.H. Newell, also submitted a payment by results scheme and
the impression is given that these senior officials were vying with one another
for position and favour. Keenan's plan envisaged reduced classification salaries
for teachers, to be augmented by results fees determined by individual examination of pupils who had made ninety attendances in the results year. The
'ninety' attendance was a first step to secure a basic level of attendance, when
compulsory attendance was a long way off in the future. Also included was a
scheme to have managers' results fees, based on quarterly examinations by
school managers, and intended to involve them more closely in the superintendence of schools. Keenan showed himself to be a skilful and diplomatic
adviser before the Powis Commission. It is likely too that Keenan's influence
with the inspection staff may have contributed significantly to their general
unanimity of opinion concerning the introduction of payment by results to
the national schools.

Within a year of the publication of the Powis Commission's report, the
National Board gave consideration to both Newell's and Keenan's schemes for

21 *Report of CNEI for 1858*, appendix, p. 186. 22 *Powis Commission*, vol. i, *Report*, p. 299. 23
Powis Commission, vol. vii, Minutes of Evidence, p. 71.

payment by results and decided to adopt Keenan's proposed scheme.[24] It was envisaged that a sum of almost £100,000 would be paid in 1871–72 to augment teachers' incomes by results payments. However, the government was prepared, as a temporary arrangement, to allow only probationer and third class teachers to benefit by the results scheme. Consequently, a mere £12,504 was paid for results that year.[25] The first general application of payment by results came the following year, 1872–73.

In July 1871, the Commissioners considered a memorandum from Keenan discussing payment by results, local taxation in aid of public education, a scheme of pensions for teachers and the necessity for regularised contract forms for teachers.[26] That it was Keenan who was to the fore in exploring means to implement the Powis recommendations shows how prominent a force he had become in Marlborough Street. Already honoured as a Companion of the Bath, Keenan was shortly to succeed Alexander Macdonnell as Resident Commissioner in December 1871. Thus, at 45 years of age, the main architect of payment by results in the national schools had become not alone a member of the National Board but its foremost commissioner, the first inspector to achieve such prominence.

As early as 1850, the Board had requested managers of schools to enter into agreements with their teachers but now the payment of results fees was made conditional on the signing of contract forms prescribed by the Commissioners. This caused delay in the actual payment of fees to teachers due to considerable controversy over the acceptance of such contracts by managers. After a compromise was reached early in 1873, whereby an alternative to the Board's form of agreement was permitted, teachers got the benefit of a contract of employment, providing for three months' notice of dismissal, and their results fees for 1872.[27]

For the teachers, the introduction of payment by results meant a substantial improvement in income and as such, this was a much overdue benefit. Coinciding with its implementation, however, the Commissioners decided that from October 1872, good service salaries would no longer be payable for new cases. In 1872 also, the gradation of teachers' class salaries was simplified. Instead of the former eight scales, there were now four different salary rates with six categories of classification and modest increases were given in the lower divisions. The main effect of this was to simplify the promotional procedure, though examination was still essential for movement from a lower to a higher class.

Thus commenced a slow and gradual improvement in conditions for the national teachers. In 1875, legislation was passed providing loans for the erection of residences for teachers. A few years later in 1879, legislation estab-

24 Minutes of the CNEI, 28 February 1871. 25 *Report of the CNEI, for 1871*, pp 21–22. 26 Minutes of the CNEI, 4 July 1871. 27 John Coolahan, *Irish Education: History and Structure* (Dublin: IPA, 1981), p. 27.

lished a pension fund for national teachers and compulsory retirement was introduced for males at age 65, and for females at age 60. These measures, though slow to have widespread effect, brought about notable improvement in the circumstances of the teachers.

At the commencement of payment by results, the grant was regarded as experimental and to be continued for only three years. At the end of this period, the government increased the class salaries of teachers and renewed results grants but proposed also to supplement these sources of income by raising a local contribution through the poor law unions. By the National Teachers' Act of August 1875, Boards of Guardians were authorised to become contributory for a third of the full results fees payable to teachers, the government undertaking to provide a corresponding third, contingent on the contribution.[28] The remaining third of results fees was to be unconditional. Because Boards of Guardians had the option of striking a rate for education or refusing to so do, thus remaining non-contributory unions, it is hardly surprising that the 1875 Act met with very small success. The great majority of unions did not contribute and extremely limited funds were derived from this source. Naturally enough, great dissatisfaction arose when teachers in the non-contributory union areas received only one-third of their results fees and this caused much controversy in the period up to 1881. Under considerable pressure from managers and teachers, the government and Treasury, while attempting to preserve the principle of requiring a local contribution towards education, gave concessions which eased the situation notably by 1881. Nevertheless, right through to the 1890s, teachers did not always receive in full the results fees due to them because of the provisions of the 1875 Act, illustrating that it was the teachers who were penalised by the unwillingness of the local unions to raise rate-aid for education. The failure of the 1875 Act had serious consequences for education in Ireland. Because of its partial success, it helped to postpone consideration and action concerning local funding and control of education, issues which were increasingly important from that time.

28 CNEI, *History of the Vote*, p. 94.

3

Primary Inspection during the
Payment by Results Era, 1872–1900

THE PAYMENT BY RESULTS SCHEME

Under the payment by results system, national education was to embark on a significantly new course in which greater attention and interest would be directed towards the secular curriculum and towards the attainment of children.

In order to arrange the detailed procedures for payment by results, the first of a series of conferences of the senior officials and head inspectors presided over by P.J. Keenan as Resident Commissioner was convened in July 1872. Held in the Office in Marlborough Street, this lasted for three days during which the detailed programmes and fee scales together with instructions for inspectors were drawn up. This was essentially the blueprint for payment by 'ascertained results' as Keenan called it. The Commissioners quickly approved the plans.[1]

Inspectors were to be circularised and also to receive instructions from the head inspectors as to the mode of conducting results examinations especially with a view to securing uniformity in the tests applied. The requirements for awarding passes in the various subjects, along with the detailed programme of instruction for each class were thus communicated to all the inspectors.

The new system envisaged the individual examination by the inspector of all children who had made ninety attendances in the previous results year. Annual results examinations were to be held in every school normally in the same month each year after 1873. Each school was to have its own results year ending on the last day of the month prior to the inspector's visit, notice of which would be given in advance. Teachers were to complete examination rolls and include only those children qualified by attendance and other conditions to be examined. Inspectors were to ensure that the complicated rules were observed and enter on the examination roll the pass or fail marks given in the various branches of the programme. This was to be transmitted to the Office and, some time later, the teacher could anticipate payment for the results achieved.

1 Minutes of CNEI, 30 July 1872.

Obligatory subjects included reading, writing, arithmetic and spelling with grammar and geography added from third class, and agriculture for boys from fourth, while girls commenced needlework at second. Later, bookkeeping could be substituted for older boys in towns in the place of agriculture. Fees for the obligatory subjects ranged from 2s. in first to 2s. 6d. in sixth class for reading. Arithmetic in first earned only 1s. while in sixth it was worth 3s. An infant at most could merit 3s. and a sixth class pupil could gain 14s. 6d. for the teacher on the obligatory course.[2]

Optional subjects to be taught during or after school hours included vocal music, drawing, geometry and algebra which were worth between 3s. and 5s. in sixth class. Extra subjects could be taught outside school hours and selection could be made from a wide range which included Greek, Latin, French, and scientific areas such as higher geometry and algebra, trigonometry, magnetism and electricity, botany, physiology and geology. Results fees of 10s. per pupil were applicable for Greek and Latin.

The notes governing the operation of the system can only be described as labyrinthine, their complexity compounded by minor adjustments from time to time. Pupils between four and seven years who made the required 90 attendances could be presented for examination as infants though their individual examination could be dispensed with if there was provision made for their systematic training.[3] A pupil who earned fees for the teacher in reading, writing and arithmetic could not be presented a second time for examination in the same class. If a pupil failed in one or more subjects, he could be examined the following year in the same class and try to pass in the subjects failed previously. Only one fee for each subject could be paid for a pupil in any class no matter how long the pupil remained in the class and, under no circumstances, could a pupil be presented for examination more than twice in the same class except infants, fifth and sixth. From an early date, both fifth and sixth classes were divided into two stages in each of which the pupil could earn results fees. This meant that there were eight class gradations above infants, the last four of which could be represented as 5^1, 5^2, 6^1, 6^2.

The programme of instruction was highly specific and attempted to measure out and demarcate exactly the amount of knowledge to be acquired at every level of the national school. The lesson books of the Board were the basis of the reading, for example:

Third Class
Reading – Fee, two shillings and six pence – (a) To read with ease and correctness the lessons of the Third Book. (b) To be fairly acquainted with the meanings of words and the subject-matter of

2 *Report of the CNEI for 1873*, appendix, p. 60.   3 The attendance requirement was raised to 100 days from 1 March 1878, see *Report of CNEI for 1877*, p. 22.

these lessons (c) To repeat correctly five of the pieces of poetry contained in Third Book.[4]

Writing consisted of transcription from the lesson books and required the
production by the pupil of at least ninety pages of copy-book work written on
different days, signed and dated by the pupil and to be 'kept neat and free
from blots'. This of course was intended to prevent falsification of attendance.
Fourth class arithmetic for 2*s*. 6*d*. required the pupil to know numeration and
notation well and all the more useful arithmetical tables, to do easy exercises
in addition and subtraction mentally and work on slate or paper 'accurately
and speedily' a sum of seven lines in addition of money and questions 'in all
the compound rules and reduction'. Geography, for a mere one shilling and
sixpence in the higher classes, required knowledge of the maps of the world,
Europe and Ireland. Agriculture paid 3*s*. for senior boys and was based on
knowledge of the Board's *Agricultural Class Book*. More practical but equally
lucrative for senior girls was needlework requiring proficiency in cutting out
articles of dress and skill in sewing and knitting. Equally specific but more
arcane were the requirements in all the extra branches of the programme. In
all, there were seven obligatory subjects and a long list of extras.

The programme did not change greatly over the years. Occasionally a
new subject was added to the list of extra branches. For example, Irish was
admitted as an optional subject from 1879 when the Board acceded to a
request for its inclusion from the Society for the Preservation of the Irish
Language.[5] The scale of fees did not alter much either, modest increases
being granted only sparingly. Thus, the system of payment by results drawn
up in the early 1870s assumed and maintained a notable degree of permanence in the national schools lasting right up to the beginning of the twentieth century.

THE NATURE OF INSPECTION UNDER PAYMENT BY RESULTS

Payment by results was in full operation in Ireland from 1872. Although the
inspectors had been accustomed to a form of individual examination, payment
by results represented an enormous change in the manner and method of
their work. At the commencement of the results system, the inspectors in
their annual reports reflected a broad welcome for the new system. While
opinion among the inspectors concerning the effects of payment by results
varied depending on the individual, a representative view was to welcome the
new arrangements and perceive them as promising for the advancement of
education. Inspectors generally were anxious to see teachers' earnings

4 Ibid., p. 56.   5 Minutes of CNEI, 2 July 1878.

improved and believed that the results system offered a healthy stimulus for the advancement of education in the schools. Inspectors noted that the new system offered an incentive to good teachers, that it held promise for an improvement in attendance and that it would lead to better progress in the schools generally. However, some inspectors expressed reservations about the results system noting particularly that it emphasised mechanical teaching approaches at the expense of the intellectual development of children.

For both children and teachers the inspector's examination was now an event of some consequence and looked forward to with a mixture of trepidation and excitement. For the children obtaining a pass was a mark of achievement while every pass awarded brought a modest increment of payment for the teacher. Initially there were some difficulties of adjustment to the new circumstances. For example, many teachers found it difficult to accept that a child, though well prepared and likely to obtain a pass in various branches, was not eligible to be examined if he or she had not made the requisite attendance. Many teachers falsified the records of attendance in an attempt to maximise their potential earnings. In the early years of payment by results, cases of falsification abounded and many warnings were issued to managers and teachers in an effort to stamp out the practice. In spite of this, hundreds of cases of falsification were dealt with over the years and it continued to be a special duty of inspectors to scrutinise school accounts with great care.

For the inspectors, the early years of the results system brought a sharp increase in the demands made on them in carrying out the programme of inspections on time. Unanticipated factors such as illness or inclement weather often caused delays in the examination programme with notable pressure on individual inspectors to try to make up for time lost. There was intense pressure on both the head inspectors and the district inspectors to get results examinations done on time. The great complexity of the detailed provisions of the system ensured that many hours had to be given to the individual examination of every child. Initially also the inspectors had to complete a large amount of clerical work to assist the Office in paying teachers in accordance with the results found. The inspectors had considerable clerical work to do in their own homes calculating and tabulating the money value of the results examinations and transferring data from marking sheets to examination rolls. This significant increase in the volume of their office work, encroaching on Sundays even in some instances, added greatly to the pressures imposed on inspectors by the new system.

It was envisaged from the beginning of the results system that instead of the former practice of completing one primary and two secondary inspections per year in each school, the most that could be expected from inspectors would be the new annual results examination and one secondary inspection if possible. However, the difficulty that many inspectors experienced in completing the essential results examinations precluded the holding of secondary inspections in the majority of schools. Thus, the main thrust of inspection for a long period was concentrated on the results examinations and on occasional incidental visits. All duties in connection with classification of teachers, model schools, applications for aid, special inquiries and so on, were unchanged despite the heavy burden of individually examining every child in the district in seven or more subjects. Inspectors had to organise their time with the greatest economy to fulfil all their obligations. The average number of schools per district was about 120. Small schools could be examined for results in one day but larger schools could take two or more days to examine. This meant that over half an inspector's working year was given over completely to results examinations.

Within a short time of the full commencement of the results system, it was accepted that as much clerical work as possible connected with the results examinations should be done centrally in the Office. The efficiency of the inspectors in discharging their duties was recognised and improvements in their conditions were proposed. These were given practical effect with the abolition of the classification of inspectors in addition to a substantial salary increase for all inspectors. Of significance also was a recommendation that inspectors' assistants should be employed on an experimental basis to do some of the examining in populous areas. These would be paid at a much lower rate than inspectors and could help to reduce the number of inspectorial districts in Ireland. This was essentially a transference of the practice introduced in both England and Scotland with the Revised Code, of employing a subordinate class who could do work of a routine nature under the supervision of 'full' inspectors. At this time the Treasury under its permanent secretary R.R.W. Lingen, was increasingly assertive in limiting and controlling expenditure by the National Board and the fact that local funding for education in Ireland was so meagre made the Treasury reluctant to permit additional demands on the exchequer. The granting of substantial salary increases to inspectors and administrative staff made it all the more imperative for savings to be made in the cost of inspection. Keenan and the Board resolutely opposed the appointing of inspectors' assistants on the basis that inspectors in Ireland practically determined the income of the teachers and therefore, it was desirable to employ only 'first class and thoroughly reliable men'.[6] Lingen advised the Irish government that the inspectors' assistants scheme introduced with the Revised Code in Britain had 'answered there perfectly well', and eventually the Treasury view prevailed with the appointing of four assistants in 1877–78. However, the number of assistants in Ireland remained comparatively low throughout the results period.

Not surprisingly, relieving the inspectors of much of the clerical work associated with the results examination shifted the huge burden of this work

6 CNEI, _Report on the Possibility of Cheapening the Cost of Administering the Vote for Public Education, Ireland_ (MS Private and Confidential), 1884, pp 60–62.

over to the inspection office in Marlborough Street necessitating extra staff almost immediately. Within a decade, there were close to eighty persons employed there, double the staff of 1874. Some of the extra work derived from the legislation of the 1870s, especially the contributory unions measure, but the greatest pressure was caused by results business. The scale of work in the Office is adequately conveyed by the estimation made in 1884 that over 142,000 items of inbound correspondence – of which almost 14,000 were inspectors' reports and almost 10,000 letters from inspectors – were handled in a year while over 217,000 items were sent out.[7]

With the tedium of calculating the pounds, shillings and pence due to the teachers now taken over by the Office, the inspectors still had intensive work in schools under the results system. Individual examination of all qualified children in all the various subjects was extremely time-consuming and necessitated longer hours in schools than heretofore. Every school had its own results year with its results examination conducted in the same month from year to year. Thus, a teacher whose school results examination was anticipated in the month of March devoted his efforts towards preparing his pupils for the inspector's visit that would determine the amount of results fees payable for that particular year. The custom was to send home the younger children when examined and continue on with the older children until eventually the pupils on the higher class books, fewer in number but perhaps prepared in extra subjects such as Latin or Algebra, could be finished. Marks assigned, accounts checked, some hurried entries in the school's Observation Book, and at last inspector and teacher were released from their exertions perhaps in the dim light of a wintry evening. It was not uncommon for a results examination to continue later than 5 o'clock whereupon the inspector journeyed back to his centre. At the end of the day or certainly before the following Saturday's post, he had to make out the results report, a foolscap page or two, commenting generally on the proficiency of the pupils, the school accounts and the condition of the schoolhouse. Extracts from this were in due course furnished to the manager and to the teacher. Taking into consideration the tribulations of travel especially in the more remote areas, it is apparent that the results system greatly added to the travails and cares of the inspector's work.

The mode of inspection in Ireland was excessively minute and complicated, and the time necessary for examining a given number of children was longer than that required in England. The system as arranged in Ireland was much too time-consuming for inspectors and the large number of small schools added further to the relative inefficiency of the system of inspection overseen by the Commissioners of National Education.

7 Ibid., p. 257.

CONFERENCES WITH THE HEAD INSPECTORS, 1872–82

It was understandable in the circumstance of the early 1870s with the anxiety of the senior officials of the National Board to get payment by results started, that the system devised would be less than perfect and would in the course of experience be found to need adjustment. The question arises therefore about the extent to which the head inspectors and senior officials modified the results system in the light of experience.

There were six conferences held over an eleven-year period at which the six head inspectors and the most senior officers of the Board attended, and which were reported in the minutes of the Board. It is unlikely that other conferences were held without being recorded though it should be borne in mind that the Resident Commissioner and Secretaries and Chiefs of Inspection were in close contact permanently at the Office. However, the more formal gatherings requiring the presence of the six head inspectors began with the introduction of payment by results and ended when the system was well established. Strange as it may seem, these occasional conferences of the head inspectors disappeared completely after 1882 as if to suggest that once the detailed arrangement of the results system was refined, there was no further need for conferences.

As mentioned previously, the programme of instruction and scale of fees were drawn up at the 1872 conference with the head inspectors. Detailed advice as to the conduct of examination was also prepared. For example, arithmetic was to be tested by giving five sums in different rules and awarding a pass if three were worked correctly. Penmanship in senior classes could be marked on dictation exercises. Pupils who had not 90 attendances need not be examined unless the inspector had time. The fact that the Board approved all the recommendations of the conference with merely one minor amendment indicates that almost complete discretion in deciding the arrangements rested with Keenan and the senior personnel. Every one of these was, or had been at one time, an inspector.

Two years later, a further conference with the head inspectors arranged the classics programme, decided that fifth class should have two stages, and instructed inspectors to draw up calendars of results examinations to be completed before the end of February. The 1874 conference also directed that the head inspectors should conduct check examinations in each district, without prior notice to the district inspectors. The flavour of Keenan's command and dominance may be seen in the following:

> The Resident Commissioner reminded the Head Inspectors of the rule forbidding the making of speeches at Public Examinations of Model Schools. He further impressed upon them that their special function is to superintend the District Inspectors and exhorted them

to do so with energy and vigilance, and, where necessary, to be fearless in the discharge of their special duty.[8]

Similar conferences held in 1875 and 1878 dealt with other minor aspects of the results system. Inspectors were permitted to have an office day other than Saturday for doing their reports and were no longer required to make any report in respect of incidental visits unless some irregularity came to light. Further reduction in the clerical work included the simplification of marking sheets and secondary report forms and the ending of weekly reports on the model schools. The district book was to be revised and to be of the simplest character possible.[9] Later, other minor adjustments were made to the scale of fees, test cards were revised for arithmetic and, generally, the arrangements for results examinations were smoothed and refined.[10] Indeed, the whole point of these conferences with the head inspectors was to eliminate difficulties that had been found through experience, and to fine tune, so to speak, the details of results examinations in the national schools.

It is not possible to say whether the conference deliberations of the senior personnel and head inspectors included discussion on such questions as class examination or inherent weaknesses in the results system. If they did, the deliberations of the Board did not include any mention of such matters. It certainly does not appear to have been the case that any of the Commissioners entertained significant reservations about the system as the conference recommendations were invariably accepted with ready approval. It is apparent that for much of the period after the introduction of payment by results, the Commissioners, both as a body and as individuals, did not manifest notable interest in the detailed working of the system over which they presided.

However, within the Office, particular cases of incompetence raised concerns about the lack of uniformity of practice among inspectors as regards examinations generally. Thus, a major weakness in the inspection system – its variability from one inspector to another – came to the attention of the most senior officers of the Board very often by means of complaints from teachers and managers. While the lack of uniformity extended to many aspects of inspection, the question of results examinations came to particular notice within a decade of the commencement of the results system. The Resident Commissioner took action in an attempt to resolve this problem when uniformity of standard in conducting results examinations was the major feature of the longest conference of head inspectors on record. Clearly, Keenan was concerned in January 1881 when he directed the head inspectors to meet in one of the practising schools in Marlborough Street and examine the school as if it were for results with the view of arriving at a 'common uniform standard of examination and marking.' They were to devote a day to discussing the programme and prepare typical questions, and then

8 Minutes of CNEI, 24 March 1874.   9 Ibid., 16 March 1875.   10 Ibid., 19 March 1878.

after their return to their respective Circuits, they should assemble
the District Inspectors associated with them, at some convenient
centre, examine a school for Results with them, and endeavour to
make them thoroughly conversant with the uniform standard agreed
upon among themselves.[11]

It is likely that the convening of the district inspectors here envisaged was the
first occasion since results was introduced that inspectors came together to
discuss strategy and this was very likely a novel and helpful development.
Indeed, for all concerned it must have occasioned considerable thought and
study about the process of inspection and underlying issues affecting education and teaching. The experiment does not appear to have been repeated
however, though Keenan was wont to refer to the practice in evidence to government commissions.[12] However, check inspections by head inspectors did
become a more common feature of the results system and these were of some
benefit in reducing the variability of standards among the inspectors.

The last conference with all the head inspectors present was held in
February 1882. This dealt only with matters of detail relating to results as if
the question of uniformity had been satisfactorily disposed of. The fact that
only minute points of detail were amended and more significantly, that further conferences appear to have been deemed unnecessary, strongly suggests
that the senior personnel of the Office were at last confident that the results
system in Ireland was now as perfect as it could humanly be made. The
Resident Commissioner, Sir Patrick Keenan, who had directed all the conferences and whose governance was more than a trifle presidential, had championed the results system for close on two decades and was doctrinaire in his
certitude of its efficacy in education. When asked in 1883 if it had improved
elementary education in Ireland, he answered:

I think the greatest educational blessing that ever befell Ireland was
the introduction of that system.[13]

There is nothing to suggest that Keenan ever modified his view of payment
by results during the remaining ten or so years of his tenure. Quite the opposite indeed, as he lost no opportunity of extending its benefits at home, in the
secondary schools through the 1878 Intermediate Education Act, and abroad
in Trinidad and Malta where he was sent in an advisory role on behalf of the
government. Results ascertained by inspection became a dominant motif in
the national schools of Ireland and associated thinking included the belief that
the percentage pass rates in reading, writing and arithmetic were a reliable
and valid index of comparison for school proficiency as between England,

11 Ibid., 25 January 1881. 12 *Royal Commission on Technical Instruction Second Report*, vol. iv,
Evidence relating to Ireland (c.3981–iii), HC 1884, xxxi (i), pp 134–39. 13 Ibid., p. 139.

Scotland and Ireland. A prevailing view in Marlborough Street throughout the 1880s was that payment by results *per se* had contributed enormously to reducing illiteracy as gauged by the census returns.

The sixth conference of the head inspectors in 1882 was the last time for a long period that the most senior inspectors came together to discuss the detailed operation of inspection. There followed a lengthy period of apparent immutability in the functioning of the national school system. Regrettably from the point of view of inspection of schools, the overall administration of the system, and above all, the quality of teaching and education in the schools, the termination of the 1882 conference of head inspectors marked the beginning of a long period of staid and dreary routine in the internal affairs of the Office. Whereas apparently capable officials filled the senior posts each in their turn, there is little evidence of fresh thinking on particular issues, or of difficulties in the national system being identified and addressed, or indeed, any substantial development internally in these years. Whereas the main purpose of the conferences had been to iron out the operation of the results system, they could have provided a useful mechanism for the adumbration of new ideas and new policies or even the significant modification of payment by results. Sadly no such internal dynamic was in evidence during the long period in which the results system had supremacy in the national schools of Ireland.

Though the inspectors were often assigned responsibility for special inquiries, these almost always referred to particular incidents that had arisen in schools and such inquiries had little significance for the overall operation of the system of national education. While the Commissioners for National Education had upwards of eighty inspectors in their employ, little or no use was made of the inspection corps for analytical or developmental tasks. Instead, the inspectors were preoccupied with their work in schools and this increasingly meant that they were more and more engaged in results examinations. The preoccupation with results examinations became more accentuated with the passage of time.

INSPECTION IN IRELAND AT VARIANCE WITH DEVELOPMENTS ELSEWHERE

As Ireland was perfecting its system of payment by results in the early 1880s, England had commenced a process of gradual retreat from the policy of payment by results. As early as 1875, the results system in England underwent notable modification with the introduction of class subjects which did not necessitate individual examination but could be judged by inspectors on the basis of the proficiency of whole classes.[14] Further modifications of inspection

14 Balfour, *Educational Systems of Great Britain and Ireland* (Oxford: Clarendon Press, 1903), p. 38.

followed and attitudes to payment by results gradually altered so that by 1885, the process of dismantlement was well under way. The dismantling of payment by results was assisted by the recommendations of the Cross Commission which reported in 1888 and by 1895, the last vestiges of the results system had been removed from English schools. By this time, the influence of child centred and Froebelian thinking on the education of young children was making itself felt in English discourse on education. Scotland also mitigated the effects of payment by results following closely English example in 1886 and again in 1890 when individual examination disappeared as the basis of payment for the ordinary standard work of the schools. Instead, capitation grants were introduced and these were supplemented by modest merit payments depending on the quality of the teaching as assessed by inspection.[15]

Despite the fact that payment by results was perceived to be outmoded in England and in Scotland, there was no hint of any significant change in Ireland's national school system. In fact, a remarkable degree of rigidity accompanied the operation of results in Ireland. For example, when kindergarten approaches were introduced from the mid 1880s, under the results system, it was almost as if kindergarten was an extra subject to be taught to infants rather than an actual approach to infant teaching generally. That individual examination of infant pupils was not dispensed with for kindergarten and class examination introduced as a matter of course for this aspect of school provision gives insight into the lack of flexibility in the national school system. Class examination was not mentioned in the rules at any time and this was testament to an extraordinary rigidity of practice within the inspection system. It is indicative of the all-pervasive grip of payment by results on virtually every aspect of national education for a very lengthy period. Apart from minor details, neither the programme of instruction nor the method of inspection changed in any significant way throughout almost thirty years of payment by results.[16]

There were many signals about the baneful effects of payment by results given by inspectors in their annual reports which were published as appendices to the annual reports of the Commissioners. These reports were littered with references to significant deficiencies in the quality of work in schools. In particular, the teaching of the key obligatory subjects of reading and arithmetic was commented upon very unfavourably by many inspectors suggesting that reading was mechanical and unintelligent while arithmetic featured an undue concentration on written work and a lack of emphasis on understanding and facility with number. Many other elements of the work in schools were criticised by many of the inspectors with frequent references to rote learning, the lack of creative work in writing, memorisation of textual

---

15 Ibid., p. 134.   16 J.M. Coolahan, *The Origins of Payment by Results Policy and the Experience in Irish National and Secondary Schools*, unpublished MEd thesis, 1975, TCD.

material with little or no understanding of content and various other criticisms. Though inspectors were indirectly critical of the results system, they frequently made suggestions within the parameters of results payments as for example recommending that a special results fee should be payable for explanation in the case of the teaching of reading.

It appears likely that inspectors were loath to be critical of the results system given the fact that the Resident Commissioner was well known to be a devotee. Keenan was wont to refer to the improvements that had come in tandem with the results system and in this, it may be suggested, he was correct to a notable degree. Results had brought a greater concentration and focus on the secular curriculum. It had encouraged the better progression of pupils through the classes and up to the higher classes of the national schools with considerable benefit for the proficiency of pupils. It had also provided a stimulus to the system of schooling and given teachers some modest benefit in terms of payment. However, the benefits it brought were increasingly diminishing as time marched on without any modification or development of the system. In fact, the failure to reform or develop the inspection system in the late 1880s and into the 1890s became a grievous matter as the national schools became more obviously locked into an outmoded system. The concentration on individual results examination became more intense as time moved on and, in certain ways, sight was lost of more important considerations. For example, the secondary inspections were dropped completely in the late 1880s owing to pressure of work in carrying out results examinations. The head inspectors were assigned districts of their own in order to assist in the completion of results examinations at about the same time as secondary inspections were dispensed with. Both of these moves at this time signalled a desperate reliance on individual examination of pupils when it would have been most timely for inspection to take on a new form with far less recourse to minutiae and larger emphasis on overall school work and quality. Both the head inspectors and the chiefs of inspection as well as the other senior officials of the Board displayed a notable lack of acumen at this time in the discharge of their responsibilities as leading officers in charge of the administration of the very large school system under their control.

Thus, the carrying out of the results examinations that only determined about one third of teachers' incomes took precedence over virtually all other considerations in the national school system. This was a serious and enduring failure on the part of the administration of the national school system and had detrimental effects on the quality of work carried out in the schools for a long time. Although the programme of instruction and the results system were matters absolutely under the control of the Commissioners and that could have been modified at their discretion, acting on the advice of their inspectors and officials, an unwavering and rigid sameness was steadfastly maintained. The management and direction of national education were affected by a notable lassitude during the payment by results era, most notably in the period after 1888.

An important aspect of the national education system during Sir Patrick Keenan's period of office as Resident Commissioner was that the inspectors had virtually complete hegemony over the most senior posts in Marlborough Street. Several of the inspectors who reached the position of Chief of Inspection secured further promotion to the two secretary-ships. Thus, during the payment by results period, a whole succession of former inspectors came to occupy the position of Secretary. These included Michael Fitzgerald, John E. Sheridan, W.R. Molloy, W.R. O'B. Newell and J. Morrell. A further dimension to their elevation inside the Office was that a number of these also secured appointment as commissioners where they had the opportunity of presiding over all the business of the national schools at its highest level. It is all the more surprising then that so little was done to ameliorate or reduce the ill-effects of payment by results given that so many former senior inspectors had positions of power at the nerve-centre of the entire school system.

TRANSITION TO A NEW CURRICULUM AND MODE OF INSPECTION,
1894–1900

The Commissioners of National Education had ultimate responsibility for what occurred in the national school system and it is fair to say that the Commissioners failed to distinguish themselves in the quality of their contribution to the overall administration of the system for a considerably lengthy period. All this was to change dramatically by the mid-1890s with the influence of a number of new Commissioners on the board. Chief of these was Archbishop William J. Walsh of Dublin who accepted an appointment to the board in 1895, becoming the first leading Catholic ecclesiastic to occupy a seat for decades. Other Commissioners who manifested a special interest in the development of the national school system were Lord Chief Baron Christopher Palles, a prominent judge, and Professor George F. Fitzgerald, a scientist from Trinity College, Dublin. With the demise of Sir Patrick Keenan in 1894 and his replacement by Christopher Talbot Redington, a period of transition commenced during which many influences were at work. A development of particular significance was the assertion by the Commissioners of greater control over the detailed operation of the system of national education. At this time, the Board manifested a notable loss of confidence in its senior officials and inspectors and this was to have major repercussions as new trends emerged. For the inspectors, an inquiry in 1895 into the administration of the July examinations for training college students proved damaging in the longer term and precipitated a significant crisis internally at the Board's headquarters in Tyrone House. This was but one of a number of items that displeased leading commissioners and caused them to take a more active interest in particular aspects of the functioning of the system.

At this juncture, in March 1896, the Commissioners took the very unusual step of ordering that the inspectors as part of their usual annual reporting 'be invited to furnish their views at length and unreservedly as to the working of the present Results system' and furthermore, the inspectors were asked to give special attention to aspects such as reading, explanation and mental arithmetic.[17] As a result of this initiative on the part of the Commissioners, inspectors had a notable opportunity of expressing their views on what had become a critical issue. In their reports, the inspectors commented on many of the defects of the results system and expressed dissatisfaction in varying degrees with aspects of its operation. There were many recommendations that individual examination could be dispensed with in certain subjects, that class examination would be more suitable in some instances, that merit grants ought to be introduced, that some subjects could be made optional, and that various combinations of the foregoing could be applied to the inspection system. The most incisive of the inspectors were Peter Connellan and Samuel E. Stronge, both of whom were head inspectors and had been noted critics of the operation of payment by results for a protracted period. However, nothing was done in Tyrone House to implement any changes to either the programme of instruction or the inspection system in advance of the major inquiry that was initiated by the Commissioners in the summer of 1896. In effect, the dismantlement of payment by results was postponed pending whatever actions the Commissioners themselves would take at a later time. This may be seen as a significant failure on the part of the administration in Marlborough Street to introduce some interim reforms of the results system despite an acute need and a relatively clear consensus among inspectors that change was necessary.

A number of Commissioners including Walsh, Palles and Fitzgerald were alert to a movement in education towards practical and manual subjects. At this time, the Recess Committee convened during the parliamentary recess in 1896, had given consideration to technical education as an issue of importance for the economic and social improvement of Ireland with a particular interest in all facets of education including the national schools. Leading Commissioners proposed an official commission of inquiry for primary education and, following a determined representation to government, were successful in achieving their aim. In January 1897, the Vice-Regal Commission on Manual and Practical Instruction was appointed under the chairmanship of Lord Belmore. Decisive factors in the appointment of the Commission were the influence of the Recess Committee and the political climate of constructive unionism which sought to ameliorate social and economic conditions in Ireland generally.

17 Minutes of CNEI, 3 March 1896.

The remit of the Commission was narrow. It was to 'inquire and report with a view to determining how far, and in what form' manual and practical instruction should be included in the programme for national schools. The Commission took account of new patterns of practical instruction emergent in Britain, Scotland and on the continent focusing particularly on curricular and pedagogical aspects with limited reference to contextual factors such as the administration or financing of education. In all, the Commission took evidence from 186 persons and held 93 meetings before its final report was ready for publication in June 1898.

REPORT OF BELMORE COMMISSION

Although its terms of reference were narrow, the Belmore Commission managed to range widely on curricular policy and associated issues. The final report proposed sweeping changes in the primary school curriculum and implied significant reorganisation of national education. Kindergarten was recommended to be extended as far as possible to all schools, hand and eye training and educational woodwork were suggested as suitable for older children, and drawing, singing, drill and physical exercises were recommended to be taught to all children. Elementary science including object lessons and simple experiments, was also recommended. Cookery, laundry work, domestic science and needlework were included as suitable for girls. The report envisaged the gradual introduction of the new subjects and the employment of expert advisers to assist teachers in the implementation of the recommended programme. Most importantly, the Commission was strongly of the opinion that results fees depending on individual examination of pupils ought not to apply to the new subjects but instead the industry, methodology and effectiveness of the teacher should be the main focus of inspection of schoolwork.[18]

Taken as a whole, the Belmore Commission represented an important landmark in national education in Ireland. A changed conception of the meaning and purpose of education was enshrined in its final report while a new and enlightened view of childhood animated its thinking. The report recognised the one-sided nature of primary education and proposed forms of experience and observation as important avenues for learning at school. It called for less dependence on book knowledge and rote learning and instead recommended training in habits of correct reasoning and the acquisition of hand and eye skills for educative purposes. The report concluded that manual and practical training would benefit pupils by stimulating their intelligence, increasing their interest in schoolwork and making school life brighter and more pleasant while it was believed that the literary aspects of study need not suffer adverse effects. It envisaged the development of technical education at post-primary and higher

18 Ibid., pp 2–4.

levels and acknowledged the need for primary education to prepare pupils suitably so that they might benefit from any form of further education be it literary, scientific or technical. This represented a notable advance on the view that primary schooling was in itself a complete education. Now the emphasis was on a wider curriculum so that the primary school might provide a suitable foundation for a broad range of further education and training.

New thinking about the three Rs was in evidence deriving partly from greater awareness of the ways in which children learn and attributable mainly to better understanding about infant teaching. Arithmetic was to be linked more with every day experience, reading was to be seen as a key to information and writing was to be based more on the observation and experience of children.[19] Another distinctive feature of the report was the emphasis placed on the inter-relatedness of school subjects. Local circumstances were to be taken into account in deciding how to approach the teaching of certain subjects and the greater freedom for teachers that this entailed was a very significant development. The report mentioned in-service training and greater cooperation and liaison between schools as necessary to support the satisfactory implementation of the new curriculum. Whereas some of the ideas outlined in the report could be regarded as honourable aspirations unlikely to be translated into reality, the report voiced strong disapprobation for payment by results and signalled the necessity to follow English and Scottish developments, holding out definite promise of change on this central issue.

Although the report was impressive in its discussion of the various educational aspects explored, it was not without serious flaws. The most obvious of these was that the report did not examine the national system with a view to determining appropriate measures for the introduction of the desired change in curriculum. Major infrastructural deficiencies received scant attention. Important matters such as inadequate buildings, poor amenities and equipment, small schools, irregular attendance and untrained teachers, did not receive studied consideration but were assumed to be satisfactory or perhaps not regarded as germane to the issues of manual and practical instruction. The Commission was deeply influenced by the evidence taken abroad where circumstances were entirely different. The Commission viewed curricular policy and practice as an element in isolation and, consequently, found it easy to recommend the transposition to the national school system of all that was best in England, Scotland and to some extent Sweden. As a result, the report proposed an ambitious scheme to be superimposed on the existing programme with only minimal adjustments to the overall system of national education. This was a substantial flaw in the work of the Belmore Commission.

Just as serious was its failure to examine the financial implications of the proposed changes. The final report acknowledged that considerable expendi-

19 Ibid., p. 13.

ture would be necessary and, glossing over the financial complexities, expressed confidence that the state would not hesitate to provide the funds required to improve the system. This was certainly disingenuous since it was well known among the members of the Commission that the Treasury was very unlikely to be enthusiastic about proposals for increased spending. The Commission made no attempt to consider the enormous intricacies of teachers' salary payments. Regrettably, the final report did not give useful guidance on essential financial changes that would require careful planning in advance nor did it help to prepare the way for transition to implementing the recommended curriculum. The Commission did not attempt to analyse the implications of its proposals for such key groups as inspectors or the administrative staff at the National Education Office. This was disappointing since these groups had a crucial role to play in facilitating the gradual movement towards changing the curriculum.

The narrow focus of the Belmore Commission, combined with its lack of thoroughness in examining relevant contextual issues, left behind many unanswered questions and much unfinished business. Although the members of the Commission had accomplished a great deal in elucidating the parameters for a new curriculum and hastening the abandonment of payment by results in primary education in Ireland, there were many underlying issues affecting national education that remained unresolved and which would necessitate particular attention in the following years.

TOWARDS A NEW CURRICULUM AND THE ENDING OF PAYMENT BY RESULTS

Following on from the publication of the Belmore report, a two-year period of uncertainty and hesitation ensued during which the administration of national education seemed almost paralysed and incapable of taking decisions to give effect to the recommendations of the Commission. This was an especially fraught period in the affairs of national education and some extraordinary tensions were in evidence among the most senior personnel in Tyrone House. What was most obviously apparent was that the administration was very poorly prepared to address the very significant issues that now presented themselves for action and resolution. The death of C.T. Redington and the retirement of some of the leading officials contributed to a delay in introducing changes for the primary schools of Ireland. Eventually, a new curriculum and a new salary system for national teachers were drawn up and were to be put into effect at the commencement of the new century. At the same time, a major restructuring of the inspection corps was decided upon and this also was to come into effect in 1900–01.

4

The Primary School Inspectorate, 1900–22

The year 1900 represented the dawn of a new era for national education in Ireland. The ending of payment by results, the introduction of a new salary system for teachers, the publication of a new programme of instruction coupled with the appointment of a new staff of organisers to assist its introduction, rearranged procedures for inspection and a reorganised inspectorate, ensured that for all associated with primary education 1900 was indeed a watershed. It was the beginning of a remarkably different epoch in the affairs of national education, one in which controversy and discord seemed to take the place of the relative tranquillity and calm of the results era. The new century ushered in a period of extraordinary turbulence in national education and various issues attracted enormous public interest so much so that national education was almost constantly in the news. The provision for the teaching of Irish, as a subject and as a medium of instruction, became a major focus for public controversy when the Gaelic League was especially active in the campaign for greater attention to the teaching of Irish. The new programme of instruction was also a focus for considerable debate and criticism, while the new salary arrangements for teachers were a source of great concern for many years. Other issues such as the reform of Irish education, the managerial system and school conditions, also attracted enormous interest and debate. Thus, the early years of the new century were packed with incident, and education questions commanded unusual and sustained public attention against a background of important political, social and cultural change.

The efforts to reform many features of the national school system were to be affected by inadequate resourcing. Ireland depended to a very large degree on central exchequer funding for the support of the national school system. The Treasury considered that per capita expenditure on Irish primary schooling was too high. Furthermore, in the early years of the century, the government sought a restructuring of the administration of Irish education, which would allow more scope for local authorities and for local funding of schools. Such plans were successfully opposed. As a response, the Treasury kept limitations of its expenditure on education. This resulted in tensions between policy makers and funders, and continued to act as a brake on the achievement of policy aspirations.

THE STARKIE ERA, 1899–1920

The appointment by the government of Dr William J.M. Starkie as Resident Commissioner in 1899 marked the beginning of the new era in the national school system. A distinguished classicist and former president of Queen's College, Galway, Starkie had no previous connection with the national schools and took over at a time of momentous change. Within a year of his appointment, a new curriculum was being drawn up and a major restructuring of the inspectorate was also devised. A new salary system for teachers had to be created as it was intended to abandon the results system in one swift administrative change. These reforms came at a time when the circumstances of the public finances were not the most propitious as the Boer War had begun in South Africa and the government insisted on economies in the National Education Office. The inexperienced Starkie gave promises that proved difficult to maintain in the course of time in the light of these developments. His career as Resident Commissioner lasted until his death in 1920 when the country was on the brink of new political arrangements.

NEW SALARY STRUCTURE FOR TEACHERS AND THE
LINK TO INSPECTION

The most complex task facing Starkie was to create a new salary structure for teachers to replace the results system. After much deliberation, a consolidated salary system was finalised by the summer of 1900. The main feature of the new system was the division of teachers' salaries into first, second and third grades, with first grade being further divided into two sections, with fixed salary for each grade, and with scales of continued good service salary accruing by increments in each grade. Teachers would be eligible for increases of salary at intervals of not less than three years so that the increments were known as triennial. An important feature of the new system was that the higher grades of salary could only be paid to teachers who worked in schools with larger average attendances, so that for example, first grade salary required at least 50 children in average attendance. Promotion from grade to grade now depended on schoolwork alone and this meant that inspection of schools was to have a huge connection with teachers' salary payments especially as regards upward movement in the salary grades. An important corollary to the new grade system was that the Board was constrained to agree with the Treasury that the maximum number of teachers to be recognised in the different grades above the third grade should be definitely fixed. Known as 'standard numbers', these strictly limited the numbers of teachers who could be promoted to the highest salary grades. The Board had very little scope to allow flexibility in resolving individual teachers' salary claims as the financial constraints imposed by the

Treasury were severe and quite unsuited to the very complicated salary arrangements that were now being devised.

Throughout 1900 and later years, there was a great deal of confusion about the exact implications of the new grading system. The magnitude of the task of transferring some 12,000 teachers' salaries from the old classification system to the grade system posed enormous difficulties for the Office. The complexities of rearranging teachers' salaries stretched its administrative resources far beyond the limit, with the result that for more than a decade, all sorts of anomalies cropped up, causing considerable irritation among the teaching force and adding greatly to the difficulties of administering national education. The situation in the Office verged on the chaotic in the initial stages of the grading system. A major casualty arising from this was the resignation from the Board in 1901 of Archbishop William J. Walsh in a blaze of publicity. Walsh publicly criticised the officials in Marlborough Street for incompetence and Starkie was obliged to defend his administration though he had been himself critical in private of the same officials. Starkie was rueful about the loss of Walsh, perceiving it as a calamity for the Board. The changeover to the new salary system was badly managed and remained a source of considerable grievance among teachers for many years.

While inspectors formerly had a connection with both teachers' incomes and promotions, through results examinations and classification examinations, the new grading system required that all triennial increments and grade promotions would be based absolutely on inspectors' reports subject to other conditions being met. This meant that teachers' prospects of increments and promotions would depend solely on the recommendations of the inspectors. Whereas previously the inspector's results examination might determine a third of a teacher's income, the new grading system made a teacher's advancement in the service almost completely dependent on inspectors' ratings. This was a marked change from the results era when a strict inspector might not give the benefit of the doubt to some pupils under examination but which would cost the teacher a relatively small sum in lost earnings. Under the grade system, an unfavourable inspector's report could depress a teacher's income considerably and could have a severe cumulative effect over a period of years. Simply stated, the salary arrangements of 1900 imposed a much heavier burden of responsibility on inspectors than had previously been the case. Nothing of particular significance was done to prepare the inspectors for their new responsibilities and the system took effect with a notable degree of uncertainty and confusion about many aspects of teachers' remuneration.

REORGANISATION OF THE INSPECTORATE, 1900

A thorough restructuring of the inspectorate was proposed by Starkie within a short time of his appointment. The fact that leading Commissioners had lost confidence in some of the most senior officials was a large factor in the plans drawn up at the end of 1899. The single most dramatic reconfiguration of the inspectorate that had ever occurred was unveiled in the early months of 1900. All inspectors were to receive new titles, a new organisational structure was devised, salary scales were to be revised, the competitive examination for entry was to be abolished and teachers were to be eligible for promotion to the position of junior inspector in certain circumstances. The district system was to be replaced with an arrangement whereby the country was divided into 22 inspection circuits, in each of which a senior inspector and two junior inspectors would be based. A notable feature of the reorganisation was that a cut of about 20% in both staffing and expenditure was envisaged, though it was known that this could only be accomplished over a considerable period through natural wastage. The principle of denominational balance as between Catholic and Protestant appointments as inspectors was continued up to 1922.

The title Chiefs of Inspection was changed to that of Chief Inspectors. A critical and dramatic aspect of the restructuring was that the Chief Inspectors would no longer be an integral part of the administration in Marlborough Street but rather be in charge of all aspects of inspection. No longer would it be deemed appropriate for them to aspire to appointment as Secretaries in the Office. Instead, they were expected to oversee the detailed operation of inspection in the schools and training colleges. This aspect of the restructuring was a major cause of conflict between the senior inspectors and Starkie and the other Commissioners. In what was one of the most extraordinary developments of Starkie's career in charge of national education, both Chiefs of Inspection, Edmund Downing and Alfred Purser, were suspended from duty by order of the Board in early 1900. These two senior officials subsequently returned to service. Starkie was opposed to their reinstatement and how seriously he viewed the issue can be gleaned from the following quotation:

> During the first year of the new system the incapacity and disloyalty of some of the senior officials was so injurious to its success that I was constrained to use very strong language to some of my colleagues ... I pointed out that the Chief Inspectors had been disloyal to the Board from the beginning and I disapproved of making them pass judgment on a scheme which they had tried to kill.[1]

Underlying tensions and conflict were to fester and be the cause of various difficulties for a protracted period. Whereas various attempts were made by inspectors to modify aspects of the proposed restructuring, the Commissioners resisted all efforts to alter the new arrangements.

1 W.J.M. Starkie, *Confidential Evidence to the Vice-Regal Commission of Inquiry into Primary Education*, 1913 Appendix [CD. 6829], pp 5, 6.

THE REVISED PROGRAMME OF INSTRUCTION IN
NATIONAL SCHOOLS, 1900

Doctor Starkie was responsible for the preparation of a draft programme to take account of the Belmore report and a number of individuals contributed to this in one way or another. Eventually, the final draft of the programme was approved by the Board and was circulated in September 1900 as the Revised Programme of Instruction in National Schools. A detailed syllabus, representing a year's work, was specified for each of six standards in every subject of the Revised Programme.

Taken as a whole, the Revised Programme amounted to a major redefinition of the aims, principles and content of instruction in the national school system. All the elements that the Belmore Commission had recommended were incorporated into this new curriculum. The familiar subjects, English and arithmetic, were given a new orientation and made more purposeful. Kindergarten was extended and linked to manual instruction while object lessons and elementary science were completely new. Drawing, singing and physical drill were to be features of instruction for all children. School organisation was fundamentally altered with the arranging of six standards after infants and the delineation of approximate ages for the different standards. The Revised Programme had enormous implications for the improvement of school buildings, furnishings and equipment but this aspect was not given studied attention at this juncture.

An important aspect of the revision of the curriculum was the decision to appoint a number of organisers, many of them from England, to assist in the introduction of the new subjects into the schools. Thus, organisers for music, elementary science, drawing, cookery and laundry work, and needlework were nominally the responsibility of the Chief Inspectors. The intention was that the organisers would train teachers sufficiently to be able to introduce new subjects into their schools or, in the case of vocal music, drawing and needlework, improve considerably the teaching of subjects with which teachers had some familiarity. Appointed initially for a five-year term, the organisers arranged courses for teachers throughout Ireland and met with varying levels of success. Drawing, elementary science, needlework and singing progressed very well under the tutelage of the organisers. The work of the organisers, despite the lack of success in some respects, was quite remarkable. Hundreds of short courses were arranged for teachers all over Ireland. Holiday periods, Saturdays and evenings were all utilised to disseminate information and skills relevant to particular aspects of the Revised Programme. Teachers responded extremely well to the opportunities offered and were enthusiastic in their attendance and participation in the new courses. The organisers combined courses with visits to schools where they endeavoured to demonstrate teaching techniques for the benefit of teachers. Although the services of some of the assistant organisers were dispensed with in 1905, the Board retained a staff of organisers on a permanent basis. Kindergarten organisers were later deployed to concentrate on infant training while a number of Irish language organisers were appointed to focus on the teaching of Irish in the national schools.

The organisers made a very notable contribution to the dissemination of the Revised Programme and to the improvement of teaching methods generally. The inspectors cooperated well with the staff of organisers. Inspectors gave assistance to the organisers with regard to the selection of centres for courses and in drawing up lists of teachers who might be invited to attend. In their reports, inspectors adverted to the work of the organisers and hoped that further training would be made available to the teachers in particular aspects of the programme. Inspectors praised the enthusiasm of teachers in regard to attendance at courses and acknowledged the benefits that were evident in teaching practice in schools. Inspectors themselves attended organisers' courses in Dublin between 1901 and 1903, when arrangements were made to release twelve inspectors at a time, to attend science and manual instruction classes for a few weeks each. For their part, the organisers were conscious of the influence of inspectors in relation to the introduction and continuance of their subjects in the schools.

INSPECTION UNDER THE REVISED PROGRAMME OF INSTRUCTION

The Revised Instructions to Inspectors issued in July 1902, provided the basis for inspection for a long period. The instructions reiterated the leading principles of the Revised Programme and commented on many detailed aspects of the curriculum outlining desirable practice in classrooms. The main thrust of the instructions was that the Revised Programme necessitated new methods of inspection. These were to consist mainly of observation of teaching methodology and oral examination of pupils on a class or sample basis with a view to formulating an estimate of the quality of work done. An annual report would be furnished on every school based on a formal inspection with advance notice, but also taking into account other incidental visits, during which aspects of schoolwork would be assessed. The main object of incidental visits was to be the promotion of good teaching methods and inspectors were to take careful account of the quality of work observed.[2]

Inspectors had been habituated to inspecting in a particular way under the results system and this contrasted sharply with what was expected in the new dispensation. For inspectors and for teachers the degree and extent of change required for the Revised Programme was enormous. Not surprisingly, there were many difficulties encountered in the transition to the new system. An important difficulty that accompanied all the changes introduced in 1900–

2 CNEI, *Appendix to the Rules and Regulations 1903* (Dublin: Thom, 1904), pp 1–11.

01 was that a number of the most senior inspectors were alienated by the drastic reorganisation of the inspection system. As a result, the management of the inspection staff during the early years of the Revised Programme was significantly affected. For much of the first decade of the twentieth century, inspection did not have good leadership and this was a significant contributory factor to both the troubles that beset Starkie's administration and the difficulties experienced by some teachers.

Relations between Starkie and the Chief Inspectors remained very strained and this had very serious effects on the management of the inspectorate in the new climate of the Revised Programme. Relations within the National Education Office were soured in all sorts of ways and for several years bitterness and disaffection were factors of note within the administration with serious consequences in some respects. One of the Chief Inspectors was superannuated eventually by the Board at Starkie's request though this did not end the conflict.[3] Some features of the day-to-day work of the inspectors did not appear to receive the attention that they might have been accorded. For example, conferences of the senior inspectors relating to the revised curriculum were convened only belatedly in 1903 and 1904 to explore some of the detailed aspects of inspection in the changed context of the schools. Similarly, the Chief Inspectors did not create any new definition of their role in the new circumstances preferring to yearn for their former roles within the Office. As a result, the management of inspectors was lacking strong directional control and monitoring.

An important aspect dealt with at the conferences in 1903 and 1904 was the system of marking to be used in schools under the revised curriculum. With the abolition of the results examinations, an annual general inspection of every school was now intended with the assignment of a merit mark to individual teachers and schools. Six merit marks were now decided on and these were to be the terms Excellent, Very Good, Good, Fair, Middling and Bad. Securing uniformity among inspectors was the intention of the senior inspectors and seven criteria of assessment were agreed:

> An *excellent* school is one in which (1) the whole programme is taught in a highly creditable manner; (2) in which the best methods of teaching are in use; (3) the educational equipment ample; (4) the tone and discipline of a high order; (5) order and tidiness exemplary; (6) the school records neat, correct, and complete; and (7) house and premises of a good class and in good order.[4]

Though it was stated that it was 'obviously impossible to formulate precise definitions' for each of the six gradations of school merit, the senior inspectors

3 Minutes of CNEI, 5 January 1904.   4 *Vice-Regal Commission of Inquiry*, Appendix to First Report, p. 223.

proceeded to postulate approximate descriptions for each of the terms. Thus, it was arranged that 'Fair' would be taken to mean a school which was neither praiseworthy nor blameworthy as regards programme, methods, tone and discipline, order and tidiness, but whose premises were in fair repair, whose equipment was fairly adequate and whose records were correct and complete. A 'Bad' school would mean a school which was unsatisfactory in every respect. The senior inspectors drew up a tabular summation of this marking system and gave definitions for highly efficient and efficient teachers:

> A *highly* efficient teacher should show *special* aptitude in developing the intelligence of his pupils; in cultivating habits of order, neatness, attention, and industry, and in maintaining a firm but pleasant discipline. His preparation for work should be thorough, and his pupils should attain a *highly* creditable proficiency.[5]

An efficient teacher was defined as above with the omission of the italicised words.

This was the most important matter agreed at the 1903 conference and it decided, more or less, the common parlance of inspection in primary education in Ireland for close to fifty years. What was especially relevant for inspectors were the merit marks to be assigned to the teachers and to the schools on the occasion of the annual general report. It is evident that the senior inspectors realised the enormous difficulty attaching to exact description of the various marks but it seems likely that they underestimated the complexity of securing uniformity among all inspectors in the allocation of merit marks. Another significant difficulty was that the seven criteria chosen did not distinguish between a teacher's work and factors outside the teacher's control. Whereas it might be deemed correct to expect a teacher to maintain school records properly, it was hardly correct to evaluate any teacher partly on an assessment of the repair of house and premises and the sufficiency of school equipment. A further complication was that the merit of an individual school principal was intertwined with the merit of assistant teachers, and all were tied up with premises and equipment in a way that confused issues considerably. Another awkward feature was that there were six different merit categories, loosely demarcated, and certain to produce unreliable estimates of merit when applied by different inspectors.

This was the system of merit marks which was used for well over a decade but which was not properly understood by teachers for much of that time. Defined by the conferences of senior inspectors, the merit marks were a vital part of inspection and had particular significance for the award of increments and promotions. This was necessitated by the salary system with its grade

5 Ibid.

salaries and increments which were to be based absolutely on the merit marks assigned by the inspectors at the time of the annual general report. In a move which was indicative of a revision of the reorganisation of the Office arrangements of 1900, Starkie was obliged to assign an inspector to duties in Marlborough Street in 1903 dealing almost exclusively with teachers' promotions and increments derived from the merit marks given by inspectors over successive years. Both Samuel E. Stronge and A.N. Bonaparte Wyse were assigned responsibilities within the Office to augment the administrative side in relation to the intricacies of teachers' increments and promotions.

There were few national conferences after 1904. Instead there were regional or circuit conferences that were to be relied on in future to ensure uniformity of inspection and to facilitate the arrangement of business. In addition, the Chief Inspectors were supposed to preside at a conference in each circuit at least once a year, though it may be surmised that this proviso was not always adhered to. However, the fact that conferences at circuit level were part and parcel of inspection work from 1901, made it possible to think that there was very good provision for exchange of views and consultation about aspects of inspection. While it seems certain that circuit conferences were helpful in many ways to all inspectors, these meetings were primarily local and had as their main focus operational despatch and effectiveness. Policy and planning considerations were not the functions of small gatherings where senior inspectors spoke to two or three junior inspectors. The group of senior inspectors did not have and did not seek to have any opportunity to come together to discuss their work and look to its improvement and refinement. Thus, senior inspectors did not play a distinctive role in the overall management of inspection in the post-1900 period. The failure to continue the conferences of 1903–04 was a mistake since it is reasonable to think that meetings such as those would have, in time, enabled the overall management of inspection to be modified and strengthened. The Chief Inspectors did not bring forward any notable initiatives to improve the management of the inspection corps at this time and the inspection system continued to function in general terms as it had done in the past.

ISSUES AND CONTROVERSY AFFECTING INSPECTION

In the early years of the new century, various issues and notable controversies arose and many of these had links with the inspectors. In a notable public address in Belfast in 1902, Starkie commented upon various aspects of Irish education, offering a wide-ranging and candid critique of the system.[6] In so doing, Starkie broke with the tradition of silence and reserve set by his pred-

6 W.J.M. Starkie, *Recent Reforms in Irish Education, Primary and Secondary, with a view to their co-ordination* (Dublin: Blackie, 1902).

ecessors who avoided public discussion of educational issues. Among the topics referred to in his address was the question of the managerial system and local interest in education. Starkie drew attention to the neglect of proper maintenance of national school buildings and the lack of heating, cleaning and general comfort and hygiene in schools, relating these to issues of funding, control and interest in local facilities for education. This led to a storm of protest and a protracted and vigorous controversy ensued. Starkie was obliged to explain that he had spoken in a personal capacity only and not as a representative of the National Board. Of particular interest is the fact that Starkie drew on inspectors' reports to support his views on the managerial question and later, when his Belfast address was published, Starkie included several pages of extracts from inspectors' reports to buttress his arguments and challenge his critics. In what was a carefully edited and very selective use of inspectors' reports, Starkie asserted that managers were generally indifferent to the practical needs of education, that the ordinary supervision of the schools was insufficient, that the upkeep of school buildings was neglected and that, apart from the managers themselves, there was virtually no interest in education at the local level.

Major structural changes in education in Britain, along with the many changes that had taken place in primary, secondary and technical education in Ireland, helped to focus greater attention on the overall functioning of the Irish education system after 1900. Issues relating to the financing, administration and co-ordination of Irish education became politically important and the establishment of a department of education was under consideration during this time. In the event, there was determined opposition to the proposals for major reform and no significant restructuring of Irish education resulted.

An important development as regards the national schools was the appointment of an English inspector, F.H. Dale, to survey the conditions in Irish primary schools and to compare their circumstances with those of England. Dale spent over two months visiting schools in selected centres throughout Ireland and was accompanied by the local inspectors, having earlier been given their reports on particular schools. Starkie spent a considerable amount of time in Dale's company travelling to schools. Dale's report was a model of clarity and objectivity and provided the contextual background to national education that was sadly overlooked by the Belmore Commission six years previously.[7] Dale pointed out a wide range of radical defects in the national school system in comparison to elementary education in England. His report detailed serious deficiencies in regard to school premises, equipment, staffing, attendance, infant education and instruction generally. Many of the difficulties were seen as attributable to the multiplication of small schools, the lack of local interest and financial accountability, and the effects of payment

7 *Report of Mr F.H. Dale, H.M. Inspector of Schools, Board of Education, on Primary Education in Ireland* (Cd. 1981), HC 1904, xx.

by results. The report highlighted the need for some modifications to the Revised Programme and recommended that specimen schemes, adapted to various types of school, should be circulated to teachers. Convent schools were found to be superior in terms of repair, cleanliness and quality of instruction than almost all other schools, including the model schools. A special appendix listed defects in the model schools including insufficiency of classrooms and unsuitable organisation, and concluded that even though they were superior to the average national school, they did not in any meaningful sense afford models of primary education. Even the Central Model Schools in Marlborough Street, the practising schools for the training college, merited some stern observations by Dale.

Dale showed particular discernment in relation to inspection. He pointed out that since the existing state of instruction in the schools was very deficient as regards intelligence and method due to the results system, it would take a considerable time before improved methods would be practised generally. Dale stated that much depended on the Board's inspectors during the period of transition but he added that their time was taken up with the holding of detailed annual examinations of all schools, so that they had little opportunity of paying incidental visits directed towards suggestions and advice to teachers. Therefore, he recommended that inspectors should be relieved of the necessity of holding formal examinations except in cases where schools were unsatisfactory. Dale also realised that inspectors could not discharge the functions of an effective local authority in matters such as cleaning and sanitation in schools, aspects which were widely neglected by school managers throughout Ireland. Similarly, inspectors could not hope to have sufficient knowledge of, and contact with teachers, to be able to discharge the responsibility for teachers' promotions, which were the responsibility of the local authority in England. With particular perspicacity, Dale noted that teachers would avail of every means to secure promotion and he inferred that teachers and inspectors were on a collision course when he predicted that there would be increasing numbers of appeals against the judgment of inspectors.

Dale also commented at length on the salary scheme in Ireland and he concluded that teachers had genuine grievances in regard to its operation. He contended that the arrangement whereby all teachers commenced at the lowest grade of salary, irrespective of the size of school, was not just to the teachers, and he recommended that the size of the school should be a larger factor in determining a teacher's income.

Although Dale's comments on inspection were perceptive, they were but a small part of his report so that his forewarning about appeals against inspectors' judgments and the likelihood of pressure over promotions, did not receive much attention. When his report was considered by the government and by the Board, inspection did not feature as an issue for concern and Dale's observations did not prompt notable alteration in its functioning.

However, some changes were introduced in response to Dale's report. Specimen programmes were issued to assist teachers in different types of schools and manual instruction was dropped from the curriculum. New rules were drafted to provide for the amalgamation of small schools for boys and girls adjacent to each other, and to provide for the instruction of boys under eight years by women teachers.

While the government later appointed Dale and another inspector, T.A. Stephens, to examine intermediate and technical education, including the co-ordination of Irish education generally, neither their report nor Dale's earlier report on primary education resulted in significant reform of the structure of education in Ireland. Throughout this period, the government adopted a policy of rigorous control over expenditure on education, refusing claims for extra funding and limiting spending as much as possible. Government attempts to reform Irish education had serious consequences for national education, especially in relation to expenditure on virtually every aspect, but most acutely felt in regard to building grants. The annual reports of the National Board during these years were filled with accounts of the attempts made to gain Treasury sanction for various new proposals that were initiated primarily by Starkie. These included proposals for higher grade national schools, scholarship schemes, grants of free books to pupils, fees for school gardens, heating and cleaning grants and extra payments for principals of large schools. In accordance with government policy, the Treasury maintained a firm control over spending, thus severely hampering the Board's attempts to improve national education.

In an important lecture in 1911, Starkie made government policy and Treasury parsimony towards national education a major theme of his forthright address. Explaining why the building of schools had virtually come to a standstill during the previous years, he characterised the Board's predicament as follows:

> We are sent from post to pillar. We are sent from the Treasury to the Development Grant; from the Development Grant to the rates; and from the rates back again to the Exchequer. Such is the disgraceful position in which Irish education is ... The rule of the Treasury in dealing with us is invariably that of the White Queen in 'Alice through the looking glass', 'jam tomorrow and jam yesterday – but never jam today'.[8]

Starkie was highly critical of the way in which the National Board had been treated over a long period and it was indicative of his courage and independence that he did not hesitate to give public expression to his views.

8 W.J.M. Starkie, *The History of Irish Primary and Intermediate Education*, address at Queen's University Belfast, 3 July 1911 (Dublin: Thom, 1911).

During the early years of the new century, there was considerable controversy about the teaching of Irish in the national schools. In response to public pressure from the Gaelic League, a small but important cadre of Irish language specialist inspectors was appointed in 1904. The Bilingual Programme, introduced that year, broadened the scope for the teaching of Irish in districts where it was used as a vernacular, while Irish could also be taught as an extra subject for special fees. A further related development was the appointment of six organisers of Irish language instruction in 1907. In this the Board was responding to a powerful new cultural influence that was spreading throughout the country and heralding the emergence of significant new political realities.

Throughout these years, Starkie made a point of visiting schools himself all over Ireland. It became his practice to set aside a few weeks each year to devote himself almost exclusively to school visitations sometimes combining a tour of inspection with family holidays in places such as Donegal, Sligo and Cork. Normally, he was accompanied on school visits by inspectors or senior officials of the Board or others with an interest in education. Starkie prided himself on his knowledge of schools and his acquaintance with the circumstances obtaining in education throughout Ireland. He evinced particular concern for school conditions and sought to improve provision for sanitation and accommodation. Most important of all, Starkie was strongly committed to the promotion of the principles of the Revised Programme and he lent his weight and authority to the raising of standards of education throughout the country.

TEACHERS' DISSATISFACTION AND THE DILL INQUIRY, 1913

Increments and promotions were a constant cause of concern among the teachers throughout the first years of the new salary system and the INTO brought forward many representations on behalf of its members. Since inspectors' merit marks had immediate impact on the remuneration of the teachers, it was little wonder that the salary arrangements held the potential for major contention. Two particular organised claims came to notice a decade after the system had commenced. A group of Belfast teachers petitioned the Board, stating that grave discontent prevailed in the Belfast circuits due to the lowering of merit marks and consequent loss of increments and promotions. Essentially, it was believed that the standard of marking by inspectors was stricter in Belfast than elsewhere. A conference of senior inspectors was convened by the Board in May 1911 to consider inspection and a new circular was issued in June in response to the various criticisms put forward by the teachers. While the Belfast teachers' claims were not upheld, the new circular, popularly referred to as the 'tone' circular, sought to underline the necessity of cultivating friendly and cordial relations with managers and teachers while emphasising that the tone of a school was its most important characteristic. The circular also stressed that a school's merit mark could not in future be altered unless a joint mark had been agreed by junior and senior inspectors.[9]

Shortly after the Belfast case, a similar claim was brought forward by teachers in Clonmel. Protracted correspondence and investigation resulted and considerable tension developed around the issue and the personalities involved. Finally in 1912, the Board took the severe step of dismissing Edmund Mansfield a prominent INTO figure and spokesman for the Clonmel teachers.[10] A veritable storm of protest greeted the dismissal and, under severe pressure from various representative bodies such as local councils and Gaelic League branches, the government agreed to set up an inquiry. Chaired by Sir Samuel Dill, the inquiry was directed to examine the rules, regulations and practice of the Commissioners concerning inspection and to provide recommendations as to what changes were desirable in the system of inspection and associated matters. In effect, the inspectors and the Office, Starkie and to some extent the Board, were on trial on charges particularly linked to increments, promotions, appeals, and general procedures and relations between teachers and inspectors.

The inquiry began in January 1913 and its report was ready exactly one year later.[11] The report made nineteen recommendations six of which suggested changes in the incremental, promotional and grading system for teachers. Other recommendations included better appeal mechanisms, public disclosure of circulars to inspectors, advance consultation with managerial and teacher interests about new regulations, the creation of new posts of divisional inspector, an extended probationary period for new inspectors and the abolition of inspectors' observation books.

Though the Dill inquiry had trawled extensively through many elements of the Board's administration of national schools, it did not manage to shed imaginative light on many of the problems that beset the teachers. While minor changes were suggested, the inquiry did not produce a comprehensive analysis of the inspectorate nor of its linkage with the Office administration. Relations between the INTO and Starkie continued to be rancorous and the inspection system continued to be viewed with suspicion and distrust. The controversy left a considerable legacy of acrimony and hostility associated with the overall administration of the national school system at a time of gradually changing political realities.

A new circular was issued in January 1915 to give effect to the changes that the Board agreed in the light of the Dill report. A related development was the appointment of three divisional inspectors in 1917 and it was hoped

9 CNEI, *National Education Circulars 1900–1913* (Dublin: Thom, 1914).   10 *Vice-Regal Commission of Inquiry*, Appendix to First Report, pp 200–22 and T.J. O'Connell, *History of the INTO* (Dublin: INTO, 1968), pp 401–11.   11 *Vice-Regal Commission of Inquiry, Final Report.*

that these new posts would secure as far as possible a uniform and correct standard in inspectors' estimates of the efficiency of schools and teachers. The divisional grade was to augment also the managerial role of the chief inspectors and this was a notable feature of an important new tier in the inspectorate.

END OF AN ERA

A period of great political uncertainty in Ireland followed Asquith's Home Rule bill of 1912. The First World War, the Easter Rising of 1916, the threat of conscription and the Sinn Fein electoral success of 1918, the setting up of Dáil Eireann in 1919, the strife and war in Ireland in 1920 and after, all combined to make this a period of intense uncertainty and disturbance in Irish society. Tumultuous events and rapid changes in the political sphere overshadowed developments in the educational field. A Vice-Regal Committee of Inquiry into Primary Education (under Lord Killanin) reported in February 1919.[12] It recommended improved salary scales for teachers and a number of administrative changes for primary education. It did not deal with school inspection. The Killanin Report fed into the ill-fated Education bill of 1919.

For the inspectorate, 1915 to 1921 was a time of little development in regard to the overall structure and pattern of its functioning. The established patterns of recruitment and training of inspectors continued though a new and significant element was the recruitment of a small number of women about this time, and this pattern was to continue under native government.[13] Certain aspects of school life appeared to prosper most notably perhaps the curriculum in the schools. Starkie and some of the inspectors were increasingly discomfited by the political developments of the period with the rise of nationalistic feeling which viewed them as part of the crown's administrative machinery. In the latter half of 1920 and in the period leading to the truce of July 1921, the ordinary functioning of the inspectorate was notably circumscribed in some parts of the country. Starkie suffered poor health and died in 1920, his position left unfilled. Eventually, under the terms of the Government of Ireland Act of 1920, arrangements were made for the division of the country into two parts, Northern Ireland and Southern Ireland, each with its own government and education department.

At the end of January 1922, a special meeting of the National Board was summoned at the instance of Fionan Lynch, Minister of Education of the Provisional Government. Acting on his behalf, Pádraig Ó Brolcháin addressed the Commissioners and informed them that as chief executive officer, he proposed to take full control of and responsibility for primary education in

---

12 *Report of Vice-Regal Committee of Inquiry into Primary Education* (Killanin) C.60. 13 Mary Mulryan-Maloney, 'Women Teachers in the National Education System, 1870–1922', Unpublished PhD dissertation, National University of Ireland, Maynooth, 2005.

Ireland, including the full administrative and executive functions of the Board. In accordance with the directions of the Provisional Government, Ó Brolcháin was to take over charge of the Office on 1 February 1922, effectively disbanding the Commissioners of National Education after more than ninety years of existence.[14] A new epoch had begun.

14 Minutes of CNEI, 31 January 1922.

5

Inspectorate for Intermediate (Secondary) Schools: the Beginning

Secondary, or intermediate, education as it was then referred to, developed on very different lines from the national school system. The issue of secondary school inspection was also to prove much more disputatious than that of primary school inspection. Within the context of laissez faire ideology of the nineteenth century, it was not generally regarded as the business of the state to provide secondary education. Such education was regarded as a matter for middle and upper class parents who might subscribe to it as they saw fit. Most of the secondary education which was available was provided by private organisations or individuals. There were no state regulations affecting it and, as for instance the 1871 census indicates, there was great variety in the providers of the system and in the quality which prevailed. Nevertheless, the demand for such schooling grew in the second half of the nineteenth century, with the opening up of public service occupations to recruitment on the basis of merit as recorded in public examinations. The 1871 census showed that while Catholics formed 77% of the population, only 50% of the 21,225 pupils who were enrolled in secondary-type schools were Catholic. In the 1870s, political pressure was being applied to moderate the canons of laissez-faire policy and to secure some state support for secondary schooling.

The schools were anxious to receive state support, but were very jealous of their independence and the freedom they enjoyed as private institutions. The key aim was to secure public funding but to delimit as much as possible the influence which the state might presume to exercise in return for its subventions. The highly state-regulated system which had evolved at primary level was regarded as very inappropriate for secondary schooling, and was to be resisted. The Intermediate Education Act of 1878 was the legislative mechanism through which state funds were made available to secondary schools. This was through a payment by results scheme which set up a public examination system for secondary school pupils. Based on pupil success rates in the examinations the state paid results fees to the managers of the schools in which the pupils were enrolled, while prizes and exhibitions were made available to the most successful pupils. The powers of the Intermediate Commissioners, established by the Act, were limited to devising programmes, conducting the examinations and paying awards. The Act took no cognisance of the need to support, equip or found schools. The Act made no mention of teachers and laid down no conditions for teacher competence or remuneration. Apart from engaging with the examination process, schools remained free to conduct their affairs as they saw fit. Yet, through the operation of the public examinations the Commissioners exercised a great influence on the content and method of secondary education throughout the country, as the vast majority of schools participated in the examination system.

It is noteworthy that, as the 1878 bill was being drafted, Catholic Church authorities indicated that they did not want the bill to include state building grants for schools or a state inspection system. Such measures would be regarded as a too intrusive role by the state. For instance, Bishop Conroy writing to the chief secretary, on behalf of the hierarchy, regarding the drafting process stated:

> I trust that your plan for the improvement of Intermediate Education will not include a demand of the right to inspect Catholic Schools *otherwise than by testing their results in the examination.* We should be jealous of such inspection; and to claim the right of making it would signally interfere with the success of the proposed scheme (original emphasis).[1]

This opposition to inspection in secondary schools was sustained for many years. The Intermediate Education Act only contained the most summary mention of inspectors – 'The Assistant Commissioners shall also act as secretaries, and, when required, as inspectors'.[2] In the roll-out of the legislation, this potential role of the commissioners acting as inspectors was never activated.

Arising from limitations and problems associated with the operation of the payment by results process of the Intermediate Education Act (1878), a commission was established to review the system, after twenty years of operation, in 1898. The Commission, under the chairmanship of Chief Baron Palles, received oral and written evidence from many interested parties. The issue of inspection was raised by proponents and opponents of inspection.

The minutes of the Palles Commission also make clear that the issue of school inspection was a very divisive one among the Commissioners. Some members such as Archbishop Walsh and Lord Palles were in favour of a strong role for school inspection, while others wished the results examinations to be retained as the central plank of state aid for schools. The final report of the Commission favoured the retention of examinations as its first recommendation stated 'that a public general examination of students should be retained as the basis for the calculation of the school grant'.[3] Only a limited and vague role was envisaged for school inspection.

1 Quoted by T.J. McEllgiott, *Secondary Education in Ireland, 1870–1921* (Dublin: Irish Academic Press, 1981), p. 23.　2 *Intermediate Education (Ireland) Act, 1878*, Section 3.　3 Áine

The report failed to clarify and define the role which an inspectorate ought to play, and this was to give rise to considerable difficulty later. Following the publication of the Commission's report in 1899, the Intermediate Education Act, 1900, was enacted. Section 2 of the Act stated:

> The Board may, if they think fit, with the sanction of the Lord Lieutenant, and with the approval of the Treasury as to number and remuneration, appoint persons to act as inspectors in addition to, or instead of, the Assistant Commissioners.[4]

In 1901, the Commissioners appointed six 'temporary' inspectors for intermediate schools. They were required to report on such matters as the efficiency of the teaching, the sanitary conditions of schools, the timetable, the qualifications of staff and the equipment used for the teaching of practical subjects. The names of these first *six* inspectors were Messrs. Shuckburgh, Cassie, Stegall, Mayfield, Brereton and Roberts. They were all Englishmen.

An effort was made in the rules for 1902 to dilute the importance attaching to individual student results in the examinations. Thus, the fees to schools were now to be in the form of a capitation grant based on the general performance of the examinees of a school, seen in relation to the number of pupils on the school roll. As a condition precedent to the payment of such a grant, the school manager had to consent to have the school inspected.

Then, on the basis of inspection, bonuses could be paid to schools at the rate of 10% or 20% of the normal school grant depending on whether the school was deemed 'satisfactory' or 'highly satisfactory'. This bonus scheme operated for the year 1902 on the basis of the reports of the temporary inspectors. In no case was the school grant reduced on the basis of an unsatisfactory report by an inspector of any particular school. In the school year 1901–02 these inspectors visited over three hundred schools. Four temporary inspectors were appointed for the school year 1902–03. The reports of the temporary inspectors for the school year 1901–02 and 1902–03 were published in five volumes.

The inspectors reported:

> The work of the schools as a whole is mainly a preparation for the Intermediate Examinations ... But there are many important parts of education that cannot be tested by a written examination. These we have found to be largely neglected.[5]

Hyland and Kenneth Milne (eds), 'Intermediate Education (Ireland) Commission', 1899 (Palles Commission) in *Irish Educational Documents*, vol. I (Dublin: CICE, 1987), p. 212.   4 Hyland and Milne, 'Intermediate Education (Ireland) Act, 1900' in ibid., pp 217–19, p. 218.   5 *Selected from the Reports of the Temporary Inspectors, 1901–02*, published by the Intermediate Education Commissioners, 1902, p. 3.

Regarding school staff, they highlighted the very varied pattern of teacher qualifications which existed:

> Some had taken university degrees in honours and some in pass sub-jects, while many had not yet completed their university course. A considerable number held certificates from various boards for their respective subjects. A very large number had no qualifications except more or less experience.

They expressed concern about small schools in country districts where 'one teacher is compelled to give instruction in all the subjects of the curriculum, with the result that the teaching sometimes suffers, as the attainment of the teacher in one or other of the subjects is insufficient.'

The temporary inspectors were also critical of the general condition and upkeep of some schools. They stated:

> With some conspicuous exceptions there was often a lack of cleanli-ness. In many schools windows had not been cleaned, floors had not been recently washed, or swept, and the premises were ill-kept throughout. In many schools the classes did not meet in separate rooms. The noise from the simultaneous teaching of several forms is distracting, and renders effective teaching difficult, if not impossi-ble.... In nearly all schools the supply of blackboards was insufficient, and the surface of many was defective.[6]

Methods of teaching were regarded on the whole as unsatisfactory, as were arrangements for light and ventilation. There was a shortage of suitable desks and the inspectors found very few school libraries. The criticisms made by the temporary inspectors left a residue of resentment among school managers, who considered their work too intrusive.

The Commissioners considered that the work of the temporary inspectors was valuable to the system. Under Rule 56B bonuses were paid to schools deemed 'satisfactory' or 'highly satisfactory'. In June 1902, the Commissioners applied to the under-secretary at Dublin Castle to obtain the sanction of the chief secretary for the establishment of a permanent inspectorate, with the appropriate funding. They outlined the work of the temporary inspectors and urged that a permanent inspectorate would be an improvement for secondary education. A six-year conflict ensued between the Commissioners and the Chief Secretary's Office on the issue of a secondary school inspectorate. The chief secretary opposed a permanent inspectorate because the Commissioners did not propose to reduce the expenditure for examinations by an amount

6 Ibid., p. 4.

equivalent to that of the cost of inspection. The central government did not wish the inspectorate to be a further expense added to the costs of the examinations. The Intermediate Board took a very different interpretation of the situation stating that

> whilst the Act of 1900 authorised inspection, it, upon its plain and undoubted construction, so authorised it as supplemental to, not as substitute for, the general examination prescribed by the Act of 1878.[7]

As well as the issue of economy involved regarding the inspectorate, there is also evidence that the government would have favoured a system based on inspection, rather than results examinations, which the Palles Commission had retained. A stalemate ensued on the issue with intransigent positions taken by both sides in the dispute.[8] The direct outcome was that following the school year 1902–03, the temporary inspectors were not re-appointed and the work of inspection fell into abeyance.

Further difficulties arose from changes in the rules and programme for the results examinations introduced by the Board for 1902, with a view to reform. This involved changes in subject groupings, mark allocations and the conditions for passing the examinations. One immediate effect of the operation of the new rules was a calamitous failure rate in the examinations of 1902, requiring special 'doctoring' measures as a rescue operation.[9] The shift towards a school grant on general performance of pupils also failed and, in 1903, the original scheme of payment on the basis of individual students' performance was reinstated. With the demise of the temporary inspectors, the bonus payments to 'satisfactory' and 'very satisfactory' schools were also terminated.

Thus, by 1904, the intermediate education system had, to a large degree, relapsed into the state of ill-health which had called forth the Palles Commission of 1898–99. The affairs and policy of the Intermediate Board, by 1904, had reached an unsatisfactory impasse. In that year, the government appointed two English inspectors, Messers Dale and Stephens, to survey the system of intermediate education in Ireland and to make recommendations thereon. Their appointment, with extensive terms of reference, so recently after the Intermediate Commission of 1898–99, would indicate that the Government did not have confidence in that Commission's Report, or in the Intermediate Board whose members had formed the Palles Commission. Among the terms of reference for Dale and Stephens were, 'To what extent, if any, inspection might take the place of the examinations conducted by this Intermediate Board'. Dale and Stephens submitted a searching and thorough

7 SPO File CSORP 1914. 1839 – Letter from Intermediate Board to Dublin Castle, 30 June 1902. 8 Áine Hyland, 'The Setting Up of the Intermediate Inspectorate, 1900–1909', in *Proceedings of the ESAI Conference 1978*, pp 159–70. 9 *Report of the Intermediate Board for 1902*, p. vi.

report, in 1905, which gives a valuable picture of many aspects of intermediate education in Ireland at that time. There was clarity and precision in the analysis and its recommendations were definite and unambiguous. Among other issues, Dale and Stephens set out major defects of the payment by results system, with a detailed explication of the causes of the defects. It recommended the abolition of the payment by results examinations and their replacement by internal school examinations, 'under the general supervision of the inspectors', and external examinations for two school certificates, conducted by the Central Authority which would replace the Intermediate Commissioners. It was recommended that the Central Authority set out criteria for the recognition of intermediate schools. The efficiency of the recognised schools 'should be secured by inspection'.[10] Schools recognised as satisfactory would receive annual, block capitation grants. The report envisaged comprehensive duties for the inspectorate including the obligation to report on:

> the suitability of the site with a view to facility of access for the pupils, the relations between the school and the local educational authorities, the fees paid by pupils, the sanitary condition of the school, the suitability of the buildings and equipment, the conditions under which teachers worked and the salaries of the teachers, the sufficiency of the staff, the suitability of the instruction to the scholars and the locality.[11]

As well as examining these and many other aspects of the scholastic life of the school, they were also to have powers of inquiry into such things as the provision for games and physical training, the hours of work of the pupils, the arrangements for boarders. The role of the inspector was seen as a vital link between the Central Authority and the school. If implemented, it would involve an unprecedented intrusion by public officials into the schools which were private institutions.

Even before the publication of the Dale and Stephens Report, in 1905, Chief Secretary Wyndham announced in parliament in April 1904 that the government intended to introduce significant policy changes to education in Ireland.[12] However, in June 1904, the Catholic hierarchy expressed their strong opposition to any proposed changes in the educational status quo.[13] Wyndham did not remain long in office and was succeeded by Walter Long in 1905. The Liberal Party won the general election of 1905. In the context of the political climate of the time, the radical blueprint for change in inter-

---

10 Hyland and Milne, 'Report of Messrs. Dale and Stephens on Intermediate Education', 1905, in *Irish Educational Documents*, pp 219–26, p. 224. 11 Ibid. 12 David Miller, *Church, State and Nation in Ireland, 1898–1921* (Dublin: Gill & Macmillan, 1973), p. 122. 13 *Freeman's Journal*, 23 June 1904.

mediate education proposed by Dale and Stephens was allowed to lapse and their main proposals had to wait for twenty years, to be implemented by an altogether different regime.

Chief Secretary Walter Long had a Consultative Conference convened of representatives of the Boards of National and Intermediate Education and the Department of Agriculture and Technical Education. The Conference was asked to advise on how better co-ordination might be achieved between the three systems under existing powers. The Report of the Conference, presented to the new chief secretary, James Bryce, in January 1906, made three key recommendations. One of these was the need for 'a permanent staff of Inspectors under the Intermediate Board.' The Conference expressed itself forcefully on the matter as follows:

> The reform which we deem most urgent in the interests of co-ordi-
> nation is the appointment of permanent inspectors on the staff of the
> Intermediate Education Board ... we have to record our conviction
> that the appointment of an inspectorial staff to that Board is an
> absolute necessity.[14]

Meanwhile, the Intermediate Board carried on its clash with the Chief Secretary's Office on the matter of school inspection and this was interlinked with broader policy concerns. The reports of the Intermediate Board for the years 1902, 1903, 1904, 1906 and 1907 all requested permission to appoint a permanent inspectorate, persisting in seeing it as supplemental to the results in examinations, rather than in the manner advocated by Dale and Stephens. The Board's pleas were to no avail and the measure of their discontent and the degree of tension which existed are indicated by the following resolution of the Board sent to Lord Lieutenant Aberdeen in 1908:

> That in the opinion of the Board, the time has arrived when it is nec-
> essary for them to consider whether it is possible for them, in the
> interests of true education, to continue the administration of the
> funds entrusted to them for the promotion of Intermediate Education
> in Ireland in the absence of a system of inspection the establishment
> of which was provided for by the legislature in the Intermediate
> Education Act of 1900.[15]

The forceful tone of this resolution, with its threat of resignation, made an impact, combined with the conciliatory approach of Chief Secretary Birrell, so that on 22 September 1908 the Board received word that the Treasury had

14 *Report of the Consultative Conference on Co-ordination between the Education Sectors* (Private and Confidential), (A.T. and Co., 1906), p. 5.   15 *Report of the Intermediate Board for 1908*, p. viii.

sanctioned Birrell's recommendation on the appointment of six inspectors on a permanent basis.

The Board at its meeting on 30 September decided on the salary scales, which were approved by the Treasury. Two inspectors were to be at the scale £350–£700; two at £500–£700 and two at the scale of £700–£800. Advertisements for the posts were issued in December 1908, with an upper limit of 45 years, and a warning that 'canvassing, directly or indirectly, will be regarded as a disqualification.' Interestingly, at a meeting between members of the Intermediate Board and representatives of the Heads of Intermediate Schools on 5 February 1909, the Heads requested that the inspectors to be appointed 'should be Irish and practical educationalists', which was agreed. This meeting also recorded the view that six inspectors were insufficient for the work to be undertaken, but that was all that was authorised.[16] As might be expected, competition was keen for these very well-paid employments. There were over 400 applicants for the positions, and the appointments were made at the Board meeting on 18 March 1909, subject to the sanction of the lord lieutenant and the approval of the Treasury. The six appointed were: Charles Kerin, Ernest Ensor, Joseph O'Neill, John Maguire, Thomas Rea, Charles Wright. Whereas the temporary inspectors appointed in 1901, were all Englishmen, it was noteworthy that the permanent inspectors were all Irishmen and had previous experience of intermediate education in Ireland. They began their active service in October 1909, having been allowed an orientation period. The Board, by a majority vote, decided not to appoint any woman inspector.

Lord Lieutenant Aberdeen approved the regulations for the inspectorate. Among the extensive powers allocated were the following:

> The inspectors shall inspect and report on the character of the teaching in each school, the sanitary condition of the school, the arrangements as to ventilation and light, the character of the text-books used, the timetable, and the reasonableness of the arrangements as to hours for classes, recreation, and study. The inspectors may test the efficiency of the teaching in the schools by examining the students, by having the classes taught in their presence, or otherwise as they may think fit.[17]

No notification as to the date of inspection was to be furnished to any school. The inspectors were required to forward a journal of the work done by them in each week, and their tours of inspection were to be arranged by the Assistant Commissioners.

16 Intermediate Education Board for Ireland, *Reports of Conferences, 1909–1912* (Private and Confidential), Report of Meeting, 5 February 1909.   17 Intermediate Education Board for Ireland, *Rules Relating to Inspectors* (Private and Confidential), 1909.

The issue of school inspection, or more specifically the nature of the powers to be exercised by the inspectorate, continued to be contentious, now in the context of school managers' attitudes. That the inspection issue was one of major concern and sensitivity is clearly evident from the report of a meeting between members of the Intermediate Board and representatives of the Heads of Catholic and Protestant Intermediate Schools held on 5 February 1909. The Heads had submitted, in advance, an agenda of eleven points relating to inspection on which they had concerns. These included an appeal process, limitations of inspectors' powers concerning methods of teaching, uniformity of inspectorial assessments, limitations to inspectors' role in commenting on teacher qualifications and staffing ratios, costs of inspection not to be a charge on the money available to schools. The debate on many of the issues was intense and robust. The Heads insisted that the inspectors must accept 'the results of the written examinations as the most potent factor in determining the nature of the work in schools and the distribution of the school grant', even if the Board members did not concur. The issue which got the most extended and heated debate was the challenge by the Catholic Heads to the Board's view that inspectors should have the right to inspect the facilities of boarding schools, such as dormitories and kitchens. The Catholic Heads considered this to be *ultra vires* for the Board. The meeting ended with agreement on some issues, but disagreement on other aspects of the planned inspection process.[18]

In the autumn of 1909, the Catholic Schoolmasters' Association and the Heads of Convent Intermediate Schools passed resolutions stating that they were prepared to accept inspection in the limited manner recommended by the Palles Commission of 1898 but adding:

> we regard as outside the legal powers of the Board any extension of the scope of inspection so defined and, in particular, the inspection of the residential departments of boarding schools, of the academic degrees, or diplomas, of teachers, and of the financial arrangements of the schools.[19]

The elaborate role of the inspectorate as set out in the Dale and Stephens Report and in the new rules for inspection were not satisfactory to these private institutions. In December 1909, another conference was held between a committee of the Board and the Joint Consultative Committee of the Headmasters' Associations which again discussed issues of concern regarding inspection. The different contexts of Catholic and Protestant schools were discussed, most of the former being under the control of bishops or religious con-

18 Intermediate Education Board for Ireland, *Reports of Conferences, 1909–1912* (Private and Confidential), Report of Meeting, 5 February 1909.   19 Report of the General Meeting of the Catholic Headmasters Association and the Convent Intermediate Schools, in *The Irish Educational Review*, vol. III, Oct. 1909, p. 56.

gregations. Religious staff were appointed to these schools on a different basis to appointments in lay protestant schools. It was also pointed out that the provision of university education satisfactory to Catholics was a major cause of contention for Catholics, and they were placed at a disadvantage in obtaining university qualifications. A looser form of 'qualification', other than a university degree, would be more acceptable it was felt. Intrusion on the area of remuneration of staff in Catholic schools was regarded as unwarranted and inappropriate. The Board representatives, however, expressed concern about the 'sweated' labour of some lay teachers in these schools. It was agreed that returns supplied to inspectors by schools were to be confidential to the Board.

The tone and emphasis of the Catholic concern can be gleaned from the statement of the Revd Andrew Murphy at the meeting:

> We have at present absolute freedom apart from whatever obligation we have taken in connection with the Board's Examinations ... but if we allow the Intermediate Board to walk in and take charge of the qualifications of our teachers and the salaries paid to them, and if, after we have allowed that, the Board ceases to exist in a few years time, we shall not be in the same position to treat with the new body as if we had retained our freedom.[20]

The abstract of the meeting drawn up by the Assistant Commissioners put the issue clearly and succinctly when it stated:

> There is a political aspect to this question which cannot be ignored. The democratic tendencies of the times must be considered. By any such surrender of liberty as is involved in the present requirements of the Board, Catholic schools cannot but weaken their position if they are compelled to defend themselves against the encroachments of a popular elective body that may possibly succeed the Board.[21]

Thus, quite clearly, the issue of school inspection was part of a broader religious, political and economic concern, and this impinged on the inspectors' reports.

The work of the inspectors was supplemental to the results examinations which, because of the reliance on the income they generated, continued to dominate the work of the schools. It was usual for two or three inspectors to visit a school on the same day, or days. Their reports followed a set template. The first section set out the name of the school, the date(s) of inspection, the inspectors who visited, the management of the school and the number of students. The second section was devoted to details on the staff of the school.

20 Intermediate Education Board for Ireland, *Reports of Conferences, 1909–1912* (Private and Confidential), Report of Meeting on 2 December 1909.   21 Ibid.

The section on 'General Description of Schoolhouse' required detailed reportage on aspects such as the condition of the premises, the dimensions of each classroom, ventilation, heating, lighting, sanitary arrangements, school requisites – desks, blackboards, maps, libraries. The next section related to dormitories and cubicles. Under 'School Work', details were recorded on school hours, attendance, vacations, homework, discipline, mode of punishment. The 'Recreation' section inquired about games, size of playgrounds, drill, periods of play on dry and wet days. The final section – 'Detailed Report of Classes Inspected' – listed the subjects examined, the names of the teachers and commented on the quality of the teaching and pupil responses. Each subject report was signed by the inspector who examined the classes. There was a significant difference in the reports on Catholic and Protestant schools. In the case of the latter, details were recorded on the qualifications, experience and salary of each staff member. This information was not filled in for most Catholic schools. Furthermore, reports were not made on the 'dormitories and cubicles' of Catholic schools, reflective of their stance on the private and independent nature of these institutions. The reports on the schools for each year were bound, printed and marked, 'Confidential printed for members of the Board only'. They were not intended to provide information to the general public, the media, or parliament. For the year 1909–10 the inspectors recorded reports on 368 schools. They visited schools throughout the island from Skibbereen to Ballymena, and from Ballinrobe to Arklow. The schools visited by each inspector were listed in the reports as follows: Mr Kerin inspected 102 schools, Mr Wright 105, Mr Ensor 108, Mr O'Neill 129, Mr Maguire 91 and Mr Rea 120. Inspectors often visited schools in pairs.[22]

A reading of the reports indicates that the inspectors were independent-minded, professional and hard-working. When commenting on the inspection of individual subjects their analyses were accompanied with wholesome praise, when deserved, but they were also blunt and frank in their criticism when they considered this was needed. In the sections entitled 'Detailed Report of Classes Inspected', individual teachers were named and frank and detailed comments were recorded on their presence, mode of teaching, use of textbooks, style of questioning, and so on. The flavour of the comments may be gained from some representative quotations. On a lesson on the mountains of Asia the inspector recorded:

> No general principles were laid down, and neither the imagination nor the reasoning faculties of the students were called into use. The teacher is slow and heavy in manner and does not seem to have either a wide knowledge of his subject or a clear idea of its practical value. The boys answered rather carelessly.[23]

22 Intermediate Education Board for Ireland, *Report of Inspectors, 1909–10*, 3 vols (Confidential: Printed for Members of the Board Only).   23 Ibid., vol. I, Rep. No. 23, p. 4.

An inspection of French teaching recorded:

> The teaching is almost entirely on traditional lines, with a view to the examination. The teacher has some idea of pronunciation, but not enough to enable him to correct properly, consequently the pronunciation of the classes was very bad. An unsuitable book on antiquated lines is used to teach grammar and composition.[24]

While a majority of comments on the quality of teaching were negative, the inspectors also acknowledged the ability of teachers they observed, as for instance, regarding an English lesson:

> The master had an excellent manner, bright and quick, and he distributed his questions among all the boys in a proper manner. He taught with a plentiful variety of illustrations, and he showed some humour when dealing with foolish questions. Nothing seemed to be missed in his treatment of the essay.[25]

Inspecting a French class in a well established girls' school, the inspector stated:

> This class is taken by Miss _____, one of the finest French teachers I have ever seen. The first ten minutes were devoted to phonetic drill, a sound-chart being used, and the result was admirable. The rest of the lesson was entirely on Reform lines; all the questions were put, and answered in French, great attention being given to grammar which was taught inductively. The class-room was well equipped with pictures relating to France and the French, a French atmosphere thus being to some extent created.[26]

Cumulatively, the reports gave an intimate and fascinating insight into the conditions of schools and the quality of teaching and learning in them at the time. Great variations both in conditions and quality were revealed, reflective of the diverse, on-the-ground educational circumstances of the period. A striking feature, which emerges repeatedly, is the small number of pupils in many schools and, hence, the very small numbers in many of the classes being inspected. It is also worth noting that as well as observing teaching, the inspectors took an active role in questioning pupils, and, sometimes in demonstrating teaching. The report on each school was distinctive and reflective of the context being inspected. There is nothing of the bland formula about the reports. As such, they were much more engaged with, and revealing of the life of the school than a later approach to secondary school inspection, discussed in subsequent chapters.

24 Ibid., vol. I, Rep. No. 25, p. 3. 25 Ibid., vol. I, Rep. No. 33, p. 9. 26 Ibid., vol. III, Rep. No. 252, p. 5.

The office base for the intermediate inspectors was in Hume Street, Dublin, where the Commissioners for Intermediate Education were located. The inspectors benefited from high salaries and good expenses. The number of inspectors was small and this helped them to develop a close esprit de corps. They were well educated, scholarly men and they enjoyed a social status and prestige. When not on tours of inspection they conveyed an impression of enjoying working hours and conditions which contemporary society saw as appropriate to gentlemen. Anecdotal evidence exists that leisurely coffee breaks and lunches at the nearby Shelbourne Hotel were not unusual occurrences. The intermediate schools, as independently owned institutions, were not at all as controlled by rigid regulations as the national schools. Neither were the intermediate inspectors as tightly controlled by Commissioners, or as tightly regulated by rules and procedures as the national school inspectorate. The character of the intermediate inspectors' work was less onerous than that of the national school inspectors, and they had much less influence on the career prospects or remuneration of teachers than their national school counterparts. Both inspectorates operated in professional isolation from each other.

It was interesting that the first year of operation of the permanent intermediate inspectorate, 1909, was also the year which saw the establishment of the Association of Secondary Teachers of Ireland (ASTI), which was set up to promote and protect the interests of lay secondary teachers. It had four main aims to secure for teachers: registration; adequate salaries; security of tenure; and pension rights.[27] The dire condition of lay secondary teachers at the time was well captured in the Dale and Stephens report of 1905. It pointed to their meagre salaries, poor qualifications, insufficient training, insecurity of tenure and lack of pension provision. The report calculated that the average salaries for male and female teachers, respectively, were £82 65s. 7d. and £48 25s. 7d. per annum. The Report came to the doleful conclusion:

> It is not surprising that from every source from which we obtained information we learnt that no Irish graduate, save in exceptional circumstances, will enter the (secondary) teaching profession if any other career presents itself to him.[28]

The ASTI was in favour of the investigative role of the inspectorate in the hope that it would bring to light statistical data on conditions of employment which it could utilise in its campaign for improvements.[29]

By 1912, the Intermediate Board had changed its policy on inspection vis-à-vis results examinations as a mode of giving state support to school managers. The Board's report for 1912 records its view as follows:

27 John Coolahan, *The ASTI and Post-Primary Education in Ireland* (Dublin: ASTI, 1984), p. 14.   28 *Report of Messrs. Dale and Stephens on Intermediate Education* (Cd. 2546).   29 Coolahan, *The ASTI and Post-Primary Education*, p. 15.

The school grant should be a capitation grant, paid to schools which satisfy the required conditions, on all pupils between the ages of 12 and 19 years, who have been in regular attendance during the year. The conditions to be fulfilled by schools should include:

(i) That the schools should be certified as efficient by the Inspectors of the Board;

(ii) That a reasonable proportion of the pupils should pass the certificate examinations;

(iii) That the teachers should possess qualifications to be approved by the Board.

A bonus grant might be paid to schools of more than average efficiency shown either by a high proportion of passes in the certificate examinations or by a high proportion of success in the honour examinations.[30]

This represented a major change of policy and, if implemented, would have largely abolished the results examinations in favour of an inspection system as the basis for payment. It would also suggest a vote of confidence in the nature of the work being conducted by the recently established inspectorate. The Board submitted its views to the chief secretary.[31] The chief secretary introduced a bill in January 1913 which provided that the Board need no longer hold examinations other than examinations of students competing for exhibitions and prizes and giving the Board power to provide for the payment to managers of fees dependent ...

(a) on the results of inspection of schools or

(b) partly on the results of such inspection, and partly on the results of honour examinations.[32]

However, school authorities took a different viewpoint and opposed the bill. This bill was withdrawn in the light of the opposition and a more modest measure, the Intermediate Education Act, 1913 (3 and 4 geo. 5, c. 29) was enacted. This merely empowered the Board to substitute school inspection for results examinations, in the awards of grants to schools for pupils under 14 years of age. What this meant in effect was that the Preparatory Grade results examination was abolished and, in its place, the reports of inspectors on the quality of the education of pupils under 14 years of age was the basis for payment to school managers.

One reason for the abolition of the Preparatory Grade Examination was that some schools were submitting pupils for this examination which were not regarded as genuinely intermediate schools at all. Interestingly, at a consultative meeting between members of the Board and representatives of Christian

30 *Report of the Intermediate Board for 1912*, p. viii.　31 *Report of the Intermediate Board for 1911*, p. x, and *Report for 1912*, p. vi.　32 *Report of Intermediate Board for 1912*, p. vii.

Brothers' Schools, on 5 January 1912, Brother Crehan concluded, 'The scheme has another advantage; it is gradually feeling the way towards a complete scheme of inspection.' Father Tom Finlay, of the Board, responded, 'It is the first step to it. If it works well it will be easy enough to get power to extend it.'[33]

This exchange would suggest that the work of the inspectorate, since its establishment in 1909, was viewed with satisfaction. However, the optimism that inspection would replace the other results examinations proved to be misplaced. The results examinations continued to operate for the Junior, Middle and Senior Grade Examinations, even though the Board continued to reiterate its dissatisfaction with this system.

In 1918 a Vice-Regal Committee was established to inquire into the conditions of Service and Remuneration of Teachers in Intermediate Schools, and on the distribution of grants from Public Funds for Intermediate Education (Molony Committee). The committee involved itself in a consideration of all aspects of the system of intermediate education in Ireland. It concluded that 'Piecemeal reform is not sufficient – what is needed is that the whole system be reconstructed.'[34] In that context, it considered that 'The abolition of the present system of payment by results is an essential preliminary to reform.'[35] The committee recommended that in place of the payment on examination results that 'A capitation grant should be paid, at a flat rate, in respect of all pupils between certain prescribed ages who have been in regular attendance throughout the year, to every school recognised by the Central Authority.'[36]

The principal test of the efficiency of a school would be inspection, but examinations should have a direct, but subordinate place. Furthermore, the Committee stated that inspection should not be confined to the grant-earning classes, but that a school should be inspected as a whole. It recommended that instead of the existing results examinations, there should be two certificate examinations – an 'Intermediate' and a 'Leaving Certificate'. Thus, the Vice-Regal Committee was endorsing the recommendations of the Dale and Stephens Report (1905), and the views of the Intermediate Board since 1912, seeking to give a central role to the inspectorate whose reports would form the basis of state support for the schools. However, the issue was caught up in a complex, political controversy which raged from late 1919 to late 1920.

Arising from the recommendations of the Vice-Regal Committee (1919) and from a similar Vice-Regal Committee on primary education (Killanin), which also published its Report in March 1919, the government prepared an Education bill, which got its first reading on 24 November 1919. The bill

33 Intermediate Education Board for Ireland, *Reports of Conferences, 1909–1912* (Private and Confidential), Report of Meeting, 5 January 1912.   34 *Report of the Vice-Regal Committee on Intermediate Education (Ireland) 1919* (The Molony Committee) (Cmd. 66) xxi, 645, p. 675.   35 Ibid., p. 668.   36 Ibid.

embodied fundamental changes for the administration of education in Ireland including the abolition of the existing boards and their replacement by a Central Authority for all sectors of Irish education. It also incorporated a provision for county education committees. Powers relating to compulsory attendance, provision of school books, school transport were also included in the bill. There was to be an education rate levied with popular control of education attached in the form of county and local education committees. While not specifically included in the bill, the understanding was that the payment by results examinations would be abolished, and that the inspectorate would take a more central role in determining schools' efficiency for the allocation of capitation grants.[37] The Education bill was strongly opposed by the Catholic church authorities, and a bitter controversy ensued through 1920.[38] Eventually, the government abandoned the Education bill and it was withdrawn on 13 December 1920, days before the Government of Ireland Act was passed, establishing partition on the island. The defeat of the Education bill 1919–20 left the plight of intermediate education unchanged and ameliorative measures were perforce postponed. The government had replied to the Board's requests for reform and greater financial support with the statement that 'the settlement of the matter awaits the passage of promised legislation.'[39] The Board was given no new funding and the defeat of the Education bill as well as the passing of the Home Rule legislation made the likelihood of such funding very remote. Yet, the system had to be carried on, and results examinations continued to be the lodestone of the intermediate system, with the inspectorate rather on the margins. There is a strong tone of frustration in the Board's Report for 1920 as it reflected back on the experience of the forty-two years since it was established, in 1878:

> It is difficult for us at this juncture – when the whole edifice of secondary education in Ireland is toppling to destruction – to refer to these matters in language of moderation and restraint.[40]

Thus, the intermediate education system which was inherited by the newly independent state in 1922 was in a very unhealthy condition and in need of much reform. A consolation, however, was that an inspectorate had been founded and had established itself as a credible and valuable agency. Though small, it had given useful and important leadership in the short period of its existence up to 1922.

37 *The Education (Ireland) Bill* (MacPherson) 1919 (214), i, 407.   38 John Coolahan, 'The Education Bill of 1919–20: Problems of Educational Reform', *Proceedings of the Educational Studies Association of Ireland* (Galway University Press, 1979), pp 11–31.   39 Quoted in *Report of the Intermediate Board for 1919*, p. viii.   40 *Report of the Intermediate Board for 1920*, p. x.

6

The Inspectorate for Technical Instruction under the DATI, 1900–22

Under the terms of the Agricultural and Technical Instruction (Ireland) Act, which was passed in 1899, a system of technical education suitably designed to meet the requirements of industrial and agricultural development was introduced. Unlike primary and intermediate education which were administered by nominated boards of commissioners, technical education came under the aegis of Ireland's first government department, the Department of Agriculture and Technical Instruction which became operative from 1 April 1900. Its headquarters were in Upper Merrion Street, Dublin. Under Section 7 of the Act an advisory committee, the Technical Instruction Board was set up to assist the Department. Under Section 23 of the Act, a Consultative Committee of Education with a representative of the commissioners for primary and intermediate education, the Technical Instruction Board, and the Agricultural Board was established with the aim of 'co-ordinating educational administration '. A total of £55,000 per annum was allocated to technical education in addition to the grants formerly administered by the Department of Science and Art at South Kensington and the grant in aid of technical education as defined in the Technical Instruction Act of 1889. The Act defined technical education as 'instruction in the principles of science and art applicable to industries' and was not to include 'teaching the practice of any trade, or industry or employment'.[1]

The Department of Agriculture and Technical Instruction (DATI) in its first annual report set out the aspirations for its educational role. It stated:

> To the educational part of its work the Department looks at as the most powerful and abiding means of promoting the end in view ... experience has amply proved that it is to the *individual and national resourcefulness* [original emphasis] and the confident characters thus developed by an educational system, more than to any other cause, countries which have in recent times achieved marked industrial success owe their progress ... The Department feel that if the people be placed in full possession of the benefits of such an educational system, they will have the instrument of their own salvation in their hands.[2]

1 *The Agricultural and Technical Instruction (Ireland) Act 1899* (300), i, 93. 2 Department of Agricultural and Technical Instruction (DATI), *First Annual General Report,* 1900–01 (Cd. 839),

The Department viewed its role as working in co-operation with the primary, secondary and higher education systems, and it saw all sectors of the system as incorporating a technical education dimension, as well as the 'specially technical institutions'. The DATI in its early policy and reports reflected the optimistic mood regarding the potential of education for economic and social development which prevailed at the turn of the new century. It also incorporated the widespread view of the time in the value of a more practical dimension in education and in discovery and experiential type learning.[3] The Department also caught the mood of the time when it identified its role as 'to evoke and fortify the self-reliance, enterprise and sense of responsibility of the people.'[4]

Technical education was to be promoted by a combination of central and local popular control. At local level the councils of county boroughs, urban districts and counties set up local statutory committees which prepared schemes of technical instruction for their areas which, if approved by the central Department, were put into operation subject to annual review. Local funding had to be forthcoming before the Department could assist local schemes from central funds. The new Department did not see itself as establishing a compartmentalised educational system in rivalry with existing bodies; rather it saw itself as a supportive agency to local effort and resources aimed at improving the industrial resources of the country. It saw as an early priority the improvement of scientific and practical subjects in the secondary schools. Science teaching had reached a very low ebb, with only 673 pupils presenting science at the Intermediate Board's Examinations in 1899. Such science teaching as existed was largely theoretical and verbal and there were only six secondary schools with laboratories in 1899.

The approach taken by the Department towards the secondary schools was 'principally from the point of view of general education, which is the first concern of the secondary schools, and secondarily, from the point of view of those specialised applications of education to which the secondary school should lead'.[5] In this context, new programmes were drawn up straight away, for the first two years of secondary schooling, in experimental science, drawing, domestic economy and manual instruction. The courses for third and fourth year were made available in the school year 1902–03. However, domestic economy and manual instruction never proved popular subjects in secondary schools and were only taken by a very small minority of students. Following a meeting of a sub-committee of the Intermediate Board with officials of the Department, the Board passed a resolution on 21 February 1901 agreeing to adopt the Department's programmes. This had significant implications for Science teaching, in particular. Book learning and rote learning

p. 21.   3 John Coolahan, *Irish Education History and Structure* (Dublin: IPA, 1981), pp 33, 87.
4 DATI, 1st *Report*, op. cit., p. 21.   5 Ibid., p. 22.

were to be replaced by a practically oriented approach, using research methods, observational and activity methods. To achieve the new policy aims it would be necessary to equip schools with laboratories and apparatus, to have a suitably trained teaching force, and to replace the written, results examinations by new forms of assessment. The Intermediate Board agreed to accept assessment by the DATI's inspectorate in place of their traditional written examinations for these subjects. This was a significant breakthrough in the prevailing system of secondary education at the time. It is noteworthy that while secondary school managements opposed the institution of a school inspectorate in place of the results examinations for most of the work of the school, they accepted the DATI's inspectorate in relation to Science and Drawing. The likelihood is that toleration of the latter was linked to the DATI's limited and specific brief relating to these subjects, rather than to the general life of the school. Furthermore, the grants made available were of significant assistance, with few strings attached.

The DATI took a very pro-active stance in assisting in the provision of science laboratories. By the end of 1902, 101 permanent and forty-nine provisional laboratories had been established at a cost of £30,000 to the Department.[6] By 1904, 243 laboratories had been established and equipped.[7] The DATI also took the issue of teacher training very seriously, remarking, 'The Department regard the question of the qualifications of teachers as of the utmost importance.' Among other supports for teacher education the DATI set up a celebrated scheme of summer courses for in-career teachers and this was maintained over the years. In the first year, 293 teachers from 196 schools participated in these summer courses. The courses were usually of four weeks' duration, from 10 a.m. to 4 p.m. and were taken in teachers' own time, but teachers were paid their expenses to attend. Teachers with degrees and diplomas were accepted for a time, but the DATI wanted all to have had a practical course in an approved laboratory. Teachers who successfully completed a summer course were given a certificate of proficiency and after five such successful courses were awarded 'permanent recognition'. The courses remained popular for teachers. For instance in 1913–14, 529 teachers participated and, even during the war years, well over 300 attended each summer. The Department paid tribute to the earnestness of the teachers' engagement with the courses and noted, 'The Department have established courses of instruction for every type of teacher engaged in their schemes, and to this circumstance they attribute in large measure the success with which these schemes have been attended.'[8] A valuable factor in sustaining the cordial relationships between the Intermediate Board and the DATI was the establishment in 1901–02 of a consultative committee of the Heads of

6 DATI, *Report for 1901–02* (Cd. 1314), p. 16.   7 DATI, *Report for 1903–04* (Cd. 2509), p. 56.
8 DATI, *Report for 1901–02*, p. 60.

secondary schools operating the DATI programmes and the quality of the DATI's engagement with this committee.

The key agency which enabled the DATI to achieve its objectives with regard to partnership with the secondary school system was the new inspectorate which it appointed. The inspectors were involved in drawing up the new programmes and in facilitating the setting up and equipment of the science laboratories, as well as in the teacher training courses. The inspectors shared the sense of new beginning, the fresh impetus with which the Department sought to infuse Irish education at the turn of the century. The Department referred to the change that was involved 'as something of a revolution'[9] and relied on the professional skills and diplomatic efforts of the inspectorate to ensure that it proceeded smoothly. With regard to the science laboratories the inspectors were closely involved in drawing up the plans and 'in almost every case it meant a visit or several visits, the inspector giving such aid to the schools as was possible'.[10]

The subject courses designed by the DATI were not intended to be tightly prescriptive of content and school managers were allowed latitude to adjust them to suit local circumstances. In a circular issued to schools the Department set out the assessment process as follows:

> The work will be tested by inspection, without notice usually; but, towards the close of the school year, the Inspector will give notice of his visit of final inspection for that year. On all such visits, but especially on the visit of final inspection, it will be within the discretion of the inspector to test any or all of the classes by practical exercises in the laboratory, or by viva voce examination of classes or of individuals, or by written examination, or by a combination of these methods. You will observe that the Grants to be paid may be increased by one tenth or reduced by one or more tenths, as the Department may determine on receipt of the Inspector's report.[11]

The procedure adopted for inspection was that following occasional visits to schools during the year, final inspections took place in April and May. These were conducted by the inspector of the district, accompanied, usually by a colleague. The inspector had to satisfy himself that the pupil attendance rates as presented by the school were accurate. Most of the inspection was through oral examination or checking of practical work. The report of the DATI for 1901–02 remarked, 'considering the previous absence of inspection in secondary schools in Ireland, it might be said that the smooth working of the system of inspection during the last session has been remarkable.'[12]

9 DATI, *Report for 1907–08* (Cd. 4430), p. 75.   10 *Report of the Departmental Committee of Inquiry on the DATI*, 1907 (Cd. 3572) p. 90.   11 DATI, *Report for 1901–02*, Appendices, p. 181.   12 DATI, *Report for 1901–02*, p. 62.

The Department hoped that the system of payment for work done on the result of inspection rather than written examination would give scope to the exercise of initiative by the teacher and not force teaching 'into a narrow groove, nor mould it into a stereotyped form,' which was alleged to have happened to much of the secondary school programme.

Most of the first appointees as inspectors for the DATI were Englishmen. In 1901, Mr George Fletcher became Senior Inspector, at a salary of £700 per annum, plus travelling expenses. He was very committed to technical education, supported the heuristic method in science teaching, and was very keen to promote craft industries as a complement to agricultural pursuits in rural areas. By 1904 he had seven inspectors working under him. Fletcher was appointed Assistant Secretary of the DATI in 1904, but he retained a keen interest in the work of the inspectorate.[13] As the work expanded, so did the number of inspectors so that by 1911 there were fifteen inspectors in the DATI.

From the year 1902–03, and up to the war years, the DATI annual reports contained reports by the inspectors, under their own names. These were detailed and informative. The career grades of the DATI inspectorate gradually evolved as Senior Inspector, Inspector and Junior Inspector mirroring the nomenclature of the national school inspectorate at this time. They reported for relevant districts such as 'the Southern District', the 'North-Central District, 'the Northern District'. Names such as Fletcher, Dixon, Turnbull, Smail, Garrett, McCaffrey, Ingram, McGann were those of the early pioneering group who were in the forefront of the Department's educational efforts. Other inspectors such as Mr Sullivan, Miss Anderson, Miss Lough focused on individual subjects such as art, home economics or domestic economy. For many years the reports focused on six themes as follows: Secondary Schools; Local Authorities' Technical Instruction; Teacher Training; Central Institutions; Scholarships and Drawing and Manual Instruction in primary schools, indicative of the spread of responsibilities under the Board of Technical Instruction.

It would appear that relationships between the schools and the inspectors were cordial and co-operative. The DATI report for 1905–06 records that 'The Principals and teachers have ever welcomed the visits of the Inspectors and their suggestions as to improvements either in detail or in the general work.'[14] In a general assessment of the first seven years of operation the DATI stated:

> In almost every secondary school in Ireland there is now in operation a systematic course of instruction in Experimental Science and

13 Susan M. Parkes, 'George Fletcher and Technical Education in Ireland, 1900–1927', in *Irish Educational Studies*, vol. 9, no. 1 (1990), pp 13–29.   14 DATI, *Report for 1905–06* (Cd. 3543), p. 64.

Drawing ... The payment in aid of such teaching is based upon the amount of work done, and its excellence is tested by an inspection alone.[15]

The DATI also casts interesting light on how the inspectorate dealt with sensitive roles and contexts. The Report for 1908–09 makes the following revealing comment:

This substitution, for an impersonal examination test, of personal inspection as a means of ascertaining the efficiency of a school, carried with it, however, certain risks contingent upon the personnel of the inspectorate, the mode of organising it and of dealing with its recommendations and reports. It is satisfactory to record that almost without exception inspection has been cordially welcomed by the schools, even where the Inspectors' reports have been adverse ... It has been found possible for inspectors to assist constructively in the organisation of schemes at the same time that they have had to fulfill the role of judicial critics of the manner in which the same schemes have been carried out. The visits of inspectors have been found to be as useful to the schools as they were necessary for the Department.[16]

The report recorded that a demand existed for more frequent inspections but that it was not possible to satisfy this demand.

While the DATI laid great stress on its promotion of Science and practical subjects through the existing secondary schools it, of course, was also keen to support the work of the local technical instruction committees as they became established and drew up schemes for technical education. As the historian of the Department has noted, 'There were, however, many difficulties to be overcome. Outside the cities and a few of the larger towns there were no technical schools; teachers were in short supply; and over most of the counties there were no manufacturing industries with which technical instruction could be linked.'[17] Yet, by 1902–03 the inspectors were also working with the local agencies, on the ground. In that year, twenty-seven county schemes, twenty-four urban schemes, and six schemes for county boroughs were introduced. In his report for 1903–04, Mr Fletcher, as Senior Inspector, reported on the satisfactory progress in working with the urban and county schemes. The difficulty of securing suitable accommodation and of obtaining qualified teachers for such technical education schemes caused problems. However, by 1907–08, the DATI could report 'as regards the work of Technical Instruction proper, the Department have now arrived at a point where the

15 DATI, *Report for 1907–08* (Cd. 4430), p. 74.   16 DATI, *Report for 1900–08* (Cd. 5128), pp 78, 89.   17 D. Hoctor, *The Department's Story: A History of the Department of Agriculture* (Dublin: IPA, 1971), p. 88.

local authorities of every county and nearly every urban authority in Ireland have in operation schemes of technical instruction.'[18] As well as part-time provision throughout the country, there were, by 1908, nine Day Trades Preparatory Schools.

Interestingly, inspectors commented retrospectively on the difference they found in promoting Science and Drawing in Secondary Schools to that of establishing an altogether new system of technical instruction on a largely 'Greenfield' context of local authority provision. Inspector Garrett reflected on the issue as follows, in his report for 1911–12:

> In the early days of Technical Instruction in Ireland the inspection of secondary schools was by far the most onerous section of the work of an inspector. To install a new system in existing schools was one thing; to call into existence a whole set of Technical Schools and to build up a system of Technical Instruction suited to the needs of the country was a much more difficult and onerous task. The former was a matter of a few years work, the latter is still far from completion.[19]

Apart from the DATI staff's favourable reportage on the work being undertaken, there is also interesting collaboration available from other sources. In 1905, Messrs. Dale and Stephens presented their commissioned report on intermediate education. They included a significant section on the relationship of intermediate and technical education within their report. Referring to the successful promotion of Science within the intermediate schools the report commended 'the tact' of the DATI's inspectors as well as the public spirit of the school managers. Pointing to the increase from 705 pupils sitting the Science examination in 1898, the report celebrated the increase to 5,950 in 1903, with grants to schools amounting to £12,353. It concluded:

> It is hardly possible to over–estimate the importance of this reform in Irish education. For the first time in Ireland genuine instruction in Science and Drawing has been rendered possible, and the old methods of purely theoretical work, based solely on textbooks and examination papers – work which was not merely futile in itself, but absolutely prejudicial to any proper grasp of scientific method – have been superseded by a system under which every student is forced to familiarise himself with the procedure of investigation by actual experiment. It would be superfluous to dwell on the educational gains involved.[20]

18 DATI, *Report for 1907–08* (Cd. 4430), p. 74.   19 DATI, *Report for 1911–12* (Cd. 6647), p. 115.   20 Report of Messers F.H. Dale and T.A. Stephens, *Intermediate Education Ireland* (Cd. 2546), 905, p. 29, par. 90.

Dale and Stephens, however, also pointed out that the more favourable treatment of Science was in danger of injuring provision for subjects such as the classics.

Another body, the Departmental Committee of Inquiry reported on the work of the DATI, in 1907, and gave revealing insights on the work of the Board of Technical Instruction and of the inspectorate. The report stated, 'The evidence we received and our own observations amply support the testimony which the experts gave as to the remarkable results already obtained in this section of education work.'[21] In his evidence to the Committee, Mr Fletcher, now Assistant Secretary in the DATI, stated, 'I think I may say that the advice and criticism which the Inspectors have always been ready to offer have been universally welcomed, that the Inspectors and Heads of schools are on excellent terms.'[22] With regard to the work with the local authorities he also considered that the inspectors have shown 'much ability and tact in the discharge of their duties.'

In its report the Committee considered that staff in the DATI were over-worked and that 'a strong case exists for additional staff.'[23] The Committee went on to record a remarkably favourable opinion of the staff of the DATI, including the inspectors – 'We think that in point of zeal, devotion to duty, practical good sense and ability, the staff of the Department ... is entitled to a high place in the records of the Civil Service.'[24] Overall, the Committee reported in favour of the role of the DATI, considering that it carried out its functions on lines well adapted to meet the temporary and permanent necessities of the country on matters under its remit from the 1899 Act.[25] In evidence to the Committee, details were given on the mode of inspection of schools with inspections without notice throughout the year and the final inspections towards the end of the year, when an inspector from another district accompanied the local inspector. For students entering for Honours examinations the inspectors first carried out a practical test, which was a qualifying one, and for those qualified they conducted written tests, to satisfy the Intermediate Board regulations. It was made clear that this written test was not required by the DATI regulations. It was done 'to bridge over the difficulties and to enable the system to be worked. The method has worked exceedingly well.'[26] It was also reported that the inspectors held periodical inspectors' conferences, 'in which every detail of inspection is fully and freely discussed, in no high and dry academic manner, but quite freely to seek to secure uniformity of action'.[27] There was also provision for appeal against inspectors' decisions, but such appeals were 'remarkably few'. In 1912, T.P. Gill of the DATI informed schools that while the efficiency of schools would continue to be tested by inspection and that occasional inspection would take

21 *Report of Departmental Committee*, op. cit., par. 170.   22 Ibid., p. 177.   23 Ibid., par. 323.
24 Ibid., par. 259.   25 Ibid., par. 258.   26 *Minutes of Evidence to the Departmental Committee of Inquiry* (Cd. 3574) 1907, par. 2180.   27 Ibid., par. 2188.

place without notice, 'special inspections of a more thorough character' would henceforth be held no more frequently than one inspection in three years, for any school.

The number of students in secondary schools for whom grants were paid by the DATI increased impressively over the years, as is indicated in the following table.

Table 6.1: The number of secondary pupils for whom DATI grants were paid in certain years

Year	No. of Schools	No. of Pupils	Amount of Grant
1901–02	154	6,615	£ 9,575
1906–07	278	12,816	£25,151
1909–10	283	13,450	£28,100
1919–20	247	16,077	£36,000

Source: Compiled from Annual Reports of DATI.

The early progress surprised even the inspectors who remarked in 1903–04 that, 'the progress made is far greater than could have been looked for'.[28] By 1909–10, Mr Dixon, Senior Inspector, considered that 'the teaching of Experimental Science and Drawing may now be regarded as having reached its normal volume, and no material increase can be expected for some time to come.'[29] This was true in terms of schools assisted, which declined somewhat in later years, but the number of students continued to increase and, accordingly, the grant paid to schools.

The inspectors were also in a position to record steady progress in the work of technical instruction under the local authorities. The table 6.2 indicates the growth in student numbers and expenditure on technical schools and classes in the early years.

However, teaching conditions were often very poor, and inspectors' reports tell a tale of situations in which heating, lighting and ventilation were poor, buildings were damp and facilities limited.

The DATI report for 1912–13 stated that the work for secondary schools having been successfully accomplished, 'efforts are now being concentrated on the rapidly developing system of technical education.'[30] That this rapid expansion had occurred is evidenced in that, by 1912, schemes of technical instruction were in operation in all the counties and in 91 of the 96 urban districts, and a total of 45,341 students were enrolled in the courses.[31] In 1906, the

28 *Report of DATI for 1903–04*, p. 58.   29 *Report of DATI for 1909–10*, p. 95.   30 *Report of DATI, 1912–13* (Cd. 7298), p. 99.   31 Ibid., p. 99.

Table 6.2: Student numbers and attendance grants for technical education
for 1902–10

Year	Student Nos. Technical Schools/ Classes	Attendance Grants Paid £	s.	d.
1902–03	29,513	£5,979	6s.	6d.
1903–04	39,398	19,956	11s.	6d.
1904–05	40,345	23,673	7s.	3d.
1905–06	43,520	26,414	13s.	9d.
1906–07	43,520	37,220	12s.	6d.
1907–08	44,458	41,765	9s.	4d.
1908–09	41,242	45,691	10s.	
1909–10	42,909	49,110	8s.	11d.

Source: *Appendix to the Report of the DATI for 1911–12*, p. 314.

Department devised new programmes which included attendance grants payable for co-ordinated courses of instruction. Students could take two or three subjects from a range of different groups which were laid out in courses of three and four years' duration. Extra capitation payments were paid for the later stages of the courses to encourage students to persevere. In 1911, the regulations allowed attendance grants to be also paid for single-subject courses, which helped rural schemes of technical education. In 1913, the Department instituted its own schemes of Technical School Examinations, whereas up to then they used those of English examining bodies. Most of the technical education was conducted on a part-time basis, but a number of Day Trade Preparatory schools were established in cities, amounting to ten by 1910 and to fourteen by 1919. They were seen as a bridge between national school and employment, offering part general and part technical education. In the year 1914–15, 45,930 students were enrolled in the various technical instruction courses, and the figure tended to remain around 45,000 over subsequent years.

The workload of the inspectorate in support of the Board of Technical Instruction programmes was both varied and very extensive. The flavour of the work is captured in the report of one inspector who stated, 'work for the year included the usual course viz. – inspection duty, test examinations, visits of inquiry, office work, correspondence, and occasional visits as judge at county shows'.[32] Other inspectors' duties included such roles as advice on the design of science laboratories and equipment, advising on technical instruction schemes for local authorities, design of new programmes, reportage on

32 *Report of DATI for 1910–11* (Cd. 6107), p. 138.

developments in technical instruction. Mr Fletcher, in his evidence to the Departmental Committee of Inquiry in 1907 reported how the inspectors worked flat out when on inspection duties to the extent that 'what would happen, if an inspector were to fall ill, I hardly know.'[33] The Commission of Inquiry itself strongly endorsed the scale and quality of the work of the inspectorate.

The work of the inspectorate, as with other aspects of the DATI's activities, was affected by the First World War, 1914–18. Difficulties included the reduction to the Departments staff and in the teaching staffs of schools through enlisting in the armed forces for the war effort. There was also curtailment of schemes and the postponement of building plans.[34] Interestingly, however, there was no appreciable diminution of attendance, except in and around Belfast. Technical Instruction Committees also found themselves in difficulties due to war-time inflation. The Treasury came to the rescue, somewhat, in 1918, with funds which allowed the payment of war bonuses to the Committees' employees.

The post-war period witnessed a general desire for educational reform in Britain and Ireland. In May 1919 Mr MacPherson, chief secretary for Ireland, set up a five-man drafting committee to draft an Education bill which would incorporate proposals of the Killanin and Molony Committees, which had been presented earlier that spring. Mr Fletcher of the DATI was one of the drafting committee. The draft bill was completed by 24 July 1919. The Education bill (1919) got its first reading in parliament on 24 November. Among its radical proposals was the establishment of a central education department which would take over responsibility for primary, secondary and technical education. The Vice-President of the DATI was to become Vice-President of the proposed Department of Education. The bill gave rise to very intense controversy. Interestingly, the Technical Instruction Association opposed the idea of technical education coming under the control of the proposed Department of Education.[35] In the light of the more general and clerical opposition to the measure, the government did not proceed with the bill. It was withdrawn on 13 December 1920, a week before the Government of Ireland Act, establishing partition, was passed into law.

A parliament was established in Belfast and began to function in May 1921. A new Department of Education was formally established for Northern Ireland on 7 June 1921. On 1 January 1922 responsibility for technical instruction in the six counties of Northern Ireland was transferred to it from the DATI. The transition was eased somewhat when some senior staff of the

33 Minutes of evidence, op. cit., par. 2184. 34 Seán MacCartáin, 'The Department of Agriculture and Technical Instruction, 1899–1903', in Norman McMillan (ed.), *Prometheus Fire* (Tyndall Publications: Carlow, 2005), pp 211–37, p. 227. 35 John Coolahan, 'The Educational Bill of 1919: Problems of Educational Reform', in *Proceedings of the ESAI Conference 1979*, pp 11–31, p. 19.

DATI transferred to Belfast.[36] Meanwhile, in the south of Ireland the War of Independence, followed by the Civil War hampered the work of the DATI and the Technical Instruction Committees. Inspectors, as well as others, faced danger and difficulty in travelling, particularly at night. Itinerant instruction and night classes were particularly affected. Interestingly, in the context of the cultural revival movement of the time, Irish classes, provided by the committees in these years proved very popular. The DATI continued to control technical education under the government of the Saorstat (Free State) which assumed the transfer of power on 1 February 1922. Following the Ministers and Secretaries Act of 1924, a Department of Education came into operation in June 1924. It then took over responsibility for technical education. Of the DATI it has been said:

> The Department of Agriculture and Technical Instruction was founded at a time of significant social and economic change. Its officers established a powerful trajectory of growth and development by responding to increasingly enthusiastic calls for educational provision, while initiating their own innovative projects.[37]

The DATI's inspectorate had played a distinctive role in the DATI's achievements. Its mode of operation was very different from the tradition which had developed in primary education, and from that of the secondary school inspectorate, established in 1909. The DATI inspectorate was not focused closely on the work of individual teachers and it was less hidebound by detailed regulations. Its role was seen more as advisory and supportive of the work of local authorities and of school authorities endeavouring to provide Science and Drawing in their curricula. While the DATI inspectorate had an evaluative role linked to Departmental grants being made available for educational effort, it was generally received as an agency with benign benefits for schools. Its mode of operation differed in tone and practice from that which had come into effect during the payment by results era for national schools, for instance. The DATI inspectorate saw itself in the vanguard of a new, progressive initiative in Irish education, and through the inspectors' efforts, the DATI realised many of its objectives.

---

36 Kieran Byrne, 'Laying the Foundations: Voluntary and State Provision for Technical Education, 1730–1930', in John Logan (ed.), *Teachers' Union (TUI)* (Dublin: Farmer, 1999), pp 16–36, p. 32.   37 Ibid., pp 29–30.

7

Change in the Administration of Education in the New State

Prior to the achievement of political independence in 1922, there were two currents of thought relating to reforms in the education system. One was a movement towards administrative and structural reform which was reflected in the Education bill of 1919–20. This bill included provision for the establishment of a department of education to have responsibility for all educational sectors. This was to be assisted by a representative advisory council on education. Local education committees were to be established which would aid, maintain and equip schools. Provision was to be made for free school meals, school books and requisites. A scholarship scheme was to be introduced and care of afflicted (*sic*) children was to be undertaken. The bill also included clauses on compulsory attendance, and evening and continuation schools. An education rate was to be levied and would be added to departmental funds to resource the system. Payment by results was to be abolished in secondary schools, with a scheme of incremental salaries and pensions introduced for teachers.[1] This was by far the most comprehensive attempt to restructure the education system in Ireland. The bill encountered strong opposition, particularly from the Catholic Church. It was withdrawn in December 1920, a week before the Government of Ireland Act established a partition settlement on the island.

The other current of thought favoured curricular reform, rather than administrative change. Inspired by the ideology of cultural nationalism, the adherents of this movement sought a much more central place for the Irish language, together with an Irish emphasis in subjects such as history, geography, and music, contributing to a Gaelic ethos in the schools. It was considered that the schools ought to be prime agents in the revival of the Irish language and native tradition which, it was held, were the hallmarks of nationhood and the basis for independent statehood. The awakening of interest in the Irish language, literature, history, mythology, games, music and dancing which manifested itself in the late nineteenth century created a momentum for a new curricular emphasis following independence. Many nationalists considered that the main purpose of education in a free Ireland was the re-establishment of a Gaelic civilisation.

---

1 *Bill to Make Further Provision with respect to Education in Ireland*, HC 1919 (214) 1.407 and HC 1920 (35) 1.563.

On the establishment of the Irish Free State, it was the curricular reform movement rather than the movement for administrative restructuring which got the main government support and attention. Energies were harnessed for a cultural revolution based on the schools. Apart from establishing a Department of Education in 1924 with responsibility for all sectors of the education system, the inherited pattern of administration, financing and control remained very much as they had been under the British regime. No commission was officially established to review the administration of the system and no effort was made to introduce comprehensive legislation for the education system. The official transfer of powers to the Provisional Government took place on 1 February 1922. Pádraig Ó Brolcháin was appointed the new chief executive officer for national education. He informed the Commissioners of National Education that they were being disbanded on the eve of the transfer of powers. He also informed them of the new direction which was being taken for education policy as follows:

> In the administration of Irish education it is the intention of the new government to work with all its might for the strengthening of the national fibre by giving the language, history, music and tradition of Ireland, their natural place in the life of Irish schools.[2]

On 8 June 1923 the Board of Commissioners of Intermediate Education was dissolved and it was replaced by two Intermediate Education Commissioners, Seosamh Ó Néill and Proinsias Ó Dubhthaigh. Technical education remained under the aegis of the Department of Agriculture until 1924. At the time of the partition settlement, civil servants were given the option of transferring to whichever of the two new administrations on the island they preferred. On the establishment of the Department of Education on 1 June 1924, all branches of education came under its control. This included the reformatory and industrial schools, which were placed under the control of the Reformatory and Industrial Schools Branch (RISB). These institutions were placed in the charge of an Inspector of Reformatory and Industrial Schools, distinct from the schools' inspectorate. The inspectors of schools did not have responsibility for the reformatory and industrial schools, but they did inspect the schools that were attended by pupils who lived in these institutions. Later, for a short period, 1997 to 2005, a schools inspector was appointed as the Inspector for the five reformatory and industrial schools which remained under the aegis of the Department. In 2005 these institutions were transferred to the Department of Justice, Equality and Law Reform.

Seosamh Ó Néill, who had been one of the secondary school inspectors appointed in 1909, became the first Secretary of the new Department of Education. In preparing for the establishment of the Department of Education, Seosamh Ó Néill contacted the permanent Secretary of the Board

2 Quoted in the *Irish School Weekly*, 11 Feb. 1922, p. 127.

of Education in London and the Secretary of the Scottish Education Department on staffing issues including the 'Delineation of the powers and authority of the Chief Inspectors as compared with Assistant Secretaries of each branch.'[3] The advice given was that the Chief Inspectors had free access to the Secretary and 'in this respect are on an equality with the chief administrative officers, and they have complete liberty to represent to me the harmful effects which they consider might result from administrative action.' It was also reported that relationships between the Chief Inspectors and Chief Administrative Officers were 'so close that if there is any conflict of opinion the officer who submits the matter to me is quite certain to inform me that his colleague differs from him.'[4] Both in the case of Scotland and of England it was reported that inspectors were not categorised in relation to sectors such as primary and secondary, but 'that all inspectors are expected to take part in the general inspection of schools within their area, irrespective of whether these schools are providing primary, intermediate or secondary education'.[5]

The Irish officials gave some consideration 'to amalgamate at least to some extent, all inspectors into one branch',[6] but this did not come to pass, nor would it have been easy to achieve because of the traditional differences of role by the three inspectorates. It was also considered desirable to bring the three branches geographically closer together by bringing the secondary branch from its traditional location at 1 Hume Street into Marlborough Street, where the primary branch was, and locating the inspectors of the Technical Instruction Branch in Talbot House, adjoining Marlborough Street. Some thought was also given to having an advisory council set up of external representatives to assist the Minister for Education. In the event, the inspectorate was established as subordinate to the senior administrative staff, inspectors only inspected schools in their own branch of the Department, the secondary branch stayed in Hume Street, and no advisory council was established. This situation endured for decades.

It is significant that for the first forty-five years of the new administration the four Secretaries of the Department during that time had all been secondary school inspectors. The four were Seosamh Ó'Néill (1923–44), Micheál Breathnach (1944–56), Labhrás Ó Muirthí (1953–56) and Dr Torlach Ó Raifeartaigh (1956–68). This tended to give a predominant voice to the secondary school inspectorate in the policy and administrative area. Furthermore, the fact that the offices of the Minister for Education and the Secretary of the Department were located in the building occupied by the secondary branch of the Department, at 1 Hume Street, into the 1930s also conferred an aura of the secondary branch to the image of the Department. However, in terms of scale, the primary school inspectorate greatly outnumbered the inspectorate of the

3 National Archives (NA) 2006 Box 120/2, Letter from Joseph O'Neill 24/10/23.   4 Ibid., Letter from Sir L. Amherst Selby-Biggs 2/11/23.   5 Ibid., Letter from Mr McDonald 23/10/23.   6 Ibid., Memorandum of Mr Butler on re-organisation of the Department of Education 30/1/23.

other two branches for many decades. Primary education was universal, with over 5,000 schools, about 13,000 teachers, and 493,000 pupils in 1924–25. There were 278 secondary schools, with 1,398 registered teachers (735 unregistered), and about 22,800 pupils. There were 64 technical schools with 21,637 pupils, with a further 34,000 attending classes elsewhere than in established technical schools. There were 1,035 teachers, between full and part-time in technical education.[7] Thus, the scale of operation of the primary inspectorate was much more extensive and, as the other sectors remained relatively small until the expansion of post-primary education in the 1960's, the number of post-primary inspectors was quite small relative to the primary inspectorate.

As was noted in the first annual report issued by the Department of Education, in 1926, for the school year 1924–25, the three branches – primary, secondary and technical – 'had little in common when they were taken over by the Department. They had come into being at different times, had different origins and were administered on different lines'.[8] The one form of co-ordination identified as possible by the Department was 'the unification of aims and methods by the co-ordination of the curricula of the various systems and the creation of administrative machinery which would keep the work of all three branches in harmony.'[9] The Department set up a standing Council of General Inspectors from the three inspectorates – Messrs Kerin, Muilleoir and MacNicholl. It is interesting to note the role this Council was envisaged as playing. The Department report stated:

> The main work of this Council consists in the co-ordination of the inspectorial staffs of the three branches as far as the different nature of the work permits, the unification or correlation of their programmes and methods, the preparation for schemes for reforming any sections of those branches that are defective or not consonant with one another and, in general, the formulation of the best methods for correlating or carrying into effect as one whole the educational policy of the Department.[10]

This discourse regarding co-ordination and correlation was more aspirational than effective, and there is no evidence that the standing Council operated as a unifying force for inspectorial action. In practice, the inspectorates continued to be organised and administered as largely discrete entities. The inspectors of each branch focused on their specific responsibilities in a largely compartmentalised way, with administrative headquarters in different buildings. Each of the three inspectorates had its own esprit de corps shaped by the context and traditions of the sector for which it had direct responsibility. Séamus Ó Buachalla records the situation as follows:

7 *Report of the Department of Education for 1924–25*, Appendix 1, pp 96–97.   8 *Report of the Department of Education for the School Year 1924–25*, p. 6.   9 Ibid.   10 Ibid., pp 8, 9.

> Each of the three branches (of the inspectorate) operated according to
> different traditions and norms, had different relationships with the
> schools and contrasting internal authority patterns; the Starkie legacy
> of administrative hegemony over the professionals survived unchal-
> lenged in the primary branch; in the secondary branch as late as 1940
> the highest administrative officer was at assistant principal level while
> in the technical instruction branch the chief inspector was both pro-
> fessional and administrative head.[11]

Regarding the secondary branch, it is interesting to note that W.F. Butler
(Dr de Buitléar), who had been Assistant Commissioner with the Intermediate Board since 1910 became principal officer in the secondary branch up to
his death in February 1930. The Department of Education's *Annual Report*
for 1928–29 (published July 1930) records in tribute to him that 'his services
during the transition period (1922–25) were particularly valuable'.[12]

The issue of the unification of the inspectorate emerged periodically over
the years. In March, 1933 the Secretary of the Department of Education
sought improved salaries for senior inspectors, and an upgrading of the T.I.B
inspectors' salaries from the Department of Finance. The extensive role of
the inspectors was set out in detail in his submission. However, the Minister
for Finance stated that he was not prepared to consider any proposal 'except
in connection with a scheme for a unified inspectorate for your Department
as a whole.' The Department of Education could not agree with the concept
of an integrated inspectorate. Assistant Secretary Ó Dubhthaigh replied, on
10 November 1933, that 'If co-ordination is interpreted as meaning the setting up of a common inspectorate whose members would deal with all classes
of schools – primary, secondary, technical – it is not a practicable proposi-
tion'.[13] No breakthrough occurred on the organisation of the inspectorate. In
1946, the Department of Finance was again urging the Department of
Education to unify the three inspectorates as official policy.[14] The issue also
emerged in the late sixties, and in the late eighties, but became a reality only
in the nineties. As might be expected, the character of the work of the different inspectorates varied in intensity, linked to the contextual circumstances
in which they operated. For instance, in his autobiography, Micheál
Breathnach who had been appointed as one of the 'Twelve Apostles' with a
special brief to promote Irish as a primary school inspector, was promoted to
the secondary inspectorate in 1924, and recalled, 'Bhí difear mór ar gach uile
bealach idír an dá shaghas cigireachta' (there was a great difference in every
way between the two types of inspection). He found much less regulation

---

11 Séamus Ó Buachalla, *Education Policy in Twentieth Century Ireland* (Dublin: Wolfound Press,
1988), p. 253. 12 *Report of the Department of Education for 1928–29*, p. 7. 13 NA Box 2006
120/16, Letters from Seosamh Ó Neill, 8 March 1933, from Department of Finance, 10 June
1933 and letter from P. Ó Dubhthaigh, 10 Nov. 1933. 14 Ó Buachalla, op. cit., p. 252.

applicable to secondary school inspection and he found it to be easier and more relaxed than primary school inspections.[15] The tradition of recruiting secondary inspectors from the primary branch was quite common in the 1920s; Labhras Ó Muirthí, a later Secretary of the Department, as was Breathnach, was another in this category.

In seeking to establish the inspectorate on a good financial footing, the Department of Education stressed to the Department of Finance, 'It is our aim to make the inspectorate a profession of a superior grade to which the best of our teachers in all the branches of the service may be attracted.' As an indication of this, Pádraig Ó Brolcháin, the first CEO for primary education, in 1923 drew up a scheme for the 're-organisation of the inspectorate' (primary) with salary maxima as follows: Chief Inspector £1,000; Deputy Chiefs £850; Divisional Inspectors £700; Class I Inspectors £600 and Class II Inspectors £500.[16] Inspectors would also benefit from expenses and subsistence allowances. These aspirational salary scales were well ahead of those of teachers at the time, and reflected a view of the inspectors' role as being one of considerable social status.

However, over the first four decades of independence, the proportion of public expenditure applied to education reflected a declining pattern, as is indicated in the following table:

Table 7.1: Educational expenditure as a percentage of the
public sector budget, 1926–61

Year	Total Public Sector Budget in £ million	Total Educational Expenditure as % of Public Sector
1926–27	34.0	14.1%
1931	32.0	16.1%
1941	49.0	12.1%
1951	118.0	9.3%
1961	214.7	9.5%

Source: Adapted from D.H. Akenson, *A Mirror to Kathleen's Face* (1975), p. 8.

This lack of resourcing for education over this period had significant impact on qualitative developments within the system. The inspectorate as the key professional link between the Department of Education and the school system operated within narrow parameters regarding the administrative/economic framework of the system which existed at that time.

15 Micheál Breathnach, *Cuimhne an tSeanpháiste* (Baile Átha Cliath, Oifig and tSoláthair, 1966), p. 238.   16 NA Box 2006, 120/16.

It is interesting that appointment as Secretary of the Department in those years was not a structured, competitive one. Micheál Breathnach records that he entered no competition for the post and was informed of his appointment by a phone call from his predecessor in the office. Séamus Ó Buachalla records how Minister Mulcahy had arranged with Minister of Finance McGilligan in 1951, that Labhrás Ó Muirthí and Torlach Ó Raifeartaigh should be the next two Secretaries of the Department – which is what transpired.[17]

Overall, the structural changes, the shift in educational ideology, the new curricular emphases, the personnel arrangements were accommodated with no significant upheaval on the transition to independence. Despite the difficult conditions which operated in the post-civil war context, no significant opposition manifested itself to the new configuration of arrangements for the education system. The main question was: Could the aspirations for a cultural revival through the Gaelicisation policy be accomplished? The inspectors would have a crucial role to play in this regard.

17 Ó Buachalla, op. cit., p. 275.

8

The Primary School Inspectorate, 1922–60

TRANSITION PERIOD FOR NATIONAL SCHOOL INSPECTION, 1922–34

Inspection of national schools was affected in various ways throughout the period of the War of Independence and its aftermath. The transition to native government in the Irish Free State was accompanied by major change in the inspection corps, in its personnel and in its organisation and administration. Curricular policy also underwent major redefinition and this also was a major alteration in the circumstances bearing on schools, teachers and inspectors. The period of transition from about 1922 to 1934 was one of important reshaping and redefinition of many features of the national education system as it entered upon its second century of existence. Despite many significant changes however, it is remarkable that the system in its essentials changed very little under native administration. Indeed the enduring structures and patterns of Ireland's national school system and its functioning are in some ways quite extraordinary. An important feature under the new regime was the harnessing of the national school system and its modification as necessary to suit the aims and aspirations of the emergent state. Understandably, the political, cultural and national considerations of the time took precedence in many aspects of education during this period.

All the key features of the national school system remained in place under native government. Thus, the structures of patronage, management and staffing of schools continued as before. The overall regulation of the system continued with the occasional issuing of the Rules for National Schools while the patterns of annual reporting on the system continued after a fashion. Inspection changed but little in the new era apart from different personnel and new emphases. The most obvious and notable change was in the curricular policies pursued by the government. Another significant modification was in the administration and control of the system under new political masters.

In many respects the character and leitmotif of national education for the future was signalled clearly by the order of the Provisional Government issued in February 1922 when it ordained that from St Patrick's Day 1922, the Irish language should be taught or used as a medium of instruction for not less than one full hour each day in all national schools where there was a teacher competent to teach it.[1] The appointment of Eoin MacNeill, a founder

1 Public Record Office, *The National School System, 1831–1924, Facsimile Documents*, p. 72.

member of the Gaelic League and closely identified with its educational aspirations, as Minister for Education in 1922, underlined the government's commitment to Irish as an integral part of education policy. The State's intentions were further elaborated with the approval of the constitution later that year, including the provision that Irish was to be the national language while English would be recognised as an official language.

The appointment of Pádraig Ó Brolcháin as Chief Executive Officer in charge of the National Education Office in Marlborough Street was an early indicator of the government's attachment to prominent figures in the Gaelic League and the role expected of them in native government and administration. Ó Brolcháin was deeply committed to the Gaelic revival and was assiduous in his pursuit of it throughout his twelve-year tenure as executive head in Tyrone House, up until his death in 1934.

Another important appointment was that of Joseph O'Neill, or Seosamh Ó Néill, who became Secretary to the Ministry of Education with effect from 1 May 1923. O'Neill, had spent two years as an inspector under the National Board before joining the intermediate schools' inspectorate in 1909. O'Neill had his office in Hume Street where the Intermediate Education Commissioners were located. O'Neill was a committed revivalist and remained Secretary for a very long period up to 1944.

With the foundation of Saorstát Éireann, some inspectors took up appointments in Northern Ireland and a number of inspectors took early retirement under the terms of the Treaty. For the 54 national school inspectors who remained under Dublin's control, the transition to the new state was accompanied by a notable redefinition of priorities within the service. Proficiency in Irish swiftly emerged as a critical feature for all future work and especially for appointments and promotion. Fewer than half of all the inspectors left in the service were proficient in Irish as established by an internal office survey of June 1922 though the degrees of proficiency at the time were somewhat simplistic. The inspection staff included a chief, a divisional, 11 senior inspectors, 3 pre-1900 district inspectors, 36 junior inspectors and 2 women inspectors. These were deployed in 14 circuits comprised of 33 sections. An immediate issue was the reorganisation of the country for the territorial deployment of the inspectors. The circuit and section system dating from 1901 was replaced by a divisional and district arrangement, whereby 7 divisions comprised of some 46 districts were devised. One Chief Inspector and two deputy chiefs were to be responsible for the general direction of the inspection and organising staff. Seven divisional inspectors were to have charge of six or seven districts each, to exercise a supervisory role over district inspectors. All existing staff were to be assimilated to the new system and existing rights and privileges were accorded special consideration. The most significant aspect of this was that district inspectors, for salary purposes, were divided into two classes with differential salaries. However, both the class 1 and class 2 district inspectors had exactly similar duties. In the course of time, the Department of Finance permitted some modification of the staffing arrangements, but it is noteworthy that the organisational framework of the primary inspectorate determined in 1923 was not subsequently altered. A notable feature was that about twenty organisers, in subjects such as music, kindergarten and domestic economy, were also under the control of the Chief Inspector, remaining an integral part of the national school system.

The altered organisational framework was good. The restoration of the district title, with independent powers but answerable to a divisional inspector with wider territorial responsibility, was especially notable. The creation of a cadre of divisional inspectors along with the appointment of deputy chief inspectors, based in the Office, offered the prospect of a more co-ordinated and better structured inspectorate. An inescapable conclusion to be drawn from the rearrangement was that the pre-1900 organisation was restored in essence if not in all details. The divisional grade corresponded with the head inspectors of old, districts were back in vogue, while the Chief and deputy chiefs were mainly to be occupied in Tyrone House. It is likely that O Brolchain and T.P. O'Connor, the Chief Inspector, both of whom worked for the National Board pre-1900, were responsible for the reorganisation. However, there was little sign of any change in the linkages between the inspectorate and the administrative arm of the national education system.

An important factor in the promotion of many individuals at this time was competence in Irish and this was also a major consideration in the first competition for new inspectors held under the aegis of the Irish Free State. Twelve vacancies were advertised bilingually in the *School Weekly* in May 1923, and an estimated 700 applicants competed for the positions.[2] The former conditions governing appointment and training appear to have been ignored while particular emphasis was placed on competence in Irish and availability to oversee Irish courses commencing in July. That month, the successful candidates were announced and these were: A. Walsh, M. Breathnach, M. Hughes, M.McGeehin, B. Ní Mhurchadha, M. Kinsella, D.J. O'Connor, S. O hAodha, J.B. Dolan, L.J. Murray, T. Ó Tuama and C. Watters. Of these, seven were secondary teachers, two were national teachers, one had been an inspector of Irish under the Department of Agriculture and Technical Instruction, and two were training college lecturers. Sometimes referred to as 'dáreag aspal na hathbheochana' or 'the twelve apostles of the revival', the description is more than apt. Almost at once, however, some of these were transferred to secondary school duties and further vacancies arose in the primary inspectorate.[3] Among those who transferred were Micheal Breathnach and L. Ó Muirthí, both of whom became Secretary of the Department of Education in later years.

2 *Irish School Weekly*, 12 and 26 May 1923.   3 Micheál Breathnach, *Cuimhne an Seanpháiste* (Baile Átha Cliath: Oifig an tSolathair, 1966), pp 236–37.

Throughout these years Gaelicisation was a major theme for the top officials of the new Ministry of Education. Both O Brolchain and O'Neill were strong advocates of policies aimed at transforming Ireland through the gradual intensification of Irish language teaching in the school system. Gaelicisation was the paramount concern in many respects and nowhere more centrally than in the primary education sphere. Preparatory colleges for prospective teachers were established in 1926 and seven in all were brought into operation within a few years. These residential colleges were designed to provide secondary education with Irish as the medium of instruction and special arrangements were made to attract native Irish speakers into the colleges so that later on, there would be a steady stream of fluent Irish speakers into the training colleges. Admission to the preparatory colleges depended on a competitive entrance examination held at Easter each year and this included oral tests in Irish carried out by inspectors. Such policies found ready support among government figures including MacNeill and Ernest Blythe who as Minister for Finance gave crucial support for the establishment of the preparatory colleges to underpin the Gaelicisation programme. In spite of many constraints and constant shortages of State money, the government made every effort to advance its policy of Gaelicisation in many facets of public life. The establishment of An Gúm to publish educational texts in the Irish language, in 1926, as part of the Department, underlined the government's prioritisation of the Irish language and identity at this time.

THE PRIMARY SCHOOL CURRICULUM 1922–34 AND INSPECTION

Among the most obvious features that underwent change for Gaelicisation purposes was the school curriculum. In a series of steps beginning in 1922, the primary school curriculum was radically altered to make provision for the teaching of the Irish language as a language in its own right and also as a medium of instruction. Whereas a minority of schools had made provision for Irish as a language in the early years of the twentieth century, the proposals introduced under native administration far exceeded such provision in terms of range and depth.

NATIONAL PROGRAMME CONFERENCE, 1921–22

Against a backdrop of grave civil strife and political turmoil in Ireland, the INTO took an important initiative in 1920 in convening a conference to produce a new programme for national schools. Relations with the administration in Tyrone House and its inspectors were very poor at this time and the conference proceeded without reference to officialdom. By early 1922, a new programme had been devised and was to come into effect at the beginning of April, having been adopted by the Minister for Education of the Provisional Government.[4] Called the National Programme of Primary Instruction, this set out a notably different curriculum for primary schools that was in accord with the nationalist ideals and aspirations of various groups at the time. It immediately presaged the abandonment of the curricular reforms of 1900 and subsequent years. In outline, Irish, English, mathematics including algebra and geometry, history and geography, singing, needlework and drill were to be obligatory subjects, while subjects such as drawing, elementary science and nature study were made additional subjects for which special fees might be paid. Every pupil was to receive at least one hour's instruction in Irish each day. Where parents objected to the teaching of Irish or English as an obligatory subject, their wishes were to be complied with. However, in a contradictory way, a programme for infants was also outlined and was prefaced with a note that 'the work in the infant standards is to be entirely in Irish'.[5] The programme set down benchmark principles for instruction in Irish and these were to have profound implications for generations of children for half a century and more.

SECOND NATIONAL PROGRAMME CONFERENCE, 1925–26

Within a short time, the INTO had cause to request a review of the programme so speedily introduced in 1922. On this occasion, the Minister for Education took the initiative and appointed the Revd Lambert McKenna SJ as Chairman of the Second National Programme Conference which included representations from managers, teachers, county councils, the Gaelic League as well as eleven nominees of the Minister for Education. Inspectors were strongly represented at the conference and even more significantly in the background as advisers to the ministry. The Second National Programme Conference was given a very narrow brief, merely to consider the programme in operation, and to make recommendations as regards 'alterations which may seem desirable'. Following a complex and tense series of deliberations with some evidence taken in public, including that of Professor T.J. Corcoran of UCD, various compromises were agreed among the parties especially among the teachers' representatives and inspectors. The Chairman, two teachers and two divisional inspectors drew up a revised programme which was finally amended and ratified early in 1926. Soon after, the Minister for Education, J.M. O'Sullivan, accepted the programme as the official programme for use in national schools.[6]

4 T.J. O'Connell, *History of the INTO* (Dublin: INTO, 1969), pp 343–51.   5 National Programme Conference, *National Programme of Primary Instruction* (Dublin: Educational Company, 1922).   6 *Report and Programme of the National Programme Conference, 1925–26*

The Report of the Second National Programme Conference and the appended Programme of Primary Instruction reflected fully the compromises and selectivity that had characterised the private deliberations of the conference. The report endorsed the policy of the previous conference and introduced a few adjustments to assist a more gradual approach to the realisation of the State's aims. The key principle of teaching infants through Irish was reaffirmed with the modest change that English could be used before 10.30 each morning. Higher and lower courses, written in English, applicable to Irish and English in tandem, were now set out and intended to be used to suit the circumstances of each school. A preliminary note explained that where the attainments of both teacher and pupils justified the use of Irish as the school language, the higher course was to be taken in Irish together with the lower course in English. Those who adopted the alternative lower course in Irish and the higher course in English, were to be expected to advance gradually towards the higher course in Irish with a consequential reduction in English.

Also significant was an adjustment to the programme requirements in mathematics, history and geography as the ministry and representatives of the teachers moved towards a reduction of expectations to facilitate the teaching of Irish.

As the conference concluded, the INTO secured an assurance that the inspection system would be examined in the context of the new requirements affecting teachers and schools and this apparently was a factor in the decision to sign the Second Conference Report.[7] The INTO representatives, in a special note appended to the report, stated that a radical reform of the inspection system was necessary to assist the successful implementation of the programme and it was hoped that a joint committee of inspectors and teachers would soon undertake this task.

THE COMMITTEE ON INSPECTION OF PRIMARY SCHOOLS
(McKENNA COMMITTEE)

Almost immediately, a committee to examine inspection was appointed by the Minister. The group constituted to inquire into inspection was almost entirely comprised of men who had served on the programme conference. Thus, Lambert McKenna, as Chairman, and ten others, including representatives of school managers, teachers and the Christian Brothers, were appointed as a Committee on Inspection by Minister J.M. O'Sullivan in June 1926. The same inspectors were nominated as members of the Committee, so that it almost resembled a sub-committee of the conference. Once again, the brief

(Dublin: Oifig an tSolathair, 1926).   7 Ibid., p. 55.

was narrow, simply to investigate inspection and the award of merit marks, and to report if changes or reforms should be considered. Significantly however, the Committee was also instructed to advise as to the desirability of instituting a primary leaving certificate examination. A thirty-nine point questionnaire was dispatched to various individuals and heads of institutions, inviting suggestions and views about inspection and a primary leaving certificate examination. Apart from one inspector, no witnesses were examined. Instead, it was agreed that the Chairman, who had Jesuit friends in many of the chief cities of Europe, should be sent abroad for the purpose of securing first-hand evidence 'as to the practical working of foreign inspection systems, and of obtaining other indispensable information which could not readily be procured by correspondence'.[8]

At the public expense, grudgingly approved by the Department of Finance, Fr McKenna went on an extended tour of five countries, visiting twelve cities and meeting teachers, inspectors, and others, during September and October 1926. Although McKenna's account of his visits in Europe yielded a forty-page addendum to the final report of the Committee, not a single idea of any consequence was mentioned in the recommendations of the Committee. Instead, the report contained a number of minor recommendations in relation to inspection suggesting more frequent incidental visits and more thorough general inspections. The report drew attention to the controlling aspect of the inspection system but did not manage to provide any significant modifications for the future. An appeal board against inspectors' ratings was recommended. This was a significant change to allay teachers' concerns and came into operation soon after. The Committee also recommended that a primary school certificate examination should be introduced and this recommendation was adopted with alacrity with the introduction of the primary certificate as an optional examination in 1929. Apart from recommending the establishment of the appeal board and suggesting many minor changes in inspection procedures, the Committee had little further to offer. It put forward no significant statement about the recruitment, training, staffing, workload or management of the inspectorate. Not a word was uttered about the Office or its linkages with the inspectorate. Although the Committee had gathered some evidence, notably some returns from the Office and various submissions from inspectors and others, none of this was published. The McKenna Committee represented one of the few occasions under native government that any body considered the inspectorate with reference to its functioning in the education system.

Despite the report of the McKenna Committee, the INTO continued to voice concerns about inspection and especially about the rating of teachers in the context of increments of salary as arranged in the 1920 salary agreement

8 *Report of the Committee on Inspection of Primary Schools* (Dublin: Stationery Office, 1927), p. 5.

that linked pay to efficiency of teaching. In the meantime, the ministry continued to exert certain pressure to speed up the implementation of the Gaelicisation programme with emphasis given to tightening regulations governing appointments and promotions to principal and vice-principal positions. Though in many ways the ministry maintained good communication lines with the INTO, tensions about inspection and aspects of the programme continued to be a feature of the period. A circular of July 1931 exhorted teachers to extend instruction through the medium of Irish as it pointed out that the use of Irish as the teaching medium was obligatory once the teacher was competent to give the instruction and the pupils were able to assimilate it. A further indication of the government's intent in relation to Gaelicisation was the announcement in 1931 that the salaries of Gaeltacht teachers would be augmented in some cases by as much as 10%.[9]

At this time, Fianna Fáil, under the leadership of Eamon de Valera, was an important and emergent political party, marking the government closely in Dáil debates on education issues. Soon, it came to pass that de Valera's party formed a government and Tomás Derrig became Minister for Education in March 1932, a position he was to retain until 1948, apart from one short interlude. De Valera, in a St Patrick's Day broadcast, announced his intention to make changes in Irish education but Derrig was more specific when he addressed the INTO Congress in 1932. Making use of Irish and English, he told the teachers:

> The heart and core of all our work in the creation of a National State must be the revival of the national language as the spoken language of the people, for in the Irish language lies enshrined for us the genius of our race. If we lose our language we lose our national heritage. In its songs, its prayers and its proverbs are expressed the Gaelic soul of our people.[10]

Thus, it can be understood that in the 1931–32 period, administrative and political influences were strongly assertive in the restatement and reinforcement of the cultural and national aims underlying the programme of instruction in the primary schools. Of interest here is the nature of the evidence available to the education ministry concerning the question of Irish teaching in the primary schools at this time. At the end of 1930, a very substantial body of divisional and district inspectors' reports was compiled on foot of an instruction to submit confidential accounts about teaching through the medium of Irish. The reports of the inspectors provided a valuable catalogue of the problems being experienced in schools and affecting children and teachers to a serious extent. The reports provided very definite evidence to

9 *Irish School Weekly*, 27 June 1931.   10 *Irish School Weekly*, 2 April 1932.

suggest that the policies being pursued for Irish were inimical in many ways to the education of very large numbers of children in Ireland. However, the reports of the inspectors were not accorded serious consideration. The published annual report of the Department of Education for 1930–31 bowdlerised the inspectors' accounts beyond recognition. In a three-page summary entitled 'Teaching through Irish', an anodyne description presented a bland picture, admitting progress was slow, but looking hopefully to fifteen or twenty years henceforward, when teaching power would be such as to enable the work in all national schools to be done entirely through the medium of Irish.

As may be understood from the foregoing, the publication of inspectors' reports had undergone a mutation of extraordinary proportions under the new administrative and political arrangements of the Free State. In this there were clear signs that the inspectorate had reached a low point in its fortunes when its commentary on the school system could be disregarded and kept from publication.

THE REVISED PROGRAMME OF PRIMARY INSTRUCTION, 1934

Throughout the period 1930 to 1934, the INTO remained critical of the inspection system and linked its criticism of the inspectors with criticism of the programme of instruction. A small number of inspectors, those with strong Irish language credentials within the Department, were influential in advising the senior officials such as O Brolchain and O'Neill, as well as the ministers of the day about possible modifications of the programme. At one point, a joint committee of leading INTO representatives and inspectors was set up to consider the programme in detail in a series of meetings in October and November 1933.[11] This committee failed to agree a report and the INTO provided its views in detail to the ministry in February 1934.[12] The teachers' representatives urged that nature study or rural science should be eliminated from all schools, and that algebra and geometry similarly should be eliminated from most schools except the larger ones. The tone and spirit of the document placed before the Minister at this juncture conveyed the message that a lightening of the programme was all that was necessary to make progress with Irish. This was the message that soon found acceptance inside Tyrone House as the Minister, Tomás Derrig, in an unprecedented move, arranged for a hurried consultation with all inspectors in June 1934. Within days, a new programme was being prepared and in September 1934, the *Revised Programme of Primary Instruction* was printed. An Roinn Aistriúchán in Dáil Éireann translated it into Irish soon after under the title *Clár Nuadh na mBun-Scol*.

11 Department of Education, Registered File 34809, *Clár 1931; An Chomhdháil de Chigirí agus Oidí agus na Moltaí.* 12 Department of Education, Registered File 34809, *INTO Report 28 February 1934.*

Thus, the last step in the evolution of the primary school curriculum of the Free State was completed with the issuance of a revised programme. This was the slimmest programme produced for over thirty years. Not since the days of payment by results had such a narrow curriculum been prescribed for use in national schools. Obligatory subjects included Irish, English, arithmetic, music, history and geography for senior standards, and needlework for girls. Rural science or nature study was optional in all schools, and algebra and geometry were optional for all schools except larger boys' schools where one branch was to be taken up. There was no mention of subjects such as drawing and physical training which had been optional. A course based on the previous higher course was set out for Irish. English was 'no longer permitted' in infant classes where the teachers were competent to do the work through Irish alone. English was optional for the first standard and no syllabus was set for this standard. The new programme in English was less ambitious in scope than that previously in operation. Only rudimentary written work was prescribed and composition, which had thrived to some extent in earlier years, was not even mentioned. Recitation was not stipulated while oral work in English was equated with reading and explanation of the lessons. The word 'Kindergarten' disappeared from the infant programme and 'games' were substituted for 'drill'. It was stated in the preamble that the lightening of the programme was expected to lead to more rapid progress in the teaching of Irish and in the spread of teaching through Irish. A strong authoritarian note was struck in the very first words of the preamble which announced:

> The Minister for Education has decided on certain modifications in the programme of instruction for Primary Schools. These come into operation immediately.[13]

OVERVIEW OF THE CURRICULUM, 1922–34

The three distinct stages of the evolution of the national school curriculum came to an end with the publication of the 1934 revised programme. The abandonment of the programme that had been introduced in 1900 and the reversion to a three R approach with Irish writ large, was indeed a profound change in the circumstances of primary education. The programme as produced in 1934 remained largely in place until its eventual replacement in 1971. Thus a long period of rigid, narrow and uninspiring fare for teachers and children was ensured in the national schools as a result of the curricular policies determined during these first years of independence.

With regard to the involvement of inspectors in the evolution of the programme, it may be noted that only a minority of inspectors, carefully chosen

13 An Roinn Oideachais, *Revised Programme of Primary Instruction* (Dublin: Stationery Office, 1934).

for their Irish language credentials, were closely associated with the process in 1925–26 and again in 1933–34. Ironically, for the second time in thirty years approximately, though for very different reasons, major revision of the curriculum was accomplished without the clear support of all the inspectors of the day. It seems clear that Padraig O Brolchain and Seosamh Ó Néill were especially influential in seeing through, in the national school system at least, the almost total subordination of the curriculum and school-life generally to the promotion of revivalist aims. The 1934 revision of the programme was to remain, without major modification, the curriculum of the national schools for the following three decades and more.

INSPECTION UNDER NATIVE GOVERNMENT

The character and operational patterns of the primary inspectorate were established very definitely in the early years of independence. The inspectorate assumed a distinctive style of its own very clearly founded on what had gone before but now modified by the ideals of Gaelicisation and national independence. Remarkably, more than forty new appointments were made in the period from 1923 to 1930. This was perhaps the most significant intake of new inspectors in a short period to occur until the early years of this century. In a sense it demonstrated the great commitment of the State to matters educational at a time of particular stringency in the public finances. All of these new inspectors appear to have been selected on the basis of an interview, emphasis being placed on qualifications and experience but especially on fluency in Irish and ability to teach through the medium of Irish.

The primary inspectors were deeply embedded in virtually every aspect of primary education. Inspectors were involved with teachers and schools, with school managers, with building matters, with Gaeltacht areas and summer courses for teachers. Inspectors carried out special inquiries, prepared notes for teachers and assisted with arranging the work of the organising staff in music, kindergarten and domestic economy. The primary inspectorate also vetted and sanctioned the textbooks which publishers prepared for the use of schools. Cast always in the role of carrying through the wishes and instructions of the Department, the inspectors at district and divisional levels had little opportunity to influence the policy aspects that underlay all day-to-day business.

While the bulk of inspection work consisted of visiting and reporting on schools, work connected with the State examinations became a substantial element of inspectorial business under native government. Prior to 1922, national school inspectors had responsibilities in connection with the training college Easter entrance examinations in addition to the final examinations for the students in training. This work expanded rather dramatically in the course of the 1920s with the introduction of examinations for Irish certificates, scholarship examinations and preparatory college examinations, while oral Irish tests in each of these, added further to the workload of inspectors. The introduction of the Primary School Certificate examination in 1929 added significantly to the burden of work involved in setting, superintending and marking State examinations. The examination section of the Department's Primary Branch which had responsibility for administering these examinations, gradually assumed a much larger engagement with the school population as the numbers of candidates increased with the passage of time. When the Primary School Certificate became a compulsory examination for sixth class pupils from 1943, inspectors were more than ever weighed down with examination work. There was hardly a month in the year without some element of examination work. Easter Week was the time reserved for oral tests in Irish and English, and for the practical tests in Needlework for girls, the so-called 'Easter Orals'. All available inspectors and organisers were committed to this work at Easter and the correction and collation of marks had to be completed by the end of the third week of May. Soon after Easter, the scholarship examination was held and its marking had to be completed by a group of inspectors within three to four weeks. Next came the preparatory college examination which required the same length of time to correct but necessitated a large group of inspectors for marking. The Primary School Certificate examination, on the second Friday in June, demanded the full attention of every available inspector to arrange markers, to visit examination centres and to supervise the correction of papers. This was not completed when the training college final examination was begun in June lasting for ten days. Only a few inspectors were deployed superintending these examinations but every inspector in the service was involved with the subsequent marking of the students' final examination. This was carried out in July while early in August, the revision of marking of both the first year and final year students was completed.

As may be understood from the foregoing, examination business was a prominent feature of inspectorial work throughout the year's round. Whereas factors such as seniority, qualifications and location had a bearing on the amount of examination work allocated to an inspector, all inspectors had to devote a considerable amount of time to the arrangement, superintendence and marking of examinations. Although the examination burden was demanding, particularly from 1943 onwards, it was not without some notable benefits. Firstly, in the absence of any national assemblies or conferences of inspectors, the necessity to hold marking conferences in Dublin enabled inspectors to meet and become acquainted with colleagues who might otherwise have remained totally unknown to them. Secondly, the setting and marking of examination papers, especially the training college examinations, provided a stimulus for many inspectors to keep in touch with the training college programme of study. Despite the difficulty that this posed for individuals who were at a considerable remove from the day-to-day life of the colleges, there was an obligation on many inspectors to maintain, as best they could, an academic interest in particular aspects of the training college courses.

THE RATING SYSTEM

The main sphere of work for the inspectorate was, as always, visiting and reporting on schools. The core of inspection was the assessment of teachers' work in schools. This was regulated by the *Rules and Regulations for National Schools* and by the circulars that issued from time to time. Whereas there were changes made in some of the details, the operation of inspection continued to follow much the same pattern as that established prior to 1922.

Under the provisions of the salary agreement for teachers of 1920, merit marks assigned by inspectors assumed a new significance. A key feature was that the status and emoluments of teachers should bear a distinct relation to the efficiency and ability with which they discharged their duties. Teachers whose work was deemed to be very satisfactory, were eligible for special increments over and above the ordinary salary scale for teachers. The salary system was inextricably linked to the inspection of schools. The intention was that a teacher whose work was highly regarded by the inspector, would be paid more and would have better prospects for promotion or for securing a better position than teachers whose work was less highly regarded. Commonly referred to as the rating system, it categorised teachers as highly efficient, efficient and non-efficient.

Highly efficient was defined to mean that a teacher's work as regards the programme of instruction, general discipline and pupils' progress, was very good. Efficient was understood to mean that the teacher had not neglected any subject while overall performance was good. Non-efficient denoted a standard below efficient. What was crucial in the circumstances of Saorstát Éireann was the change in the programme of instruction, especially the provision to be made for the teaching of Irish, since this was to be a critical factor in the determination of highly efficient and efficient ratings.

Annual reports on teachers and schools were still at the heart of inspection though every teacher was not required to have an in-depth report each year. Frequent incidental visits were to be an important aspect of inspection so that inspectors would be familiar with the schools and would have opportunities for observing teaching methods and for assisting and advising teachers. Annual general reports were to be obligatory for teachers with a rating below efficient, for teachers on probation or with less than five years' service, and for those teachers whose work was deemed to have deteriorated. There was provision for teachers who wished to apply for a general report on their work in the hope that a higher rating would be granted. In addition, inspectors were required to provide general reports on a certain number of other teachers each year so that all teachers over time would undergo a general inspection of their work. Now called 'Mór-thuairisc', the general report was to be a thorough and comprehensive affair, every class and every subject being carefully tested, and the teacher being given every opportunity to show what the children had actually done, and to display their knowledge and accomplishments. Three days' notice of the precise date of a general inspection was to be given to the teacher and to the school manager. The inspector was to take careful account of schemes of work, progress record, weekly syllabus and the teacher's preparation for work. In judging the quality of the professional work of the teacher, the deeper purposes of education were not to be overlooked by the inspector who was enjoined to

> keep constantly before his mind the extent to which the education given has contributed to the formation of character, the training in good habits, the development of the pupils' intelligence, the strengthening of the sense of personal and national self-respect, and generally the preparation of the pupils to take their place as good and useful citizens of their country.[14]

The general report was to provide a comprehensive and balanced account of the teacher's work. Instead of the brief minute customary in the past, there was to be a fuller account of the work, and mention was to be made of any abnormal circumstances which might have affected the teacher's work. The efficiency table was altered so that in addition to the merit mark for each subject of the programme, the inspector would also provide a comment on the efficiency of the teaching in each subject so that the report would leave no doubt as to how the inspector judged the teacher's work. Considerations such as the proficiency of the pupils, the teacher's attitude and preparation for work, the manner of teaching, handling of lessons, the discipline and power of holding the pupils' attention, the personal influence on children and the observance of official regulations, were all mentioned as factors to be taken into account by an inspector in formulating an assessment of the teacher's work. Having regard to the multiplicity of factors to be kept in view by an inspector, it seems little wonder that the Irish term *mór-fhiosrú*, literally meaning a great inquiry, passed into common parlance among teachers as an apt description of the major manifestation of official interest in their work. It is apparent that in the primary sector, school inspection was extremely close and tightly arranged. Though the basic design was an inheritance from the past, the reformulation that occurred in the Irish Free State had the effect of

14 Reports of the Department of Education for 1925–27, pp 9–15 and circular entitled 'Inspection of Schools-Revised Instructions to Inspectors', p. 11.

consolidating many of the requirements and expectations that were part of the teachers' role. Of major importance were the provisions relating to Irish. As far as possible, the requirements of the official programme had to be carried out, particularly the use of Irish as a medium of instruction. In addition, for a highly efficient rating, a teacher's work in oral Irish had to be very good. Thus, the use of Irish, both as a subject and as a medium of instruction, was intended to be a decisive factor in the award of highly efficient ratings with consequential salary increments and enhanced promotional opportunities for successful teachers.

It was through the inspection system mainly that the State could assert rigorous control over the implementation of its policy relating to Irish. There could be no mistaking the seriousness with which the Department proposed the speedy transition to teaching through Irish in the national schools. It was in the national school system particularly that the Department had sufficient power and control to secure compliance with its aims for Irish, the very ambitious nature of which was clearly not fully appreciated. In the rating system as it was commonly known, the Department found a convenient but very powerful harness for keeping a tight rein on the national teachers who were to be in the forefront of the attempt to make Irish the vernacular. By means of the rating system, the inspection corps was to have a mighty influence on classroom practice throughout the twenty-six county state. Unlike the secondary school system, where the whole school was more the focus of inspection and where the visit of an inspector was a rare event in any case, the national school teacher was ever and always anticipating the visit of the district inspector whose reports were of immediate significance to the teacher, determining his or her official standing and reputation as a teacher. Indeed, it was the closeness and detailed nature of inspection that more or less guaranteed that national teachers would do all in their power to endeavour to comply with the Department's objectives in relation to Irish. Thus, in a very real way, the inspectors came to be the mainspring and driving force behind the revivalist intentions of the Department and its political masters for the foreseeable future.

Inspectors were closely associated with the production of a series of Notes for Teachers in which were set out explanatory comments and ideas to assist teachers in various aspects of the curriculum. For example, the *Notes for Teachers – Irish*,[15] which appeared in 1933 was the forerunner of a number of booklets providing advice to primary teachers and students in training. Though densely written, these were helpful to teachers in certain respects. One of the booklets *National Tradition and Folklore*,[16] issued in 1934 advocated that national teachers should undertake the compilation of local tradi-

15 Department of Education, *Notes for Teachers – Irish* (Dublin: Stationery Office, 1933).   16 Department of Education, *National Tradition and Folklore* (Dublin: Stationery Office, 1934).

tion from local sources, in manuscript books to be supplied by the Department, and listed various subheads and suggestions that might guide teachers in their efforts. This foreshadowed the scheme arranged in conjunction with the Irish Folklore Commission to collect material through the national schools. The scheme prompted schools to get pupils in the fifth and higher standards to gather stories and traditions in their homes or districts and operated from September 1937 until December of the following year. This reflected the interest in, and preoccupation with, elements of folklore, local tradition, songs, place-names, and social, religious and archaeological data, that were perceived as key aspects of national consciousness and identity at this period.

In 1936 the INTO initiated an inquiry into the use of Irish as a teaching medium to children whose home language was English. An interim report on the use of Irish as a medium of instruction for the infant school was produced in March 1939, and submitted to the Minister for Education in May of that year. The final report was published in July 1941.[17] It was largely based on a questionnaire distributed to teachers who used Irish as a teaching medium for children from non-Irish speaking homes, supplemented with a historical introduction and commentary. While stressing that 'the National Teachers of today and their Organisation are whole-hearted supporters of the movement for the revival of Irish',[18] the report was critical of many aspects of the method used in employing Irish as a medium for children from non-Irish speaking homes. The Department of Education based its policy response largely on the solicited views of the inspectorate. The view was recorded that inspectors considered the report as representing 'the views of the middle-aged, somewhat tired and not too well linguistically equipped teachers.' They went on to assert: 'The next twenty years are likely to be the critical ones. Utmost use must be made of school hours and all our efforts concentrated on giving the children the power to speak Irish as their national language.'[19] Further to this, the Chief Inspector submitted a twenty-six page document, with a further six pages of summary, as a critique of the INTO report.[20] This response re-affirmed the Department's education policy on the pedagogy of Irish.

An important and notable feature for the divisional grade and more senior inspectors throughout the years was the annual conference arranged in Dublin. To its credit, the Department from an early stage facilitated the holding of these conferences of the senior inspectors. This was the most significant type of conference in evidence during these years. It was customary to hold the conference of the senior inspectors in January during the school holiday period. The chief inspector and the divisional and deputy chief inspectors met in Marlborough Street, usually with the Assistant Secretary

17 INTO, *Report of the Committee of Inquiry into the Use of Irish as a Teaching Medium to Children Whose Home Language is English* (Dublin: INTO, 1941).   18 Ibid., p. 67.   19 National Archives, File S. 7801 A.   20 Ibid.

for Primary and perhaps one or two others of the administrative staff present. It was the custom for the Minister to attend for some short while and perhaps address the conference on some issues of importance. For example, in 1940, shortly before the Primary Certificate Examination became compulsory, Eamon de Valera attended one such conference at the time that he was Minister for Education, as well as Taoiseach. The conference on that occasion devoted some time to discussing points raised by him including the teaching of Irish and arithmetic. The first item on the agenda posed the question, 'how best to give effect to An Taoiseach's policy – i.e. 'A little done well.'[21] It is apparent that the annual conferences of senior inspectors gave attention to many aspects of the Department's affairs and were important for a number of reasons. Interestingly, it was customary also for the senior inspectors to have a meeting with representatives of the INTO at some stage during or after the conference. Items and issues from the conferences also featured at the divisional conferences held from time to time with the district inspectors. In this way, some useful dissemination of information was part of the functioning of the primary inspectors throughout the years.

THE PRIMARY INSPECTORATE AND THE NEW DEPARTMENT OF EDUCATION

With the enactment of the Ministers and Secretaries Act in 1924, a government order brought the Department of Education into being in June 1924. Various educational services and institutions were gathered into one ministry. From then on, the major education services were commonly referred to as national education or Primary Branch, the Secondary Branch and the Technical Instruction Branch. The Department also took over responsibility for reformatory and industrial schools. The different education services were brought under the control of the Minister and the Department. However, each service had its own origin and its own tradition, and the patterns of structure and administration were distinctively different. For various reasons, the Department did not blend all the services into a single unified entity for administrative purposes. Instead, the main branches retained their separate identities and this was notably underscored by the physical separation of various sections and offices. The Hume Street offices were the location for both the Secretary and the Minister up to 1939, and this may have been a factor in conferring a certain precedence on the Secondary Branch. On the other side of the Liffey, the National Education Office retained its own identity. Although Marlborough Street was to be eventually the main locus for the Department of Education, it seems that for a very considerable period, right

21 Department of Education, miscellaneous file, *Comhdháil na gCigirí, 1940.*

up to modern times, a cardinal feature of the administration was the almost total compartmentalisation of the various executive sections. This was reflective of the actual functioning of the whole education system where the different sectors, in virtually every single facet of their operation, remained more or less hermetically sealed, one from another.

The Department came into being not as a result of legislation tailored to alter the education system, but rather as a part of the political and administrative arrangements necessitated by the transfer of powers with the foundation of the Irish Free State. A very notable feature of the Irish education system ever since has been the paucity of legislation for education. Of particular relevance is the fact that no comprehensive legislation for education was enacted until 1998. Therefore, the Stanley letter and the Royal Charters of 1845 and 1861 still had significance as part of the legal basis on which national education rested. For all practical purposes, the Chief Executive Officer, the Secretary and the Minister were the major figures in charge of national education.

Although fundamental reform of the education system was not embarked on, some measures of note were adopted for primary education. A scholarship scheme was instituted to enable bright pupils to proceed to secondary education by the allocation of money awards of modest amounts. The new state also introduced compulsory attendance legislation for children from six to fourteen years of age. The School Attendance Act of 1926 was a notable legislative measure and took effect at the beginning of 1927 and led to a significant improvement in average daily attendance. Efforts were made to tackle the serious difficulties that existed with regard to the financing and provision of new schools and the care and maintenance of existing buildings. A discreet policy of amalgamating adjacent boys' and girls' schools was also pursued and a modest element of co-education was gradually extended through the school system, almost exclusively in the smaller rural districts. Another measure initiated in 1933–34 was the decision to provide Gaeltacht grants of £2 to support Irish-speaking families. This led to the creation of special Gaeltacht districts for inspectors and, in 1954, Seán Ó Casaide, Pádraig Ó hEidhin and Tomás Ó Laoi were the three designated inspectors for what were termed the 'Fíor-Ghaeltacht' regions in Donegal, Galway and Kerry.

Within the Department of Education, the Primary Branch dwarfed the other branches in terms of pupil numbers and State expenditure. The primary sector, by virtue of its size and history, was the branch which had the greatest experience of State involvement in, and administration of education. Because of its sheer size and cost, the Primary Branch, in many senses, was the Department of Education up to recent decades. While the Gaelicisation programme was notably new, a considerable part of the identity of the Department derived from the traditions and practices of the previous era in the National Education Office. Continuity was a corner-stone of the

Department's operations for many years, and in common with other departments and State institutions, there was no radical or revolutionary restructuring of the internal management of the Department of Education. The Primary Branch, largest in terms of staff and size of sector, occupying the building that was to become the headquarters of the Department, had a signal influence on the gradual evolution of the Department of Education as it assumed the identity familiar even today.

The main elements of the administration inherited from the previous era were preserved intact. Rules and regulations and circulars were the mainstay of control and communication. Virtually all the precedents of the past were observed. Much of the documentation and standard forms of earlier years were kept on though certain items were translated into Irish as time went on. Office routines were preserved as before, as for example, the requirement that all communications from outside should be addressed to the Secretary, or the practice of entering county, name and roll number of a school at the head of all letters and instructions concerning that particular school. Thus, the overriding features of the Department's administration were continuity and conservation rather than any notable reshaping of its working practices. In this, the Department of Education was not unlike the other departments under the new Dublin government.

Not everything was preserved however. In many important respects, there was erosion and contraction at the headquarters of national education in the first decades of independence. As part of the Department of Finance's search for economies, substantial rearrangement and cost-cutting measures effected significant reduction in staffing within the Department. Premier sections of the office were reconfigured and certain duties were assigned to more junior staff while old practices lapsed or were forgotten. There were important changes in the manner of handling inspectors' reports and the post of examiner, a remnant from the 1900 period, was suppressed. What had been termed the Inspection Branch was renamed to be the Payments and Administration Branch and this remained the title assigned to the main executive sections dealing with primary schools in the Department of Education and Science for many years. Inspectors' reports were to be dealt with in future by lower executive officers who could refer difficult cases to more senior officials. The statistical section was downgraded in the reorganisation and inspectors no longer had a role in gathering data from schools. The Department of Education, in its annual reports, contrasted very unfavourably with the former practices of the Commissioners in the publication of information and statistical data about primary education. Not alone was statistical reportage jettisoned, but the ordinary annual reports of inspectors on the state of education virtually disappeared at this time. Substantial cuts were effected at the uppermost level of the Department with the disappearance of the dual secretariat of old and its replacement by a chief executive officer to be replaced in 1934 by an assistant secretary on a lower rate of pay. In terms of the administration of education, all the reductions and alterations of these early years had long term effects and acted as serious limitations for the successful operation and development of the primary education sector right up to the 1960s and later.

The Department of Education was structured on a dual administrative and professional basis. Recruitment to the professional wing, including the inspectorate, was always on the basis of suitable qualifications and relevant experience, normally teaching experience of some kind. The administrative side was staffed by career civil servants recruited under the norms set by the Civil Service Commission. Career and promotional prospects were quite different and a number of other factors accentuated the notable divide between the administrative and professional arms of the Department.

The primary inspectorate throughout the years remained a highly contained service within itself. Few of its personnel transferred to the other inspectorates, and fewer still transferred to administrative duties within the Department. The only presence the primary inspectorate had within Marlborough Street, throughout the years until the 1960s, was the few senior inspectors accommodated on the ground floor of Tyrone House. The Chief Inspector and the deputy chief inspectors were normally the only inspection personnel located within the Department. All other national school inspectors were 'outdoor' staff in the fullest sense. At no stage was there a focal point within the Department for inspectors. While the Chief and deputy chief inspectors had rooms in Tyrone House, their functions were primarily advisory, particular cases and matters being referred to them regularly for their advice. However, their role was limited and narrow. While the Chief Inspector might have some influence over policy considerations generally, the senior inspectors in many respects were not accorded and did not take a prominent role in many policy matters. All in all, the primary inspectorate was subordinate to the administrative wing of the Department of Education.

With the passage of time, the bureaucratic and hierarchical structure of the Department consolidated and reinforced the concentration of power in the hands of the small number of very senior officials at the top. Thus, for all intents and purposes, through to the 1960s, the Secretary and the two Assistant Secretaries, with respective charge of the primary and secondary sectors, were 'the Department'. In an important sense too, the Minister was 'the Department' since under the Ministers and Secretaries Act of 1924, the Minister was a 'corporation sole', accountable to parliament for the Department, and obliged to present to parliament its annual reports.[22] Legal powers were vested only in the Minister but obviously there was an informal delegation, even if strictly illegal, to the top officials who could be relied on to know the mind of the Minister.[23] It may be said that 'the Department' was legally

22 Ministers and Secretaries Act 1924, No. 16 of 1924, Saorstát Éireann.   23 T.J. Barrington,

the Minister, but functionally, it was the three top officials, acting in accordance with the Minister's instructions, or in the absence of stated instructions, acting as they best saw fit. In practice, 'the Department', in certain instances, might simply be one man, acting as he thought best in a particular situation.

It is useful to mention the individuals who held the position of Minister of Education during the decades up to the 1960s. Tomás Derrig had the longest tenure of any Minister, in all about fifteen years with a short break in the middle, during which Sean T. O'Kelly but more notably Eamon de Valera, held office for a little while. Although de Valera was Minister for less than nine months, he was wont to take particular interest in the affairs of the Department and in education generally from time to time. Richard Mulcahy was Minister twice in the inter-party governments of the late 1940s and 1950s. Sean Moylan was Minister for three years in the early 1950s while other Fianna Fáil holders of the office included Jack Lynch and Patrick Hillery. Because the national school inspectorate was fairly contained within itself, under the immediate control of the Secretary and the Assistant Secretary who interposed between the senior inspectors and the Minister, there was not a great deal of connection between inspectors and the Minister throughout the years.

THE PRIMARY INSPECTORATE UP TO 1960

The most significant feature of the primary inspectorate as the years passed was that very little changed. The arrangements of the early years of national independence took on a permanence and durability that was in some respects surprising. Native government and deep regard for education did not produce notable ongoing change and responsiveness to circumstances as they developed. Instead, a long period of sameness and stasis ensued and right up to the 1960s there were few notable alterations within the primary sector generally.

Economic circumstances, the enormous constraints imposed by the Second World War and its aftermath, emigration and various other matters were important background aspects during the 1940s and 1950s. Inspection continued to have a profound role and influence in the primary education system. Although there was occasional criticism emanating from teachers' representatives, centring mainly on the rating system, controversy was relatively rare. An exception to this was the section on inspection in the INTO's *A Plan for Education* published in 1947. It contained a strong critique of the current mode of inspection. Among highly critical comments the following was stated:

The Irish Administrative System (Dublin: IPA, 1980), pp 31–32.

On the inspector's side there is only too often a traditional lack of sympathy, so that even the best teachers dread the inspector's visit. ... Under the present system, we regret to say, the inspector gives practically no help to the teacher, and the majority of teachers have never got as much as one really helpful suggestion from any inspector. The formal reports are vague, stereotyped and unreal, and though the need for improvement is often alleged the diagnosis is rarely accompanied by a prescription.[24]

The forcefulness of these charges was directly attacked by the Minister for Education, Tomás Derrig, at a Senate Debate which took place on the *Plan*, during which he put up a spirited defence of the inspectorate. The INTO *Plan* also strongly attacked the rating system. It concluded by putting forward a new design for the work of the inspectorate, and proposals for its recruitment and training.[25]

The rating system was modified notably in 1949 as part of the *rapprochement* following the bitter seven months' strike of teachers in Dublin in 1946. The highly efficient rating was dropped after a series of meetings in Marlborough Street with representatives of the INTO, the Department and managerial authorities including Archbishop J.C. McQuaid of Dublin. The effect of the change was that no longer would inspection have a direct connection with teachers' emoluments once a teacher achieved a rating of 'Satisfactory' on completion of probation. A few years later, the INTO successfully negotiated further changes to inspection and these included the ending of general inspections for the majority of teachers. An important new circular on the inspection of schools was issued in July 1959 superseding previous circulars and altering some features of its operation.[26] More cordial and co-operative inspector-teacher relationships ensued.[27]

This period brought only minor changes to the organisation and operational aspects of the primary inspectors. Significantly, recruitment of inspection personnel was maintained and also, the organisers for kindergarten, music and domestic economy continued to play an important role most notably in providing summer courses for teachers. A signal development from their ranks was the publication in 1951 of *An Naí-Scoil* which outlined new emphases for infant teaching and prefigured major curricular change to come twenty years later.[28] In sharp contrast, the Report of the Council of Education published in 1954 after laborious deliberation on the function and curriculum of the primary school, did not lead to the introduction of any notable change in primary education.

24 INTO, *A Plan for Education* (Dublin: INTO, 1947), pp 33–34. 25 Ibid., pp 34–38. 26 Department of Education, *Circular 16/59*. 27 T.J. O'Connell, op. cit., p. 420. 28 Department of Education, *An Naí-Scoil: The Infant School, Notes for Teachers* (Dublin: Stationery Office, 1951).

Throughout these years the Department itself, and the various ministers, played a rather limited and timid role in education generally. The Department's reportage on education dwindled notably, particularly in regard to inspectors' reporting on the school system. This may be seen as symptomatic of the period and it was to come to pass in 1964 that the Department ceased completely to provide any report at all on the education system, apart from statistical data. There were many manifestations of administrative and political shortcomings throughout these years. An important example from the point of view of inspection and visitation of schools and institutions was the failure to develop some cohesion and cooperation among the various groups of inspectors in the employ of the Department. As in many other matters, this appears to have been a result of administrative compartmentalisation of remarkable endurance and effect. The overall administration of the primary education sector was far from impressive in these years. The main reasons for this would appear to have been a combination of political and administrative weakness and inertia, to some extent reflective of the period. The lack of renewal and restructuring within the Department, allied to settled and unchanging civil service practices, limited the effectiveness of the ministry. Public service frugality may have been a factor in limiting the capacity and scope available to the personnel of the Department. Notably and crucially lacking was a broad perspective on the whole education system and a commitment to seek its development and advancement. Leadership was not a strong feature within the overall education system throughout these years.

9

The Secondary School Inspectorate, 1922–60

From the first annual report of the Department of Education, for 1924–25, it was quite clear that the State did not intend to interfere with the inherited structure of the private secondary school system. It saw no role for the State to establish such schools or to support their establishment. The report put the issue of the State's role vis-à-vis the school very clearly when it stated:

> The Secondary system is largely a private one in which schools ... retain their full autonomy in all matters of appointment and internal organisation. The State at present inspects these schools regularly and exercises a certain amount of supervision through its process to make grants to schools as a result of their inspectors, but it neither founds secondary schools nor finances the building of them, nor appoints teachers or managers, nor exercises any power of veto over the appointment or dismissal of such teachers or the management of the schools ... the Secondary system remains as hitherto one of purely private management.[1]

The State's main concern was the curriculum and the assessment processes. It took the decision which had been advocated by the Dale and Stephens Report in 1905 and the Molony Report of 1919 of abolishing the payment by results examination system. The first Dáil Éireann appointed a Commission on Secondary Education which held its first meeting on 24 September 1921, 'to draft a programme which would meet the national requirements, while allotting its due place to the Irish language'.[2] Its deliberations were forwarded on 7 December 1922 to the Minister of the Dáil as a series of subject committee reports. Some of its recommendations formed the basis of the new programme for secondary schools which became operative on 1 August 1924. In June 1924, the Intermediate Education Amendment Act had been passed which allowed changes in the programmes of instruction and in the public examination system.

The influence which the State could exert on secondary education in the new political context was through the programmes for public examinations

---

1 *Report of the Department of Education for the School Year, 1924–25*, p. 7.   2 Dáil Commission on Secondary Education, Subject Committee Reports (Unpublished, in Library Department of Education).

and through regulations concerning the granting of recognised status to schools. Regulations were laid down concerning the qualifications of teachers who would receive State incremental salaries, as well as the 'basic' salaries paid by the school managements. Grants to schools were no longer to be payable on examination results but were to be paid on a capitation basis for pupils who passed entrance examinations, who followed an approved course of study and who made 130 attendances per annum. The result was that while State control was limited and indirect it could, nevertheless, affect a great deal of what went on in the secondary schools. The secondary school inspectorate was to play a central role in the implementation of the State's mechanisms of influence.

From August 1924 the old three grades of results examinations were abolished and they were replaced by two certificate examinations – the Intermediate Certificate and the Leaving Certificate Examinations. Irish became an obligatory subject for the award of the Intermediate Certificate from 1928 and for the Leaving Certificate from 1934, a regulation which lasted up to 1973. From 1932 all recognised pupils had to study Irish. Furthermore, to encourage secondary schools to give a more prominent place to Irish than just provide it as a school subject, the Rules and Programme of 1924 recognised three types of secondary schools – Grade A, Grade B (which became sub-divided into B¹ and B²) and Grade C. Irish was to be the official language in the Grade A schools and all subjects other than English were to be taught through the medium of Irish. Irish was also to be the official language of the Grade B schools and was to be the medium of instruction for some subjects. In the Grade C schools, Irish was just taught as a school subject. There was an extra grant of 25% based on capitation paid for Grade A schools, and Grade B schools got an extra financial incentive based on the extent of teaching through the medium of Irish. An incentive to pupils to use Irish when answering examination papers came in the form of bonus marks. To help provide textbooks in Irish, An Gúm was set up in 1926 as a State-supported publishing house. Inspectors were in a position to earn extra emoluments by writing and translating textbooks for An Gúm.

Although the abolition of the results fees had removed a distasteful pressure on schools and pupils, the public examination system continued to exercise a huge influence on secondary education, and vestiges of the attitudes engendered by the results system continued to influence the system. The Department published each student's results by his/her examination number and named the schools at the top of the list of numbers. The unhealthy rivalry was further exacerbated by many schools publishing the success rates of their named pupils, as advertisements in the public press. The tendency for a predominantly literary, grammar-school type curriculum continued to prevail in the secondary schools.

One of the striking new features of the curricula for schools was the introduction of more 'Open' courses whereby the old tradition of prescribing set texts for study for the examinations was dropped. The closely prescribed courses were replaced by curricular guidelines from the Department of Education, and textbooks were not prescribed for any language subject. The aim was to give Irish secondary teachers more freedom to plan their courses, select their textbooks and devise their pedagogic strategies. The design of examination papers in relation to the more open approach to course content presented problems for those setting the examinations. Specimen papers were prepared during the school year 1924–25 and issued to schools in advance of the examinations. This change of policy towards more open courses was proposed by a sub-committee of the Commission on Secondary Education, which reported in 1922. One of the key shapers of this policy was the Revd Tim Corcoran, Professor of Education in UCD. He exercised a huge influence on curricular policy for primary and secondary education in the new state. It was not the inspectors who were the main influences on curricular policy. This was acknowledged by Seosamh Ó Néill, Secretary of the Department, in an obituary notice on the death of Corcoran in 1943. He stated:

> In the reconstruction of the Irish State he was from the beginning the master builder in Education. The Commissions on Education set up in 1921, were guided so largely by him that it may be said that the curricula, aims and methods in primary and secondary education which emerged from them were in the main, the work of his hands.[3]

Corcoran also took a hands-on role with the inspectorate in the early years in preparing sample questions and preparing a memorandum on approaches to the treatment of texts by teachers.[4]

The inspectors took the major responsibility for preparing the examination papers for the public examinations, for their administration, and for monitoring the assessments. As the system expanded, over time, this responsibility for the prestigious public examinations consumed a considerable amount of the time of the secondary inspectorate. From the start, co-ordination was established between personnel in the universities with the inspectorate for the drawing up and marking of the papers for the Leaving Certificate Examination, and for university scholarship schemes.

Under the new arrangements teachers were required to submit at the beginning of the year the programmes which were proposed for each class for the year and the inspectors reviewed these for their suitability in quality and extent. According to the annual report of the Department of Education for the school years 1925–26–27, published in 1928, 'The interchange of views

3 Joseph O'Neill, 'Prof. T. Corcoran – The Educationalist' in *Studies*, xxxii, 1943, 160, p. 158.
4 John Coolahan, 'The Secondary School Curricular Experiment 1924–1942: The Case of English', in Vincent Greaney and Brendan Molloy (eds), *Dimensions of Reading* (Dublin: Educational Company, 1986), pp 42–62.

with the Department's inspectors with regard to these matters of organisation (re programmes) gives evidence of an educational co-operation of a harmonious character'. The new entrance examinations were also taking root and the Department also reported satisfaction on their development:

> On the whole, the Entrance Examination has been well carried out by the schools and has served a useful purpose. There are naturally varying standards throughout the country, but these will gradually be aligned by the inspectors' assessments.[5]

The many-sided role of the inspectorate is also in evidence by the interesting development in the school year 1928–29 of establishing 'Standardising Committees' for the public examinations, which became operative for the examinations of 1929. A letter from the Minister was issued on 26 March 1929, inviting six representative associations of secondary school interests to nominate representatives for these committees to act in association with inspectors. While no expenses were to be paid for attendance at the meetings in the Department in Hume Street, during the first week of July 1929, it is striking that all agencies participated. They were to advise the Minister on the standard of the questions and the suitability of the papers, and to advise on the standard of marking of candidates' scripts. The Standardising Committees helped to bring the views of school personnel and of the inspectors closer on examination issues, and teachers appreciated the consultative role. The Department published a summary of recommendations and decisions arising from the Standardising Committees which provided useful guidelines to teachers.

The Department of Education issued a circular on 24 January 1928 which set out new proposals for the introduction of Higher and Lower courses for some subjects in the Intermediate and Leaving Certificate Examinations. The minimum time requirement for each Lower Course would be half that required for a Higher Course in that subject. The Department decided not to proceed with this strategy at the time and adopted an alternative approach of changing the methods of calculating examination results, involving a reduction in the standard of difficulty of papers. However, the Higher and Lower Course scheme was resurrected following Fianna Fáil's election success in 1932. From 1932–33 there would be a Full and Lower Course operating in English and Irish for Intermediate and Leaving Certificate Examinations. The Lower Courses in languages were geared towards the functional use of the languages. The following year, Full and Lower Courses were extended to include French, German and science. Teachers objected to the unilateral, non-consultative role being adopted by the Department of Education, and the issue was raised in the Dáil, on 14 February 1934. Later that year, teachers were consulted when changes in mathematics and Latin courses were being contemplated.[6] The public examinations had again assumed a central place in educational concerns and debate. The inspectorate was the main agency which oversaw the whole process.

Important as the initiation and conduct of a new curricular and examination schema was for the inspectors, it was by no means their sole function. Initially, the Chief Inspector for secondary schools was Seoirse Mac Niocaill who was very much a pro-active champion of the cause of the Irish language in the schools. There were six district inspectors, each with a wide geographic spread of schools to be visited. Because of the paucity of numbers they were expected to deal with a wide variety of subjects. For instance, Micheál Breathnach recounts that he supervised the teaching of Irish, history, geography, mathematics and commerce, until he was appointed as a special inspector for Irish, with a twenty-six county brief, in 1931. He was appointed Assistant Chief Inspector in 1934. The fact that the secondary schools were private institutions had a major influence on how inspectors were received, and how they operated within the school. The inspectors were the legitimate officials of the Department of Education who were entitled to investigate if regulations were being implemented. Nevertheless, the owners of schools liked to emphasise that they were 'guests' in the school, with limited functions to perform. They did not have the same sense of authority of established officers of the system as had become habitual for the national school inspectorate. Condition 7 for the recognition of schools set out a much more low key concept of the role of the inspector than was set out by Lord Lieutenant Aberdeen in 1909. It stated, 'The Manager shall permit the Department's inspectors to visit the school for the purpose of testing the efficiency of the instruction given, and of ascertaining if the Department's regulations are being observed.' The Regulations concerning Irish as compulsory for the award of the certificate examinations, and as a compulsory subject for pupil recognition, as well as the scheme of A, B and C grade schools were significant challenges to some schools and, at times, called for diplomacy and understanding from the inspectors, as the regulations became bedded down.

In the early years of the new state the secondary inspectors were much more in evidence in schools than became the pattern later, when they became very much absorbed with the public examinations and various forms of administrative work. T.J. McElligott in his memoir, *This Teaching Life*, recalls the contrast in his early years of teaching to the later years when the inspector in a secondary school became 'a quasi-extinct occupational species'. In the mid-thirties he stated:

6 John Coolahan, *The ASTI and Post-Primary Education, 1909–84* (ASTI, 1984), pp 123, 124.

Inspectors were very much in evidence in those years; they were the eyes and ears of a Department as yet unsure of itself. They prowled and probed, recommended texts, not infrequently those they had written ... for all the power inspectors had over teachers and the curriculum, they seemed powerless to effect any improvement in the physical conditions within the school.[7]

From the evidence available, it would appear that recognition of a secondary school was rarely withdrawn by the Department on the basis of reported inadequate infrastructure or equipment.

The Department of Education secured, in 1925, against pressure from the Department of Finance, that the inspection of science, and practical subjects continued, for many years, to be the responsibility of inspectors from the Technical Instruction Branch. With the expansion of vocational education in the late thirties the TIB sought the full services of its own staff. Following the appointment of two secondary inspectors for science in 1939, this role was taken over by the secondary branch of the Department. A significant dimension of the Department's annual reports was the section on 'The Work in the Schools'. These accounts of the work done in the schools in the various subjects was 'based largely on the reports of the General Inspectors in charge of those subjects.' The accounts set out the strengths and weaknesses encountered in the observation of the work in the schools. For the first few years, the accounts were informative and did not flinch from making targeted comments on deficiencies and difficulties observed.

However, the quality of the reports declined. Indeed, in the years 1930–31, and 1931–32 no comments were made except for the teaching of Irish. As regards other subject areas the reports stated 'there was nothing to add' to previous reports. From 1932–33 the limited reportage was presented through the medium of Irish. When it occurred, the comment was often based on the results of the public examinations rather than on observed teaching in the schools. As well as the desultory and superficial reportage on the work of the secondary schools, the inspectors gave no indication of recommended action and follow-through concern. This contrasted with the reportage of the inspectors in the technical instruction branch, and represented a missed opportunity by the secondary inspectorate at doing useful evaluation of the quality of teaching and providing recommendations and guidance for good practice. Unlike the vocational sector, no up-skilling courses were conducted for secondary teachers, and the inspectors seem to have had no contact with teacher education departments of the universities.

However, in the post-war years an improvement took place in the reportage by the inspectors on the teaching of the various subjects, as pub-

7 T.J. McEligott, *This Teaching Life* (Dublin: Lilliput Press, 1986), p. 30.

lished in the annual Departmental reports. Throughout the 1950s the reportage was quite extensive on what was happening in the schools. Yet, it gives the impression of being cast in a general commendatory style with only rare reference to weaknesses and no discrimination between schools in different circumstances and locations. The reportage focused on individual subjects and tended to be patterned. No reference was made or inferences drawn from the statistical data which accompanied the reports. There was no comment on drop-out rates through the secondary school system, or to timetable balance, or to the number of teachers teaching subjects in which they had no competence, or on the conditions and equipment found in schools. When the Investment in Education team in the early years of the next decade asked more fundamental questions a very different image of the quality of, and engagement with secondary education emerged. This may possibly be the reason why from 1964 the Department published no general report or commentary on the progress of the schooling system. In the report for 1963–64, it was announced that 'In future statistical tables will be issued annually as a separate publication. A report on progress and developments in the field of education generally, will be published at intervals of three years.'[8] This latter promise was not honoured and, from then only statistical tables were published, with no general commentary or evaluation at all. In fact, statistical tables were not always published annually, and the report for 1971–72, covered the four previous years, back to 1968. The lack of a public report by the inspectors on the system from 1963 was a weakness; potentially professional comment by the inspectorate could have been very valuable, at a period of great change in education.

While the Registration Council for Secondary Teachers came into operation in 1918 and the transition arrangements for existing teachers expired in 1925, the Department of Education in its reports expressed concern at the continuing pattern of employment of unregistered teachers in secondary schools. For instance, in 1929–30, the percentage of unregistered teachers was 42.2%, in 1931–32 it was 45.3% and in 1933–34, the proportion of unregistered teachers in secondary schools was 47.2%.[9] Thus, almost half of the teaching force was unregistered in the mid-thirties. Apart from expressing a concern about the trend, the Department of Education took no action on the matter, and the problems involved seem not to have merited comment by the inspectors, who had a responsibility for promoting teaching efficiency in the schools. Registered teachers were required to have a degree, a Higher Diploma in Education and three years satisfactory probationary experience. Many of the unregistered teachers were members of religious congregations who owned the schools and who could be employed, but could not benefit from state incremental salaries due to their unrecognised status.

8 *Report of the Department of Education for 1963–64*, Prefatory Note.   9 John Coolahan, *ASTI and Post-Primary Education*, pp 107–10.

Mr Tomás Derrig, who became Minister for Education under the Fianna Fáil government of 1932, was an ardent supporter of the revival of the Irish language through the schools. On 5 January 1935 he convened a meeting of the secondary school inspectors. He posed three issues to them – could the progress of gaelicisation be accelerated in the secondary schools, could the present programme be revised so as to give greater encouragement to the study of Irish; and could an extra examination be introduced at the end of second year.[10] Despite the Minister's desire for change, no agreement was recorded and no change occurred in the programme at that time from this Ministerial intervention.

While Mr Derrig was the Minister for Education, it was known that Mr de Valera, the President of the Executive Council, took a keen interest in the education brief. He had been a founding member of the ASTI in 1909 and retained a keen interest in educational matters, particularly in mathematics. Mr de Valera had sought changes in the secondary programme in contact with Minister Derrig in 1935, but in July 1937, he took the initiative of convening a special conference of the Minister for Education, the Secretary of the Department, the Chief Inspectors and the District Inspectors of Secondary Schools. The move to change policy on the secondary school programme, introduced in 1924, provides an interesting insight into the interplay of professional and political influences on the shaping of policy at that time. Mr de Valera summoned the Conference

> as a result of his own experience and the experience of a considerable number of people interested in Secondary Education, he felt that it was time to examine thoroughly once more the programmes and examination courses and papers for secondary pupils.[11]

Mr de Valera maintained that there was a very general opinion amongst educationalists that the programmes were too extensive and too vague and the examination papers made thereby too difficult for the average secondary pupil. He also held that the programmes should not be overloaded, since the progress in Irish and in the work of Gaelicisation generally would be much more difficult. In language subjects definite books should be prescribed and the mathematics course should be made as definite as possible. In Mr de Valera's view, the aim throughout should be a training in accuracy and thoroughness rather than attempting a wide range with the corresponding risk of vagueness and indefiniteness, 'a little, but that well', should be the motto.[12] This approach involved a fundamental change of approach from that which had been adopted in 1924. Mr de Valera, building on his basic concepts, proposed a new curricular framework for the secondary schools and invited the

10 NA Box 2006, 120/1 Inspectors Conference with Minister, 5/1/'35.   11 Official Notes of the Conferences 23, 28 July 1937 Department of Education Archives.   12 Ibid.

secondary school inspectorate to review the existing programmes with a view to agreeing an alternative.

In the course of discussions it became clear that the inspectorate did not concur with all that was being proposed, nor even on the question 'as to whether the present programmes were in fact too extensive and too vague.' In the light of this, it was decided to postpone a decision on the points under review until the inspectors had given them 'full consideration at their September conference' in 1937. However, the inspectors took the opportunity at the July Conference of stressing the insufficiency of inspectorial staff to 'ensure expert supervision and guidance of the specialist teaching of the higher ranges of all the main subjects.' It was noteworthy that the District Inspectors of secondary schools used the opening provided by the discussion at this conference to prepare a memorandum on the unsatisfactory position of the inspectorate, as they saw it. Having drawn attention to the diverse and demanding duties they were expected to perform they concluded:

> It is quite clear that the inspectors cannot possibly have an adequate amount of time at their disposal to give expert advice and guidance on purely educational matters during their inspections. The tendency towards de-specialisation has been further accentuated in recent years as individual inspectors have had (in the interests of economy) to inspect all, or nearly all, the subjects in some of the schools. It happened last year that one inspector had to deal single-handed with all the subjects in a very considerable number of schools.[13]

They stated 'that the whole system of inspection would require to be revised.' They also called for the recruitment of three new district inspectors and three new inspectors at headquarters.[14] It is not clear if this memorandum went officially to Mr de Valera's office, but his Secretary, Mr Maurice Moynihan, recorded receiving it from 'a private source.'[15] In any case, no revision of the system of secondary inspection took place, nor was there increased recruitment arising from the memorandum.

At the inspectors' conference in September 'there was no unanimity among inspectors on the best way forward, but the principle of prescribing content and textbooks was accepted by a majority for a number of subjects.'[16] In a detailed memorandum, the Chief Inspector, Seoirse Mac Niocaill, stated, 'I think a set of unanimous recommendations is out of the question.'[17] The majority was prepared to accept prescribed texts for classics and modern lan-

13 NA File S10107 A, 'Memorandum from the District Inspectors'.   14 Ibid.   15 Ibid., Moynihan's note dated 15 Oct. 1937.   16 Interview with T. O'Raifeartaigh, inspector present at meeting – in John Coolahan, 'The Post-Primary Curricular Experiment 1924–42', p. 58, and NA Box 120/16 Inspectors' Response to Review of Secondary School Programme.   17 NA File S10107 A, 'Chief Inspector's Memorandum'.

guages and for the poetry section of the English and Irish courses. Adjustments to the secondary school programme were being prepared within the Department during the spring of 1938. Mr de Valera took a keen interest in all developments. A circular was prepared for issuing to the various school associations signalling changes ahead and inviting responses. Mr de Valera had the circular submitted to him for his personal approval, and he also sought a copy of the responses submitted by the associations.[18]

On 3 December 1938, Seosamh Ó Néill, Secretary of the Department of Education, sent a copy of the planned programme changes to Mr de Valera stating he would 'be glad to learn whether the Taoiseach had any objection to this proposal.'[19] The Taoiseach met with the Minister for Education to discuss the programme on 4 January 1939. Among changes Mr de Valera sought were prescribed prose, as well as poetry, for Irish and English, an elementary course in mathematics for girls at Intermediate Certificate level, three instead of four books of Euclid at Intermediate Certificate, and a reduction in the general science course. Mr de Valera also met some delegations from school associations on the planned programme. For instance, he met a Christian Brothers delegation on 17 January 1939. A report of this meeting stated, 'The Department's proposals were disclosed by the Taoiseach to the deputation on strict confidence.'[20]

The Taoiseach convened a meeting in his office, on 18 January 1939, of the Minister for Education, the Assistant Secretary in the Department, and the secondary inspectors in charge of the different subjects. These were S. Mac Niocaill, Chief Inspector (Irish and Mathematics); M. Breathnach, Assistant Chief Inspector (Irish); J. Bithrey (Classics and English); L.Close (Mathematics and Geography); T. Ó Raifeartaigh (History); G. Ó Dubháin (French and German). A detailed four-hour discussion took place. Among points in the report of the meeting were that changes needed to be made on the prescribed texts for English, the Irish course was to be tightened and rewritten, the history course for Leaving Certificate to be revised 'according to An Taoiseach's suggestion', Calculus was to be dropped from the Leaving Certificate Honours mathematics course in line with An Taoiseach's wishes. Work went ahead on the new programme and, up to June 1939, Mr de Valera is recorded as making detailed amendments to it.[21]

During his period as Minister for Education in 1939–40, Mr de Valera informed the Dáil, in his speech on the education estimates in 1940, 'I have therefore arranged that the vague and extended programmes in language and literature hitherto in operation in secondary schools should be replaced by precise courses with prescribed texts, and that the courses in other subjects should as far as possible be made equally precise.'[22]

18 Ibid.   19 Ibid.   20 NA File S10107, 'Report of Deputation of the Christian Brothers to An Taoiseach'.   21 NA File S10107 B, 'Letter from M.Ó Muimhneacháin to S. Ó Néill,' 1 June 1939.   22 NA Box 2006/120/16.

Arising from Mr de Valera's initiative an important change occurred which had an impact on secondary schooling for decades. Between 1939 and 1941 the new programme for secondary schools was finalised. A key element was that set courses were laid down for all subjects. Prescribed texts were laid down for all language subjects. 'Honours' and 'Pass' categories were introduced for subjects at Leaving Certificate level, and for mathematics at Intermediate Certificate. De Valera also took the initiative of establishing closer links between the university and the secondary school Leaving Certificate. Following a series of conferences between inspectors and university staff there was a co-ordination of subjects for the Leaving and Matriculation Examinations. Uniform courses and texts were agreed upon for the examinations of 1942, and a pass in the Leaving Certificate from 1942 was regarded as equivalent to a pass in the corresponding subject of the Matriculation Examination, conducted by the National University.[23] A significant change was also promoted by Mr de Valera for the examinations of 1942 by inviting university staff to set the Leaving Certificate Examination papers and control standards. The ASTI opposed this move and while their arguments impressed the Minister for Education and his senior officials, Mr de Valera remained convinced of the rectitude of the decision, and the university personnel were retained in this role until 1949.[24] In response to continued criticism of this situation by the ASTI the Minister responded that the university personnel were seen in the role of external examiners.[25] It is noteworthy that it was external political intervention that led to the changes in secondary school programmes in 1939–42, and not the initiative of the professional staff of the Department. There is evidence that at least some of the inspectors were not in favour of the changes. There is also some evidence that the greater influence given to university personnel on the Leaving Certificate Examinations from 1942 caused problems to inspectors in monitoring the type of questions put forward by university staff.[26] Overall, it could be concluded that the inspectors were being over-ridden, to a degree, by a strong politician with a clear sense of purpose. Following the programme and examination changes introduced in the early forties little significant change occurred for many years. Unlike England, Northern Ireland and some other European countries in the post-war era, Ireland, though it had been a neutral in the conflict, introduced no reform plan for education. There had been a significant growth in the number of secondary schools and pupils from 278 schools with 22,897 pupils in 1924–25 to 409 schools with 45,413 pupils by 1948–49, but no parallel expansion took place in the secondary school inspectorate.

A memorandum in the Department of Education on secondary schools in 1950 gives an informative overview of the structure and work of the secondary inspectorate at that time. It stated:

23 *Report of the Department of Education for 1940–41*, p 23. **24** Coolahan, *The ASTI and Post-Primary Education*, p. 109. **25** Ibid., p. 169. **26** Ibid.

The inspection of secondary schools is carried out by a staff of eleven inspectors, under the direction of two Assistant Chiefs and a Chief Inspector. There are three inspection divisions, with normally three inspectors in each division. The remaining two inspectors are especially responsible for French and Music in the schools in general. To each inspector is assigned the inspection of a certain group of subjects in all schools in the division. They are grouped as follows: (i) Irish and history (ii) classics and English (iii) mathematics, science and geography, and to each is also allotted special responsibility for school organisation, i.e. entrance examinations, timetable, curriculum, staffing etc., in about one-third of the schools in the division. It is a function of each inspector to advise a teacher regarding methods of teaching and the textbooks used and to direct him [*sic*] generally. Particular attention is paid in the course of inspection to new schools and to new and inexperienced teachers. Copies of the inspectors' reports on the subjects and classes inspected are issued to school managers. In addition to the work of inspection, the inspectors set the Examination Papers, act as advising examiners at the Certificate Examinations, as the Department's representatives on co-ordinating courses and examinations for the Leaving Certificate and Matriculation of the National University, and advise the Minister regarding the programme, and courses as prescribed, and other problems relating to secondary schools.[27]

Quite clearly, the fourteen secondary school inspectors had a full remit. Each of the nine inspectors working in the three divisions had over forty schools to deal with, on a widely scattered geographical base. They needed considerable versatility regarding subject competence. Their advice to teachers, particularly inexperienced teachers would seem perforce to be attenuated, bearing in mind all the other duties, particularly in relation to the public examinations. There is no specific mention of their role in the case of any chronically inefficient teachers, nor were they required to report on the conditions of work, equipment and classroom facilities which they might encounter.

The fact that the Council of Education, established in 1950, was deliberating on curricular issues from 1950 to 1960 was used as an excuse by government to inhibit interested parties from a more active grappling with educational reform during that time. In the context of the national economic difficulties in the 1950s, there was no willingness from the Department of Finance to engage with any costly investment in education.[28] Where possible, it sought cutbacks instead. While no significant changes occurred in the character of secondary education in the 1950s there was a very significant increase

27 'Memorandum on Secondary Schools' 1/12/1950, in NA Dept. of Taoiseach 12981B.   28 Coolahan, *The ASTI and Post-Primary Education*, pp 216–22.

in the number of pupils attending the schools. In 1951–52 there were 50,179 pupils enrolled, but by 1961–62, ten years later, the number had increased by 60% to reach 80,400 with the number of secondary schools increasing by 25%, from 434 to 542.[29] Public interest in secondary schooling was developing apace, and it was clear to commentators of the time that policy changes were badly needed. The sixties were to bring radical changes, including new approaches to the work of the inspectorate.

29 Ibid., pp 184, 185.

10

Vocational/Technical Instruction Inspectorate, 1922–60

When the Department of Education took over responsibility for education in the new state there were 49 Statutory Committees with responsibilities for technical education. The vocational schemes continued to be funded from central and local funds. Each committee revised its scheme annually, with the help of an inspector if necessary, and schemes were then submitted for approval by the Department. Each scheme was intended to provide a series of courses of instruction linked to local industrial conditions. Students who reached a standard of education equivalent to the old Junior Grade, or the new Intermediate Certificate could attend specialised courses of instruction involving progressive studies for a period of four or more years. In May, each year, examinations in the subjects of these courses were conducted by external examiners in co-operation with the Department's inspectors for students who voluntarily entered for the examinations. Courses in the County Borough and Urban Schemes could be quite comprehensive in range and were usually located in permanent technical schools. The rural and county schemes were provided with a more limited range of courses, of short duration, and delivered by itinerant teachers.[1] The number of students enrolled in classes in technical schools in the early years was as follows:

1924–25	*1925–26*	*1926–27*
21,637	22,336	22,718

Source: *Report of the Department of Education, 1925–26–27*, p. 69.

The number of students enrolled in classes under County Schemes elsewhere than in established Technical Schools were:

1924–25	*1925–26*	*1926–27*
33,625	41,417	35,437

Source: *Report of the Department of Education, 1925–26–27*, p. 70.

1 *Report of the Department of Education for 1924–25*, pp 51, 58.

During the academic year 1924–25 there were 65 technical schools in operation, 22 conducted by county borough and urban committees, and 43 forming portion of the schemes conducted by county committees. The main work of the schools was carried out in evening classes over two or three evenings a week, attendance at which was voluntary. There was no definite link between the workplace and the technical school, and there had been a lack of appreciation by industry of the value of systematic technical training, which differed from the practice in other countries.[2]

On assuming authority for technical education the Department organised a survey of the activities of the Technical Branch and 'as a result of special reports prepared by the Chief Inspector and the Senior Inspector it became clear that a thorough investigation of the facilities for industrial and commercial training in the Saorstat was necessary'.[3] A Commission on Technical Education was established, 'to enquire into and advise upon the system of Technical Education in Saorstat Éireann in relation to the requirements of Trade and Industry'.[4] The Commission included representatives of employers, teachers and of the Departments of Education, Industry and Commerce, Agriculture, and Finance. Two experts from Switzerland and Sweden added an international dimension to the Commission. It began its work on 5 October 1926, under the chairmanship of John Ingram, who was Senior Inspector of Technical Instruction. Ingram had been an inspector with the Department of Agriculture and Technical Instruction since 1912. He was Senior Inspector with the Technical Branch of the Department of Education from 1923 to 1927. In 1927 he became Chief Inspector of the Technical Branch and combined this role with that of Principal Officer of the Branch, with responsibility for administration and finance until he left the Technical Instruction Branch in 1944. Over the years, he fulfilled many key technical education and other roles for the state and was held in very high esteem. He was regarded as one of the most influential figures in the development of vocational and technical education in the new state. The fact that an experienced inspector was appointed as chairman of the 1926–27 Commission helped to give a well informed view of the strengths, weaknesses and needs of technical education to the members.

In a letter to the first meeting of the Commission the Minister for Education, John Marcus O'Sullivan, elaborated on the terms of reference, and the letter's contents clearly indicated that the government sought a comprehensive report based on the 'fundamental principle that Technical Instruction can have and should have as profound an educational and civic value as any other form of education'.[5] The Commission took a thorough approach, held

2 *Report of the Commission on Technical Education* (Dublin: Stationery Office, 1927), p. 17.   3 *Report of the Department of Education for 1925–26–27*, p. 69.   4 *Report of the Commission on Technical Education*, 1927, p. vi.   5 Ibid., p. ix.

75 meetings and took evidence from 129 witnesses including 8 inspectors of the Technical Instruction Branch. It visited many institutions, including the Shannon Power Development Schemes and the Irish Sugar Beet Factory, Carlow, then flagships of the new government's approach to the establishment of semi-state bodies for the development of industry in the new state. The Commission reported on 5 October 1927, and the report was published in February 1928.

In its analysis of the existing take-up of technical education the Commission reported, 'We are, however, left with the disquieting result that the large majority of the schools in the Saorstat are concerned with commerce and domestic economy and rarely with technology, art and craftwork.'[6] It concluded that 'the work of the school in more important districts bears too little relation to the local requirements of trade and industry and that a general change of outlook is required.' The Commission also regretted the trend whereby very few students on a 'course' system persevered to the third or fourth year of the course. The committee found that much of the work of the technical schools was being distorted from technical education *per se* because they were obliged to provide 'introductory courses' for students, with very low standards of achievement coming from national schools. As regards the instruction given in rural areas it was seen as mainly relating to the life of the farm. As regards the ten Trade Preparatory Schools, there was no definite link between them and apprenticeship. It was reported that while much of the instruction in these schools was of a high standard, they did not attract large numbers of pupils, and most pupils did not complete the third year of the course. These and other findings led the Commission to recommend a set of proposals which sought radical changes on the provision of technical/vocational education. The Commission stated that as a result of their investigations they had 'come to the conclusion that radical changes are necessary to meet the existing and probable requirements of trade and industry'.[7] The Commission made 92 recommendations affecting a very comprehensive range of issues. Those included curricula of primary and secondary schools, the establishment of a scheme of continuation schools for 14–16 year olds, apprenticeship arrangements, technical education in relation to specific trades, higher technical education, restructuring of local statutory committees for continuation and technical education, teacher training, financing arrangements.[8]

The main recommendations of the Commission on Technical Education formed the basis of the Vocational Education Act, which became law in July 1930. This was a landmark piece of legislation. The term 'vocational' embraced two distinct elements incorporated in the Act – continuation education and technical education. Under the Act, the 49 local technical instruction committees were restructured as 38 vocational education committees

6 Ibid., p. 18.   7 Ibid., p. 150.   8 Ibid., pp 145–52.

(VECs), smaller in composition and intended to be more effective in operation. Each VEC had a chief executive officer who proposed schemes and administered policy. Under the new legislation, the VECs had the duty to set up schools in each local authority area, with the support of a compulsory rate. The new regulations led to a striking amount of building activity resulting by 1936 in 46 new schools, extensions to 21 others and the initiation of building plans for 48 other schools.[9] Under the Act, continuation education was designed 'to continue and supplement education provided in elementary schools and to include general and practical training in preparation for employment in trades etc. and general and practical training for improvement of young persons in the early stages of employment'.[10] It was intended for young people aged 14 to 16, and as a preliminary to technical education proper from age 16 onwards. Technical education was seen as pertaining to trades, manufacturers, commerce, and other industrial pursuits. The schools were to be under secular control and were non-denominational, although VECs were encouraged to make provision for religious education. This was a matter of concern to the Catholic hierarchy, who sent a delegation to relay their concerns to the Minister of Education in October 1930. In response to these concerns the Minister emphasised in a detailed written reply to the bishops that continuation education did not involve 'general education' and was to be severely practical and vocational in emphasis. It would not be allowed to infringe on the type of education provided in national and secondary schools. He also assured them that he had been most careful not to introduce a new principle of control in education. The Department would require proposed courses to include specific provision for religious instruction for those who sought it. He also tried to allay Episcopal apprehensions about co-education and night schools, under the Act.[11] Thus, the Minister went to great pains to alleviate concerns of the Catholic hierarchy regarding the new system, but the unease of the Church re-surfaced later. Yet, O'Sullivan's conciliatory movement meant that the hierarchy did not formally oppose the Act, which, if it had happened, would have greatly impeded early efforts to get the new system off the ground.

There was a sense of excitement in the Technical Instruction Branch, located in Talbot House, Talbot Street, in getting the new system under way. The inspectors prepared an explanatory memorandum in 1931 setting out the framework within which each VEC should devise its curriculum. The curriculum should be of a general vocational character, with a bias towards the

---

9 John Coolahan, *Irish Education: Its History and Structure* (Dublin: IPA, 1981), p. 97.　　10 *Vocational Education Act, 1930* No. 29, in Public Statutes of the Oireachtas.　　11 Letter from J.M. O'Sullivan, Minister for Education, to Most Rev. D. Keane, bishop of Limerick, 31 October 1930; reproduced in Appendix 3, of Seamus Ó Buachala, *Education Policy*, pp 399, 403.

local economy. It emphasised that 'the methods of instruction employed should differ radically from those of the primary and secondary school. A definite break both as to subject matter and its treatment is needed all through the vocational course'.[12] The continuation courses were to be planned on a two-year basis and were organised in groups. The main subjects for boys were Irish, English, mathematics, general science, rural science, art, mechanical drawing, woodwork, and metalwork. The subjects for girls generally included Irish, English, arithmetic, commercial subjects, and domestic economy. The courses were to be whole-time and involve between 25 and 28 class hours per week. The inspectors made a virtue of the fact that they did not prescribe course details but allowed discretion and flexibility for local needs. The inspectors also prepared new regulations, official forms etc and issued these in good time.

While Section 114 of the Vocational Education Act gave the statutory authority for the inspectorate to inspect any school or course assisted by a vocational education committee, the memorandum of 1931 was more specific regarding the inspector's role. It stated:

> The schools must be open to the Department's Inspectors who will visit them periodically with or without notice. They will ascertain and report upon the efficiency of the instruction and the organisation of the work of the scheme.

The new VECs held their first meetings in the early autumn and prepared their schools for the financial year 1931–32 by 1 December 1930, the date prescribed in the Act. However, some CEOs were not always well prepared with their classes and programmes so that they only became available 'well after the opening of the 1931 school year.' Subsequently they were required to have them approved by early July each year, for publication in August with a view to efficient implementation at the start of the school year in question. The Department for Education report for 1930–31 (published 1932) commended the work of the VECs, stating that they

> have faced their new responsibilities with earnestness and intelligence, and undoubtedly have at heart the welfare of the schemes they manage.[13]

Inspectors also visited various locations and held conferences with VECs on implementation issues.[14] The Annual Departmental Report gave extracts from inspectors' reports on different subjects, from time to time.

12 Department of Education, *Vocational Continuation Classes: Memorandum for the Information of Committees*, 1931.   13 *Report of the Department of Education for 1930–31*, p. 47.   14 *Report of the Department of Education for 1931–32*, p. 52

One of the problems encountered by inspectors for many years was the quality of instruction in the general subjects such as English and geography in the continuation schools. They found the techniques poor, on lines used in primary schools, and giving rise to bored pupils. The Report for 1932–33 stated, 'Very decided efforts on the part of teachers are required to create a different atmosphere for the instruction and to get their students to respond with interest'.[15] The inspectors took a pro-active stance in seeking to improve the situation they found. Many conferences were held by the inspectors with principals and teachers at which the policy to be adopted was explained, and advice given. A summer course was organised in 1933 'at which teaching methods and treatment were discussed and suggestions given as to syllabuses and lessons'.[16] The inspectors also prepared notes for teachers on the teaching of English, mathematics, geography and farm accounts. These interventions were recorded as bringing about improvements in the day-to-day teaching in the schools. Competence in Irish was sometimes a problem in the recruitment of TIB inspectors. In some instances, personnel were appointed on the promise that they would achieve a competence in Irish during the probationary period.

The hands-on approach of the Technical Instruction Branch inspectors was maintained over the years. The tradition of summer courses for teachers on a variety of subjects was maintained. In April 1937, in response to a request from the Irish Technical Education Association a number of committees were established to review teacher training in six subject areas and each committee was chaired by the Chief Inspector.[17] The outcomes of the committee work fed into the courses being provided. During the three school years 1939–40, 1940–41 and 1941–42 a scheme of 'Special Inspections' was undertaken whereby 'the work of every whole-time teacher and many part-time teachers has been carefully examined and the results secured and methods used were discussed with each teacher, immediately the test was over. The results as far as the teaching of individual subjects is concerned are very encouraging.'[18] The inspectors reported 'in nearly every case the advice given was accepted and more efficient work was being done'.[19]

In 1934 an inter-departmental committee was set up to examine whether the school-leaving age should be raised. The committee was chaired by John Ingram, Chief Inspector of the TIB. In its report published in 1936 it did not favour raising the age as a general measure, but recommended that some pilot schemes be initiated in urban areas. Its key recommendation was as follows:

> The provisions of Part V of the Vocational Education Act might be put into operation in two or three carefully selected areas, all

---

15 *Report of the Department of Education for 1932–33*, p. 74   **16** Ibid.   **17** *Report of the Department of Education for 1936–37*, p. 57.   **18** *Report of the Department of Education for 1941–42*, p. 31.   **19** *Report of the Department of Education for 1940–41*, p. 32.

employed juveniles in those areas being required to attend classes for not more than 180 hours per year, and all unemployed juveniles in the areas being required to attend whole-time schools.[20]

In 1937 a pilot scheme was initiated by the Cork Vocational Education Committee and inspectors held conferences with the CEO and teachers on the issues involved. In subsequent years, this pilot scheme was extended to Limerick and Waterford VECs, but it was not extended countrywide. A committee of Inquiry on Industrial and Reformatory Schools was also set up in 1934. Chief Inspector Ingram prepared a report on relevant issues for the committee which the committee adopted in full and incorporated without change in its report for the Minister for Education. Regrettably, few of the recommendations for reform contained in this report were implemented. In 1936 Ingram and another senior TIB Inspector, Mr Morgan Sheehy, devised a new scheme of Technical School Examinations leading to the award of Trade and Technological Certificates. This scheme was accepted and put into operation immediately. Entrants for these examinations increased from 9,158 in 1936 to 13,183 by 1943. Some candidates continued to sit for examinations such as those run by the City and Guilds.

Early in 1938, Chief Inspector Ingram sought a restructuring of the T.I.B. inspectorate. At that time there were two Senior Inspectors, Messrs. Hackett and Burke. There were four Class I Inspectors – Messrs Barrett, Sheridan, MacCionnaith and Ó Sithigh. There were 5 class II Inspectors – MacColum, O'Keeffe, O'Flanagan, McCann and Kirwan.

There were four other inspectors for subjects such as art and domestic economy. Thus, the full complement of staff was sixteen. The salaries of the TIB were lower than those in the other sectors. Ingram sought improvements on the salaries and a restructuring of the TIB into divisional and district inspectors. He also withdrew TIB inspectors from inspection work on science and practical subjects in secondary schools, due to the expanding work in the vocational sector.[21]

The new Constitution adopted by the Irish Free State in 1937 highlighted the state's philosophy on the relative roles of the state, the churches and parents in education, and emphasised the role of religion in society. The Constitution reflected a Catholic Church ethos. In the years following its adoption, unease at the low profile of religion within the vocational system was expressed in several articles by clergy, such as the Revd Professor Martin Brenan of St Patrick's College Maynooth.[22] The Irish Technical Education Association (ITEA) was stung by such criticism and urged the Department to issue a memorandum which would up-date the rationale of continuation

20 *Report of the Inter-Departmental Committee on the Raising of the School Leaving Age* (Dublin: Stationery Office, 1936 [p. no. 2086]), p. 32.   21 *NA Box 2006/120/16.*   22 Revd Martin Brenan, 'The Vocational Schools', *Irish Ecclesiastical Studies,* lvii (1941), pp 13–27.

education and give more precise guidelines than the 1931 memorandum. The Department prepared such a memorandum, largely authored by Mr Joseph P. Hackett, a senior inspector with the T.I.B. The memorandum, known as V40, was published in 1942. This twenty-six page document changed the emphasis of the original conception of continuation schooling as set out in the 1930 Vocational Education Act. In particular, it gave a much stronger cultural nationalist role to the system and it sought to ensure a central place for religious instruction.

Memorandum V40 stated:

> Continuation education must be in keeping with Irish tradition and should reflect in the schools the loyalty to our Divine Lord which is expressed in the Prologue and Articles of the Constitution. In all schools it is essential that religious instruction be continued and that interest in the Irish language and other distinctive features of the national life be carefully fostered.

It went on to state:

> It is necessary not only that religious instruction be given at certain times, but also that the teaching of every other subject be permeated with Christian Charity, and that the whole organisation of the school, whether in work or recreation be regulated by the same spirit.[23]

The document re-emphasised the practical bias intended in the courses being taught with the immediate object of enabling boys and girls to make themselves useful as soon as possible in the economic and household spheres. The document concluded by emphasising the role of women in the home, as set out in the Constitution and advised that the domestic economy programme should be focussed on the home needs and family role of girls. Memorandum V40 became a key framework of reference document for vocational education for many years.

Reports on the efficiency of schools in the annual reports of the Department now contained specific comment on religious instruction as, for instance, in the report for 1942–43, 'Religious Instruction on a well organised basis now forms part of whole-time continuation courses'.[24] Reports also commended practices such as school retreats and the celebration of masses at the opening of the school year. In 1941 a new training course for teachers of Irish was introduced, An Teastas Timire Gaeilge. This aimed at producing a high

---

23 Department of Education, *Organisation of Whole-time Continuation Education, Memorandum V40*, 1942.   24 *Report of the Department of Education for 1942–43*, p. 30.

degree of fluency in the language as well as cultivating enthusiasm for the culture and folklore associated with the language. During the 1940's the graduates of these courses – Timirí – attracted large numbers to evening Irish classes where they participated in Irish language, drama, dance and 'oicheanta Gaeilge'. However, after a few years the interest petered out, and while the Irish language continued to be taught in the schools it did not have this broader cultural impact.[25]

The conditions which arose from the outbreak of the Second World War 'had a marked influence on the progress of vocational education'.[26] The Chief Inspector of the TIB held conferences with groups of CEOs seeking economies in administration. As the war went on more difficulties were encountered on many issues including transport, books, paper, heating, and lighting. Pupil attendance also suffered in that teenagers were often kept at home for cutting and saving turf and for manual assistance with farm work. Despite adverse circumstances the vocational education system continued to operate and inspectors continued to commend the teaching in both day and evening classes, albeit the work in the general subjects was still regarded as weak.[27]

During the war years, on 20 October 1944, a unique and tragic incident occurred in the shooting dead of Joseph Kirwan, Divisional Inspector of the TIB, for the Munster region. While Kirwan was on an inspectorial visit on that day to Hospital Vocational School in East Limerick a man entered the principal's office, where Kirwan was having a cup of tea, and shot him dead. The assailant had been employed as a temporary engineering instructor in the school from 1934 to 1942. But, following a special inspection at the school in May 1942, the Department withdrew recognition from him as a teacher. Despite his efforts he was not reinstated, and he blamed Kirwan for his situation. In subsequent proceedings at the Central Criminal Court medical personnel gave evidence that he suffered from a mental disorder which took the form of delusions of persecution and he was confined in a mental home.[28] This tragic event gave rise to much public concern and debate at the time, and entered the folklore of teacher-inspector relationships. Among other bodies, the Irish Vocational Education Association (IVEA) paid generous tribute to Joseph Kirwan's contributions to vocational education, and passed a formal vote of sympathy to his family. Happily, it was an isolated incident, and while tensions could exist in inspector-teacher relationships, nothing like this ever happened again.

At the Technical Instruction Congress of 1943, the Irish Technical Education Association (ITEA) urged that the Department of Education

25 Muiris Ó Riordáin, 'Vocational Education; The Cultural Emphasis', *Proceedings of the Educational Studies Association of Ireland 1977*, pp 194–200. 26 *Report of the Department of Education for 1940–41*, p. 25. 27 *Report of the Department of Education for 1942–43*, p. 35. 28 *Irish Independent*, 16 January 1945.

should establish a Committee to devise a system of examination for day vocational schools. The Minister agreed to this and nominated three inspectors to sit on this committee. To assist the Committee with its work, the inspectors conducted a pilot study in twenty-six vocational schools. Eventually, a scheme was devised, which became known as the Day Group Certificate and it became operative from the school year 1947. It was considered that the availability to pupils of a certificate of achievement based on such an examination would enhance employment prospects. The examinations were organised in five groups. However, success rates proved disappointing, particularly in the early years, as the following table indicates.

Table 10.1: Success rates in the group certificate examination, 1947, 1948

	% Pass 1947	% Pass 1948
(i) General Certificate in Commerce	37.5	60
(ii) Secretariat Certificate	28.7	55.8
(iii) Certificate in Domestic Science	61.1	74.9
(iv) Certificate in Manual Training	58.8	61.2
(v) Certificate in Rural Science	37.6	32.0

Source: *Report of Dept. of Education 1948–49, and 1949–50*

The numbers taking the examination expanded rapidly over subsequent years increasing from 2,470 in 1949 to 37,884 in 1959, in which year the general failure rate was down to 30%.[29]

The introduction of the Group Certificate cut across the earlier aspirations of the Department of Education which sought to encourage local variation of courses in line with local economic and industrial needs. However, the scheme probably helped to standardise approaches and give more clear guidelines to CEOs and school principals. The inspectors reported in 1949–50 as follows:

> As the syllabuses of the whole-time day courses were based mainly on the Day Group Certificate Examinations, there was more systematic teaching ... and the State certificate gave students an incentive to study.[30]

---

29 *Report of the Department of Education for 1948–49, and for 1959*, p. 89. **30** *Report of the Department of Education for 1949–50*, p. 30.

The Day Group Certificate examinations continued until they were absorbed within a reformed post-primary Junior Certificate Examination in 1989, to be taken by pupils in both vocational and secondary schools.

During the 1940s as well as experiencing financial cut-backs associated with war-time conditions, the vocational education system came under serious questioning within the policy arena. In 1942, the Secretary of the Department of Education, Seosamh Ó Néill, submitted a memorandum to the Taoiseach on agricultural education in the schools. The memorandum was critical of the vocational system particularly regarding the promotion of rural and agricultural education. The memorandum proposed a radical restructuring of the primary school system as the best way forward. Primary schools, it was suggested, should be organised as dual entities. The 'Junior' sector should provide traditional primary education for children up to twelve years of age. The 'Senior' School would provide a four-year course of full-time schooling of a practical and literary type suited to the needs of an agricultural economy. The schools would be under the primary school management system.[31] The report of the Commission on Vocational Organisation, published in 1944, was strongly critical of the curriculum of vocational schools, particularly in their non-inclusion of agricultural education (which had been retained under the auspices of the Department of Agriculture in 1930). The tenor of the criticism is reflected in the following quotation:

> Thus, we have the amazing fact that in the small towns of Ireland, where there is no industry worth speaking of, elaborate and expensive buildings have been erected and classes maintained to teach, not agriculture, but commerce and domestic economy.[32]

It also criticised the lack of involvement by the Department of Industry and Commerce with the vocational school system whereby there was a lack of 'co-ordination to secure that industry receives an adequate supply of trained workers and that trained workers get employment'. It went on to remark, 'But even within the sphere of the Department of Education's control there is a lack of co-ordination e.g. there is no link between the primary and the vocational schools, and in many towns there is overlapping between secondary and vocational schools and the higher standards of primary schools.' The report concluded, 'Continuation education has at times been provided at great expense for unsuitable students; the work could possibly be done by lengthening the course at the primary schools or extending the existing secondary schools'.[33] In its response to the Commission's Report the

31 NA Dept of Taoiseach S. 14392 + Box 2006/1201/27.   32 *Commission on Vocational Organisation* (Stationery Office, 1944), par. 351.   33 Ibid., par. 352.

Department of Education remarked that its 'comments consist mainly of sweeping generalisations and inaccuracies which do not give a correct estimate of the work done in vocational schools.'[34] The report of the Commission did not find favour with the government, and it was allowed to lapse into obscurity.

However, a further threat to the continuation schools came in the report of an internal Departmental Committee on possible post-war reforms of the schooling system which was established in March 1945. This Committee was chaired by Labhras Ó Muirthí, and it included inspectors from all three branches of the Department.

This initiative followed from a letter from Taoiseach de Valera to the Minister for Education, Mr Derrig, in which he drew attention to the white papers on education in which Great Britain and Northern Ireland were planning post-war educational reform. Mr de Valera urged that these papers should be examined carefully by the Department of Education, if it had not already done so. The Taoiseach also called for a thorough examination of the educational system in Ireland, including primary, secondary, vocational, agricultural and university education.[35] When the committee was established in March, it had the same broad terms of reference as listed in the Taoiseach's letter, albeit translated into English. However, neither in the committee's interim report of August 1946 nor in its final report in 1947 did the committee explore these terms of reference. Rather, it confined its attention to the educational needs of 14 to 16 year olds. It would seem that the Taoiseach was impatient at the pace of work, and on 29 August 1945 the Minister for Education wrote to the Taoiseach stating that the preparation of a white paper would be premature until the committee had progressed its work.[36] In the event, its report only dealt with a limited issue and could not form the basis of a white paper.

The Committee's recommendations bore much resemblance to the memorandum by the Departmental Secretary in 1942. It suggested that a Junior primary school would cater for pupils up to twelve years of age. A new Senior school should be established whose curriculum would provide mainly for continuation work, but it should also include manual training and general science or rural science for boys and craftwork and domestic economy for girls. In the later stages, the curricular emphasis should be increasingly on practical subjects.[37] A sub-committee of inspectors, who were members of the committee, submitted a report to it on key problems relating to the operation of the three branches of the Department.

---

34 NA Dept of Taoiseach S. 13552.   35 NA File S 10107 A, Letter from Mr de Valera to Minister Derrig, 16 Dec. 1944.   36 NA File 12891 B, Letter from Minister Derrig to Taoiseach de Valera, 29 Aug. 1945.   37 'Report of the Departmental Committee on Educational Provision', June 1947, par. 28, NA Dept of Taoiseach 12981B (unpublished).

J.P. Hackett who had chaired the group who produced Memorandum V40 in 1942, was a member of this Departmental Committee. Noting the criticism of non-religious control of continuation education, he remarked that memorandum V40 had been 'an effort to effect a reconciliation by the denominationalism of continuation education'. He ruefully concluded, 'I am now satisfied that no reconciliation is possible and that there is no real future for continuation education under vocational committees as at present constituted, notwithstanding the success of their day courses and the value of the work which has been done to date.'[38] In the event, this proved to be the nadir of the policy approach to vocational education. The 1947 report was not acted upon, nor published, and it dropped out of public consciousness. The practitioners involved with vocational education continued their work, despite war-time privations and the impact of the extremely harsh weather conditions of 1946–47. At Easter 1946, the inspectors held a two-day conference with the CEOs to review the work and they recorded a satisfactory verdict.[39] Such meetings continued in subsequent years and facilitated good working relationships between the inspectors and the CEOs. The Day Group Certificate Examinations in 1947 gave a fillip to the system.

The Fianna Fáil government was replaced by an Inter-party government at the general election of 1948, with Minister Mulcahy as Minister for Education. Significant education policy change was not on the agenda. In 1950 Minister Mulcahy established a Council of Education. In announcing the Council, Minister Mulcahy stated that it would be particularly important for its work that 'the advice and direction of these with active experience in and close contact with the work of the schools would be available', yet no inspector was appointed to the Council.[40] Its first role was to report on the function and curriculum of the primary school, which it did in 1954. Its second allocated job was to report on the curriculum of the secondary school which it did in 1960. The establishment of the Council, the roles it was given, and the slow manner in which it conducted its work, took the policy spotlight off vocational education, which carried on its work with little public controversy.

The tradition of holding annual meetings of the CEOs and inspectors, over two or three days in Dublin each May continued each year through the 1950s. They focussed on issues and problems within the vocational system. They were sometimes addressed by the Minister for Education. The agenda was enriched on occasion by inputs from the CEOs 'research committee', which met three or four times a year and which had involvement from the inspectorate. These opportunities fostered good communication and rela-

38 NA Department of Taoiseach S. 12891 B, J.P. Hackett, 'Note on Continuation Schools' 18 July 1947.   39 *Report of the Department of Education for 1949–50*, p. 25.   40 Department of Education, *A Council of Education: Terms of Reference and General Regulations* (Dublin: Stationery Office, 1950), p. 10.

tionships between the inspectors and the CEOs. During the fifties, joint delegations of CEOs and inspectors made study visits to the United States and Scandinavia, aided by funds external to the Department, to study and report on aspects of the education system in those countries. The inspectors also organised conferences at various locations with groups of subject teachers – rural science, commerce, Irish, domestic science and woodwork – during the fifties. Some of these conferences were also attended by CEOs. They focussed on improved methodologies including planned visits of pupils to business and industry sites, the use of visual aids, silent films, filmstrips, the application of the project method. This latter was particularly emphasised for rural science teaching. In 1951–52, the inspectors issued an addendum to Memorandum V40 on rural science teaching, urging a much more practical bias to it. In 1956, the Department issued a circular letter which urged CEOs, principals and teachers to extend the use of Irish as the ordinary language of the school as much as possible, and not to confine its use to the Irish class. In general, the reports of the inspectors on the efficiency of instruction in the schools in these years was favourable, with the exception of the teaching of English and geography, which was a continuous cause of concern.

The appointment of Mr Seán Moylan as Minister for Education in the Fianna Fáil administration of 1951–54 was favourable to vocational education as he had an allegiance to it, and the vocational school building programme benefited. The Department's Report for 1950–51 commented on 'the strong demand' which was in evidence for both continuation and technical education. It reported that at many centres 'long lists of students were awaiting admission' and enrolments at country VECs 'taxed to the maximum the available accommodation.'[41] This became a regular theme in the Reports of the fifties which recorded the building of many new schools, and extensions to others. The capital funding for vocational education increased from £164,668 in 1951 to £328,295 in 1956.[42] While many of the country vocational schools tended to be small, their presence became a regular feature on the Irish rural landscape and brought forms of practical and vocational education close to the people.

Overall, despite difficulties encountered, the vocational education system expanded well over the early decades of its existence. In 1932 there were 98 schools with 676 full-time teachers and 598 part-time teachers; by 1959 the number of schools had grown to 272 with 1,574 full-time teachers and over 500 part-time teachers. Enrolments in whole-time day continuation courses rose from 7,925 in 1931 to 17,978 by 1950, to reach 25,608 by 1957. Enrolments in part-time course reached 11,992 in 1959. The demand for

41 *Report of the Dept of Education for 1950–51*, p. 23.   42 *Report of Department of Education for 1955–56*, p. 15.

evening and adult courses was impressive, and by 1959 there were 86,343 students attending these classes.[43] The pro-active and close engagement of the inspectorate in the technical instruction branch can be regarded as highly significant for the promotion of continuation and technical education during the first four decades of political independence.

43 John Coolahan, *Irish Education*, p. 103.

11

An Era of Educational Change and its Implications for the Inspectorate

In contrast to previous decades, the 1960s witnessed a dramatic increase in governmental and the general public interest in educational policy and practice. A range of investigative bodies was established to analyse, appraise and report on all aspects of the education system. A much more pro-active governmental policy approach ensued which greatly altered the inherited shape of the education system. Education came to be seen as a form of investment in promoting human resources and economic growth and development. Educational change formed a part of wider social, economic, technological and cultural change in Irish society.[1] A notable landmark in this regard was the first Programme for Economic Expansion, in 1958, which signalled changed attitudes to economic and industrial development. Subsequently, the Irish economy began to expand, and it was realised that a more industrial and technological society needed a skilled workforce and could, in turn, provide greater financial resources for education. Shortly after assuming office as Taoiseach, in 1959, Sean Lemass announced that an immediate policy of the government was to increase the facilities available for post-primary education, and this became one of the key leitmotifs for education policy over subsequent years.[2]

A great deal of appraisal and analysis was undertaken by a range of agencies on many aspects of the Irish education during the 1960s. The outcome of these investigations, combined with the policy initiatives which evolved from them, greatly transformed the structure of the education system and the patterns of participation, particularly at post-primary and tertiary education levels. Such changes had far-reaching consequences for the school inspectorate but no formal re-appraisal, restructuring or re-formulation of its role took place. Thus, it found itself seeking to continue its traditional roles with multifarious new responsibilities, within a fast-changing, and expanding system, without the sufficient personnel, resources and support staff which were required. As a consequence, particularly at post-primary level, the role of the inspectorate lost clear focus and, became involved in many and varied activities, involving circumstances which gave rise to tensions and some loss of morale over subsequent decades.

1 John Coolahan, *Irish Education: History and Structure* (Dublin: IPA, 1981), pp 131–39. 2 *Dáil Proceedings*, vol. 177, cols. 470–71, 28 October, 1959.

To understand the work of the inspectorate in this era, it is necessary to outline some of the key developments of the sixties which impacted on the education system and the inspectorate's work environment, while other changes are incorporated within the relevant chapters which follow. One report which did not impact much on the system was the long-awaited report of the Council of Education on 'The Curriculum of the Secondary School', which was completed in 1960. The report was oriented much more towards the past than to the future. It identified the dominant purpose of the secondary school as 'the inculcation of religious ideals and values'. It interpreted the prevailing curriculum as of 'the grammar school type, synonymous with general and humanist education',[3] and it endorsed this model. It expressed a sense of concordance with most existing practices and reflected complacency on many issues. In its short paragraph on the inspectorate it praised the freedom the inspectorate allowed to schools on curricula and methods, and remarked, 'None of the organisations consulted by us has expressed any dissatisfaction with the system of inspection'.[4] This could be interpreted as a compliment to the inspectorate, or as a lack of rigorous inspection which suited secondary school authorities. A scheme of a free secondary education for all was regarded as 'untenable and utopian', but it favoured an extension of the scholarship scheme.[5] By the time the Council of Education report was published, in 1962, more incisive and dynamic thinking was taking place which would be influential for policy and practice.

In June 1962, a committee was formed in the Department of Education, on the instruction of the Minister, Dr P.J. Hillery, 'to consider the present position of post-primary education, particularly in its social aspect and to make recommendations.' The committee was chaired by Dr Duggan, Deputy Chief Inspector, and its secretary was Dr Finbarr Ó Ceallacháin, also an inspector, who drafted the report. Three other inspectors completed the team. They issued an interim report in December 1962, which was not published. The report stated, 'We unhesitatingly recommend a compulsory and free period of post–primary education for all Irish children'.[6] In planning for the future, the authors stated, 'We reject entirely the basis on which pupils enter secondary and vocational schools at the present time.' Instead, they considered that the existing distinction between these two types of school, should be replaced by the concept of a comprehensive system whereby a common form of post-primary course extending over a three year period should exist in both types of school. They considered that this common, comprehensive type curriculum would have many advantages and tend 'to eliminate social barriers currently created by educational cleavages'.[7] This course would be followed by a three-year senior course with some subject specialisation, and accompanied by a

3 Council of Education, *Report on the Curriculum of the Secondary School* (Dublin: Stationery Office, 1962, Pr. 5996), p. 256.   4 Ibid., 248.   5 Ibid., p. 252.   6 Section of Report published in A. Hyland and K. Milne (eds), *Irish Educational Documents II* (Dublin: CICE, 1992), pp 555–60, p. 556.   7 Ibid., p. 558.

service of pre-employment courses for some pupils, vocational in nature and of one year's duration. The Committee recommended that local statutory committees, of a representative character, should be set up for post-primary education. While this report was not adopted, it reflected fresh thinking from a group of inspectors about post-primary education which was to be influential.

The following May, 1963, Minister Hillery delivered a major speech with four new policy initiatives. The most significant was that the state intended to undertake the building of a new type of post-primary school – the comprehensive school – in areas not being currently served by a secondary or a vocational school. To help put vocational schools on an academic and social par with secondary schools, Dr Hillery announced that the two-year course in vocational schools would be extended to three years and that a new Intermediate Certificate programme would be available to both types of school. To promote technical education he announced that a new Technical Leaving Certificate would be introduced. Furthermore, new educational institutions, to be known as Regional Technical Colleges would be established to boost technical education and to help align educational provision with manpower needs.[8] Minister Hillery also introduced the first scheme of state grants for the capital needs of secondary schools in 1964.

During these years, the Investment in Education Team, established by the Minister in 1962, was at work on a major analytical and statistical study of the education system. The study was conducted in association with the OECD. Mícheál Ó Flannagáin, Chief Inspector of the Technical Instruction Branch of the Department served on the National Steering Committee of the project, while Pádraig Ó Nualláin, inspector of secondary schools was a member of the four-man Survey Team, headed by Professor Paddy Lynch. The report, published in 1966, was a large-scale, detailed report which focused predominantly on four major themes – education and manpower needs, patterns of participation in education, curricula, and the use of resources. Under these four areas of inquiry it found very serious shortcomings which would need to be addressed if the education system was to respond satisfactorily to the needs of a fast-changing society. Looking to the future, the report urged the setting up of a special educational development unit within the Department of Education, which should include an inspector.[9] In the event, the unit included an inspector from each of the three sectors, Dr Finbarr Ó Ceallacháin, Séamus Ó Buachalla and Brian Coyle. Many implications for reform arose from *Investment in Education* findings. Sean O'Connor, who was appointed first head of the Development Unit, aptly commented that the report 'has signposted the direction of educational reform and, by highlighting our deficiencies, has offered a challenge that cannot be ignored'.[10]

8 Speech delivered by Minister Hillery at a press conference, 20 May 1963.   9 *Investment in Education Report* (Pr. 8311) (Dublin: Stationery Office 1966), p. 352.   10 Sean O'Connor, 'Post-Primary Education: Now and in the Future', *Studies* (Autumn 1968), pp 233–49, p. 233.

The challenge was already being faced, and during these years major transformative changes were undertaken, so that by 1975 the education system had been significantly re-configured. The following is a summary of the main changes affecting primary, post-primary, special education, and some aspects of tertiary education.

At primary level, preparation for a new curriculum was underway from 1966, which in 1971, became official curricular policy reflecting a dramatically different ideology and approach from that in operation since the 1920s. It was a child-centered curriculum, with a wide range of subjects and it advocated active and discovery pedagogic methods. The Primary School Certificate was abolished in 1967. 'Secondary Tops' in primary schools were to cease and the normal transfer age to post-primary education was set at twelve years of age. From 1966 the policy was adopted of closing small primary schools, particularly those which were old and in poor condition. In many parishes, outlying townland schools were amalgamated into central village schools. New standards were introduced in the provision of new school buildings. The policy aim of improving teacher-pupil ratios was only gradually achieved due to the pressure of a growing population, with the census of 1966 recording the first inter-census increase of population since the Famine. Teacher education was reformed and, by 1974, the teacher education course for primary teachers was developed into a three-year BEd Degree course, validated by the universities. Teacher Centres were provided on a regional basis from the early 1970s, which were to act as a support resource for teachers in all sectors of the system. The provision of in-service education for teachers gathered new momentum in the early seventies, in conjunction with the implementation of the new curriculum. Changes in primary school management were also underway and, from 1975, management boards, comprising representatives of the patron, the parents and the teachers became operative in primary schools.

Among key changes at post-primary level was the introduction by Minister O'Malley of the free education and free school transport scheme in 1967. This added great momentum to an already existing trend of increasing pupil participation. The number of pupils enrolled in post-primary schools increased from 136,000 pupils in 1965 to 335,000 by 1985. Teacher numbers increased from about 7,300 to almost 20,000 over the same period. Such increases had huge implications for the provision and nature of post-primary schooling. Two new types of school were introduced – comprehensive and community schools, with new forms of management and financing. The status of vocational schools was changed so that they could now offer both the Intermediate and Leaving Certificate, as in other post-primary schools, as well as their traditional Group Certificate. A comprehensive curricular policy was adopted for all schools whereby the traditional academic and practical subjects would be combined, with pupils being offered an extensive subject menu to suit their talents and interests. Subject content in subjects such as science, mathematics and languages was reformed. A massive school building programme was initiated, with new buildings containing the type of rooms, equipment and resources required to serve new curricular policies. The public examinations came under scrutiny and improvements were made in the examination papers, now being taken by massively increased numbers of examination candidates. Improvements were made in pupil-teacher ratios, though these were not sustained during the cutbacks of the 1980s. Initial teacher education programmes were reformed and extended, and various forms of in-service education for teachers became operative. Subject associations, such as the Science Teachers' Association, were formed from the early sixties, and teachers participated in syllabus committees for the various subjects, in association with Departmental inspectors. Curricular experimentation including pilot initiatives, came to the fore in 1970s, and, in 1977, the Department of Education established a Curriculum Unit. Pre-employment courses, with the support of EU funding, were instituted in 1977. Guidance counselling was introduced to schools, and a psychological service was established within the Department of Education in 1965, primarily as a resource for pupils in post-primary schools.

Education for pupils with disabilities was given greater attention by the state during these years. In 1959 the first inspector for special education, Tomás Ó Cuilleanáin, was appointed and, in 1960, a Special Education Unit was established in St Patrick's College of Education. The report of the Commission on Handicap in 1965 led to increases in the provision of special schools and special classes. Better provision was made for the education of pupils experiencing hearing and sight disabilities.

A notable instance of an increased concern for the education of the socio-economically disadvantaged was the establishment of the Rutland Street Project in 1969. This was a forerunner of many later projects targeted at the needs of disadvantaged pupils. In 1970, the *Report on the Education of Itinerants* (Travellers) was published and highlighted the needs for enlightened initiatives to cater for the educational needs of traveller children. Also, in 1970, the Kennedy Report on Reformatory and Industrial Schools was published; it made wide-ranging recommendations for reform but, while some improvements followed for children in care, many of the recommendations were not implemented. The psychologist Tony Gorman represented the Department of Education on this committee. Such initiatives reflected changing social attitudes towards the rights of all pupils. At first, the emphasis was placed on special provision for various categories of pupils with special needs, which later gave away to a policy of pupil integration in mainstream education by the 1990s.

New educational institutions came into operation in the early 1970s – the Regional Technical Colleges. Originally announced by Minister Hillery in 1963, a more precise brief was prepared for the colleges in the Report of the Steering Committee on Regional Technical Colleges published in 1967. A vocational school inspector, Mr Jerry Sheehan, was secretary to this Committee and another inspector, Dr Finbarr Ó Ceallacháin assisted the team. Originally, these colleges were conceived as providing senior cycle post-primary courses, apprentice and technician courses as well as a range of tertiary courses of an applied character. As they evolved, however, they committed themselves to a tertiary education role. For about twenty years of their existence, up to 1992, they operated under the aegis of the Vocational Education Committee in whose geographical location they were placed. During these years the inspectors attached to the vocational section of the Department exercised various responsibilities in relation to the Regional Colleges.

Inspectors contributed, in a variety of capacities, to the various reports and policy initiatives which re-shaped the structure and provision of educational services. In turn, their professional work pattern was greatly altered by the new configuration and by the changing pattern of relationships which evolved in the interface between the education system and the general public. The advent of a national television station in 1961 and much more extensive coverage of educational affairs on radio and in the press highlighted the need for briefings for press conferences and media presentations by ministers and senior officials. Many new educational organisations came into being and established a tradition of holding conferences and seminars at which Ministers for Education or their nominees were expected to present addresses. The Irish tradition of the availability of ministers for the opening of new buildings or the presentation of reports gathered momentum, as more frequent opportunities presented themselves, which called for informed speech-making. In the changing culture, many committees were established to deal with particular issues and Departmental representation on committees became much more extensive. Inspectors were called upon to assist and participate in all such activities.

Ireland's entry to the European Economic Community (EEC) in 1973 was a significant historical landmark which had huge ramifications for the development of Irish society. In the educational and training arena, Ireland was to prove to be a very influential member state, and, in due course, benefited greatly from social and structural funds to help develop its workforce and economy. This work placed new demands on personnel within the Department of Education, as in other departments.

The multiplicity of changes and developments at all levels of the education system gave rise to many demands, challenges and responsibilities for the Department of Education. From the foundation of the state, this had been a very centralised administrative structure, with the vast bulk of decisions being made at the centre. There were no regional education authorities to share the burden of educational administration. While the vocational education committees had responsibilities affecting vocational and technical education, all their significant decisions were subject to Departmental approval. A number of bodies such as the Higher Education Authority (HEA) and the National Council for Educational Awards (NCEA) were set up to deal with specific functions. Yet there was no fundamental re-structuring of the Department of Education in the context of the very changed educational system which was developing. Traditionally, all significant issues affecting each individual school and institution were relayed to the Department for decision. From the 1960s, this continued to be the case but, in addition, a great range of issues affecting the many new institutions, organisations, and matters arising from new policies were now added to the Department's agenda. While the establishment of regional education authorities was mooted periodically, they were never established. It was only gradually from the mid-eighties that bodies external to the Department were established for specific functions, which alleviated some of the heavy workload at the centre.

The traditional structure of the inspectorate continued without any significant re-adjustment until the 1990s. Some increases in staffing were secured to help cope with the expanding workload. However, this was not sustained, and an embargo imposed on public service recruitment from the early eighties impinged hugely on staffing within the inspectorate with deleterious consequences throughout the eighties and into the early nineties. A pattern also occurred of deploying inspectors in specialised units within the Department. Instances of this included the Development Unit in the 1960s, the Building Unit in the early seventies, and the Curriculum Unit from the late seventies. This facilitated an interchange of perspectives and skills between different categories of staff within the Department, but could deplete inspectorial staff relating with schools. Inspectors also took on the job of editing and writing contributions for the Department's education journal, *Oideas*, which began publication in 1968.

However, the incremental development of the functions of the inspectorate did not lead to any co-ordinated initiative to stand back and examine what was happening, and whether the role and function of the inspectorate were losing their focus and becoming too multifarious. The role of the inspectorate changed due to evolving circumstances, rather than through a conscious re-interpretation of the role. Events rather than formal policy tended to dictate the pattern of development. In this context also, the relationships of the inspectorate with the administrative side of the Department changed and led to a weakening of the inspectorate in the policy arena. It is of interest that from 1968 it was almost thirty years before an inspector, John Dennehy, achieved the Secretary General's role, which the inspectorate had dominated for over forty-five years prior to 1968. However, positions such as Principal Officer and Assistant Secretary did open up for the inspectorate. Inspectors such as Risteárd Ó Foghlú, Tomás Ó Floinn, Finnbarr Ó Ceallacháin, Donnacha Ó h-Éalaithe, Pádraig Ó Nualláin, and John Dennehy held positions as Assistant Secretaries during the period. As in similar contexts in other countries, some tensions existed between the administrative and the professional sides of the Department. Some of this could be linked to promotion aspirations and some to the expertise and experience of the different categories of staff. The internal administrative staff would be exposed in their career path to issues such as budgeting matters, personnel issues, industrial relations and the variety of political issues affecting the policy process. The experience of many inspectors would have been school teaching and expertise in subject areas, often to a high academic level, but sometimes in a compartmentalised context. The nature of the work of senior administration may not always have been congenial to them, and sometimes, administrative staff were disappointed with the nature and quality of the policy advice they got from the inspectorate. Administrators could not be promoted in the inspectorate and, in some instances, they did not welcome promotions of the inspectorate to their sphere of activity. It is noteworthy that up to 1991, the Chief Inspector was not a member by right of the Top Management Team which comprised of the Secretary and Assistant Secretaries.

When, in the early 1980s, a tradition of ministers appointing external personnel as personal advisers on policy was introduced, there was an initial unease within both the inspectorate and the administrative staff, which dissolved before long. One such adviser who has written about his experience is Dr John Harris, who advised Minister Gemma Hussey in the early eighties. He regretted the relatively small influence exercised by the inspectorate on policy and administration issues, and pointed to a regrettable gulf which sometimes existed between the inspectors and the administrative staff.[11] Harris favoured the joint inclusion of administrative staff and inspectors on committees advising on policy. Of a number of Departmental working parties, set up in those years, Harris remarked, 'Both administrators and inspectors were involved in most cases, as a matter of deliberate policy.'[12]

In the context of the changes affecting post-primary schools operating a comprehensive- type curriculum and presenting pupils for the same public examinations, an effort was made to unite the secondary and vocational inspectorate as a unified post-primary inspectorate. Apart from nomenclature, this initiative met with very little success. The sub-cultures and mode of operation of each sector had been different. They had been, and continued to be organised as separate trade union branches. While individual personal relationships of inspectors in each sector were generally cordial, there was no sustained tradition of joint working or co-operative initiatives, although instances of co-operation occurred periodically. To officialdom, there was a logic at this time of establishing a joint post-primary inspectorate, but the reluctance of the protagonists presents an interesting case study of how difficult

11 John Harris, 'The Policy-making Role of the Department of Education' in D.G. Mulcahy and Denis O'Sullivan (eds), *Irish Educational Policy: Process and Substance* (Dublin: IPA, 1989), pp 7–26, p. 15. 12 Ibid., p. 17.

it can be to merge two such Departmental entities, each of which regarded its own role as distinctive and tended to regard the work of the other as of lesser importance.

As part of the re-organisation of post-primary education Minister George Colley, in January 1966, sent a letter to vocational and secondary schools urging that they should change from operating as 'two rigidly separated post-primary systems, each with its own schools, its own curriculum and courses of study, its own examinations and its own cadre of teachers'. In place of this segregated pattern he sought 'a pooling of forces so that the shortcomings of one (type of school) will be met from the resources of the other, thus making available to the student in either school the post-primary education best suited to him'.[13] This was in the interests of promoting the comprehensive curricular policy and the provision of the Intermediate Certificate course in vocational schools. The new comprehensive schools, followed in the early seventies by the community schools, reflected the government's ideal of comprehensive curricular provision, which the vocational and secondary schools were encouraged to emulate, as far as possible. Moves were also afoot at this time to promote a common salary scale for the three categories of teacher – national, secondary and vocational. The Ryan Report of 1968 endorsed this policy, and while some difficulties occurred regarding its implementation, by 1971 all teachers had a common salary scale with a common system of conciliation and arbitration.

Against this background it was not surprising that efforts were made in the 1970s to promote an integrated inspectorate, particularly regarding the work of the post-primary inspectorate. Hitherto, the three sectors of the inspectorate operated as separate entities, with little crossover in work responsibility. The primary inspectorate was by far the largest, the longest established and exercised the most tightly regulated form of inspection. It had a clear sense of purpose and had a myriad of responsibilities in relation to the primary schools. The secondary inspectorate was comprised of honours university graduates, who were conscious of, and enjoyed a high social status. Their mode of inspection of the private secondary schools with their academic, grammar school type of curricula was of a light model. They did not have the power to remove ineffective teachers, although they could alert school principals to inadequate teacher performance. Their role in managing and administering the public examinations of Intermediate and Leaving Certificate was regarded as of great importance, a role which they cherished and which became more extensive as time went on. The vocational inspectorate had a wide range of functions in relation to vocational and technical education. They liaised with the VECs, conducted detailed school inspections,

13 'Letter from George Colley, Minister for Education to the Authorities of Secondary and Vocational Schools, 1 Jan 1966', in A. Hyland and K. Milne, *Irish Educational Documents II*, pp 259–61.

with the power of withdrawing recognition from ineffective teachers, conducted the Technical School Examinations, of which there were many, and participated in teacher education of vocational teachers. They tended not to have the same status as the secondary school inspectorate at that time. Even within the vocational school inspectorate there were gradations of status with, for instance, the inspectorate relating to the crafts such as metalwork or woodwork, many of whom were non-graduates, categorised as Grade B inspectors, a non-promotional grade. The three sectors of the inspectorate were on different pay scales, with differentiation between male and female salaries, and each was affiliated to a different branch of their trade union. Prior to 1969 each sector had its own chief inspector, with responsibility for his particular sector. There were no female chief inspectors.

In 1968 the vocational branch of the Institute of Professional Civil Servants initiated negotiations for a salary increase. In the course of the negotiations, the official side indicated that a new structure for the inspectorate was being envisaged, which would yield salary increases as well as changes in career structure. Agreement was reached with the vocational inspectors on 9 December 1968,[14] and the new framework for the inspectorate overall came into operation in January 1969. It took some time to iron-out details of the new scheme but, from 1 April 1971, a common salary scale became operative for all inspectors.[15]

Under the new arrangement the secondary and vocational inspectorates were amalgamated, forming the post-primary inspectorate. A new post of Chief Inspector was created with responsibility for both the primary and the post-primary inspectorate. After a transititional period, the three former Chief Inspector posts were replaced by the new grade of Deputy Chief Inspector, one for each sector – primary, secondary and vocational. The career framework now had the following categorisation:

• Chief Inspector
• Deputy Chief Inspector
• Assistant Chief Inspector
• Divisional Inspector (primary) / Senior Inspector (post primary) / Senior Inspector of Guidance and Psychologists
• District Inspector (primary) / Post Primary Inspector / Inspector of Guidance Service and Psychologists.

The recruitment grade was the last one listed, and the career structure had four grades above it.

The Review Body on Higher Remuneration in the Public Sector issued a report in 1981 on 'Higher Departmental and Professional Civil Service

14 NA Box 2006/120/69, report of meeting.   15 Review Body on Higher Remuneration in the Public Sector (Chair: Liam St J. Devlin), *Higher Departmental and Professional Salary Grades, Report No. 27)* (Dublin: Stationery Office, 1981), p. 141.

Grades'. Chapter 9 was devoted to the Schools Inspectorate and it gives a valuable account of the roles of the different categories of inspector, as officially devised, and is worth quoting at some length. It sets out the position in the following paragraphs:[16]

> The Chief Inspector is the head of the Department's Inspectorate and the chief source of professional advice to the Minister and Secretary. His duties include generally supervising and arranging for the co-ordination of work as between the different branches of the Inspectorate; advising the Minister on structures and personnel matters within the Inspectorate; dealing with appeals from the Inspectorate staff in relation to matters in dispute; advising on curricular policy matters; and appraising for the information of the Minister the quality of education given.
>
> Each of the Deputy Chief Inspectors has responsibility for a branch of the Inspectorate – Primary, Secondary and Vocational. Within his area each Deputy Chief Inspector is responsible for the training and deployment of Inspectors and for the allocation of work, for ensuring that standards are maintained in schools and by teachers, for advising on resource requirements in terms of personnel and finance, and for overseeing and co-ordinating the work of the Inspectorate subordinate to him. He advises the Minister and Department on the professional content of the curriculum in his area and on related policies, approves and drafts speeches for the Minister and represents the Minister and Department as necessary. He is involved with the administrative side of the Department in negotiation with teachers' representatives on matters affecting their work. The Deputy Chief Inspectors assist and advise the Chief Inspector in the overall management of the Inspectorate. There are also duties, arising from their areas of responsibility, specific to each of the Deputy Chief Inspector posts.
>
> Assistant Chief Inspectors have responsibility for the maintenance of educational standards, ensuring that reasonable uniformity of standards and procedures are maintained. They supervise and co-ordinate the work of the subordinate inspector grades, monitoring schemes of work and records of work. They are occasionally involved in inspection, normally in serious cases calling for the direct participation of a senior officer, and deal with appeals against reports by members of the subordinate grades. They assist the Chief and Deputy Chief Inspectors in their work, provide professional information on request for the answering of parliamentary questions, provide draft ministerial speeches and serve on ministerial,

16 Ibid., Chapter 9.

international inter-departmental and departmental committees as required. Other duties and responsibilities which vary from post to post also attach to the grade. Assistant Chief Inspectors have responsibilities peculiar to their branch (i.e. Primary, Secondary or Vocational) and have specific responsibilities assigned to them, on a geographical or functional basis.

The Primary Inspectorate is organised on a geographical basis. There are 62 districts each with a teacher population of 250 to 300. The District Inspector is responsible for the inspection of all the work in the schools in his district. His role is partly inspectorial, partly advisory and partly administrative. The Divisional Inspectors supervise, co-ordinate and support the work of the District Inspectors. They are responsible for the overall planning and organising of work in their divisions, reporting thereon to their Assistant Chief Inspectors, approving innovative programmes and pilot schemes in schools within their divisions, dealing with appeals against reports of District Inspectors and conducting informal inquiries as required and/or directed by the Minister. In addition to the work assigned to them, such as work in relation to the curriculum or they may be assigned on a full-time basis to discharge specialist functions.

In the Post-Primary Inspectorate work is allocated on both a geographical and subject basis. Post-Primary Inspectors are involved in school inspections where their role like that of the District Inspectors is inspectorial, advisory and administrative. They are also involved in work relating to curriculum development, syllabus planning and the organisation of examinations. They can also be involved in work relating to the education system in general, such as in-service and pre-service training, buildings and equipment or teacher supply and qualifications. Senior Inspectors may be involved in similar work, generally at a higher level. They supervise, co-ordinate and direct the work of the Post Primary Inspectors. In their geographical areas of responsibility they plan and organise the Inspectors' work, advise and assist Inspectors as necessary, advise schools, committees and chief executive officers on education developments and take an over-view of education in their area. In their subject areas Senior Inspectors act as chairman of syllabus/curriculum meetings, act as research leaders and co-ordinate research activities. Senior Inspectors deal with appeals against reports of Inspectors. A Senior Inspector may also be given responsibility for specific areas of education such as apprenticeship training or curriculum work.

The role of the Senior Inspectors of Guidance Services and Psychologists is to organise, develop and supervise psychological services to schools. While each Senior Psychologist has certain specific areas of responsibility, geographical and functional, they are collectively responsible to the Chief Inspector for all substantive decisions concerning the work of the Psychological Service. The main responsibilities of the service lie in the areas of remedial education, pupil guidance, curriculum development, pupils with special needs, in-service training of teachers, transition from schools to work and psychological test development. The Senior Psychologists advise the Minister and Department as required, are responsible to the Chief Inspector for the operation, planning and development of the Service, supervise control and direct the work of their subordinate staff and liaise with other sections of the Department and other bodies.

In this statement of the inspectors' work it is surprising that scarcely any reference is made to the management of examinations which had become a major part of the work of the secondary and vocational inspectorate.

In its conclusions as regards inspectors' remuneration the Report made no recommendations regarding the recruitment grade or for the grade of Divisional and Senior Inspectors as they had salary claims currently lodged with the Civil Service Arbitration Board. It recommended that salary of the Senior Inspectors of Guidance and Psychological Services should be put on par with that of Divisional and Senior Inspectors. No change was recommended for the salaries of Assistant Chief Inspectors. Increases were recommended for the post of Deputy Chief Inspector. The Report considered that the Chief Inspector should benefit from a flat (non-incremental) rate, and that he should be remunerated above the grade of Assistant Secretary. The salary scales recommended by the Review Body for the inspectorate grades were very much less than had been sought by the Union in its submission. The recommended scales were as follows:

	Irish £
Chief Inspector	19,200
Deputy Inspector	14,570 x 770 (3) – 16,880
Assistant Chief Inspector	13,393 – 13,701 – 14,010 – 14,318 – 14,570
Senior Inspector of Guidance	11,304 – 11,572 – 11,841 – 12,109 – 12,378
Services and psychologist	12,644

While the statement by the Review Body of the official position in relation to the inspectorate might represent it as unified, with a clear pattern of authority and reportage, and the post-primary inspectorate as an integrated one, the reality was rather different. The changed career framework, nomenclature of positions and improved salaries won general support, but there was no enthusiasm among the inspectorates for close co-operation or integrated work.

They had been organised as distinct units with different sub-cultures, and they were loathe to abandon habituated patterns of operation for a more merged identity. In theory, the new role of Chief Inspector might be expected to act as a unifying leadership role, but the position does not seem to have had the authority, power or resources to make this real. The Chief Inspector's role in policy-making with direct access to the Secretary of the Department and the Minister was not clearly defined. Each of the Deputy Chiefs considered his role lay in directing the sector over which he had responsibility. The establishment of a close working policy and planning team of the Chief and the three Deputy Chiefs did not take place although, of course, they communicated from time to time. However, they never formed a cohesive unit as a driving force for the inspectorate. It was also the case that the top positions in the inspectorate were almost always filled on seniority. This could mean that when such leadership positions were attained the personnel would have had long experience of established work practices and may not have had the vision, energy and drive to adopt innovative and pro-active approaches as they neared retirement. It was also the case that the Chief Inspector, who would come from one of the three sectors, might not have the confidence of the other sectors that he had an accomplished grasp of their sector's work and culture.

All Chief Inspectors had distinguished track records within the inspectorate. The first Chief Inspector was Micheál Ó Flannagáin who had long experience within the vocational inspectorate. He was succeeded by Gearóid Ó Súilleabháin who had been a highly regarded leader within the primary inspectorate. Dr Finnbarr Ó Ceallacháin who had been a very innovative inspector on the vocational side followed, and when he became assistant secretary for primary education, Dr Liam Ó Maolcatha from the secondary side took the position. Pádraig Ó Nualláin, then Assistant Secretary and formerly of a secondary inspector, took over for a period.

In 1990, Seán Mac Gleannáin who had been in the primary inspectorate was appointed as Chief on the basis of new appointment procedures. On his retirement in 1997, Eamon Stack, who had had associations with the vocational sector, became Chief Inspector. From the early nineties, promotion by seniority within the inspectorate waned as reformed appointment systems came into operation.

In an effort to secure greater integration of the two sectors of the post-primary inspectorate a working party was set up in June 1976. This was chaired by the Chief Inspector, Gearóid Ó Súilleabháin, and included the Deputy Chief, Dr F. Ó Ceallacháin, Assistant Chief, Pádraig Ó Nualláin, and four other inspectors. The integration had been agreed in principle under Conciliation Council Agreed Report No. 99. The key issue was to see if this could be implemented in practice. The aim of the working party was 'to distribute the workload of the post-primary inspectorate having regard to the most efficient use of available staff and to the individual specialisations of the inspectors'.[17] The work of the post-primary inspectorate was sub-divided by the group into three areas – (a) a control function; (b) a supportive function and (c) a development function. The working party then went on to consider the extent and variety of the workload under the following headings – resources; in-service and teacher training; syllabi; teacher qualifications; examinations; representation and advice to the Department. Under each heading, the work pattern of both inspectorates was summarised. In almost all instances it was agreed that, while differences existed, they could be overcome by briefings, familiarisation sessions, and orientation sessions.[18] Despite this apparently good level of agreement achieved by December 1976, the planned integration of workload did not take place. The secondary and vocational sections of the post-primary inspectorate continued to work largely in isolation from each other and in association with the institutions to which they were traditionally related. While both inspectorates inhabited the same building from the late 1960s – Hawkins House, Hawkins Street, – the secondary inspectorate was located on Floor 3 and the vocational inspectorate was on Floor 11. It has become part of the folklore of the inspectorate how separate these agencies maintained their roles even though inhabiting the one building. In an analysis of the inspectorate by Mr Clive Hopes in 1991, he referred to the failed efforts at the integration of the post-primary inspectorate in the 1970s and applied the apt term that it was only 'technically integrated', but not in a substantive way.[19] Hopes also makes the judgment of that period, 'The integration of the post-primary inspectorate seems to have been an ill-considered and poorly planned change.'[20]

It is considered that the detailed work of the post-primary inspectorate from the sixties to the nineties is most appropriately treated under the headings of secondary and vocational inspectorates. The following chapters examine the specific work of the three branches of the inspectorate, set against the background of the changing educational system outlined in this chapter.

17 NA Box 2006/120/69, Report of Working Party's work, signed by Gearóid Ó Súilleabháin, January 1977.   18 Ibid.   19 Clive Hopes, 'A Review of the Role and Functions of the Irish Schools Inspectorate' (unpublished Report to the Secretary of the Department of Education, 1991), p. 30.   20 Ibid., p. 42.

12

The Primary School Inspectorate, 1960–90

For the primary inspectorate this was a period of great engagement and activity in which inspectors managed to have a leading role in the development and reform of many facets of primary education. There were many substantial developments in terms of curriculum, teaching methods, school design, rationalisation of school provision, special education issues, inspection of schools and evaluation of curriculum implementation. A particularly interesting development was the production by the inspectorate of a series of reports on its own work. Despite periods of financial downturn in the economy, primary education advanced and developed in many important respects. Throughout the period, though often depleted in staff numbers, the primary inspectorate provided significant leadership and advice for the improvement of educational provision at the primary level. In some ways, the primary inspectorate laid down in this period some important foundations for the long-term benefit of education in Ireland.

A NEW ERA IN PRIMARY EDUCATION

Although the First Programme for Economic Expansion issued in November 1958 contained no specific reference to education, it was apparent within a few years that new thinking on education had begun to be a prominent part of government policies aimed at improving the economic circumstances of Ireland. This was borne out by the Second Programme for Economic Expansion issued in 1963 that devoted a chapter specifically to aspects of education. The programme envisaged an improvement of the educational services commencing with the primary sector which was perceived as the foundation of the entire system. Already, the Investment in Education survey in conjunction with the OECD had commenced in October 1962 and this signalled the emergence of a new and distinctively different era in the provision for primary education throughout Ireland. Moves to reform and develop the school curriculum gathered momentum during the 1960s and primary school inspectors came to occupy a pivotal role in the transition to a major revision of the curriculum. At this time, a notable turning point in Irish education was reached. No one incident may be identified as the precursor of new developments. Rather, a range of factors gave rise to a complex and exciting series of inter-related developments and changes across the spectrum of the education system. Political, economic and social considerations especially prompted the emergence of a new climate in education generally and many aspects of education in Ireland were transformed by a remarkable period of renewal and development that brought enduring change and improvement.

Irish, both as a subject and as a medium of instruction, had dominated the primary school curriculum for about forty years. Despite many calls over the decades for change, virtually nothing had altered up to the 1960s. A few small signals of change had appeared however and these included the change in 1948 that permitted the teaching of English for half an hour per day to infant classes. The publication three years later of *An Naí-Scoil* marked a further stage on the road to a change of outlook.[1] In the 1950s, there was significant reappraisal of the official policy on Irish and changing attitudes gradually had effect. In January 1960, a major change came when the Department relaxed the requirements about using Irish as a medium of instruction. Circular 11/60 gave individual teachers the right to choose whether or not Irish should be used as a medium of instruction. Drawn up by Seán Mac Gearailt, Assistant Secretary for Primary Branch, during the ministry of Dr Patrick Hillery, this circular came as a result of increasing pressure on the Department to modify the regulations concerning Irish. Thus fell, at one stroke, the critical edict of Circular 11/31 which had made it obligatory to use Irish as the medium of instruction. As if to underline this important change, the decision to close the five preparatory colleges for Catholic students, announced by Dr Hillery in May 1960, was a clear signal that the government was adopting a changed approach to primary education. Changing the relative emphasis on Irish was the prelude to major changes in various aspects of primary education over the course of the following years.

The primary inspectorate occupied a key position at this important juncture in Irish education. Interestingly, at this time, the inspectors' association, Cumann na gCigirí Bunscoile, had demonstrated a notable degree of energy and activism in representing its members' interests. A prominent branch within the Institute of Professional Civil Servants (IPCS), the association pursued better conditions for inspectors with particular success at this time. Tomás Ó Cuilleanáin and Tomás Ó Domhnalláin were especially prominent and active in the inspectors' association at this period. Indeed, the association's influence and leadership throughout this time was especially notable. Of special significance from a professional perspective was the association's request for an annual conference for all primary inspectors. This was acceded to by the Department and took place for the first time in October 1962. Lectures and opportunities for discussion of the broad and general issues of the time were features of the two-day conference that was a historic develop-

1 Department of Education, *An Naí Scoil: The Infant School, Notes for Teachers* (Dublin: Stationery Office, 1951).

ment for the inspectorate. The association self-consciously perceived this as the beginning of a series of conferences that would increase in importance and significance from year to year. The initiative may be understood to have been an important and spearheading movement towards the development and reju-venation of the inspectorate itself, a key element towards the future reform of primary education in Ireland. The timing of this development was highly sig-nificant as it gave notice of a resurgence of vitality and dynamism within the Department of Education itself at this watershed period in Ireland's history.

At this time, a number of important initiatives occurred and these pro-vided certain assistance to the inspection corps as a period of change and reform opened up. In 1959, two inspectors, Seán de Búrca and Tomás Ó Cuilleanáin, were sent on a four-month study visit to Jordanhill in Glasgow for special education needs training. Soon after, on foot of a recommendation arising from the study visit, a new course for teachers of special schools was instituted in St Patrick's College, Drumcondra. The pace of development in the whole area of special education quickened remarkably from 1961, the year that the government appointed a commission of inquiry on mental handicap. The Department of Education was represented on the commission by a prin-cipal officer and an inspector both of whom worked in close collaboration for a period during which a major expansion of special education occurred.[2] A few inspectors were very closely involved with the emergent pattern in spe-cial education and there is little doubt but that, working in tandem with the Department's officials, they contributed notably to the overall pattern of developments. In a sense, special education provided inspectors with an opportunity to show initiative and it was an opportunity that was taken up in an incremental way.

If special education prompted some comparisons with educational provi-sion abroad, there were other aspects of primary education in Ireland that were coming under similar scrutiny at this time also. School building was the subject of particular investigation when a divisional inspector, accompanied by an architect of the Board of Works, travelled to England and Scotland in May and June 1962. A comprehensive report detailed major differences in primary education between Britain and Ireland. School design, classroom size, furniture, play areas, teaching methods, curriculum, the role of head teachers, and standards of attainment, were among the topics dealt with in this influ-ential report in the last months of 1962.[3] This report, along with the recent developments in special education, appears to have had a catalytic effect on thinking within the Department. A new approach to the design and furnish-ing of national schools followed swiftly in response to this report and school buildings changed remarkably at this time. Gearóid Ó Súilleabháin, at that

---

2 Interview with T.A. Ó Cuilleanáin, 27 October 1987.   3 Department of Education, miscella-neous file Gearóid Ó Súilleabháin, '*A Chuairt ar Shasana*', Bealtaine, 1962.

time a divisional inspector, was prominently associated with these developments. There was a growing awareness of the need to up-date teaching methodology, to apply some of the techniques and skills from special education to ordinary schools, and to review the curriculum in the light of fresh insights on the nature of the child.[4]

At about this time also, a study of the Irish language was set in train by the Minister for Education. Important and new understanding about Irish as a language and about language learning resulted, heralding the development of significantly different approaches to the teaching of Irish.[5] Inspectors were very prominently associated with these developments. In the course of time, a major new series of Irish language conversation lessons was developed by the Department for use in primary schools as part of an audio-visual method of teaching Irish. Representing a dramatic change of approach to language teaching in Irish primary schools, and known to a generation of teachers as 'the Buntús', this was a development of great significance for the time. It also had implications for teaching methods necessitating equipment such as film-strip projectors and tape recorders within a few years. Given the fact that many schools did not have electricity at this time, it can be understood that the pattern of change that was in prospect was indeed far-reaching. Closely involved in all of these developments was Tomás Ó Domhnalláin, then a divisional inspector.

A school library scheme was initiated in 1963 and every national school was provided with the nucleus of a reference library. Many new ideas were beginning to have effect in the primary schools and a notable period of transition had commenced. Aspects of education were the focus of attention in a way that was distinctively new and different. A new type of debate and discussion about matters educational opened up with the publication of studies such as that of McNamara on bilingualism in 1966, as the atmosphere surrounding education changed notably for the better. The initiative to produce a Department of Education journal of education was taken at this time also and *Oideas* appeared for the first time in 1968 with the avowed aim of disseminating information and stimulating study and thought about educational matters. This was a signal of a new approach by the Department to education issues and questions with the promise that the Department would adopt a more open and investigative attitude to aspects of education and practice. Similarly, the publication of *Ár ndaltaí uile – All our children* in 1969 marked a new departure for the Department and for the government in that a forward looking, developmental and comprehensive outline of future educational provision across all sectors was promulgated and sent to every household in

---

4 T.A. Flanagan, 'Evolution of the Curriculum in Irish National Schools, 1831–1971: Critical influences, their sources and the system's responsiveness to change', unpublished PhD thesis, 1984, U.C.G., appendix 19.   5 C.L. Ó hUallacháin et al., *Buntús Gaeilge* (Baile Átha Cliath: Oifig an tSoláthair, 1966).

the country. Under the introductory heading 'all the children of the nation' echoing the 1916 Proclamation, the Minister for Education, Brian Lenihan, talked about the rapid change that the schools were going through and compared this to 'an educational revolution'. Significantly, the minister, commenting that 'we are in a hurry' in relation to the changes that were in prospect, gave unequivocal sign that the government was impatient for movement and renewal.[6]

Education was in ferment at this time. Developments including the abolition of the Primary Certificate Examination, moves towards the improvement of the pupil teacher ratio, and the promise of 'free' post-primary education in 1967 betoken a period of great energy in education and the commencement of a new era of greater access to education beyond the primary level. The raising of the school leaving age to fifteen years, finally implemented in 1972, underlined the commitment of the state to improving educational provision for young people. The Rutland Street Project for disadvantaged pre-school children, jointly financed by the Department of Education and the Van Leer Foundation, signalled the state's concern for young children from deprived backgrounds and its interest in researching new approaches to old problems. Séamus Ó hUallacháin, a primary inspector, was prominently associated with this pioneering development as one of a number of Department officials engaged in the project. A development of particular significance for the primary inspectorate was the introduction of special training courses for untrained teachers following an agreement with the INTO. From 1966, over a period of eight years, some 800 established untrained teachers were provided with special courses by inspectors so that in future, only qualified personnel would staff primary schools.

TOWARDS A NEW CURRICULUM

In 1967, the Department of Education was engaged in the preparation of a White Paper on education. Much of the attention was directed towards primary education and the curriculum of primary schools. Although the White Paper was not proceeded with, the moves to review the primary school programme gathered momentum. A key decision was taken when it was decided that it would be preferable to produce a new curriculum from first principles rather than endeavour to revise the old programme.[7] The work of drawing up the detailed plans for a new curriculum was assigned to the inspectorate and most of its members had involvement with its subsequent development. Some thirty individual committees of inspectors were assigned the tasks of devising different parts of the curriculum and the overall work was supervised and col-

6 Rialtas na h-Éireann, *Ár nDaltaí Uile-All Our Children* (Dublin Stationery Office, 1969).   7
S. de Buitléir, 'Curaclam Nua le h-aghaidh na Bunscoile', *Oideas*, 3 (1969), pp 4–12.

lated by an overarching steering committee of senior inspectors. This key group included Gearóid Ó Súilleabháin, S.B. Ó Cléirigh, Seán de Búrca, Seán Mac Tighearnáin and Séamus de Buitléir who were reporting directly to Domhnaill Ó h-Uallacháin, then chief inspector for primary schools.[8] A working document was circulated by the Department in 1968 and wide-ranging consultations took place with interested bodies including the INTO and the Teachers' Study Group. In general, positive reactions were offered in response to the working document though issues such as training for teachers, class size, and equipment and materials were noted as important in the context of successful transition to a new curriculum.

During this time, a large number of schools were involved in a pilot scheme directed towards assisting the process of drawing up the curriculum. Arranged through the inspectors and based on the inspectorial districts, some 600 schools nationally were selected to act as curriculum centres as new methods and new subjects were put on trial while certain grants for equipment and materials were given by the Department to underpin the pilot phase. Teachers from neighbouring schools were encouraged to visit the pilot schools for short periods to become acquainted with the new developments and much of this programme of visitation was overseen by the inspectors in their districts. One of the intentions that became apparent at this time was the idea that knowledge and insight into new curricular practice and principles would be spread by means of a new type of professionalism among teachers whereby they would familiarise themselves with emergent education theory and practice through visits and study. The notably new concept of 'teacher centres' was born and within a short time the first teacher centre was opened at Blackrock, Co. Dublin, in 1971. Primary inspectors were prominently associated with all of these developments. Another important element in the movement towards change was the arrangement of one-week residential summer courses for all principals during 1970 and 1971 and most school principals had an opportunity of learning about the impending changes in the curriculum. Between 1968 and 1971 some 4,000 school principals received summer courses to prepare the way for the new curriculum.[9] Inspectors were at the centre of all of this activity and, in many ways, there was a new type of dialogue between them and the teaching personnel who were most centrally involved in the new developments and movement in education. The whole character and atmosphere of primary education had been altered irrevocably within a short period and leadership of a high degree had been shown on the part of politicians and administrators at this time. The primary inspectors were very prominently associated with the remarkable leadership that was shown as a new curriculum began to take shape around 1970.

8 Thomas Walsh, 'A Critical Analysis of Curricular Policy in Irish Primary Schools, 1897–1990', unpublished PhD thesis, Maynooth, 2006, pp 405–06. 9 Ibid., p. 433.

THE PRIMARY SCHOOL CURRICULUM, 1971

Following an intensive period of work and preparation, the Primary School Curriculum was published in 1971 in two volumes providing a dramatically changed curriculum for primary schools. This was a unique moment in the history of primary education in Ireland in that the primary inspectorate had devised, in a remarkable manner, a change of curriculum that found widespread acceptance and welcome within the sector and among the various interest groups that were affected. After a long period of torpidity and stagnation, a strikingly new and different curriculum was produced from within a relatively small corps of inspectors. Every teacher in the service received a personal copy of the two-volume curriculum.

The curriculum drew on a wide range of sources for its inspiration. An eclectic approach was apparent in the curriculum detail both as regards subject areas and in the preamble to the overall programme. Influenced by practice in other countries that were visited by inspectors in the 1960s, borrowing from sources such as the Plowden Report and adapting theoretical principles from psychologists, philosophers and sociologists including Piaget and Dewey, the curriculum was tailored specifically for the national school system at a time of significant change and renewal. Written in a bilingual format of Irish and English, the curriculum handbooks bridged the important national cultural divide. The curriculum managed to move to centre stage the key principles that underpinned its overall philosophy and these included the notably new emphases of full and harmonious development of the child, allowance for individual differences, use of the environment for learning, activity and discovery methods, and the principle of integration of disparate subject areas. Though the curriculum had many parallels with the revision of 1900, for various reasons the inspectors of the time had little detailed knowledge of what had occurred long before.

The curriculum handbooks provided a lengthy rationale for the newly developed curriculum. The handbooks produced twin new aims for primary education in Ireland based on a child-centred ideology, 'to enable the child to live a full life as a child' and 'to equip him to avail himself of further education so that he may go on to live a full and useful life as an adult in society'. The handbooks provided a changed orientation for teachers, principals and schools and went on to outline syllabi and suggested teaching approaches for the full range of subjects specified. The full page colour photographs included in the handbooks provided a remarkable and new vision for teaching and learning.

In all there were seven areas specified for study. These included Irish, English, mathematics, social and environmental studies, music, physical education and art and craft. For Irish, the curriculum laid out a syllabus for Gaeltacht and Galltacht areas and the newly-developed language courses were suggested as a modern formula for the teaching of Irish. The curriculum in English similarly allowed for the difference anticipated in Gaeltacht areas while oral, reading and writing aspects of English were given a notably new and more meaningful orientation for the future. Mathematics incorporated activities and equipment in a distinctly new manner as part of the routine study of number and concepts while an experimental syllabus was also provided for those who wished to take on further challenge in the subject. Aspects such as art and craft and social and environmental studies brought fresh and interesting new activities into primary education promising a range of experience for children such as had not been seen in previous times. The aspiration was that the whole definition of school work and its organisation were to be transformed in a profound way.

It is reasonable to suggest that this was, in many respects, the finest hour so to speak of the primary inspectorate in its long history. Not alone had the inspectors produced the voluminous material given in the two handbooks, they had been associated with each and every step of the process from its initial formulation, through the process of piloting and dissemination, through to its launch with the publication of the Primary School Curriculum. It would be difficult to locate another period when the corps of inspectors rose to the challenge and seized the opportunity in so dramatic a fashion as occurred in the few years prior to 1971. The publication of the Primary School Curriculum was a historic moment for the primary inspectorate. More importantly, for the many children and young persons who would reap some of its benefit as the years went by, the emergence of a change of curriculum was of enormous significance as indeed it was also for the country as a whole. In effect, Ireland was to gain with a modern and progressive school curriculum at the foundation level of its education system.

THE IMPLEMENTATION OF THE CURRICULUM

A critical question from the moment of publication was the issue of implementation and the degree to which the state was willing and able to support the change of curriculum. At the level of providing for new schools, the state could boast that the new design of primary school buildings facilitated in good measure the implementation of a new curriculum. In the design of the new primary schools, there was tangible evidence of a notable new outlook for teaching and learning. For example, classroom area was dramatically increased, furniture was totally different being light and easily adapted to new styles of teaching and learning while staff rooms, library/medical inspection rooms and general purpose rooms were also provided to assist with a new approach to school work. The particular design plans of the late 1960s and 1970s made extensive use of large windows providing light in abundance. A notable initiative also at this time was the experimental concept of shared area teaching under which teachers could combine their efforts making provision for teaching and learning in linked teaching spaces that allowed for flexibility of approach for groups of pupils. A significant number of schools incorporated shared area classrooms at this period though the initiative did not command strong support among teachers. Prominently associated with this initiative was Conchubhar Ó Súilleabháin, one of the assistant chief inspectors during the 1970s. The initiative was never mainstreamed and faded away in the 1980s.

The state was very active in implementing the policy recommended by the Investment in Education team of closing small schools and providing central schools as local circumstances required in many places throughout Ireland. Here, the inspectors were very prominently involved as their knowledge and understanding at first hand provided the Department with expert advice about feasible amalgamations. The closure of small schools policy initiated by George Colley as Minister in 1966 was actively pursued for more than ten years and led to the provision of many new schools of larger size with the promise of better curricular and organisational performance. Typically, rationalisation of schools necessitated meetings with local communities and inspectors were commonly involved in explaining the benefits of agreeing to the rearrangement of primary school provision within parish boundaries usually. Some of the closures were accompanied by controversy and inspectors were sometimes perceived as responsible for the loss of small schools in localities that lacked other community resources. Inspectors of the period were well used to evening and night meetings in schools and parish halls where clerical managers, parents and community representatives argued the pros and cons of particular school buildings and possible replacements with varying levels of intensity and controversy. Usually clerical managers were satisfied to adopt a neutral approach and allow the inspectors to make the case for closure and amalgamation. Very often meetings were held in buildings that were old and in poor condition lacking electricity and water and having only the most basic facilities. Open fires and oil lamps were common at the time. In some cases, particular controversy accompanied the discussion and the advice given to inspectors facing such meetings included the suggestion to have motor cars parked to facilitate speedy departure should that become necessary! In a great many cases however, the prospect of better accommodation and school transport, guaranteed into the future, was sufficient to secure agreement to rationalisation. As a result, many central schools were provided and the primary school system benefited from fewer schools with better usage of teaching power and notably better conditions for educational provision. Over the course of about fifteen years from 1965–66 to 1980–81, the number of ordinary national schools fell from 4797 to 3295, a decline of over 31%.[10] By any standard this was a remarkable transformation in a comparatively short period. That this programme of school rationalisa-

10 Department of Education, *Statistical Reports for 1965–66 and 1980–81.*

tion proceeded relatively smoothly may be attributed to the fact that there was an obvious logic to the state's intentions. The inspectors of the time contributed notably with their local knowledge and insight into the individual circumstances of each locality. For many schools that did not agree to amalgamation, some years were to pass before they could benefit from building programmes to improve their conditions while the schools that did opt for amalgamation were usually the recipients of improved conditions relatively quickly. Eventually, in 1977, the government announced an end to the policy of amalgamation of schools thereby bringing to a conclusion the programme of school rationalisation. In future, the Department would consider further amalgamations in the light of the circumstances in individual cases. However, for quite a number of years after the policy had been concluded, new central schools were still being provided illustrating the time lag that was commonly a feature of provision for new buildings.

In only one case, in Dún Chaoin in the Gaeltacht area of Co. Kerry, was an amalgamation decision and school closure eventually reversed after a period of protracted controversy. Richard Burke as Minister for Education decided in 1973 to re-open the school that had been closed a short time previously in deference to a national campaign of protest about Irish language and Gaeltacht issues.

A marked effort to assist the implementation of the curriculum was made in the early years after the publication of the new handbooks. In 1972 and 1973, three-week residential courses were held in Maynooth College for teachers from all over Ireland. Selected by inspectors on the basis of seven teachers per district, and comprising 350 teachers in each of the two years, the nominated teachers were allocated to the various subject areas of the curriculum as nearly the entire inspectorate was involved with the presentation of lectures and workshops directed at new methods and new content for all aspects of primary school work as envisaged in the new curriculum. These courses were resourced very well in many respects and included for example guest speakers on particular facets of the new programme. An open and optimistic atmosphere was a feature of the course provision while conviviality and dialogue were additional features of note. The intention was that the course participants would be able to spread the message and benefits throughout the teaching workforce by means of seminars and other courses in the various districts around the country. The hope was that by means of teachers' centres and increasing professional discourse among teachers, expertise about teaching and learning would gradually spread and facilitate the implementation of the curriculum. In general, the Maynooth courses were highly regarded by participants who found the whole experience novel and stimulating. Expansion of staff in the Education Departments of colleges of education also helped to ensure that qualifying graduates were well prepared to implement the new curriculum.

The introduction of the new curriculum and the expansion of special education services necessitated greater involvement of the primary inspectorate in in-service training than ever before. Whereas in earlier decades only music and early childhood education had featured for in-service courses, the various subjects of the curriculum as well as special education issues were to be given more attention while courses for principals of large schools, courses for staffs of particular types of school and day-release courses for the teaching of Irish were also provided by inspectors. Though courses given by inspectors reached only a small percentage of teachers in any one year, the courses had significant benefits in various ways. Inspectors themselves benefited from providing courses as they needed to take particular interest in those areas that they promoted for in-service.

Economic circumstances took a turn for the worse in 1973–74 with the arrival of the so-called first oil crisis. Funding which had been relatively generously available in preceding years suddenly became very scarce as the country faced the sharp reversal of retrenchment in public finances. Money for in-service training of teachers was reduced notably by comparison with the immediate aftermath of the publication of the new curriculum. The Fine Gael–Labour coalition government from 1973 to 1977 was characterised by a notable tightening of the public finances and funding for primary schools did not match the expectations that the curriculum raised. Throughout the 1970s and 1980s, the inspectorate continued its programme of in-service courses in summer along with other providers such as the INTO and various agencies and individuals. These courses attracted significant numbers of teachers on a voluntary basis encouraged by the granting of three days personal vacation but there was no systematic and coordinated approach to in-service provision to endeavour to ensure the implementation of the curriculum. Pre-service provision did cater in many ways for the implementation of the curriculum and the introduction of the three year degree programme for all primary teachers, with effect for new entrants from 1974, may be understood to have strengthened provision.

Within the inspectorate, there was a realisation that there were enormous needs for in-service training for established teachers. A report commissioned within the primary inspectorate in 1980 concluded that the proportion of total expenditure on primary education allocated to in-service training was insignificant and noted that there was an alarming lack of balance between expenditure on pre-service and that on in-service training. The report recommended that there should be better co-ordination of in-service provision and suggested that an in-service training unit should be established within the Department to develop and oversee a national in-service training programme.[11] However,

---

11 *Report of the Committee on Primary Schools Inspection* (Collins Report), April 1981, unpublished, pp 51–54.

a lengthy period was to elapse before a development such as this was to be realised within the Department.

To a notable extent, the new curriculum did not progress quickly in terms of implementation in schools. The Department established teacher centres in key locations around the country and courses, seminars and lectures became a common feature of the time. Though the number of teacher centres gradually grew, the centres did not have rapid effects on school and classroom practice. Despite the good efforts of many individual teachers and many of those who were to act as trainers, curriculum implementation stalled to a significant degree. Whereas there were instances where teachers managed to implement certain aspects of the curriculum or develop particular elements with success, the overall levels of implementation remained low. Facilities in many schools lagged behind curricular aspirations, pupil teacher ratios remained very high, post-primary school expectations and parental demands remained unchanged. All of these factors influenced primary teachers' practice considerably and affected the implementation of the curriculum. For various reasons the Department did not follow through on system changes that were necessary to assist and ensure implementation.

Though many aspects of the curriculum did not translate into reality on the classroom floor so to speak, many elements of primary education began to evolve under the general influence of the new era. An important dimension to the changes that came in the wake of the curriculum was the new orientation within schools as some of the new emphases gradually caught on. The pattern of improved in-school organisation was supported by the publication of Circular 16/73 that spelled out in detail the duties of principals and listed those responsibilities that could be delegated within a school. Thus commenced in a gradual way the notion of delegated responsibilities especially within the larger schools. As time went by, more and more duties and obligations were allocated among teaching staffs and this became a new aspect of internal administration in schools. School equipment began to be a larger feature as spirit duplicators, projectors, radios, tape recorders and televisions became part and parcel of provision with the Department furnishing modest grants to aid the acquisition of equipment. A distinctive and engaging initiative of the Department was the direct provision to schools of a series of film strips dealing with aspects of history, geography, nature and heritage and some inspectors were involved with their production. Inspectors were strongly supportive of school initiatives to procure modern equipment to support curricular work. Boards of management were introduced in 1975 giving further impetus to sharing of duties and responsibilities and parents came to have a small but important role to play in the running of schools. During this time also, many teachers received the support of the Department for leave of absence to pursue specialised post-graduate courses so that over time, an important pool of expertise was distributed throughout the primary sector.

A significant change in the education system came in the wake of the change of curriculum as a more enlightened approach to school discipline took effect. An important amendment to the Rules for National Schools was made in 1982 by the issuance of Circular 9/82. In accordnace with a government commitment to the abolition of corporal punishment in schools and following consultations with representatives of teacher and managerial organisations, Rule 130 dealing with school discipline was amended. The use of corporal punishment and the use of ridicule, sarcasm or remarks likely to undermine a pupil's self-confidence were forbidden. Any contravention of the rule was to be regarded as conduct unbefitting a teacher and subject to severe disciplinary action. This was a development of particular significance and was closely associated with the minister at the time Mr John Boland.

THE PRIMARY INSPECTORATE IN THE 1970S AND 1980S

During the 1970s, primary inspectors continued to be recruited in much the same manner as before. The written examination was discontinued in 1974 and in future, an interview and oral Irish test were the main means by which candidates were assessed when vacancies arose. Interview panels normally included representatives from university education departments. Training continued to be a six-month period during which newly recruited inspectors devoted their time to shadowing experienced inspectors. At the end of this time, it was customary for a test inspection to be conducted by one of the most senior inspectors in the course of which the new entrant had to demonstrate appropriate judgment about a teacher in a general inspection. In 1975, the first woman to be recruited for many years joined the service. Though there was recruitment of a significant number of inspectors from time to time through the decade, there were occasions when vacancies went unfilled for protracted periods. Application was made for an increase in the staffing of the inspectorate and on foot of this, the Department of the Public Service gave studied attention to various aspects of the primary inspectorate's work from 1979 and issued a significant report in 1981.[12] Owing to staff shortages during this time, the great bulk of the inspectorate's work was concentrated on reporting on newly qualified teachers during their probationary period. Throughout this period and for many years, inspectors had a varied set of responsibilities that included work with training colleges, in-service courses, special education matters, examination work, planning and building questions, textbook approval, committee work, summer colleges in the Gaeltacht, as well as a wide variety of special visits to schools for official purposes.

12 Department of the Public Service, 'Survey of the Primary Schools Inspectorate of the Department of Education', 1 March 1981 (unpublished).

After a period of depleted staffing, a major backlog came to be filled at the beginning of the 1980s. Two competitions in 1980 and 1981 produced a total of 29 new appointments, an exceptional intake for the inspectorate in a comparatively short period. With the large influx of new personnel by 1981, the number of inspectors in the service reached an all-time high of 93 persons not counting the organisers for kindergarten, music and domestic economy, a number of whom were still in service. However, economic circumstances played a big part when the Department of Finance decided that some of those most recently recruited would be regarded as supernumerary until such time as natural wastage brought numbers down significantly. Thus, no inspectors were recruited again until 1992 by which time staff numbers had decreased considerably. The sporadic and unpredictable nature of staff replacement in the inspectorate continued to present difficulty for a protracted period.

Although the 1970s brought considerable change to the inspectorate, many elements remained unchanged. The annual conference became a standard feature and was usually held in January in Marlborough Street. The conference normally consisted of talks and presentations from within the Department itself and featured senior administrative and inspectorial personnel focusing attention on the leading issues of the day. Irish was the main language of all discourse throughout this time and outside speakers were few. Newly recruited inspectors were expected to serve a considerable apprenticeship before they would contribute to the discussions. At this time, the conference or ollchomhdháil was held in the conference room at the back of Tyrone House, a large pre-fabricated room amidst a veritable warren of pre-fabricated buildings placed between the extension to Tyrone House and Talbot House. Although the deputy chief inspector for primary still had a room off the foyer in Tyrone House, this was soon to be forfeited as other considerations came to take precedence. The fact that the Department itself had so many of its personnel housed in pre-fabricated rooms in Marlborough Street mirrored the situation throughout the country where many schools were reliant on pre-fabricated classrooms for many years to cater for pupils. After the number of inspectors increased from 1980, it became customary for the annual conference to be held in a Dublin hotel.

An event of national significance was the Drimoleague school dispute that led to a teachers' strike in 1976. The appointment of a principal teacher in the Co. Cork school was at the centre of a dispute between the INTO and church and state authorities. An element to the dispute was Rule 76 of the Rules for National Schools that determined eligibility for appointment as principal on the basis of five years' service as a teacher. Up to this time, inspectors were part of the process whereby short-listing for principalships was customary with inspectors indicating suitability of candidates for a particular post. Against the background of the newly-introduced boards of management, the selection of a principal in this school sparked off a major dispute leading to a prolonged strike of teachers in Drimoleague. When the INTO directed its members not to enrol children from the strike-bound school in neighbouring schools, a high court case was taken by parents and both the INTO and the Department were found to be in breach of constitutional provisions in favour of free primary education. The Department was obliged to provide free transport to neighbouring schools as a matter of urgency in January 1978. Subsequently the Department succeeded in its appeal to the Supreme Court that it had not failed in its obligation to *provide for* free education. Later, the Supreme Court issued landmark rulings in relation to the constitutional guarantees for primary education while the INTO had substantial damages awarded against it. The system by which inspectors played a part in indicating suitability of candidates for appointment as principal disappeared at this time and gradually the Rules for National Schools began to be more and more out of date as events moved faster than the Department's administration could keep pace with change. As it happened, the last edition of the Rules was issued in 1965 and despite occasional promises that updated versions of the Rules would be provided, the passage of time rendered this more and more unlikely given the vast array of change that had come into the primary system. Circulars were the standard way by which the system was administered during this period and there were many significant anomalous features as substantial parts of the Rules for National Schools became totally outdated. Of particular account was the fact that employment legislation superseded many elements of the rules so that in the course of time, the rules became quite anachronistic and hopelessly unsuited to modern requirements.

An important development in 1976 was the establishment of the Curriculum Unit. Located in House 28 in Marlborough Street, this was a tiny but important adjunct to the Department that was staffed by inspectors only and, initially, on a part-time basis. Dónall Ó Coileáin, then a divisional inspector, was the first primary inspector appointed to the Curriculum Unit. The primary section of the Curriculum Unit consisted of one room that was dedicated to various small-scale research projects into aspects of the implementation of the curriculum. Assisted by various committees of inspection personnel, the Curriculum Unit carried out surveys on the various subject areas of the curriculum. Though none of these survey reports was published, some of them found their way into circulation among teachers and researchers being distributed at courses or through contacts who were interested in particular features of activity. Frequently the surveys were very limited in their scope sometimes being directed mainly at inspectors' perceptions of what was happening in the schools as an indicator of how certain curricular aspects were implemented. All aspects of the curriculum were explored in these surveys. Sometimes particular aspects such as English and Irish were studied in conjunction with outside bodies, such as the Educational Research Centre in the case of English, and Institiúd Teangeolaíochta Eireann in the case of Irish. In

1984, a committee of primary inspectors was established to survey the overall implementation of the curricular principles embodied in the 1971 curriculum. Basing its work mainly on a questionnaire survey of all inspectors and a sample of 1,000 class teachers, the survey report concluded that both inspectors and teachers perceived that factors such as class size, time constraints, post-primary school expectations and inadequate materials were among the main difficulties inhibiting the implementation of the principles of the curriculum.[13] The Curriculum Unit was a key feature of the inspectorate's functioning throughout the period providing as it did a valuable source of information about the school system at a macro level. Although the research work in some respects was comparatively unsophisticated, there was a strong sense in which the primary inspectorate pursued its remit to provide accountability on the system it reported on. At the same time, the inspectors were regularly associated with, and assisted the research efforts of the Educational Research Centre and Institiúd Teangeolaíochta Éireann in exploring aspects of English reading and Irish. Of particular note in this context was the benchmark testing of standards of English reading in Ireland in 1972, 1982 and subsequent years. Similarly important was the development and use by inspectors of criterion referenced tests in mathematics developed in conjunction with the ERC and used for assessment of curriculum implementation in mathematics.

REPORT OF THE COMMITTEE ON PRIMARY SCHOOLS INSPECTION (COLLINS REPORT)

An especially influential report on inspection was produced in April 1981 by an internal committee of inspectors. Commissioned by the Deputy Chief Inspector for primary schools, this report made a number of important recommendations that crystallised strategic thinking within the service at this period. Chaired by Dónall Ó Coileáin, the committee gave studied attention to many of the deeper issues that affected the inspectorate. In the course of a carefully argued consideration of the issues that surrounded the primary education sector at the time, the committee's report provided forty-six recommendations for the future. The committee offered many notable points for the development and enhancement of the inspection service. Chief among these was the recommendation that an annual report on the operation of the system of National Education be provided in accordance with article 19 of the Ministers and Secretaries Act 1924. Also recommended was an annual review of the work of the primary inspectorate to be appended to the annual report in accordance with requirements in the Constitution. Among the many other proposals outlined in this report were recommendations that schools would be

13 An Roinn Oideachais, An tAonad Curaclaim: *The implementation of the principles of the primary school curriculum – perceptions of teachers and inspectors: Survey Report*, June, 1987, p. 66.

reported on every four years, that criteria of evaluation of teachers' work would be drawn up and uniformly applied, that standardised tests would be used as an aid to uniformity of evaluation, that a one-year probationary period would be introduced, that teachers would be appointed to Curriculum Unit committees for specific projects, that the chief inspector for primary schools would have a budget for the Curriculum Unit, and that a management committee for the primary inspectorate would be organised on a formal basis.[14] A number of these proposals were acted on in the course of succeeding years. For example, the probationary period was shortened to one year within a few years of the report's issuance. Similarly, criteria for evaluation of teachers' work were produced soon after. Most notably, annual reports of the primary inspectorate became a standard feature throughout the 1980s and provided much detailed analysis and commentary on the functioning of the inspectorate in these years. The Collins Report of 1981 was a particularly notable and significant achievement on the part of the primary inspectorate. Providing a valuable and meritorious vision of the work and role of the inspectorate, it had important influence over many subsequent developments.

Following the recommendation of the Collins Report, a major development came in 1982 with the decision to implement the provision first given in Circular 16/59 and repeated in 1976, to provide a school report at least once every four years in the case of each school. Replacing the former *deimhin bliana*, the *tuairisc scoile* was originally intended to furnish a short report on the work of a school once every two years. Owing to shortage of personnel, the inspectorate was able to report on just 4% of schools in 1979–80. Now that there was a full complement of inspectors and with sixty-five district inspectors in service in 1982, the inspectorate commenced a programme of inspection with the intention that approximately every four years, each school would have a report on its work. This was a significant departure in that a substantial effort was henceforth to be given to reporting on the work of each school as a whole rather than on the work of individual teachers. In effect this was giving emphasis to the overall efficacy of each school in delivering an education to the children in its care and signalled a commitment to seek to develop better combination and collaboration within schools. The effort given to implementing this programme of inspection was especially notable and within a few years, nearly every school in Ireland had been reported on in the School Report / Tuairisc Scoile format. However, depletion of staff and other demands on inspectors' time had negative effects on this programme so that by 1990, instead of a four-year cycle, about seven years was estimated to be the length of the cycle between inspections.[15] In the following years, the interval between inspections grew longer and longer as staff numbers in the

14 *Report of the Committee on Primary Schools Inspection* (Collins Report), April 1981, unpublished, pp iii–xiii.　15 *Report of the Primary Education Review Body* (Dublin: Stationery Office, 1990), p. 89.

inspectorate declined significantly. Notwithstanding the inability of the inspectorate to maintain its programme of inspection, an important feature was that inspection took on a new orientation with the whole school rather than the individual teacher as the key point of reference. Ultimately this was of particular significance and would eventually have system-wide effects for both primary and post-primary education. Looked at in its historical context, it was very much to the credit of the senior inspectors of the time that their leadership and ambition for education was so clearly focused and relevant at that juncture and that such good use was made of inspection staff when circumstances permitted.

During these years, the Department through its inspectorate division continued to provide certain in-service courses for schools during the school year on particular themes. The Irish courses were a particular focus during this period but other courses also featured as for example, in 1984, when school planning became a particular topic of note at day-release courses for principal teachers nationally. In the course of the subsequent decade, school planning became a major emphasis throughout the primary system, occupying much attention and leading eventually to widespread acceptance of the necessity for schools to formulate agreed plans to guide practice. This had a transforming and dynamic effect on planning in primary schools necessitating the involvement of whole staffs in the processes of drawing up and agreeing plans across the full range of school business. Increasingly, schools became more sophisticated in formulating realistic plans underpinning all features of their work and assisting the implementation of curricular aims. In many respects this was a major change in the operation of schools and it was hugely influenced and encouraged by the programme of school reports carried out from 1982. The close connection that primary inspectors had with schools ensured that practice in matters such as planning and curriculum were key aspects of how schools were evaluated and reported on. Principals and teachers by and large were anxious to show that they were following suggested approaches as best they could. As new features came into play, such as safety and welfare issues for example, schools were able to add on particular statements or policies illustrating school practice and intent. Thus, many new elements were incorporated into school plans in a relatively smooth manner as time and circumstances required. During this period also it became standard for schools to convene staff meetings from time to time so that planning aspects could be agreed in a collaborative manner. Given that many teachers were pursuing courses and post-graduate degrees throughout these years, it may be understood that an enormous growth in expertise and skills accrued to the primary system at this time. In many respects, the primary sector showed relatively good progress throughout these years and despite the widespread programme of inspection pursued throughout the country, few if any controversies about inspection came to public attention. This was an important aspect of the increased inspection programme in schools as teachers and the various agencies accepted the external evaluation provided by the inspectors. In many respects, this was indicative of a maturity and professionalism on the part of both teachers and inspectors.

During the 1980s, the primary inspectorate as a body devoted considerable attention to formulating criteria of assessment for use in schools. Prompted by the deliberations of the Collins Committee, the inspectorate sought to develop agreed criteria for assessment of the work of teachers and schools. Known as *Critéir Mheastóireachta* or criteria of evaluation, these took the form of statements of description applicable to work in classrooms across three identified domains of activity.[16] These were the teacher domain, the domain of interaction between teacher and pupil, and the pupil domain. The criteria provided statements in respect of each of the three domains for no less than six categories of merit. The merit grades were no grade, weak, fair, good, very good and excellent or to give the Irish versions as used gan grád, lag, maith ar éigean, maith, an-mhaith and sár-mhaith. The criteria were developed for all seven areas of the curriculum and amounted to a considerable corpus of work undertaken on foot of the Collins Report of 1981. The criteria were given in Irish for all subjects except English. Committees of inspectors provided the groundwork documents that were examined and amended at annual conferences in 1983 and further refined during 1984. Though the criteria were voluminous in some respects and perhaps too detailed in ways, they were nevertheless a valuable and praiseworthy attempt to produce agreed guidelines for evaluating school work with consistency and reliability. The criteria were developed with a responsible and conscientious intent to professionalise the work of the inspectorate in such a way that subjectivity would be lessened. As such, this was an important development in inspection in Ireland. However, though the criteria infused inspectors' approach to evaluation in schools, the criteria did not reach a wide audience nor were they ever formally adopted as part of the official practice of inspectors. Like many other inspection reports and documents of this period, the Critéir Mheastóireachta volume of 1984 languished within the Department and remained unpublished.

While the criteria did not come into widespread usage among inspectors, the inspectorate did build up a considerable body of experience in evaluating whole school functioning as part of the school report process. From relatively modest beginnings in terms of reportage on the system, the evaluation of schools took on a more sophisticated aspect as time went by. Primary inspectors gradually came to be proficient in evaluating many aspects of the functioning of schools including elements of management, organisation and planning in addition to the teaching and learning within classrooms. As time went by, all of these aspects became more refined and more sophisticated

16 An Roinn Oideachais, *Curaclam na Bunscoile – Critéir Mheastóireachta*, Nollaig, 1984.

partly as a result of inspection but also as a product of improved managerial and organisational skill within the schools.

ANNUAL REPORTS OF THE PRIMARY INSPECTORATE

Another development linked to the recommendations of the Collins Committee was the commencement of the practice of supplying annual reports on the primary system. For the first time in many years, an annual report of the primary inspectorate on the year 1982–83 was completed in 1984. This was a development of particular significance as it presented formally to the Minister, Gemma Hussey, a wide-ranging account about primary education and the role of inspection in the system. What made it especially significant was that for the first time in a long period, a report was produced to provide accountability about primary education as a matter of public importance within the Department. This report recounted many of the notable developments of the preceding twenty years including the inspectorate's engagement with special education, with school evaluation, with in-service, and with committee work inside and outside the Department. The report noted that primary inspection personnel were on full-time loan or secondment to units of the Department dealing with building and educational technology thereby reducing staff numbers. The report stated that 744 school reports were furnished in 1982–83 and that more than 30% of all teachers in the primary system had been reported on either as general inspections or as school reports. The report offered many interesting insights into aspects of the implementation of the curriculum, details about school size and accommodation, the provision of special classes, as well as observations and reflections concerning the primary sector and the role of inspection.

An annual report of the primary inspectorate became a regular feature from then on. Throughout the 1980s, the annual reports of the primary inspectorate provided an important source of information and commentary about many issues of note. Though the obvious intent of the management of the inspectorate was that these would be published or made available to a wider audience, this did not occur and like many other reports produced by the Curriculum Unit, they remained hidden from public view. In truth, this was reflective of the culture of the Department at this time as many notable reports and surveys were kept under wraps within Marlborough Street and interested parties were denied access to information about aspects of the system's functioning. In a sense, this was indicative of the duality under which the inspectorate was the professional wing of the Department but had in many respects a different culture and work ethic. To a degree, it may be suggested there was a lack of coherence and mutuality about the relationship in particular aspects of work and none more so than in regard to information about the school system as it functioned. There was a powerful inertia obtaining at this time in an era before transparency and openness were vaunted at a political level. It may be suggested also that this was not a good time for the inspectorate as an entity within the Department as in many ways the inspectorate was kept in a subsidiary position for various reasons. The fact that the various branches of the inspectorate were separate did little to assist its profile within the scheme of affairs at the macro level.

APPOINTMENT OF REVIEW BODIES

In many respects, the 1980s proved to be a fraught and difficult period for education. Economic circumstances produced stringent cutbacks, most obviously in primary education with the closure of Our Lady of Mercy College of Education at Carysfort and evidenced also in the issuance of Circular 20/87. This actually increased the pupil-teacher ratio and led to vigorous protests on the part of teachers. For the inspectorate, staff numbers fell steadily although the range of special business increased in various ways. An important development, facilitated by inspectors in 1985, was the election of a representative body for parents to be recognised as the National Parents Council (Primary). A development of particular significance was the appointment of two review bodies during the ministry of Mary O'Rourke at a time of notable tension between the government and teacher unions. The Review Body on the Primary Curriculum was set up in October 1987 with two divisional inspectors appointed to act as advisers for its work. In February 1988, the Primary Education Review Body was set up with the remit of examining the structures of primary education, demographic trends and the quality of primary education and school organisation. Its report issued in 1990 provided wide-ranging recommendations about aspects of primary education and its development. The report made a number of recommendations about the inspectorate especially as regards its staffing and functioning. The report cited with approbation the recommendation given by the Department of the Public Service that there should be a complement of 107 inspectors for primary education.[17] At the time, staff numbers had fallen to 81 and the programme of inspection as planned in 1982 had fallen into serious arrears.

By the time the Primary Education Review Body had finished its deliberations, the Department had commissioned Dr Clive Hopes to carry out an independent review of the entire inspectorate of the Department of Education.

17 *Report of the Primary Education Review Body*, p. 90.

OVERVIEW OF THE PERIOD TO 1990

This was perhaps one of the most remarkable phases in their history for the primary inspectors. At the forefront of a whole series of changes in the curriculum, in in-service, in the design of new school buildings, in the introduction of new equipment and technology, in the development of special education services, and in engagement with a broad range of issues and work, the primary inspectorate forged a formidable reputation for its efficacy and success. Despite its comparatively small size and a near-chronic problem with staff numbers, the primary inspectorate exercised an extraordinary influence over developments at this time of change and renewal in primary education. A number of individual inspectors contributed remarkably to many of the developments of the period and some penetrating leadership was demonstrated in particular ways.

The production of the Primary School Curriculum was perhaps the most spectacular event of the period but the commencement of the school inspection programme of the early 1980s was also an event of great importance. The formal reports begun in 1982–83 were also a development of great significance remedying to some degree the disturbing abandonment of this obligation for about twenty years. Although the primary inspectorate remained somewhat peripheral within the Department of Education in terms of power and influence, it continued to command a high degree of respect within the education system and in the public mind. In many ways also the primary inspectorate developed a better relationship with teachers and principals with a better sense of shared work and commitment to education and to children's interests during this period as old barriers and obstacles gradually disappeared. A development of special merit during this time was that going to school took on a more positive and more pleasing aspect for the children than it had done ever before in the long history of the national schools in Ireland.

13

The Secondary School Inspectorate, 1960–90

The secondary school inspectorate benefited from seven new recruits in 1962, at a time when the grade of Senior Inspector was introduced. This brought the complement of the secondary inspectorate to a total of twenty personnel, including one woman. The team incorporated the Chief/General Inspector, two Assistant Chief Inspectors, four Senior Inspectors, and thirteen Inspectors. The recruitment process at this time involved a short-listing of applicants, a one-hour interview, a two-hour essay type assignment in Irish, and an oral Irish examination. The Irish language requirements were the same for all candidates, regardless of their subject specialism. The induction of the new inspectors was limited to one-week shadowing an experienced inspector. At that time, the secondary inspectorate enjoyed high social status and a significant differential in salary from that of teachers. Accordingly, it proved an attractive career for many candidates. However, newly-recruited inspectors were expected to be diffident to their seniors, and were inducted into a sub-culture of 'not rocking the boat' by raising awkward questions of policy or practice.

The new recruits were badly needed for the work which lay ahead. Curriculum, examinations and school re-organisation became very prominent issues for the secondary school inspectorate from the early sixties. The inspectorate was caught up in the major dispute between the ASTI and the government regarding the latter's endorsement of an arbitration award on teachers' salaries on 19 March 1964. The ASTI strongly objected to the terms of the award and, at its Easter Congress in 1964, as a pressure on the government, instructed its members to withhold their services from superintending and examining at the certificate examinations of 1964. The Minister for Education, Dr Hillery, held firm stating that the Department would hold these examinations with or without the involvement of the teachers.[1] As the practice had evolved whereby secondary teachers had formed the vast majority of the cohort of supervisors and examiners for the Intermediate and Leaving Certificate examinations, their boycott of the examinations presented a major logistical and organisational problem for the Department of Education.

1 John Coolahan, *The ASTI and Post-Primary Education, 1909–1984* (Dublin: ASTI, 1984), pp 244–46.

The stage was set for confrontation on an issue which involved great public interest. In the event, it was the inspectorate which saved the day and by herculean efforts ensured that the examinations took place and were examined. While some misgivings were expressed about the quality of the script correction, the crisis was overcome and the concerns of pupils and their parents were allayed. The issue involved a massive increase in the examination workload of the secondary inspectorate, assisted by the two other branches of the inspectorate, and it was a tribute to their professionalism that despite tensions and difficulties, the public examinations of 1964 were safeguarded. In inspector lore it became known as 'blian na raice' (the year of the conflict), and it took a heavy toll on the inspectors, as well as leaving a residue of bitterness among teachers.

Following the establishment of Telefís Éireann, the national television station in 1961, aspirations were expressed about its potential for educational programmes. In 1964, Telefís Scoile was initiated and it began to produce programmes linked to the secondary schools' examinations syllabi. Secondary inspectors liaised with RTÉ in the planning of these programmes which reached a high standard. Inspectors sat in and advised on the rehearsals of presenters. However, after early successes, the scheme suffered from a lack of long-term planning in the context of divided authority, and problems of resourcing between the Department of Education and RTÉ. The nature of the technology at that time and problems in timetabling in schools also presented problems. Cutbacks in funding in 1975 led to severe curtailment of any new material for Telefís Scoile. In 1980, the Minister convened a representative committee on educational broadcasting to advise him on future policy. The secondary school inspectorate was represented on this committee. Its wide-ranging report, which was signed unanimously by all parties, was published in 1982. However, its recommendations were never implemented, and the promising work of the inspectors and staff involved in Telefís Scoile never reached its potential impact.

Despite difficulties associated with the contretemps with the ASTI examination boycott in 1964, more co-operative arrangements between inspectors, teachers and managers evolved regarding the modernisation of subject curricula. On 15 April 1963, the Department of Education announced that it intended to introduce major changes in the Leaving Certificate mathematics and science courses in the following September, for examination in June 1965. Representations by teacher unions and management representatives got the dates for examination deferred to 1966, and joint working parties were established between inspectors and teachers to revise the mathematics and science courses. The fact that Associations of Mathematics and Science Teachers had been recently established facilitated this process. Inspectors and teachers also co-operated in curriculum reforms affecting Latin, Greek and music in 1964. Inspectors and university staff engaged in providing in-service courses for teachers, particularly in what was then referred to as the 'New Mathematics'. To promote interest in science, particularly its experimental dimension, inspectors and teachers engaged in the establishment and operation of the Young Scientists Exhibition, then sponsored by Aer Lingus, which encouraged pupils and their teachers to enter science projects in the various competition categories.

Over the years, secondary inspectors organised and provided in-service training for teachers, particularly in the context of changes in syllabi. For instance, in the area of science teaching a variety of in-service courses were provided to meet different needs. To help expand the number of science teachers in the 1960s the inspectors provided summer science courses, in a number of regions, to non-science graduates, particularly members of religious orders, to top up their qualifications to certification level. For qualified science teachers, summer courses were provided by the inspectorate for many years, a notable location being the courses given in Kevin Street Technology College. The inspectors liaised closely with the Science Teachers Association, as did other inspectors with the appropriate subject associations.

A landmark development took place in 1965 with the establishment of fourteen Syllabus Committees, charged with the task of planning the introduction of the new three-year, common Intermediate Certificate courses, which were to be initiated in 1966. The Committees were representative of the inspectorate, the teachers and school managerial interests. The work of the Syllabus Committees was very successful, and revised subject syllabi came into operation in September 1966, with pupils from vocational and secondary schools sitting for the new examination in 1969. The new forms of partnership between inspectors and teachers in syllabus design improved professional communication between both agencies, albeit the major authority remained with the inspectorate, whose members chaired the Committees and with final decisions requiring Departmental approval. An inspector also acted as secretary to the Syllabus Committees.

In 1967, the process began of restructuring and re-modelling the Leaving Certificate Programme. At first, the Department had plans for radical changes. Among other changes, it sought the grouping of subjects at Leaving Certificate, orals and practicals were to be extended to more subjects, a third senior-cycle year was to be introduced leading to an 'Advanced Certificate'. As Donal Mulcahy commented, 'Taking Ireland's own tradition in second-level education into account, this was a task which would necessitate a challenge to conventional attitudes, structures and approaches'.[2] The Department of Education set up a Leaving Certificate Committee involving inspectorial, teacher and managerial representatives, and it held its first meeting on 10

2 D.G. Mulcahy, *Curriculum and Policy in Irish Post-Primary Education* (Dublin: Institute of Public Administration, 1981), p. 21.

January 1967. A set of proposals was prepared by October of that year. Also, at that time, Syllabus Committees were established to prepare new courses for individual subjects, chaired by the inspectorate. The work of the Syllabus Committees went ahead on a productive basis and course content was reformed for individual subjects, as well as content for some new subjects, which were being introduced. However, the early momentum for more radical changes in the Leaving Certificate structure slowed down and many difficulties arose regarding implementation issues. The overall outcome was that the range of subjects available was increased, reforms took place in subject syllabi, and an alphabetical grading system for examination results was introduced from 1969. However, more fundamental changes such as the grouping of subjects only became operative on a voluntary basis, rarely adopted; orals and practicals were not introduced as planned; and the Advanced Certificate was never introduced. Thus, in the course of negotiations with the stakeholders the aspirations for reform of the Department of Education were significantly modified. Teachers were only prepared to accept proposals for school-based oral and practical assessments of subjects if in-service education was provided, extra emoluments made available and a scheme of external monitoring introduced. Discussions continued on these issues through the early seventies between Departmental representatives and the teacher unions without success.[3]

Meanwhile, a study of the Leaving Certificate Examination by researchers Madaus and McNamara, in 1970, was critical of it because of reliability weaknesses, its over-reliance on the reproduction of factual data and the over-reliance placed on the results for entry to many occupations.[4] Inspectors considered that the report did not sufficiently take into account reforms which were underway. A further pressure was placed on the Leaving Certificate results when, in 1968, universities began to operate a points system to select candidates for entry into faculties where student numbers were restricted. Arising from the Madaus and McNamara report inspectors and syllabus committees sought to improve aspects of the design of the examination papers. In 1970, a Ministerial Committee was set up to review the Intermediate Certificate Examination, which included representatives of the inspectors and teachers. The interim (1973) and final reports (1975) of this Committee were highly critical of the Intermediate Examination and proposed its replacement by a radically changed system largely school-based, but under an elaborate standardisation structure.[5] The Committee set up the Public Examinations Evaluation Project (PEEP) to explore new modes of syllabus design and assessment, using mathematics and history as exemplar subjects.

3 Coolahan, *The ASTI and Post-Primary Education*, pp 260–63   4 G. Madaus and J. McNamara, *Public Examinations: A Study of the Irish Leaving Certificate* (Dublin: Educational Research Centre, 1970).   5 *Report on the Intermediate Certificate, Examination* (Dublin: Stationery Office, 1975).

Thus, it was clear, during the late sixties and the early seventies that much attention was placed on reforming the public examinations, which were now involving a fast-increasing, and more varied pupil cohort. Inspectors were centrally involved in this process and in the protracted debates which took place with teacher and managerial interests. However, the extent of reform achieved was limited, and while some improvements were achieved no radical changes were realised and the traditional framework of the public examination process was largely sustained.

In 1971, the Department of Education prepared a report (unpublished) on an independent examination board for all State Examinations. The new coalition government which assumed office in 1973, adopted as one of its policy proposals the idea of establishing an independent examination board with responsibilities for the design and operation of the public examinations. In July 1973, the Department of Education issued a draft constitution for the proposed Examinations Board and invited responses from interested stakeholders. A working party was convened by the Minister and held its first meeting on 9 November 1973. Following a number of meetings a new draft constitution was made available on 21 January 1974. Bearing in mind the central role played hitherto by the inspectorate in the administration of the examinations it was striking that on the envisaged Board, as of January 1974, inspectors only comprised 2 of the 26 person membership. Further meetings took place with groups such as the Heads of Universities. Eventually, the text of the bill for the Examinations Board was submitted to government in March 1976. In this version the Board was to comprise 5 university representatives, 3 from other third-level interests, 8 teachers, 4 representatives of school managements, and 5 appointees of the Minister, representing 'other interests'. No specific mention was made of inspectors, but the Minister would appoint 3 'Advisers', to the Board, who would not have voting rights.[6] In the accompanying Memorandum to government, it was stated, 'The pressure of numbers, had made it increasingly difficult for the Inspectorate to continue with their present degree of involvement in the examining processes, in addition to their other duties.'[7] This represented a significant recognition of the nature of the workload on the inspectorate, in the context of the expanding system, but also, a realisation that inspectorate involvement in the administration of the examinations was not regarded as integral to the work of the inspectorate. In the event, the plans were not proceeded with. The Minister for Education, Mr Richard Burke, was appointed European Commissioner in November, the government was defeated in the general election in 1977, and cutbacks in public expenditure had become operative. While the planned initiative was not brought to a conclusion at that time, the concept re-surfaced periodically, but only became a statutory reality on the establishment of the Examinations Commission in

6 NA, Box 2006/120/69. 7 Ibid.

2003, on quite different lines than that envisaged thirty years earlier. Contemporary proposals to set up regional education authorities which, if accepted, might have alleviated the growing work burden of the centralised Department of Education, were not implemented either.[8]

Curriculum reform and renewal continued to be an area of concern through the 1970s. With the support of the Department of Education the City of Dublin VEC (CDVEC) set up its Curriculum Developmental Unit, in association with Trinity College, in September 1972. A Curriculum Development Unit was also established in Shannon Comprehensive School in 1972, and in 1977 by City of Galway VEC. A range of curriculum development projects were initiated such as ISCIP, Humanities, SESP, Outdoor Education, Transition Year, Irish Studies, Nua Chúrsa Gaeilge. These involved the inspectorate in a variety of capacities as new curriculum options were explored to fit the aptitudes of the expanded pupil clientele.[9] Eventually, in 1977, a Curriculum Development Unit was established within the Department itself, to give a more co-ordinated role to the inspectorate in relation to curriculum change. The Curriculum Unit produced eleven reports on the evaluation of pilot projects and curriculum issues in the period 1977 to 1987 but their dissemination was curtailed and their impact limited. Among the curriculum development projects engaged in by the secondary inspectors was the Intervention Project, begun in 1985, which promoted physics in girls' schools, with the help of visiting expert teachers. This project formed a case study later for an OECD publication on the promotion of science subjects.

While the issue of curriculum and examinations was a prominent one from the mid-sixties through the seventies, it was just one of a range of strands of educational policy and development which involved the inspectorate. One of these was the government's policy on the restructuring of post-primary school provision. The main planks of this policy were the establishment of comprehensive schools, the up-grading of the vocational schools to full-cycle post-primary status, voluntary co-operation between local secondary and vocational schools, the conversion of some schools into junior cycle and others into senior cycle, based on the levels of their pupil intake and accommodation, and possible common enrolment between local schools. The Development Branch set up in 1966, within the Department, which included inspectors, prepared catchment area plans based on population trends and likely enrolments, and provided guidelines for the projected re-organisation of schools. To promote these policies school rationalisation meetings were held in different regional locations where the Departmental representatives sought to provide a rationale for school re-structuring. Inspectors participated in these meetings and added their professional weight to the argumentation. This was the first time Departmental officials went out to the public arena in a structured way, to discuss post-pri-

8 Coolahan, *The ASTI and Post-Primary Education*, pp 341–44.   9 Anton Trant, *Curriculum Matters in Ireland* (Dublin: Blackhall, 2007), pp 201–02.

mary school provision, as distinct from primary, with stakeholders and the general public. However, they were not always given a warm reception and, frequently, heated exchanges took place. In particular, the ASTI and the Catholic Headmasters' Association opposed the policy of junior and senior cycle schools and common enrolment, and were largely successful in their opposition. However, the large increase in pupil numbers which resulted from the introduction of the free education and transport scheme of 1967 led to larger schools, which lessened the Department's concern on the small size of school which had existed, and which had impeded the policy of promoting comprehensive curricula.[10]

In November, 1970, the Department published its policy on establishing a new type of school, 'the Community School'. These schools were seen as a development of the comprehensive school concept, specifically adding further dimensions to the schools' activities involving community use of the school resources, and the provision of adult education. The community school policy became very controversial. The Department of Education inspectors and administrative staff held many public meetings promoting the policy, but the atmosphere at many such meetings was charged and hostile. The community school concept was, in many ways, a radical and daring one, in the context of earlier traditions of Irish post-primary schooling. Despite the difficulties encountered, the Department set about establishing the first community schools in Tallaght and Blanchardstown, two expanding Dublin suburbs, in 1971, followed by other locations nationwide. Controversy continued on the selection of sites, the boards of management, deeds of trust, and denominational aspects for many years. However, these new schools benefited from strong Departmental support in design, resourcing and equipment and won the support of parents and the general public. Interestingly, no specific policy was designed for the inspection of comprehensive and community schools and they did not come under the secondary or vocational school traditions of inspection. No process of sanction existed for a teacher or school in this sector. Inspectors did represent the Department on the management boards introduced for comprehensive schools, and inspectors also participated on interview panels for staff appointments in both comprehensive and community schools.

Even in the secondary and vocational schools, actual school inspection, per se, began to decrease, influenced by the expanding role and workload of the inspectorate. Inspectors were increasingly called on to assist in administrative work – committees, interview panels, writing politicians' speeches, preparing answers for parliamentary questions etc., in addition to their traditional professional work relating to schools, curricular policy and the examinations. Secondary school inspectors had also been members of the Secondary

10 Ibid., pp 257–59.

Teachers Registration Council since its establishment in 1918. With the greatly increased applications for teacher registration the work of this body became very extensive over the years, involving considerable work by the inspector members. The secondary inspectorate also conducted the oral Irish tests of applicants for registration. Eventually, with the establishment of the Teaching Council, in 2005, the Registration Council for Secondary Teachers ceased to exist.

Despite the decline in the presence of inspectors to evaluate the work of secondary schools, periodically members of the ASTI objected to their teaching being evaluated by inspectors observing their work in the classroom. Eventually, in January 1980, it came to a head when a group of teachers in a school objected to being asked to teach in front of an inspector, and referred to ASTI policy on the matter. A series of three meetings, beginning in April 1980, was arranged between the senior inspectorate and officers of the ASTI, which discussed the whole policy on inspection in some detail. The meetings were cordial but the kernel of the disagreement was that while the inspectorate insisted that it was an integral part of its role to appraise the quality of teaching, among other aspects of the pupils' school experience, the ASTI held that as qualified professionals its members should not be subject to such assessment by the inspectorate, except on a voluntary basis.

In an effort to place the issue of appraising teacher performance within the broader educational role of the secondary school inspectorate, Seán Mac Carthaigh, Deputy Chief Inspector (Secondary), drew up a memorandum on the rationale, approach and tradition of the inspectorate's work. It was a detailed, clear statement with eight sections, and conciliatory in tone. It was sent to the ASTI who replied formally on 28 April 1982. It commented on each of the eight sections but took exception to each instance where teacher appraisal was referred to. It did not accept the Department's view on inspection of teachers' teaching skills and concluded by stating its position 'the teacher may or may not decide to carry on teaching in the presence of an Inspector'.[11] Thus, the ASTI retained its viewpoint that it could only be on a voluntary basis that a teacher could be expected to teach and be observed by an inspector. This central issue in relation to inspection policy and procedure was not resolved at the time and remained an ambiguous area in the process of inspection. However, as the years went on the practice of school inspection on the older model of inspectorial visits fell into considerable decline. The disputed matter was allowed to drift until the restructuring of the inspectorate in the late 1990s, and new social partnership agreements became operative, when it was decided that teacher appraisal came within the terms of national agreements, in 2004. Interestingly, the Chief Inspector, Eamon Stack, and some of his senior staff met with the executive committees

11 Files in the Department of Education and Science (DES Files) (uncatalogued).

of the ASTI and the TUI on separate occasions, to help clarify and decide this important issue, and also on whole school evaluation processes.

Inspectors participated in a range of committees set up in the late 1970s and early 1980s. These included the Pupil Transfer to Post-Primary Schools Committee, the Educational Broadcasting Committee, the Teacher In-Service Committee, the Adult Education Commission, the Pupil-Discipline Committee. Despite the attention focussed on these issues little action was taken on them, the reports coinciding with a period of cut-backs in educational expenditure and the lack of prioritisation of educational development and reform by the government. Inspectors also worked on the *White Paper for Educational Development*, published by Minister John Wilson in December 1980. This was Ireland's first white paper on education, but it proved to be a disappointment, focussing more on past developments than acting as a blueprint for future educational policy. One of its proposals, that of setting up a Curriculum Council, was more elaborated on in the programme of the coalition government which assumed office in December 1982. It declared the intention of setting up a Curriculum and Examinations Board (CEB). In June 1983, Minister Hussey set up a committee to advise her on the establishment of this Board. The Curriculum and Examinations Board was set up on an ad hoc basis in January 1984, with the stated intention of its being statutorily established within the lifetime of the government. It was intended that the statutory board, when established, would take over responsibility for the public examinations.

The inspectorate would seem to have had mixed feelings about the establishment of a Curriculum and Examinations Board. Some considered that the allocation of such areas to an external agency would seriously affect the status and *raison d'etre* of the post-primary inspectorate. At a meeting of secondary inspectors on 8 March 1983, Mr Seán MacCárthaigh informed them that a number of meetings had taken place between the senior inspectorate and Minister Hussey and that 'the Minister was determined to go ahead with the proposal.' On the one hand, such a Board could be seen as allowing for an alleviation of the inspectorate's workload. For instance, an internal memo by MacCárthaigh remarked to the Assistant Secretary, 'we have an outline agenda for the development of Floor 3 (the secondary inspectorate) which can be activated once the bulk of the examination work has been transferred to the CEB'.[12] On the other hand, the rather exclusive control the inspectors had exercised on these central features of the education system was being significantly diminished. In a sense, the establishment of the CEB might be viewed as a vote of no confidence in the inspectors' performance, and the inadequate level of reform which had occurred under their watch. The CEB was established in January 1984 and an inspector was appointed to it and inspectors

12 NA, Box 2006/120/69.

acted on its sub-committees. There they participated in the discussions, debate and reports of the CEB. The policy proposals of the CEB required the endorsement of the Minister, who, of course, could consult her inspectors on such proposals.

Meanwhile, the Curriculum Unit within the Department had been experiencing difficulties. The Unit was established in 1977 with the significant terms of reference:

(a) – To review and evaluate the structure, organisation, appropriateness and implementation of current mainstream curriculum, with a view to developing a philosophy and framework for curriculum development appropriate to the needs of our time.

(b) – To recommend, support co-ordinate and evaluate initiatives in curriculum development.[13]

It was envisaged that the Unit would have a full-time staff of 8 members – a director, 2 Divisional Inspectors (Primary), 4 post-primary inspectors, one at Senior level, and a psychologist. However, this did not come to pass and by 1981 there were only two inspectors working in the Unit on a full-time basis, and a psychologist on a part-time basis. None of the inspectors allocated to the Unit were replaced within the inspectorate corps. The Unit had no administrative support structure, and it had no separate budget vote to enable it to plan and execute its programme of work. It applied to the Department's Research Committee for its funding. Despite such limitations, it did considerable work on curriculum issues and projects.

The Unit had a steering committee, chaired by the Chief Inspector, and its members comprised about 12 other staff, predominantly senior inspectors from the different branches. At a meeting in February 1981, the steering committee expressed grave concern that the inadequate staffing and resourcing of the Curriculum Unit were seriously impeding its ability to fulfil its remit. The Chairman raised the problems at a meeting with the Secretary and Assistant Secretary. Subsequently, the Minister for Education, Mr John Boland, attended a meeting of the Steering Committee on 19 October 1981. He praised the work of the Curriculum Unit and emphasised its importance. He indicated that he envisaged it working in harmony with the proposed new Curriculum and Examinations Board, and that he would establish a budget vote for the Unit. He indicated that he was aware of the staff shortages, and also of the staff shortfalls in the inspectorate in general. Despite the embargo which had been imposed on new recruitment in the public service, he stated that he had discussed with the Department of the Public Service the need for an exceptional allocation to fill vacancies which had arisen within the inspectorate in

13 DES Files (uncatalogued).

general.[14] Despite such positive assurances, neither the Curriculum Unit nor the inspectorate benefited from extra staffing, and the embargo continued to affect seriously staffing within the inspectorate. Mr Boland lost office in March 1982, as the Fine Gael–Labour coalition government lost the general election to Fianna Fáil. The coalition government was returned again to power for the period December 1982 to March 1987, with Ms. Gemma Hussey as Minister for Education from 1982 to February 1986. Following the establishment by her of the Curriculum and Examination Board in January 1984, the Curriculum Unit agreed in March 1984 to make some of its documentation available to the CEB, and a liaison committee was established between the Department and the CEB, but co-operation was not enthusiastic. The Curriculum Unit operated with two sub-sets – one for primary and one for post primary schooling. While staff shortages impeded the Curriculum Unit from achieving its programme objectives, it continued to be active and became closely linked with the programmes facilitated by the new European Social and Structural funding, linking education to the world of work.

It was planned that following two years of operation on an ad hoc basis that the CEB would be established as a statutory body. Legislation was prepared in 1986 with that intent, but a government re-shuffle in March 1986 saw Ms. Hussey replaced in the education portfolio by Mr Pat Cooney. The planned legislation was not proceeded with. Following the election of a Fianna Fáil government in March 1987, the new Minister, Ms Mary O'Rourke, reconsidered the situation of the CEB. In September 1987 she decided to abolish the CEB, and went on to replace it by a new body, the National Council for Curriculum and Assessment (NCCA), as a purely advisory body to the Department of Education.[15] This was a significant policy decision in that it clearly demonstrated that decision-making on curricular issues, and responsibility for the public examinations remained firmly under the Department of Education's control. The professional staff within the Department of Education charged with most of the work in these areas were the inspectors. From its establishment in 1987, inspectors were allocated to work with the NCCA, and its subcommittees on areas under its remit. Mr Albert Ó Ceallaigh, an inspector who had worked in the Department's Curriculum Unit, who had been appointed first Chief Executive of the CEB in 1984, also became the first Chief Executive of the NCCA. On occasion, some disagreement occurred between the inspectors and the views of the NCCA, as a whole. For instance, as regards the science syllabus, on 16 September 1988, Mr Pádraig Ó Nualláin, as Assistant Secretary, wrote to the Chief Inspector as follows:

> The Minister informed me today that she decided to accept the proposed syllabus in Science. When I referred to the objections of the

14 Minutes of meeting of 19 October 1981, in DES files (uncatalogued).   15 Áine Hyland, *The Curriculum and Examinations Board: A Retrospective View* in G. McNamara, K. Williams and D.

inspectors, the Minister said that the inspectors had made their views known at the Course Committees and were outvoted that was the end of the matter – she did not want people coming to her with objections afterwards.

In view of this principle I take it that there is no point in future in seeking the views of the inspectors on proposed syllabuses (following the deliberations of the NCCA).[16]

This was an important point which indicated to the inspectors that they did not have a veto on the recommendations of the NCCA committees of which they had been a part. The inspectors had sought to delay the introduction of the new science syllabus because they considered it needed further preparatory work. Nevertheless, the recommendations of the NCCA required the approval of the Minister prior to implementation and, in practice, NCCA proposals did not always receive a *carte blanche*.

In January 1984, Minister Hussey had published, *Programme for Action in Education, 1984–87*. This set out 'the government's approach to the priorities to be met in education over the next four years'.[17] Part of the Minister's aim in publishing the *Programme*, was to inform the public and be more transparent on the policies being pursued. This was also emphasised in her decision to publish annual progress reports on the success rates of policy implementation. She was also keen that the post-primary inspectors would resume a tradition, abandoned in the sixties, of publishing reports on the work of the schools. She asked her senior officials to explore this issue with the inspectorate. In so doing, it brought to the surface a key problem affecting the post-primary inspectorate at that time, namely that due to insufficiency of staff and extension of duties, visitation to schools to evaluate the work therein had declined significantly. The primary inspectorate had been submitting annual reports to the Secretary of the Department for a number of years, but these were used for internal Departmental reference, and were not published. In a memo, dated 30 April 1985, the Deputy Chief Inspector for secondary schools recorded, 'The Floor 3 (Secondary) inspectorate cannot at present do much more than try to keep the certificate examination system running and operate a limited number of in-service courses and action-research projects, and deal with syllabus work, emergencies and various other Departmental priorities. The examinations alone could provide full-time work for our very small inspectorate establishment. The inspection of schools is at present quite inadequate and fairly haphazard. We have not even managed to begin the much-needed overhaul of inspection and reporting procedures. The publication of an annual report should not be attempted until such issues are

Herron (eds), *Achievement and Aspiration* (Dublin: Drumcondra Teachers' Centre, 1990), pp 1–18. **16** DES Files uncatalogued. **17** *Programme for Action in Education, 1984–87 (Pl. 2153)* (Dublin: Stationery Office, 1984), p. 2.

put right.'[18] A report to the Chief Inspector on 3 May 1985, called for the formulation of a policy on inspection, and pointed out that 'reporting is a product of inspection and no amount of reporting can compensate for first-hand observation and evaluation of the actual teaching process.' It went on to state, 'It seems axiomatic that, unless there is a solid foundation of classroom inspection within the context of School and/or Scheme Reports, the game might not be worth the candle if it so happens that national reports are over skimpy and superficial in content.'[19] This statement highlighted the fundamental weakness, that in the absence of more satisfactory and regular inspectorial evaluation of the work of schools, the publication of national reports on the progress of the system would lack credibility. If inspectors were more desk-bound than school-based, on what basis could they report on the quality of schooling, in its various dimensions? Assistant Secretary Ó Ceallacháin advised the Minister that prior to the publication of an annual report consultations should also take place with teachers and school managements. The Minister accepted the advice but urged, 'Let's expedite it (the process)'.[20] However, the problems were not resolved, and while the primary inspectorate prepared reports in the 1980s, no overall reports on the inspectorate were made available until the early 1990s, and these had limited circulation.

The problems adverted to in the context of inspectorial reports were a major issue for the inspectorate by the mid-eighties, and were of fundamental importance to its capability of fulfilling its roles. The problems affected all the branches of the inspectorate, but are, perhaps, best illustrated in relation to the secondary inspectorate. On 3 March 1982 Chief Inspector, Dr Liam Ó Maolcatha, wrote directly to the new Minister for Education, Dr Martin O'Donoghue, on the difficulties being encountered by the inspectorate among which were that there was no inspector for German or Physics, only one inspector for French and two for mathematics.[21] As early as May 1982, the Deputy Chief Inspector for secondary schools, Seán MacCárthaigh, prepared a memo which as well as setting out the great array of functions being carried out by the inspectorate, raised important questions about the command structure which had developed within the Department. He stated:

> The inspectorate is seriously concerned about the lack of a clear command-structure within the Department. Their view is that the Chief Inspector is the professional head of the Department and that they should be working through him, and through him alone, to the Runaí and the Minister … Indeed the inspectorate finds it incredible that, in a matter of such national and human significance as education, the relevant state department should have become dominated by administrators rather than professionals. They are acutely conscious that their

18 NA Box 2006/120/69.   19 DES Files (uncatalogued).   20 NA Box 2006/120/68.   21 Des Files (uncatalogued).

professionalism is being used, and often misused, by administrators, who, however necessary their skills and however devoted their service, simply do not and cannot possess those insights into education that only professional training and experience can confer. The inspectorate believes that the role of the skilled administrator should be to facilitate and carry through policies decided upon by the Minister in the light of the best professional advice available to him. It is entirely unacceptable, too, that new Departmental agencies should be headed by administrators, with the inspectors working under the direction of such people. It is no exaggeration to say, therefore, that the post-primary inspector is disillusioned: it is not simply for reasons of salary (intolerable though the situation has become) that hardly any inspector or even senior inspector working to Floor 3 in Hawkins House is not actively looking for another job at the moment.'[22]

Among other things, this statement reflects the tensions which tend to exist between administrators and professional staff in departments of government. Quite clearly, this statement indicates the inspectorate's feelings of concern and disenchantment at its peripheral rather than central role in the policy process. In the inspectors' view, in the way the Department had evolved, their work tended to be viewed as very diverse, and conducted at the behest of its administrative arm, which occupied a centre-stage position. On the other hand, the administrators were faced with policy and budgetary issues over the spectrum of educational sectors and, sometimes, they considered that they received inadequate policy advice from the professionals, whose range of experience was limited, and whose expertise tended to lie in curricular subject specialism. There was also some tension on promotions within the Department. While inspectors had the right to apply for positions such as Assistant Secretary or Secretary, the administrative staff could not apply for posts such as Deputy Chief or Chief Inspectors. Inspectors could hope to obtain two of the five Assistant Secretary positions. Some aspects of the tension were to be expected, but it is also true that the command structure was obfuscatory and needed re-definition.

The tone of disillusionment among the inspectorate in the eighties was due to insufficiency of staff, working conditions, lack of clarity on role and, it would seem, lack of appreciation of their work by the higher echelons in the Departments of Education and Finance. As well as the impact of the public service embargo on appointments, introduced in 1981, which hit the inspectorate harder than other areas of the Department's workforce, the inspectorate also suffered from the departure of some experienced staff to positions outside the Department, which gave them more scope for their expertise.

A significant position paper on the 'Role and Function of the Inspectorate in the Development of Education in the Republic of Ireland,' was prepared in

22 Ibid.

the Department, in 1985. While unsigned, it would seem from internal evidence that this significant position paper on the inspectorate was prepared by Seán Mac Cárthaigh, Deputy Chief Inspector for Secondary Schools, and was partly based on questionnaire returns from the inspectorate. In the introduction to that questionnaire he pointed out that no relationship had been kept between the huge increase in post-primary pupil numbers and the number of inspectors, and that no attention had been paid to the vast increase in the range and differentiation of duties which had been allocated to the inspectorate. It is important to note that the inspectorate was analysing the situation in which it found itself and was seeking remediation for its difficulties at that time.

The paper set out 'Current trends/functions of the inspectorate', against a contextual treatment of the education system at the time. It specified the work of the inspectorate under sixteen headings, and the range of activity is illuminating. They were as follows:

Inspection

Among the many functions of the inspectorate the following are especially important:

(i) *Inspection of schools, colleges courses, etc., on a regular basis:*
Individual primary, post-primary and special schools, third-level colleges, youth and community centres are visited.

(ii) *Curriculum Development*
Initiating and/or participating in innovatory and experimental programmes/pilot schemes. Evaluating such programmes and, where appropriate, directing their dissemination.

(iii) Inspection of the work of Teachers on Probation.

(iv) Provision of a *School Report* annually, at primary level, on at least 25% of all schools in an inspector's district.

(v) *Information*
Reporting to the Minister and the Department on the educational situation in the field. Preparing documentation on educational matters for restricted or general use.

(vi) *Syllabus Development*
Chairing or participating in the work of syllabus committees.

(vii) *In-service Training*
Organising, directing, participating in courses and seminars for teachers.

(viii) *Examinations*
The post-primary inspectorate constitutes the professional core of the national second-level examining authority which is extremely time-consuming and highly-skilled work.

(ix) *Special Education*
Inspectors advise on the establishment of special schools and classes, on the provision of remedial education and on the placement of children with special learning difficulties.

(x) *Serving on Committees*
Boards of Management of Comprehensive Schools, various departmental or interdepartmental committees.

(xi) *Conferences*
Participating in conferences at home and abroad.

(xii) *Publications*
Editing 'Oideas', the Department of Education journal, production of discussion papers, articles, guidelines reports, etc., on various aspects of educational practice.

(xiii) *Public Relations*
Offering a personal liaison between the Department of Education on the one hand and schools, teachers, various organisations, public bodies and committees on the other. In this way contacts are built up with a wide range of outside interests as well as with other Government Departments and Semi-State bodies.

(xiv) Contacts with colleagues from other countries at national/international level.

(xv) Preparation of speeches for the Minister or Secretary.

(xvi) *Acting as Local Representative for the Minister*
As well as consulting with managers or schools it is standard practice for the inspector to act as liaison between the Minister and local bodies (of Regional Health Boards, Vocational Education Committees, County Library Committees) parents' groups or other voluntary associations.

In the course of a section on the inspectorate's 'method of working', the position paper emphasised with regard to 'Goals' the centrality of school inspection:

There is a certain minimum level of inspection below which the monitoring process is so incomplete that it lacks credibility. At that point, the work of the inspectorate is frustrated both in its primary and secondary functions as everything that an inspector does depends on his acquaintance with performance in the schools.

The paper reiterated the points made in 1982 by MacCarthaigh regarding the inspectors' concern 'about the lack of a clear command-structure within the Department' and dissatisfaction at the administrators' roles. The position paper also stated:

> There is a grave shortage of inspectors particularly at post-primary level and this has a serious detrimental effect on the health of the inspectorate and a curtailment on effective advisory work in schools. To offset the short – and long-term effects of this serious problem it is incumbent on the Department to initiate a programme of recruitment.

Furthermore, recognising that inspectors 'now function in an increasing dynamic and complex educational environment', the call was made for greater in-service courses and the provision of 'intensive advanced courses in counselling and interpersonal skills', for inspectors. It also drew attention to inadequate promotion prospects within the inspectorate. The position paper stated that in 1985, there were 164 male inspectors and 26 women in post in the whole inspectorate, with 54% of staff aged 45 or over.[23]

The problems facing the post-primary inspectorate were also taken up in a memorandum prepared by Denis Healy, Assistant Secretary, on 22 November 1985. He also itemised the great range of activities which inspectors were expected to engage in, under eleven headings. On the insufficiency of inspectorial staff, he stated:

> The numbers of pupils and teachers during the period 1972/'73 and 1982/'83 increased by 38% and 59.3% respectively at second level. There was no corresponding increase in the number of post-primary inspectors. Indeed the allocated number of recruitment grade inspectors remained at 57 during this period. In recent times due to the public sector embargo, it was not possible to recruit personnel to inspection posts vacated by inspectors resigning or exiting from the inspectorate. At present the number of inspectors on the recruitment grade is 46. (The number was to decrease further to 34 by 1990).[24]

Healy pointed out that the teacher to inspector (recruitment grade) ratio had been 209 to 1 in 1972–73, but had deteriorated to reach 333 to 1 by 1982–83. As an example of the seriousness of the position he pointed out that there was but one post-primary inspector of geography to inspect about 7,500 classes, even if he could devote all his time to this. There were only 3 inspectors of Irish and 2 of mathematics, at recruitment level, which would involve inspection cycles of 21 inspection-years in duration. Healy stated unambiguously, 'It is necessary to have increased number of inspectors in order to improve the quality and efficiency of instruction in second-level schools, to evaluate the effects of curricular innovations and to identify ways and means of improving the cost effectiveness of the system.' To have a reasonable

23 Ibid. 24 Ibid.

chance of satisfactory school inspection he calculated that 110 post-primary inspectors would be required, at recruitment grade.[25]

Such authoritative statements of the position of the post-primary inspectorate in the mid-eighties yielded no significant improvements. In the difficult national financial context of the time, it would appear that the Department of Finance did not view the dilemma of the inspectorate, nor, perhaps, value its role so as to give it a priority in treatment. It was not an issue which gave rise to public or political discourse, the principals and staff continued to run the schools, the public examination system operated without any major problems, so that the added value which the inspectors might give to the quality of school education would seem not to have weighed heavily with those in charge of the public purse strings, and, indeed, may not have weighed too heavily with the heads of the Department of Education in their balancing of priorities. There is evidence that the inspectorate articulated its case; it is not clear that the quality of its political networking was such as to yield desired results. The secondary inspectorate as a unit could also be seen to have been rather reactive and passive in relation to the situation they faced, whereas the primary inspectorate tended to be more proactive and innovative in similarly difficult circumstances. If the Curricular and Examinations Board had been statutorily established, as intended in 1986, it would have alleviated some of the work burden of the inspectorate. When policy changed on this, in 1987, this dashed any such hopes, and the problems continued.

Ironically, in 1986, the Department of the Public Service issued a White Paper – 'Serving the Country Better'. What became known as a 'two desk' provision was part of this paper. Paragraph 2.17 of the White Paper stated, inter alia, that:

> The excessively hierarchical work patterns, of much of the Civil Service will be changed. Fewer people in the line of command will deal with a single work item. Except in unusual circumstances, no item of work will pass across more than two desks.

Each state department was expected to carry out an in-depth review of working arrangements, and ensure that action was taken to implement the principle. As part of this process, Dr Liam O'Maolcatha, Chief Inspector, was asked to report on the situation within the inspectorate. Both the content and tone of the report by Seán Mac Cárthaigh pertaining to the secondary inspectorate are interesting, if unsurprising. He remarked in his report to the Chief Inspector, on 2 April 1986, 'The problem occasioned by the chronic understaffing of the inspectorate and by its ever-growing workload is one of underconsultation rather than the reverse.' His account of the mode of operation by the inspectorate at this time is revealing:

25 Ibid.

Individual members of the post-primary inspectorate tend to be subject specialists who are grouped into faculties ... In order to maximise
the value of the expert advice and work of the individual inspectors,
the faculties are encouraged to work together as much as possible and
to achieve consensus before reporting to the relevant Assistant Chief
Inspector ... Where possible, the Assistant Chief Inspector comes to a
decision and the matter goes no further; but this is not always the case.

The Deputy Chief Inspector is the director and general co-ordi-
nator of all work carried out on a Floor 3 (secondary branch), distributing tasks and responsibilities to or through the two Assistant
Chiefs, or directly to senior and line inspectors. He is directly and
personally responsible for advising on policy and implementing it (as
appropriate to floor 3). By tradition, however, he and the Assistant
Chief Inspectors operate as a triumvirate, and, on major issues, consult with one another and work towards consensus. By tradition, too,
every effort is made to avoid duplication of work. Unfortunately,
there is also a tradition that everything of importance must pass
through the hands of the Deputy Chief Inspector ... The Deputy
Chief Inspector and the Assistant Chief Inspectors have to act as
their own secretaries ... The position is complicated by the fact that
the Deputy Chief Inspector, and indeed the two Assistant Chief
Inspectors, have to work to a dual management structure (the Chief
Inspector and an Assistant Secretary). It is not always entirely clear
who is responsible for what, or who has the right to make decisions:
the Chief Inspector, the Assistant Secretary, the Deputy Chief
Inspector, the Assistant Chief Inspectors.[26]

This account provides a valuable insight on the internal mode of operation of
the secondary school inspectorate, exemplifying a lot of effort at co-ordination and teamwork, and a dedication to duty, but with inadequate secretarial
support and a damaging lack of clarity on areas of responsibility for decision-
making. The report concluded, 'In such a situation, the two-desk principle
cannot be fully implemented.' It went on to make the point, 'A management
study is called for, as a first step towards the rationalisation and streamlining
of structures and procedures.'[27] From the evidence available this was a very
legitimate call with regard to the inspectorate at that time. The call, however,
went unheeded and the inspectorate continued to suffer from many difficulties and constraints until a restructuring took place about a decade later, in
the last years of the century.

26 Ibid.   27 Ibid.

14

The Vocational Inspectorate, 1960–90

In his book on Irish educational development from 1957 to 1968, *A Troubled Sky,* the former Secretary of the Department, Sean O'Connor, remarked of the Technical Instruction Branch, 'The Technical Instruction Branch did not confine itself to taking 'the knock out of the pipes', but was a full and active partner with the vocational education committees in policy and curriculum development in the vocational education sector'.[1] The vocational school inspectorate was the professional agency within that Branch who had always adopted a pro-active stance in association with the CEOs in promoting the values of vocational education. During the 1960s, vocational and technical education were targeted as areas of policy priority by government and the inspectors were to experience a supportive, developmental framework for these forms of education. They readily grasped the opportunities which were opening up.

In 1962, Minister Hillery appointed a committee of five inspectors to consider the current position of post-primary education and to make recommendations for reform. The committee was chaired by Dr Duggan, Deputy Chief Inspector, and its secretary and drafter of the report was Dr Fionnbarr Ó Ceallacháin, who had joined the Technical Instruction Branch as a Grade A inspector in 1955. The Committee found that vocational schools had operated under many constraints. They were too much under the dictates of the economy, resulting in utilitarian programmes which lacked liberality of approach and neglected social and personal development, with pupils emerging from vocational schools with a 'too narrow and restricted preparation for life.'[2] The Committee identified the necessity for a review of the vocational sector and stated that 'present industrial trends provide a basis for a new meaning for skill, and the emergence of a technician as a major requirement for industry would appear to indicate that the time had arrived when vocational school patterns should also be subject to review.'[3]

Already, in 1959, a new Apprenticeship Act had been passed, which set up An Céard-Chomhairle Oiliúna (ANCO) as a new structure for the recruitment, education, examination and certification of apprentices. It was to liaise with

1 Sean O'Connor, *A Troubled Sky: Reflection on the Irish Educational Scene, 1957–1968* (Dublin: Educational Research Centre, 1986), p. 21.   2 Aine Hyland and Kenneth Milne (eds), *Irish Educational Documents*, vol. II (Dublin: CICE, 1992) pp 555–60, p. 556.   3 Ibid.

vocational education committees for the provision of courses of instruction in the nature of technical education. However, the recommendations of the 1962 Committee envisaged a much wider concept of education to be pursued by vocational education committees. In his press conference address on 20 May 1963, Minister Hillery stated that it was government policy to increase the two-year course in vocational schools to three years duration, enabling students in these schools to sit for a common, widened Intermediate Certificate Examination. He went on to state that 'The time has come to take a firm step forward in technical education. Accordingly, it is my intention shortly to establish a Technical Schools Leaving Certificate and concurrently with that to arrange with VECs for the provision of a limited number of Technological Colleges with Regional status.'[4] With this announcement Minister Hillery was indicating one of the key *leitmotifs* for future education policy, namely the promotion of vocational and technical education to a central place within the education system. The report of the Investment in Education team (1965–66) endorsed the need to develop vocational, technical and technological education for an Ireland changing fast both economically and socially.

The vocational inspectorate operated in a very different manner from the secondary and the national school inspectorates. It conceived its role as being much more intimately involved in the development of the sector with which it was associated. As well as the academic side of the work relating to curricula and teacher/school/scheme evaluation, there was also a significant administrative dimension to their role. In the past, when the vocational system was small the inspectors had developed good relationships and communication patterns with the CEOs. With the expansion of the system, this tradition continued. The CEOs had to prepare annual programmes of work and projected annual financial schemes. These needed the approval of inspectors. They wrote comments or reports on these, highlighting any weaknesses, and guiding the CEOs on how best to obtain their aims. In this way, the CEOs benefited from an 'inside track' perspective in the preparation of their submissions to the Department. Indeed, anecdotal evidence suggests that some unease existed within the Department of Education that vocational inspectors might even be aiding the CEOs in the exercise of avoiding controls of the Department! Inspectors had the right to attend and address VEC meetings, but did not have the right to vote. Inspectors were also very involved in relation to the planning and building of VEC institutions. At the request of Minister O'Malley in 1967 inspectors were obligated to sit on the VEC selection boards for teachers, whose appointment was subject to ratification by the Minister for Education.

With the expansion of the provision of vocational and technical education from the mid-sixties, the vocational inspectors viewed themselves as pro-active

4 Statement by Minister Hillery, 20 May 1963 in Hyland and Milne, op. cit., pp 247–52, p. 251.

agents in supporting such developments, and tended to see themselves in the vanguard of educational and social change. If the vocational schools were to be in a position to cope with the new common Intermediate Certificate course and examination, as well as the traditional Group Certificate, and planned extension towards Leaving Certificate courses, by at least some schools, then there was an urgent need for improvements in building, equipment and staffing. Minister Colley's plea of January 1966 for greater co-operation between local vocational and secondary schools only met with a limited response. Vocational school inspectors participated in the various school rationalisation meetings organised by the Department at this time, and also in those of the early seventies promoting the cause of community schools. Later, they engaged in the planning of community colleges, whereby some vocational schools were re-organised as community colleges, with a broader body of trustees and management. Over these years, the inspectors gave valuable assistance and advice as the vocational sector positioned itself for its new roles. In particular, the assistance on school building provision, on classroom/laboratory design and on equipment was very valuable to the sector. They also assisted on staffing issues, most obviously by their presence on VEC staff selection panels, until 2000.

The Department of Education did not proceed with its intention of establishing a Technical Leaving Certificate. Rather, in line with its commitment to a comprehensive curricular policy, the range of subjects for the Leaving Certificate programme was extended. Thus, subjects such as home economics, technical drawing, building construction, engineering workshop theory and practice, accounting and business organisation were introduced to the Leaving Certificate programme in the late sixties, with metalwork and woodwork introduced to the Intermediate Certificate programme. Some of the subjects offered a choice of syllabuses, with varied content and, to some extent varied approach. The newly introduced 'technical' subjects were first examined in the Leaving Certificate Examinations of 1971. Inspectors in the vocational sector, with specialist expertise in the technical and applied subjects, took a major role in syllabus formation. They also assumed responsibility for aspects of the correction of examination scripts in these subjects. The inspectors played a significant role in planning the resourcing and equipping of any type of post-primary school offering these subjects. A key problem which faced policy makers in promoting the technical and practical subjects was their recognition for matriculation purposes by the universities. This issue was raised by Seán O'Connor in his well-known article, 'Post-Primary Education: Now and the Future' in *Studies*, 1968. The issue became controversial, with Professor Denis Donoghue of UCD, in particular, expressing disdain towards the proposal in the same issue of *Studies*.[5] Despite the con-

5 Sean O'Connor, 'Post-primary Education: Now and in the Future' and 'Response', by Professor Denis Donoghue, in *Studies*, vol. lvii (Autumn 1968), pp 233–49 and pp 284–88.

troversy, progress was made on the recognition of such subjects for entry to higher education. The outcome was a raising of the status of technical and applied subjects, which was gratifying to the vocational inspectorate. These inspectors were also gratified by contemporaneous changes on grading and salaries, whereby Grade B inspectors were regraded to Class II inspectors, and common salary scales were established for all categories of inspectors. Secondary and vocational inspectors were now officially known as post-primary inspectors, and while the intended integration did not take place at that time, the changes affecting post-primary schooling led to some more crossover work by the two inspectorial branches.

In 1966, Minister O'Malley established a Steering Committee to advise the Minister generally on technical education and, in particular, to provide the Building Unit with a brief for the planned Regional Technical Colleges, originally announced by Minister Hillery in 1963. The Committee was chaired by Dr Noel Mulcahy and its secretary and rapporteur was Jerry Sheehan, a vocational inspector. The report stressed the need for a big expansion of technician education, spanning a wide range of occupations – technical, scientific, commercial, catering and other fields of specialisation. It called for the establishment of a national council for educational awards to act as the validating and qualification awarding body for the new colleges and for technological education generally. The report urged a flexible building design which would allow for expansion when the projected demand made itself felt. The report endorsed the eight sites for the colleges already selected by the government. It also made recommendations on buildings and equipment, the early recruitment of supervisory staff, the mode of college administration etc.[6] The Regional Technical Colleges were originally envisaged as including forms of apprenticeship and senior cycle second-level education but, in practice, their work became predominantly tertiary education, after a few years.

These institutions were an exciting new development on the Irish educational landscape. Work on the colleges went ahead apace, and the first five Regional Technical Colleges opened in September 1969, at Carlow, Waterford, Athlone, Dundalk and Sligo, with others to follow in subsequent years. There is evidence that vocational inspectors such as Dr Fionnbarr Ó Ceallacháin had favoured the establishment of such institutions for a number of years prior to their establishment. Vocational inspectors rowed in enthusiastically in their establishment and took a very active role in the design and equipment of laboratories, studios and workshops. The Colleges were seen as a vote of confidence in technical education and staff with specialised expertise were generous in their time and effort in ensuring the success of the colleges. In their development the Regional Technical Colleges (RTCs) became one of the success stories of modern Irish education. Vocational inspectors

6 Steering Committee on Technical Education, *Report on Regional Technical College* (Dublin: Stationery Office, 1967).

also sat on the governing bodies of the RTCs and also sat on many of the interview panels for staff recruitment to the colleges. The vocational inspectors continued to have an involvement with the RTCs while they were linked to the VEC sector. Legislation, in 1992, gave the RTCs new governing structures, independent of the VECs, and accordingly, of inspectorial involvement.

Vocational inspectors also assisted in the planning and equipment of the new National Institute of Higher Education Limerick (NIHEL) which took in its first students in 1972. The inspectorate also assisted in the establishment of the NIHE in Dublin, where Dr Liam Ó Maolcatha, Deputy Chief Inspector (Secondary) presided as chairman of the governing body for a number of years. NIHED received its first students in 1980. Both NIHEs were raised to university status in 1989. The vocational inspectorate also liaised with the third-level colleges of the City of Dublin VEC (CDVEC) such as those in Bolton Street and Kevin Street, and also the Crawford Institute in Cork. They had the right to inspect teachers in VEC tertiary colleges. In 1978, the six colleges of the CDVEC were re-organised into the Dublin Institute of Technology (DIT). Interaction of the DIT colleges with the vocational inspectorate continued to be productive. These involvements of the vocational inspectorate with the tertiary education sector involved a more wide-ranging remit than operated for the other two branches of the inspectorate.

The vocational inspectorate had a long-established and very direct involvement in initial and in-service education for teachers in the vocational sector. They had significant responsibilities relating to the qualifications in Irish for these teachers. They were involved in the organisation and delivery of courses for the Ceard Teastas and the Teastas Timire Gaeilge, and for certifying teachers' competence in the examinations for these qualifications. The tests for these awards were more demanding than the oral tests applied by the secondary inspectorate for recognition by the Secondary Teachers' Registration Council. The vocational inspectors were also directly involved in the training courses for teachers in the craft subjects such as woodwork, metalwork, shorthand and typing etc., which were delivered in centres such as Coláiste Charmain, Gorey; Ringsend Technical Institute, Cork RTC, and Galway RTC. The input to these courses was quite intensive, for instance, involving direct engagement with each of the three-year courses for woodwork and metalwork teachers, on an on-going basis. They also had responsibilities relating to the home economics colleges, until they were absorbed into the university sector in the mid seventies. The training of teachers of art and design also came under the influence of the inspectorate. In the early seventies the National College of Art and Design (NCAD) experienced significant upheaval reflective of much unrest and dissatisfaction by students and staff regarding the courses and facilities available. Micheál O Flannagáin, the first Chief Inspector, who was from the Technical Instruction Branch, was very involved in seeking a resolution to the issues. Eventually, the NCAD was granted statutory status with a new management structure and improved facilities. Its courses were now validated by the National Council for Educational Awards (NCEA), which was established in 1972. The NCEA was also the awarding body of qualifications obtained by students. Jack McGloinn, a vocational inspector, was the first chairman of the NCEA, and inspectors participated on NCEA course committees.

In 1970, the National College of Physical Education (NCPE) was established in Limerick, adjacent to the new NIHEL. However, the number of physical education students was small, and the Department of Education considered that it would be best to adapt the college for a more multi-purpose teacher education role. In the mid-seventies its name was changed to Thomond College and, as well as the education of PE teachers, it encompassed the education of teachers in craft subjects such as woodwork, metalwork, rural science, some business courses, shorthand and typing etc. The vocational inspectorate played a major part in the design and planning of laboratories, workshops and teaching spaces for Thomond College, as they had the practical expertise and experience to guide this aspect of the college's facilities. The establishment of Thomond College was an important landmark for teacher education in practical subjects. From 1979–80 Thomond College took over this responsibility from the inspectorate, and the older tradition of such teacher training was sundered. Thomond College was keen to establish its own independence and *modus operandi*. Its courses were validated by the NCEA, which also awarded its qualifications. Eventually in the early nineties, Thomond College was absorbed into the University of Limerick, established in 1989. The Thomond College development is best seen within a policy move of the seventies to establish an all-graduate teaching profession in Ireland. From 1974, student teachers for national schools studied for the B.Ed. degree, awarded by the universities. Home economics teachers also studied for university degrees. Most art teachers had their degrees awarded by the NCEA, at that time, later by the National University of Ireland. PE, craft, and rural science teacher education graduates of Thomond College had their degrees awarded by the NCEA, and later by the University of Limerick. This all-graduate policy was a milestone for the teaching profession in Ireland, which also now had a common salary scale and a common framework of allowances for qualifications. The outcome meant that the vocational inspectorate ceased to be involved in initial teacher education, which helped to release them for other responsibilities.

In earlier decades the Board of Works had been responsible for the building of national schools, secondary schools were built by the private owners and the vocational inspectorate had a main responsibility regarding vocational school building. This involved the relevant inspector relating to the VEC in question. With the great expansion of the schooling infrastructure which took place from the mid-sixties, a Building Unit was established within the Department of Education, with Mr Noel Lindsay, the first principal officer of the Unit. To help cope with the expenses of building the first tranche of the RTC's the government applied for and got a loan from the World Bank. Then, in 1970, a second World Bank loan was drawn down to assist in the second phase of RTCs, the proposed community schools and the new NCPE/Thomond College. The terms of the loans required the Department to prepare equipment plans for all these institutions, to which the vocational inspectorate made major contributions. The World Bank also needed evaluation reports of all funded projects. The World Bank indicated that it was desirable to strengthen the Building Unit, incorporating the expertise of architects, general educators and technical educators. Arising from this, inspectors from the different branches were re-deployed on a full-time basis to the Building Unit, which now took on responsibilities for secondary and vocational schools, but other inspectors continued to be called upon regarding teaching spaces and equipment.

The nature of the interaction of inspectors with vocational schools and CEOs was such that the personnel in the vocational sector knew each other well, and lines of communication were easily sustained. Indeed, some high level recruits to the vocational inspectorate were attracted out of the inspectorate to become CEOs themselves. While such staff were a loss to the inspectorate, in their roles as progressive CEOs they maintained useful links with the inspectorate and the Department's policies.

Vocational inspectors also engaged in night work, periodically visiting and evaluating adult education provision by the VECs. In 1969, a national association for adult education AONTAS, was founded. It was an advisory and consultative body for the promotion of adult education. In the same year, the government took the initiative of setting up an advisory committee on adult education. In its wide-ranging report, presented to the government in November 1973, the Committee (Murphy Committee) endorsed new conceptions of adult education variously termed permanent, continuing and recurrent education, and it urged that adult education provision should be taken much more seriously. Among its recommendations were the establishment of a special section within the Department of Education, with a specific budget to service adult education, and the establishment of regional and county committees who would employ specialist staff to cater for adult education in their areas.[7] While such organisational structures were not implemented, influenced by public finances constraints, a greater momentum was in evidence regarding adult education provision by the VECs and the new community schools. In 1979, the Minister for Education allowed the VECs to make fifty new appointments of what were termed 'adult education officers'. The vocational

7 *Report of Advisory Committee on Adult Education* (Murphy) (Dublin: Stationery Office, 1974).

inspectorate responded to the increased provision of adult education, providing advice and evaluation on it. This also had the benefit of bringing them in touch with adults and the parents of pupils at the day schools, who were taking night courses. There is anecdotal evidence of worthwhile dialogue over cups of tea, following sessions, which gave the inspectors a more rounded view of education and associated issues within local communities.

The 1970s was a period of initiatives and experimentation regarding the post-primary school curriculum. This included the setting up of curriculum development units within the CDVEC and the City of Galway VEC, as well as in Shannon Comprehensive School. A variety of pilot schemes was undertaken such as ISCIP, the Humanities Project, SPIRAL.[8] Inspectors engaged with the units and their programmes productively over the years. The pilot and experimental work enriched thinking on curricular and pedagogic issues and was beneficial in the restructuring of the mainstream curricula in the 1990s.

Ireland's decision to join the EEC in 1973 proved to be a momentous event in the development of modern Irish society. At first, education was not regarded as a central concern of the EEC, the prerogative in this area being seen to lie with the member states. However, socio-economic concerns relating to youth unemployment within the EEC in the 1970s prompted more pro-active concern, first of all for a policy on training which became gradually extended to incorporate education. It was realised that early school leavers were very vulnerable in a society where there was a shrinking demand for unskilled labour. In 1976, the EEC resolved to introduce initiatives to meet the problems of youth unemployment. Inspectors in the Department of Education, such as Dr Fionnbarr Ó Ceallacháin were alert to the possibilities for Ireland in this development. Dr Ó Ceallacháin had already made direct contact with the EU Commissioner and staff involved in the Social Fund in Brussels. Pointing to developments in apprenticeship training within ANCO in Ireland and the developing role of the new RTCs he secured funding for courses in hotel training apprenticeship and for courses in the RTCs for technical craftsmen. Jerry Sheehan of the CDVEC, and formerly an inspector, had by now moved to a prominent position in Brussels and was a valuable link-man in assisting such developments.[9]

In 1977, the Department of Education prepared a scheme for Pre-Employment Courses which incorporated work experience for pupils, while attached to a school. The scheme was at first confined to vocational, community and comprehensive schools, and it was aimed at those pupils who would otherwise have left school early. The scheme was accepted for support by the EEC Social Fund, and it was to be the forerunner of many EEC supported initiatives

8 For an account of such projects see, Tony Crooks and Jim McKernan, *The Challenge of Change* (Dublin: IPA, 1984) and G. McNamara, K. Williams & D. Herron (eds), *Achievement and Aspiration: Curricular Initiatives in Irish Post-primary Education in the 1980s* (Dublin: Drumcondra Teachers' Centre, 1990).   9 Interview with Dr Ó Ceallacháin, 9 July, 2007.

devised by Irish educators. Teachers within the scheme, with the help of the inspectorate, showed great imagination and ingenuity in the work experiences devised, with a lot of varied activity for pupils, which they found relevant and interesting. The pupil take-up confirmed that there was a strong demand, especially in vocational schools for a shorter, more job-relevant alternative programme to the Leaving Certificate programme. In the first year, 80 schools participated with 1800 pupils enrolling. The programme incorporated three elements – vocational studies, work experience and general studies. The number of pupils taking the pre-employment course doubled between 1977 to 1983.[10]

The EEC Social Fund was also prepared to support a network of pilot projects on the theme of transition from school to adult working life. Three such pilot projects – Humanities, ISCIP and Outdoor Education – were submitted by the Department of Education and were approved for joint funding by the EEC and the Irish government for the period 1978 to 1982. A further set of projects SPIRAL, SESP and PIPE, was approved for the period 1983 to 1986. The Department's Curriculum Unit had a significant involvement in the establishment and evaluation of these pilot curricular projects. Meanwhile, within the EEC a more structured approach to vocational preparation was underway which involved a shift of emphasis from discrete job-specific skills towards a broad approach to training in general skills. It was considered that young people needed to be adaptable, with more attention paid to their personal development and a more tangible orientation to the work environment. Initially it was conceived that the Regional Technical Colleges might have been the appropriate location for this type of education and training but by now they had concentrated on the provision of third-level education. In 1981–82, a cross-sectoral, post-primary group, locally termed the 'Group of Four' was convened in the Department to plan for this changing situation. It included

Brendan McDonagh, Senior Secondary Inspector; Albert Ó Ceallaigh, Senior Secondary Inspector seconded to the Curriculum Unit; Torlach Ó Conchubhair, Senior Psychologist; John Byrne, Senior Vocational Inspector. The Group was chaired by Tom Gillen, Assistant Secretary. Dr Cearbhall Ó Dálaigh, who was a secondary inspector assigned to the Curriculum Unit in late 1981, replaced Albert Ó Ceallaigh when Ó Ceallaigh became Chief Executive of the CEB, in 1984.

The Group of Four reviewed the Pre-Employment course framework then on offer and devised a development from that programme which became known as the Vocational Preparation and Training Programme (VPTP). In the summer of 1984, the European Social Fund extended its financial support to encompass the secondary school sector. The new one-year VPTP course commenced in September 1984. It was taken by 11,000 girls and 6,000 boys in 380 schools, including 118 secondary schools.[11] Subsequently, a further

---

10 Diarmuid Leonard, 'The Vocational Preparation and Training Programme', in McNamara et al., *Achievement and Aspiration*, pp 33–46, p. 34.   11 Ibid., p. 34

year of vocational training, known as VPTP2, was made available in a limited number of schools to young people who had concluded senior cycle schooling. The focus of the VPTP1 was on the development of core competencies, generic skills and interpersonal skills. The aim of the VPTP courses was to 'bridge the gap between the values and experiences normally part of traditional education and these current in the adult world of work'. The framework of the course involved vocational studies, preparation for working life and general studies, on the basis of 40%, 25%, and 35% of the time allocation to each respectively. The take-up of VPTP1 was impressive, reaching about 18,000 annually in subsequent years.[12] A notable gain in relation to the initiation of the VPTP1 courses was the acquisition from EEC funds of £80,000 for the in-service education of personnel for the delivery of the programmes. This precedent of training for trainers resources was further developed by the Irish authorities in subsequent years. The VPTP2 programme was distinguished by a much heavier concentration on technical skills and work experience. The inspectors made important inputs into the design and organisation of such courses. As well as the direct benefits for the pupils engaged in the pilot and VPTP courses, the experience of the new content and methodologies of such programmes benefited staff development and encouraged more flexibility of thought with regard to general curricular policy. This facilitated the development of the further education sector and Post Leaving Certificate courses (PLCs).

While it was the administrators in the Department of Education who negotiated with the EEC Social Fund officials in Brussels, it was largely the professional side of the Department which designed and organised the programmes. Within the Department of Education a European Social Fund (ESF) Steering Committee of seven members was established, involving five inspectors, which did very significant work in preparing schemes to fit European Directive Guidelines.[13] The evaluation by the EEC of the various aided programmes conducted in Ireland was highly satisfactory. The courses were seen as being well conducted and delivering value for money. Ireland showed considerable ingenuity in how EEC policy could be drawn upon for financial support of its education and training policy. On the strength of this, and with education and training becoming a more central part of EEC and, post 1993, EU policy concerns, Ireland continued to benefit in subsequent years in drawing down support from both the Social and Structural Funds for education and training purposes. This support proved highly advantageous to Ireland as it set out to develop and reform its educational system through the late eighties and the nineties. The exposure to international thinking within the EU, as within the OECD, was beneficial to the island of Ireland, but it was also the case that Ireland made useful contributions to international new thinking on education and training.

12 DES Files, uncatalogued.   13 DES, files, uncatalogued.

A long-established and important task of the vocational inspectorate was the operation of the Technical School Examinations (TS). These were initiated by John Ingram in 1935. In 1936, 9,000 candidates took the examinations and, by 1943 this had grown to 13,000 students. With the expansion of the system over the decades, these examinations assumed a great importance for many people. Eventually, between 550 and 600 examinations were provided each year for twenty-two trades. Examinations were held three times a year. The main grades of examinations were categorised as Group I, Junior Trades, and Senior Trades examinations. In most instances the examination papers were devised and corrected by inspectors. When the number of examinations expanded greatly, inspectors became 'co-examiners', supervising and co-ordinating the work of other examiners. As late as 1996, all of the twenty-six co-examiners were inspectors. The syllabi for the trades courses were revised and up-dated by the inspectors periodically over the years.

The number of entries for the TS examinations tended to be very high, peaking at 34,500 in 1984.[14] The amount of work associated with these examinations was very onerous for the vocational inspectors. These examinations got nothing like the public attention and publicity associated with the Intermediate and Leaving Certificate examinations, which were largely under the remit of the secondary school inspectorate, with more involvement from the vocational inspectorate following the inclusion of technical and applied subjects in 1969. Lack of publicity did not affect the quiet efficiency which pertained regarding the operation of the TS examinations, over a long time span.

Changes were occurring in the trades and training courses in the early nineties. For instance, there was a shift to standards-based, rather than time-based apprenticeship in the middle nineties. Within a changing context, the decision was made in 1999 to discontinue the TS examinations. The last junior trade examinations took place in 2000, and the last senior trade in 2004, albeit some tidying up arrangements continued until 2007.[15] Overall, it can be concluded that the initiative on the TS examinations of John Ingram, Head of the Technical Instruction Branch in 1935, proved to be a very valuable one for technical and applied education in Ireland, and the vocational inspectors operated these examinations over a period of seventy years in an effective and efficient manner.

With regard to the general policy and process of inspection of schools, colleges and courses conducted under vocational education committees, a document setting out full detail on these was prepared within the Department of Education in October 1981, possibly in response to some criticism of inspection being made around that time by the Teachers Union of Ireland. The document was a formal and significant statement and up-dated some aspects of traditional procedure.[16] Among the functions of the inspectorate, set out in

14 John Byrne, 'Report on the TS Examinations, 2007' (unpublished). 15 Ibid. 16 Document, 'Inspection of Schools, Colleges, and Courses Conducted under Vocational

the document were: to maintain direct liaison with Vocational Education Committees, their officers and servants; to provide a support and advisory service to them; and to evaluate the service they provided. In this three-fold relationship with VECs, it is noteworthy that maintaining direct liaison and providing support services were as much emphasised as evaluation. This was a continuation of the constructive role envisaged for the inspectorate originally in assisting VECs with plans and schemes, in a pro-active sense. As well as providing information to the Minister and the Department to help with administrative/executive decisions, the inspectors were also expected 'to identify priorities and clarify the direction of future polices with respect to vocational education.'[17] This emphasised that inspectors were expected to have a developmental, future-oriented role in relation to vocational education.

The document went on to outline that inspectors should have a comprehensive approach to their inspectorial visits to institutions. With regard to evaluating the teaching and learning processes, the tone is different from the more diffident tone adopted by the secondary inspectorate in the contemporary dispute with the ASTI on the evaluation of teaching. In this document, relating to vocational schools, it was taken for granted that the inspector had the right to evaluate the teachers' teaching. Under three headings – planning, student attainment and teacher presentation, detailed advice was given on what inspectors should do in such evaluation. Then it was stated, 'The inspector will report on the quality of the teaching/learning in a particular case and give a rating in respect of the teacher.'[18] In the event that the inspector found fault with the teaching he was required to make known the shortcomings to the teacher 'in a suitably diplomatic and discreet way', and make suggestions on means of overcoming them. On subsequent visits the inspector was to observe how the teacher was coping with his difficulties.

Where, in the view of the inspector, the teaching continued to be unsatisfactory the inspector was to submit an adverse report and set in train a process. The procedure for dealing with adverse reports was an elaborate and drawn-out one, and involved the CEO and the Vocational Committee. In the case of continuing unsatisfactory performance, the procedure involved four more inspections by varied inspectors, including at Assistant Chief Inspector level. If unsatisfactory at this final phase, the Minister would request the Committee to remove the teacher from office. This document of 1981, on inspection in vocational schools, was clear and precise for all involved parties but, it seems fair to conclude, the elaborate process in assessing incompetent teaching, involving a very long time duration for the process resulted in few dismissals from the service for incompetent teaching.

There is no written evidence available to suggest that the vocational school inspectorate experienced the same dissatisfaction with the role of the

Education Committees', 9 October 1981 in DES Files (uncatalogued).   **17** Ibid.   **18** Ibid.

administration section of the Department, as did the secondary inspectorate. Oral evidence suggests the relationships were cordial and co-operative between the vocational side and administrators. However, there is no doubt but that the vocational sector felt the impact of the embargo on appointments and the failure to increase inspectorial numbers commensurate with the scale of the expanding system and workload. For instance, in 1969, in all, there were 49 personnel between the secondary and the vocational inspectorate. In 1985, the number of personnel in post was 57,[19] even though there had been an increase of almost 200,000 pupils enrolled in post-primary schools in the intervening period, and forms of tertiary education had come into operation involving the vocational inspectorate, which were non-existent in 1969. The work on curricula, examinations, and administrative duties had expanded exponentially, but the staffing of the inspectorate was very far from being paralleled by such expansion.

The vocational inspectorate was also concerned about senior positions within the inspectorate. Following the career framework agreed in 1970, it was understood that each of the three branches of the inspectorate would have one Deputy Chief Inspector. However, this system ceased to operate in the late eighties. Máirtín Ó Lóngáin was the last vocational inspector to hold the position of Deputy Chief Inspector, in 1986. There had also been a tradition of four Assistant Chief Inspectors for the post-primary sector but, from 1984, this was reduced to three.[20] This was a cause of considerable dissatisfaction to the post-primary inspectorate, when such positions were regarded as crucial for the career profile. A variety of such circumstantial factors was not favourable to the maintenance of high morale or professional commitment. It was a tribute, however, to the inspectorate that it sustained a tradition of hard work, in a public-service spirit, for the well-being of the country's education system during these years.

19 *State Directory of Services for 1969 and 1985.* 20 *State Directory, 1984–90.*

15

Inspectors of Guidance Services (Psychologists)

In the context of new thinking on post-primary education provision in the 1960s, a new category of staff was recruited by the Department of Education – educational psychologists. The City of Dublin VEC had already, in 1960, employed educational psychologists. In 1965, the Department recruited its first three psychologists – Torlach O'Connor, Tony Gorman and Brendan Connolly. At that time, thinking in international education circles, including the OECD, highlighted the need for guidance services for the expanding pupil numbers in post-primary education. Ireland's first three comprehensive schools opened in 1966, and the concept of a *cycle d'observation* (observation period) had gained currency, whereby the aptitudes of new pupil entrants would be observed for a period and lead to guidance on the courses of study most suitable to them. The first psychologist appointees were linked to providing guidance counselling for the new comprehensive schools.

However, there was a lack of a clear job definition for the psychologists within the Department of Education, and how they would fit in with the career framework of the service had not been fully clarified. In the early years they were categorised as coming under the Development Branch, and following its demise, they were listed as the 'Psychological Service', in the State Directory of Services. In order to fit within established career patterns the psychologists had to take on the term 'Inspector' in their nomenclature. The early psychologists appointed became associated with the post-primary sector, in a mainly guidance counselling capacity. The role of career guidance teacher was becoming established in post-primary schools. Thus, the psychologists became officially known as 'Inspectors of Guidance Services.'

By 1970, recruitment to the service meant that there was one Senior Inspector of Guidance Services and eighteen inspectors of guidance services. By 1974, the posts establishment was two seniors and twenty-three inspectors of guidance. This remained the complement of approved staff over subsequent years, although by 1980 a third senior post had been created. The psychologists found some difficulty on the issues of salary and promotion opportunities. For many years, the post of Senior Inspector of Guidance had a salary equivalent to the ordinary grade (not senior) of inspector at secondary level and to the grade of Class I of the vocational inspectorate. By 1980 the senior post was upgraded to match the salary of senior inspector post-primary. The salary of all the other inspectors of guidance was equivalent to that of Class II of the vocational inspectorate or to that of the District Inspector at primary level.[1] None of the inspectors of guidance services were promoted to the grade of Assistant Chief Inspector or Deputy Chief Inspector by this date.

A need was being expressed in the late 1960s for standardised achievement tests in primary schools. Some of the inspectors of guidance went to Moray House in Edinburgh to train in the design of such tests. Achievement tests were then devised, with the co-operation of the primary inspectorate, in reading and writing, for both Irish and English, and in mathematics. These tests were welcomed in the schools and the primary inspectorate promoted and used them. The inspectors of guidance also designed pupil record cards for schools. Following the abolition of the Primary Certificate Examination, in 1967, it was the intention that it be replaced by pupil record cards which would be transferred with the pupil on to the post-primary school at which the pupil was expected to attend. The cards were designed and were used by some schools, but they did not become as universal a feature of the transfer process as had been envisaged.

It is interesting to note that while the area of special education had received greater policy attention in the 1960s, it tended to remain under the remit of the primary inspectorate, rather than of the educational psychologists. A Special Education Unit had been established in 1961 in St Patrick's College of Education, under the direction of Páid McGee, and some primary inspectors were designated as inspectors of special education. The first, and one of the most distinguished of these was Tomás Ó Cuilleanáin. Some inspectors took courses abroad or in the St Patrick's Unit on Special Education and they considered that they were best equipped to deal with special education issues at primary level. To a large degree, the work of the psychologists in the Department focussed on post-primary education, and, in the early years, on guidance counselling issues. As well as direct involvement with pupils, the inspectors of guidance services provided very many in-service courses for teachers in personal, educational and vocational guidance. Some of these courses were residential over the months of June and July. While of relatively short duration, they were intensive and participating teachers engaged with them enthusiastically. Eventually, UCD's Psychology Department, which had been running Diploma Courses in Educational Psychology since the sixties, put forward a full-time Higher Diploma Courses in Career Guidance. For a time some tension existed between the providers but, in the end, it was considered best that certification of career guidance teachers was best located within university provision. The Department of Education in-service courses by the inspectors of guidance continued for a number of years to facilitate certification by those teachers who had engaged in the part-time courses.

1 *State Directory of Services 1970s, 1980.*

Interesting pilot work was carried out by three psychologists who were assigned to areas in Dublin in the 1970s. In addition to carrying out psychological assessments, the psychologists worked closely with the remedial teachers and special class teachers in the primary schools in the selected areas. The model of engagement was regarded as very promising. However, it was not developed and gave way in the late 1970s to the expanding demands of guidance and remedial services in the post-primary schools.

Another area which got increased policy attention in the 1970s and in the 1980s was remedial education. While the Special Education Unit in St Patrick's College of Education set up courses in remedial education for primary teachers, inspectors of guidance from the Department also set up short courses for primary teachers in remedial education. However, their main role in this area was the provision of remedial courses for post-primary teachers. This work was headed up by Tony Gorman, one of the Senior Inspectors of Guidance Services. The psychologists did valuable pioneering and development work in this field. For many years cohorts of practising teachers availed of the opportunity of developing skills and understandings to apply to this important area of pupil learning back in the classroom. Eventually, this work became transferred to higher education institutions. The UCD Education Department offered a course, the Higher Diploma in Compensatory and Remedial Education in the late 1980s. In the early nineties, courses in remedial education were located, with support from the Department of Education, in UCC, UCG, Mary Immaculate College, and in the Church of Ireland College of Education. Thus, the teaching role of the inspectors of guidance services for in-career teachers in areas such as career guidance, special education, and remedial education ceased. This allowed more time to relate to the psychological needs of school pupils, which was a major area of concern, and to monitoring the quality of work in guidance counselling, special education and remedial education, in a quality assurance role.

Torlach O'Connor, a Senior Inspector of Guidance, who had headed up the guidance work of the sector, took a central role in the planning of the ESF supported pilot curricular projects on the transition from school to working life, and on the VPTP programmes. He became a member of the ESF Steering Group in the Department and did a great deal of liaison work between the Departments of Education and Labour with the EEC in securing funds for school-to-work type projects, and in ensuring the quality of such projects.[2] Psychologists also represented the Department on a variety of special committees such as the Committee on the Reformatory and Industrial School System, the Committee on Pupil Transfer from Primary to Post-Primary School, the Committee on School Discipline, whose reports were published respectively in 1970, 1982 and 1985. Psychologists also gave advice on the needs of pupils with sensory disabilities at the public examinations.

2 *DES Files, uncatalogued*

As was the case with the general inspectorate through the 1970s and 1980s, the inspectors of guidance services were also drawn into the multifarious activities of the Department. These included dealing with issues such as constituency enquiries, drawing up answers to parliamentary questions, speech writing, representing the Department at local events, sitting on committees. This type of activity tended to distract from delivering their specialist expertise, particularly in assessing and diagnosing pupil problems and providing guidance and support on the basis of such assessments. The emphasis of the role of the educational psychologists changed over the years and this tended to blur their role in the public eye. Their position within the Department of Education and their career track were not optimal in facilitating the achievement of their full potential. Yet the psychologists were a tightly knit group within the Department and maintained a good esprit de corps.

In the 1990s a good deal of reflection on and re-appraisal of the psychological service took place which was to give a significant new direction to it. A working group, chaired by Eamon Stack, eventually set out that new direction and in overview comments on the past service it stated:

> The general conclusion is that there are serious gaps in the current provision of educational psychological services for students generally, including some students having special educational needs, in both primary and post-primary schools. There is little evidence of co-ordination or regular liaison between the psychological services provided either within the Education sector, or between those in the Education sector and those in the Health Sector.[3]

No doubt the work, experience and achievements of the inspectors of guidance services, since their establishment in 1965, provided a useful platform for a more extended and focused service which was being charted, responding to the needs of Irish society in the contemporary era. Eventually, the policy decision was taken to establish a National Educational Psychological Service as a dedicated service in the Department which began its work in 1999. This greatly changed the role of the psychologists within the education system.

3 Report of Planning Group, *A National Educational Psychological Service* (Dublin: Stationery Office, 1998), p. 5.

16

The Inspectorate in Transition, 1990–98

THE CONTEXT

The 1990s ushered in a period of unprecedented economic, social and cultural change in Ireland. Over a sequence of years its economic performance far surpassed that of other developed countries and won the sobriquet, 'The Celtic Tiger'. The sustained politico-economic model of social partnership from 1987 provided a stable industrial relations environment. This, coupled with favourable taxation conditions and the availability of a well-educated workforce made Ireland an attractive location for investment by multinational companies. The effective use of EU social and structural funds also helped the quality of life for many people, as well as the physical infrastructure for trade and development. Traditional high levels of unemployment were drastically reduced to what was technically known as a full employment situation. Long-established patterns of emigration of the involuntary kind was replaced by the opposite pattern of high immigration, which helped to provide the workforce for the rapidly expanding economy.

Ireland was also greatly influenced by trends in the international, globalised economy. Accountability and transparency became pronounced features of public and private affairs. Within public administration, promotion to high office became more merit-based rather than on seniority. New initiatives such as the Strategic Management Initiative (SMI) and Value for Money Initiative (VFM) were introduced. Strategic policies and mission statements became *de rigueur*. Performance management processes were introduced, with incentives for high-level performers. The Education Department was, of course, included within the new approach to the public service and, over time, was to experience significant change.

The Irish education system in general was subject to a period of major appraisal, analysis and policy formulation. Much of this was conducted in a highly consultative manner, including the holding of a National Education Convention (1993) and a National Forum on Early Childhood Education (1998). Between 1992 and the year 2000 two government green papers and three white papers on educational reform were published, covering the whole spectrum of educational provision from early childhood to mature adulthood. An unprecedented raft of educational legislation was enacted including Ireland's first comprehensive Education Act of 1998. Increasingly, education was seen as a priority concern for national policy. As the concept of the knowledge society took hold it was seen that greater investment in its human resources through education was crucial to Ireland's continued economic growth and development. Unlike most earlier decades economic resources were available to plough into educational reform measures which, in turn, helped to form the human potential for greater achievement and, thus, created a benign economic cycle. During this period Ireland was open to the prompt-ings and stimuli of the international agencies of which it was a part, such as the OECD and the EU. This international influence was quite significant as Ireland linked it to the work of its own internal think-tanks, or policy analysts. Within the context of reform of the overall education system, it was only to be expected that a key agency such as the inspectorate came under scrutiny. International perspectives proved important in this process. The opening out to international trends and thinking on the inspectorate created a wider con-text for the appraisal of existing practice. What evolved in the process of restructuring was a combination of internal reflection and action and the stim-ulation provided by international thinking. The process was also influenced by reform moves within the Department of Education itself as part of general public service reform. While such factors created a supportive climate for the process of inspectorial reform it did not happen quickly or easily. This chap-ter examines how the process developed by firstly analysing the policy per-spectives of various reports relating to the inspectorate and, then, on how the inspectorate itself responded and operated in the period 1990 to 1998, which is viewed as a transitionary period for the inspectorate.

POLICY PERSPECTIVES ON THE INSPECTORATE

From the mid-eighties more structured engagement by the Irish inspectorate leaders with their international peers began to take place. In June 1985, Dr Liam Ó Maolcatha, Chief Inspector, and Seán Mac Cárthaigh, Deputy Chief Inspector, attended a conference in Amsterdam, organised by the Centre for Educational Research and Innovation (CERI) of the OECD. The theme was the 'Role of Central Inspectorates in Educational Change'. The discussion focused on three major themes – Roles and Tasks of Central Inspectorates; Strategies, Methods and Instruments for carrying out the Inspectorates' Tasks; and Policy Development. This was the first time that representatives of the highest levels of national inspectorates in Western Europe met to dis-cuss their role and working methods. The discussions were regarded as so satisfactory that it was agreed that the inspectorates should meet on a bian-nual basis.[1] The next conference took place in Oxford, in 1987, on 'The

1 CERI, 'Report of the International Conference of Inspectors', CERI/IE/85.9.

Inspectorates and the Process of Quality Maintenance and Development'. The Irish representatives were Dr Liam Ó Maolcatha and Seamus de Buitléir, Deputy Chief Inspector (Primary). Papers were submitted in advance of the conference by the various countries on their procedures and objectives, which provided comparisons and contrasts. A key conclusion of the conference was, 'The role towards which the inspectorate is working is that of "quality broker", working by advice, proffering guidance and advancing change by negotiation rather than relying uniquely on the legislative instrument. There is also the conviction that quality in education may be seized only on the basis of first-hand, in-depth observation culled from direct contacts with schools, pupils, parents and teachers … This organisational knowledge forms the cornerstone on which the legitimacy of all central inspectorates rests.'[2] The exposure of the Irish delegates to such discussions with their international peers is likely to have prompted further reflections on the Irish experience. In the context of the above quotation, it must have raised concerns at how removed so many post-primary inspectors had become from the primacy of experiential knowledge culled from visits to Irish classrooms, due to under-staffing and their multifarious workload.

In these years, the EEC was also concerned about the role of inspectorates and, in 1988, it commissioned a report from Dr Clive Hopes of the German Institute for International Educational Research on 'The Contribution of Inspectors and Advisers to the Quality of Schooling in the European Communities.' The Country Report for Ireland for this study was prepared by two inspectors, Seán Mac Gleannáin, Assistant Chief Inspector and Seán MacIonraic, a Post-Primary Inspector. The report was predominantly a factual account of the existing situation of the inspectorate. However, it did highlight the under-staffing, poor promotion prospects, and the lack of incentives to join the inspectorate, with teachers enjoying equivalent incomes. It drew attention to the gender imbalance within the inspectorate with only 6 females out of a total of 81 primary inspectors, and only 7 females out of a total of 54 senior and recruitment level post-primary inspectors. With the lack of recruitment the report pointed out how difficult it was to fulfil what it identified as the four-fold role of the inspectorate – inspection of schools, in-service education for teachers, conducting the public examinations and the development of the curriculum. The report also criticised the segmentation of the three branches of the inspectorate stating:

> In an age when there is growing awareness of the need for continuity and smoothness of transition within the various stages in the education process, the watertight compartmentalisation of the inspectorate is increasingly difficult to defend.[3]

2 CERI, 'Report on the Conference "The Inspectorates and the Process of Quality Maintenance and Development"', CERI/IE/87.11, p. 19.   3 Seán MacGleannáin and Sean Mac Ionraic,

The review of inspectorates conducted by Dr Clive Hopes for the EEC prompted Mr Noel Lindsay, Secretary of the Department of Education, to invite him, in April 1990, to conduct a review of the role and functions of the Irish schools inspectorate. This was the first formal review of the Irish inspectorate since the report on the primary inspectorate in 1927. Dr Hopes held a large number of individual and group meetings with inspectors and other stakeholders in the system. He presented his report in May 1991. In his introduction, Hopes signalled his views that significant change was needed stating, 'In view of the uncoordinated, independent development of the inspectorates on bases that are archaic, the need for a more coherent structure is apparent'.[4]

Part 5 of the report was devoted to 'Observations on Practice' and amounts to a severe critique of the operation of the inspectorate, within the structure of the Department of Education. It was critical of the staffing and structure of the inspectorates; the management of inspectorates; their selection, promotion and professional development; planning and communication; misuse of technical expertise; lack of administrative and secretarial support; reportage and the use of reports; level of staffing; isolation of inspectors; style of visiting schools; role in examinations; role in relation to curricula; lack of teamwork; role in in-service education of teachers. The tone of the critique was forceful as can be gauged from the following, when referring to the lack of integration of the post-primary inspectorate, which had been attempted in the 1970s:

> It was an innovation typical of the incremental, piece-meal, timid, compromising approaches to change which have been undertaken over the years with regard to the inspectorates. For example, the unclarity of the status and purpose of a Chief Inspector, the creation of the Senior Inspector salary rank without appropriately attaching a responsibility to it, the listing of the psychological service as inspectors, and finally the demise of the 'non-position' of the District/Post Primary Inspectors, introduced as an experimental idea for some future whole system model. The discontinuities, mismanagement and poor leadership throughout the period have brought the post-primary inspectorial system to a debilitated state. The absence of providing a comprehensive, analytical advisory service to the administration is a problem which should be addressed in the review on the whole approach to inspection.[5]

The critique was predominantly focussed on systems, leadership, and modes of operation, but the report respected the professionalism of individual inspectors who worked within the inhibiting systems:

'Country Background Report on the Irish School Inspectorate' (unpublished, Dept of Ed. Archives, 1990), section 8.1.   4 Clive Hopes, 'A Review of the Role and Functions of the Irish Schools Inspectorate' (unpublished, May 1991), p. 5   5 Ibid., p. 42.

In view of their utmost frustration and despondency about the lot of the inspectorate as a whole, at the personal level the enthusiasm and commitment of inspectors to their work is remarkable. This factor is a very positive indicator of the potential for a rejuvenated inspectorate, if its reform can be properly managed.[6]

Hopes prefaced his recommendations for reform by the unambiguous statement, 'Any plan for the Inspectorate, even if the decision were to keep it functioning as it now is, must include a radical increase in personnel to staff it with adequate numbers'.[7] Among the main recommendations were that the inspectorate should be re-organised as a small central staff, and a well-developed regional organisation nearer the schools. The inspectorate should be a unified, professional technical service. The inspectorate's primary concern should be with operations within schools. The formal structure of inspectorial authority would stay but the roles and functions of the Chief, Deputy Chiefs and Assistant Chief Inspectors would be re-structured and clarified. The regional offices should be assigned special cross-level, cross-school-type tasks with inspectors from all school types working together in teams on problems, and proposing solutions. Task forces should be created for such issues as curriculum, and in-service training and should cut across school types and levels. The two functions of monitoring teaching and assessing teachers should be clearly divided.

It was urged that inspectors should no longer be on syllabus committees but should focus on the assessment and evaluation of the functioning of new syllabi. It was also recommended that inspectors withdraw from their front-line, hands-on, close involvement with the public examinations, in favour of assessing the shortcomings of the examination system and proposing constructive alternatives, as well as focussing on the pedagogical functions of the schools as a whole. The report also made recommendations on recruitment and selection within the inspectorate, on the training and professional development of the inspectorate, on improved communication systems and on reportage by the inspectorate. It was urged that proper administrative and secretarial staff be available to the inspectorate. The report also recommended a scheme for the periodic secondment of expert teachers to assist the inspectorate. It was stated that, 'The misuse or lack of use of the technical advice available to the administrators is a serious flaw in the system.' As one remedy for this, it was proposed that the Chief Inspector, the Deputy Chief and the Assistant Chief Inspectors be integrated with the Administrative arm to ensure that they were properly consulted and their advice used in decision-making.[8]

The Hopes Report was the most comprehensive analysis of the inspectorate which had ever been undertaken, and what is noteworthy is its lack of immediate impact. The report got some publicity in the newspapers with sen-

6 Ibid., p. 44.   7 Ibid., p. 54.   8 Ibid., pp 55–62.

sationalist headings such as, 'Inspectors get caning from one of their own',[9] and 'School inspection system has collapsed at post-primary'.[10] The report did not, however, become a great debating issue either within the public or, remarkably, within the inspectorate itself. It may have been that the critique was too thorough and hurtful to be accepted at that time. It may have been going too far too fast for attitudes which were not ready for it. Also some of the changed roles suggested for the inspectorate may not have been palatable to inspectors, such as a much lessened role with curricula and examinations. It may also be that the nature, scale and cost of the recommendations were not appealing to the authorities in the Department of Education and Finance. It would seem that the report was not widely circulated, nor widely read. The report did not form an agenda item for the inspectors' annual conferences. This would suggest a defensiveness within the inspectorate and a failure to take the opportunity of frank appraisal as a preliminary to planning for a better future.

The author himself anticipated that significant change would not occur quickly. He stated:

> Any planned changes would take some time to bring into effect. In other words, by the time parts of the system begin to operate in new ways we shall be rapidly approaching the 21st century. A part of a system having its roots and legal regulations in the 19th century and the first quarter of the 20th century without ever really having been comprehensively up-dated is likely to experience organisational problems. The demands of the last decade of the 20th century cannot easily be met by techniques of operation which are out of date and unequal to new challenges.[11]

This was a prescient comment. While the Hopes Report had little immediate impact the ideas percolated through the system gradually, and many features of the inspectorate system as it existed in 2008 reflected the vision that Hopes had for a reformed inspectorate in 1991.

While Clive Hopes was working on his report another international agency, the OECD, had completed a national review of the Irish education system. The Review was not published until 1991, but the main text was available to the Department in the autumn of 1989. The annual conference of the post-primary inspectorate in 1989 focused on the nature and future of the post-primary inspectorate. The Secretary of the Department of Education referred to the OECD Review in his address and invited the inspectorate to meet and reflect on how they saw their future and to report to him in the light of the OECD's comments. Regional meetings of inspectors were held in

9 *The Star*, 24 March 1992. 10 *Irish Times*, 23 March 1992. 11 Hopes Report, p. 5.

Cork, Dublin and Galway in February 1990. The reports of these meetings were made available to Clive Hopes, as was the draft OECD Review. The reports of the inspectors' meetings reflect divided opinions and a general unease at a potential loss of status if they were not centrally involved in curricula, examinations and in-service education.[12]

While the OECD Review did not deal with the inspectorate in detail, the reviewers made some incisive comments. The reviewers reported that it was generally recognised that the inspectorate was 'chronically understaffed' in relation to the scope of its duties. The review stated that collectively the inspectorate constituted 'a formidable body of professional expertise.' Their expertise was not in question, 'It is rather that their full potential is far from being tapped.' The reviewers posed the dilemma as follows:

> If it is recognised that the inspectors are an indispensable link between schools and the Department, their numbers should necessarily expand and their functions should diversify in step with the quantitative and qualitative growth of the education system. In recent years, it is the reverse trend which has prevailed. The inspectorate has become under-resourced and under-staffed. The consequence has been less quality control and a weakening contribution to the overall accountability of the system.[13]

In the opinion of the reviewers, there was a need to rethink the role and specific tasks of the inspectorate in the context of the major changes which would affect the education system over the next decade. If the inspectorate was not going to be enlarged then its range of tasks needed to be reduced such as its involvement with the examinations and the delivery of in-service training for teachers, and a concentration on auditing school performance and advising the Minister and the Department. If the inspectorate corps were to be enlarged, its multiple tasks would call for a diversified staff, grouped in specialised, horizontal units, and strong central leadership. The reviewers believed that 'the system could only benefit from having an enlarged, unified and more independent inspectorate, with clearly defined functions'.[14]

In the review meeting with the Minister and her officials in Paris, on 30 November 1989, the Minister responded to the reviewers stating that she considered that the inspectorate 'should play a much larger role in the area of monitoring and advising on the performance of the system and on policy developments'. However, she added, 'as an increase in the number of inspectors was unlikely to occur, this might necessitate a gradual phasing out of their duties in connection with the examinations … This was a matter which she proposed to pursue with the inspectorate'.[15] In the event, neither of the

---

12 Appendices C, D and E in the Hopes Report (op. cit.), pp 89–135.   13 OECD, *Reviews of National Policies for Education: Ireland* (Paris: OECD, 1991), p. 44.   14 Ibid., p. 45.   15 Ibid.,

reviewers' options of increasing the numbers of inspectors or rationalising their duties took place at that time, and the status quo continued to prevail.

However, some of the ideas contained in the Hopes Report and in the OECD Review were incorporated in the Green Paper – 'Education for a Changing World', published in June 1992. It stated:

> In the context of the greater delegation of responsibility to schools, a changed role is envisaged for the inspectorate. The inspectorate's main responsibilities will be to evaluate the schools generally, to disseminate good practice and to contribute to the formulation of policy, with particular reference to ensuring and maintaining quality.[16]

The Green Paper went on to specify how these functions would be performed. Furthermore, the inspectorate was to be reconstituted as a single cohesive unit, with statutory powers. It would prepare an annual report on the performance of the school system which would be published independently. For the future, it was envisaged that inspection would be 'whole school' inspection, using a team approach and related to overall school performance. The participation of inspectors in the public examinations would be phased out with the establishment of a new agency to conduct the examinations. Inspectors would no longer participate in the actual running of in-service courses, but would be responsible for monitoring their quality. It was also proposed that teachers would be seconded for fixed periods to work with the inspectorate.[17]

These government proposals caused unease and concern among the inspectorate. Explanatory meetings were held on 11 and 13 November between senior Department officials and union representatives.[18] Various meetings of inspectors took place regionally to discuss the implications of the proposals.[19]

There were 898 formal written submissions on the contents of the Green Paper. Among these IMPACT, the public sector trade union representing inspectors, 'demanded' that examinations should remain part of the functions of the inspectorate. Neither did the proposed secondment of teachers to the inspectorate get its approval. Impact 'saw no case for the integration of the inspectorate'. It also urged that 'the current hierarchy of the inspectorate should be critically examined.' The submission urged that 'the inspectorate be centrally involved in the in-service process'.[20] The Department of Education Branch of the Public Service Executive Union in its submission expressed concern about the proposal to set up external, executive agencies

p. 121.   16 *Green Paper: Education for a Changing World* (Dublin: Stationery Office, 1992) p. 173.   17 Ibid., p. 174.   18 Report of meeting, 11 and 13 November, 1992, Dept of Ed. Archives.   19 Report of Meeting in Cork, 6 October 1992, Dept of Ed. Archives (uncatalogued).   20 Submissions to the Green Paper, vol. III, no. 749.

such as that proposed for the public examinations. It also expressed reservations of the powers intended for the proposed Teaching Council.[21]

The proposals in the Green Paper for the future role of the inspectorate got detailed discussion at the National Education Convention, held in October 1993. The Secretariat's report acknowledged that there was agreement that 'the inspectorate has an important and unique role to play in contributing to the effective implementation of the Green Paper proposals, especially those directly related to enhancing the quality of education in the system.' However, it also remarked, 'There has been a failure at official level to recognise and develop the potential of this group of individuals', due to under-staffing and over-diversified role.[22] The Secretariat reported that school managements, teacher organisations and parents had expressed concerns that inspectors would withdraw from close contact with schools, even though it was recognised that inspectorial visits to post-primary schools had been drastically curtailed. In this context, the secondment of teachers to the inspectorate was a welcome proposal but it should not be regarded 'as an excuse for not bringing the membership of the inspectorate up to a more realistic level'.

Concern was expressed on the exercise of advisory as well as evaluative functions by the same inspectorate personnel. Concern was also expressed about the preparedness of the inspectorate for the proposed new role in whole school inspection 'more especially since the views of this group are not known.' The report highlighted the type of skills and characteristics which inspectors needed to exhibit, for which special training was needed. It also stressed the need of inspectors for opportunities for private study and research. Overall, delegates at the Convention expressed high regard for the school inspectorate and gave strong support for their improved training, staffing and purposeful role.[23] The Convention Report also stated, 'The provision of a comprehensive psychological and guidance service for schools was considered a priority at the Convention', and set out how it might be best deployed, and linked to the work of the inspectorate.[24]

A valuable insight into the views of the post-primary inspectorate on the proposed changes in the functioning of the inspectorate as envisaged in the Hopes Report (1991), the OECD Report (1991) and the Green Paper (1992) is provided by a research inquiry conducted in the summer of 1994. This was a questionnaire study by John McGinty, a senior post-primary inspector. On a study of eight categories of existing work, examinations at 36% and meetings at 20% took up most of the inspectors' time. School visits only took up 12% of the time, but it was the category that most, 85%, of inspectors wished to retain. Participation on Selection Boards was the only category which a high proportion, 34%, wished 'to give up'. In the case of Examinations, 5% would 'give up', 38% would favour a monitoring role and 46% wished to retain them. On in-service work the proportions were 3%, 46% and 38% respectively ('no response', completed the 100%).[25]

Thus, there was a significant division among the inspectorate regarding the proposals to reduce their hands-on involvement with the public examinations and in-service education for teachers, with only 5% and 3% prepared to 'give them up'.

On the quality of performance on a range of inspectorial functions the following was recorded as the percentages which regarded them as 'poorly' performed:

> (a) inspecting/reporting on schools, 70%; (b) supporting/advising teachers, 60%; (c) annual report, 73%; (d) special reports, 68%; (e) monitoring probationary teachers, 74%; (f) monitoring teacher training, 81%; (g) contributing to policy formulation, 62%.

Yet these were areas which were being emphasised in policy documents as being the core elements of the work of the inspectorate, but they were being rated by high percentages of the respondents as being 'poorly' performed. A further 70% considered that senior management did not adequately utilise the inspectors in the policy-making process. When the inspectors were asked if they thought seconded teachers would free inspectors for more specialised tasks, 49% considered that they would. There was no majority support for whole school inspection but there was, by contrast, an awareness of its positive impact on work culture and effectiveness. The study revealed uncertainty in the minds of inspectors on a unified post-primary inspectorate.[26]

Overall, the responses indicated very mixed and divided attitudes on the role of the inspectorate. There was a reluctance to give up any of their existing categories of work, except for Selection Boards. While the great majority wished to retain school visits, only 12% of their time was devoted to it. Most of the inspectors considered that many of what are regarded as the core functions such as evaluation, advice, reportage and contributing to policy were poorly performed, but they did not address how this situation might be remedied. A great deal of uncertainty existed regarding new proposals on seconded teachers, whole school inspection, and the old policy chestnut of an integrated inspectorate. It would seem that, in general, the post-primary inspectorate was caught in an identity crisis where the habitual and familiar gave them a sense of career identity which new policy proposals seemed to put in jeopardy.

The Programme for a Partnership Government, published in January 1993 made a commitment to 'the development of democratic intermediate structures

---

25 John McGinty, 'Post-Primary Inspectors in Ireland: A Survey of Work Practices and of Attitudes to Proposed Changes in Their Role' (M.Sc. dissertation, Trinity College Dublin, 1994), pp 76–79. 26 Ibid.

for the management of first and second level schools.' This issue was debated at the National Education Convention in October 1993. Arising from this discussion, Minister Niamh Bhreathnach issued a 'Position Paper on Regional Education Councils' (RECs), on 11 March 1994. This paper envisaged a dual framework for the inspectorate in the future. There would be a national inspectorate which would be responsible for quality assurance and the evaluation of educational outcomes. There would also be an inspectorate operated at Regional Council level which would deal with support services to the schools in the regions.[27] The 'Report on the Round-table Discussions on the Position Paper', which took place in April 1994, urged that the inspectorate of the Regional Councils should operate on a two-tier approach, one sector as a support and advisory role, while the other cohort of inspectors would be involved in an evaluation and quality assurance role for the RECs.[28]

When the White Paper – 'Charting Our Education Future' was published in May 1995, Chapter 5, was devoted to 'The Role of the Inspectorate'. The White Paper envisaged a changed administrative framework for the education system, with regional education boards supplementing the central Department of Education. Within this framework the inspectorate was to be re-structured as a small cohesive central inspectorate within the Department, and a regional inspectorate to be seconded to the regional boards. The central inspectorate was to have three core functions – an evaluation function, a policy function and an examination function. It would evaluate and report on the standards and quality of the education provided and on the effectiveness of policies and their implementation. The policy function related to advice on policy formulation. In relation to examinations, it would supervise the operation of the national examinations. The central inspectorate would be organised into three units for these functions, under the direction of the Chief Inspector. The central inspectorate would produce an annual report, drawing on reports prepared by each regional education board.[29]

A virtue of the regional inspectorate was seen in that being closer to schools it was more likely to be more effective in providing services and working in partnership with the local stakeholders. The distinction raised at the Convention between the advisory and evaluative functions of the inspectorate was to be upheld in the way the regional inspectorate would operate. The regional inspectorate would also incorporate psychological services and provision for special needs pupils. The evaluative function would operate on a whole-school focus, and in relation to the school plan. To ensure equitable evaluation between boards, performance indicators and criteria would be

27 Department of Education, 'Position Paper on Regional Education Councils' (unpublished, 11 March 1994), pars. 11.4 and 11.8.   28 John Coolahan and Seamus McGuinness, 'Report on the Round table Discussions on the Position Paper on Regional Education Councils' (unpublished, May 1994), p. 12.   29 *White Paper: Charting Our Education Future* (Dublin: Stationery Office, 1995), pp 183–89.

developed at national level. The underlying purpose of the evaluation would be to improve the quality of education in the schools. The Department of Education would publish draft proposals for consultation with the partners in education on the whole-school inspection approach.

While a small number of psychologists would stay with the Central Inspectorate, the majority would be seconded to the education boards. There they would contribute their specialist expertise to students and schools, and also work as an integral part of the whole – school inspection teams. Teachers with recognised expertise would be seconded for specific periods on a contract basis to the Regional and Central Inspectorates. It was recognised that the proposals in this White Paper 'involve fundamental change for the inspectorate and for its relationship with schools', and intensive induction training, complemented by regular in-career training would be provided for inspectors.[30]

Whatever about the views of individual inspectors, quite clearly the policy approach had moved away from the traditional structure and multifarious roles which had come to shape the inspectorate over time. The policy reflected the concept of an integrated inspectorate operating at two levels – central and regional. At regional level there would be a two-prong approach – advisory and evaluative. The direct hands-on involvement in areas such as examinations and in-service education would yield to monitoring and oversight of such services. School inspection would be by inspectorial teams, including psychologists, on a whole school approach, in relation to school plans. The secondment of teachers to the inspectorate would be established. The proposed establishment of a Teaching Council would also remove some traditional work from the inspectorate. With the publication of government decisions, as incorporated in the White Paper, it might be expected that the evolving policy on the inspectorate had been crystallised. However, changes of government often involve changes in policy plans. Even though an Education bill, incorporating the White Paper lines of policy was drafted by early 1997, the incumbent government was defeated in the election of that summer. The incoming Fianna Fáil led government did not favour the establishment of regional education boards and new legislation was drafted reflecting this shift in policy, which would, of course, affect the plans for the inspectorate.

The Chief Inspector, Seán Mac Gleannáin, and his Deputy Chiefs, Seán Ó Fiachra and Cearbhall Ó Dálaigh, made strong and successful efforts to ensure that the inspectorate was incorporated as a specific entity in the Education Act of 1998. This was the first comprehensive education act in the history of the state. Part III, section 13, was devoted to the inspectorate, gave a statutory basis to the inspectorate, and provided a statutory basis for its functions. The most significant difference from the White Paper of 1995 and the Education bill of 1997, regarding the inspectorate was the omission of the

30 Ibid.

regional education boards and, consequently, of the regional inspectorate with its separate advisory and evaluative functions. All inspectors and psychologists would now operate under the aegis of the central Department. The key functions designated for the inspectorate followed the pattern set out for the Central Inspectorate in the White Paper, that is, to evaluate the quality and effectiveness of educational provision nationally; to assist in the formulation of policy by the Minister; and to supervise the operation of the national examinations system.[31] The approach set out for inspection was on the whole-school model; the inspectors who were psychologists would relate to the educational and psychological needs of students. In section 13.3 (3) the role regarding examinations included the phrase 'To perform such functions relating to the preparation and marking of the school examinations which are conducted in the state as the Chief Inspector shall direct', which was not in the earlier bill. This indicated a more involved role for the inspectorate with the examinations. Section 5 of the Act allowed for the secondment of teachers to the inspectorate 'to carry out any or all of the functions conferred on an inspector.' Overall, the specification of functions of the inspectorate focussed very much on what was regarded as their key roles in evaluation, maintenance of standards, and policy advice, informed by research. No reference was made to the many extra duties which had grown up such as writing speeches, researching parliamentary questions, and participating in selection boards.

The statutory definition of functions specified in the Act provided an opportunity for the leadership in the inspectorate to re-shape the work pattern of the inspectorate. The Education Act of 1998 is rightly regarded as a landmark in modern Irish education, and concerning the inspectorate it was of very great significance for its future development, albeit amendments were needed within a few years in relation to the public examinations and the psychological service.

PRIMARY EDUCATION UNDER SCRUTINY

During the late eighties primary education came under significant formal scrutiny. In October 1987, the Minister for Education, Ms. Mary O'Rourke, set up a Review Body on the Primary Curriculum and, in February 1988, she established a Primary Education Review Body. Two divisional inspectors, Liam ó h-Éigearta and Seán Ó Fiachra sat on the Curriculum Review Body, which reported in May 1990. As regards inspection of primary schools, the report recommended that external inspection both on a 'whole school' basis and on an 'individual teacher' basis should continue. However, it also recommended that inspector numbers should 'be brought up to full strength.' The Review Body

31 *Explanatory and Financial Memorandum on the Education bill (No. 2), 1997.*

also encouraged internal evaluation by the school staff, acting as a team, linked to school plans devised under the leadership of the school principal. The report urged that 'concise statistical abstracts of important features of the education system be issued regularly and promptly.'[32] On the central issue under review, namely the curriculum, the Review Body concluded:

> The curriculum requires revision and re-formulation in its aims, scope and content, in the manner in which it is implemented and in the way in which pupil progress is assessed and recorded and the way the overall effectiveness of the system is evaluated.[33]

This major and comprehensive recommendation was activated in 1990 under the auspices of the NCCA. The revision of the primary curriculum became a major task extending through the nineties, until the publication of the Revised Curriculum in 1999. The engagement of the primary inspectorate with the NCCA on this process was a major professional task throughout the period. The Review Body also recommended that a special committee be established to examine and report on issues relating to children with handicap, which was also to engage inspectors/psychologists in subsequent years.

The *Report of the Primary Education Review Body* was published in December 1990. Its remit covered all aspects of primary education. The primary inspectorate was represented by Seamus de Buitléir, Deputy Chief Inspector and John Dennehy, who acted as secretary to the Review Body. In the chapter dealing with the inspectorate a summarised statement on the work of the primary inspectorate at this time is illustrative of how varied and demanding the role had become. It stated:

> In addition to inspection and their other duties, the primary inspectorate has become more and more involved in delivering a supportive and advisory service to teachers and schools. Inspectors are assigned a wide range of specific responsibilities. They are involved in curriculum development, in–service training for teachers, special and remedial education and schemes for the disadvantaged. They advise on school buildings and equipment, act as members of committees both within and outside the Department and provide guidelines and advice to educational publishers. They conduct surveys, investigate disputes and complaints and perform other duties assigned to them from time to time. Over the years, they have been responsible for many major undertakings such as the preparation of the New Primary School Curriculum.[34]

32 *Report of the Review Body on the Primary Curriculum* (Dublin NCCA and Dept. of Education, 1990), pp 90–92.   33 Ibid., p. 97.   34 *Report of the Primary Education Review Body* (Dublin: Stationery Office, 1990), pp 88, 89.

Despite what the Review Body termed 'the mushrooming complexity of special duties which have developed over the last twenty years', the report deplored the under-resourcing and understaffing which had taken place. No recruitment had occurred since 1981, and the report urged the gradual expansion of the service from the then current staff of 81 to 107, as had been recommended by the Department of the Public Service, in 1981.[35] Among a range of other recommendations was that the Deputy Chief Inspector (primary) should be a member of the top policy making body of the Department, and he/she should control a budget for research, training and staff development. Provision should be made for 'regular and comprehensive in-service training of inspectors'. The Review Body also recommended that the inspectorate 'become involved in the publication of discussion papers, reports or pamphlets' on educational issues of public concern. In particular, a new style annual report should be issued by the Department, incorporating the professional views of the inspectorate. The report also urged 'that there be much closer co-operation between the primary and post-primary branches of the inspectorate'.[36] These significant recommendations were surfacing at a time when Dr Clive Hopes and the OECD were also reporting on the inspectorate, and while little immediate action took place on them they fed into an increasing concern that reforms were needed with regard to the inspectorate.

As regards the report of the Review Body on the Primary Curriculum, the primary inspectors took an early pro-active stance. A total of twenty-six working groups were established within the inspectorate in 1990 to report on all aspects of primary education. Two of these dealt specifically with the role of the inspector. In their review of existing practices they urged an up-dating of many traditional procedures, a more developmental role in relation to curriculum, greater in-service training for the inspectorate and greater co-ordination and cohesion between the inspectors and the administration within the Department.[37] As the NCCA undertook its major revision of the primary curriculum it set up a range of subcommittees to deal with different aspects of the work. Inspectors were very active in these sub-committees. For instance, in 1993–94, 18 inspectors functioned as members of these subcommittees, with a further 14 inspectors in advisory committees within the Department to provide advice and support for them. Inspectors were also involved in the NCCA Board of Studies and in the Co-ordinating Committee for the revised curriculum.[38] This pattern of engagement continued until the completion of the work and the publication of the revised Primary School Curriculum in 1999. It was a major contribution by the primary inspectorate to the general work of the overall inspectorate through the nineties, which is discussed in the next section.

35 Ibid., p. 90.   36 Ibid., p. 91.   37 Meithealacha Oibre Cigirí, *Tuairiscí*, 1990, uimh. 2 agus 8.   38 *Annual Report of the Inspectorate/Psychological Service, 1993, '94* (Dept of Education), p. 8.

THE WORK OF THE INSPECTORATE DURING AN ERA OF TRANSITION

When Dr Clive Hopes produced his report in May 1991, regarding the role of Chief Inspector he stated, 'The Chief Inspector should take charge of the Inspectorate. The position should no longer be regarded as a "figure head" with the two "real" chiefs, with the title of Deputy Chief, operating the primary and post-primary sectors.'[39] In that same month, Seán Mac Gleannáin was appointed Chief Inspector following a competitive appointment process. He was formerly a secondary teacher, but had wide-ranging experience as a primary inspector since joining the service in 1962. He set out to ensure that the position of Chief Inspector should be one of substantial leadership. This appointment coincided with much analysis and reflection on the role of the Department of Education within an evolving education system, and on the work of the inspectorate within the system. The Chief Inspector early secured the appointment of an inspector as his personal assistant, and modernised administrative aspects of his office. Future appointments to senior positions such as Deputy Chief and Assistant Chiefs were opened to competition, with seniority no longer the key criterion. This shift in the long-established pattern of promotion on seniority caused considerable dissension within the inspectorate, but it was an important step in reform efforts. Appointments also became cross-sectoral and were no longer tied to particular branches of the inspectorate. While inspectors in the different branches continued to do work related to their traditional areas of responsibility, more and more they joined together on cross-sectoral issues, and in committees. Moves towards closer integration were also indicated by the fact that in 1991, for the first time, both primary and post-primary inspectors attended the same annual conference. In the following year, 1992, the psychologists also joined in for the annual conference. This process was not without its teething pains as different groups considered that some issues under discussion were not central to their particular areas of interest. However, better structuring of the programme, incorporating elective as well as plenary sessions, smoothed difficulties. One of the significant outcomes of the joint conferences was the cultivation of acquaintance among personnel who might never otherwise have met each other, improving awareness of the work of different sectors, and, over time, fostering an improved esprit de corps. In 1994, the separate union branches for secondary and vocational inspectors amalgamated into one unit.

In June 1992, the Green Paper was published which stated that the inspectorate would be reconstituted 'as a single cohesive unit, with statutory functions'. The inspectorate would focus on 'whole school' inspection and publish an annual report. Since 1982 the primary inspectorate had presented a report to the Minister on its work. In October 1991 the new Chief

39 Hopes Report, op. cit., p. 58.

Inspector set about producing an annual report for the whole of the inspectorate for the year 1990–91. It took some time to compile this, but it was submitted in July 1992. As the introduction to the report points out, 'The
Report confirms that the three sections of the inspectorate/psychological service functioned as separate entities with no co-ordination of activities.'⁴⁰ The
report was mainly a quantitative analysis of the range of activities engaged in
by the primary inspectorate, the post-primary inspectorate and the psychological service, with some linking commentary. It also bore testimony to the
multifarious character of the inspectorates' work, with the linking commentary raising some doubts about the sustainability and appropriateness of such
activity. The annual report for 1991–92 was made available in November
1993, and took a similar format. It was seen as a step in the direction of producing the annual report as envisaged by the Green Paper, but it was
acknowledged, 'The reality is that the inspectorate is not yet in a position to
present an authoritative report on the performance of the system.'⁴¹ The
introduction to the report pointedly remarked:

> The Department has made increasing demands on the inspectorate in
> recent years but there has been a significant decline in the number of
> inspectors available. Inevitably the main casualty is the work of
> inspection of schools. In the year under review, there was a further
> erosion of time spent on inspection. This particular year perhaps can
> be seen as the low point in the evolution of the inspectorate.⁴²

However, it surmised that the tide might be about to turn, and commented
that the appointment of nine new inspectors in September 1992 could be seen
as a good augury for the future.

For the year 1992–93, a more attractive A3 booklet format was devised
for the annual report, which continued to be published in this way, until
1995–96. The sectors no longer reported separately on the branches' activities but related to cross-sectoral items such as curriculum and assessment, in-
service provision, and reports on the system. This was seen as reflecting 'a
more cohesive, unified inspectorate, under the general management of the
Chief Inspector'. The professional development and induction programmes
for the inspectorate were henceforth to be devised on a cross-sectoral basis.
This cross-sectoral approach was also reflected in the composition of a
number of committees, for example, The Whole School Inspection
Committee, the Research and Development Committee, the In-career Policy
Committee, the Professional Development Committee of the inspectorate.
The establishment of such committees indicated the more pro-active orienta-
tion of the combined inspectorate on policy issues. New directions were also

40 *Annual Report of the Inspectorate/Psychological Service, 1990–91* (Dept of Education, 1992).
41 *Annual Report for 1991–92*, p. 4.   42 Ibid., p. 5

observable regarding the work patterns of the inspectorate. For instance, it was decided that rather than engaging, as heretofore, in the actual delivery of in-career development courses for teachers, the inspectorate would concentrate on the identification of teachers' needs and on the monitoring of in-career development courses provided by outside agencies.[43] The provision of the courses for remedial education were devolved from the psychologists to third-level institutions with effect from September 1994. Another instance of changed work practice was the ending of the involvement of the inspectorate in the direct management and administration in the RTCs and the DIT, following the legislation of 1992 with regard to these institutions.

Early in 1994, a new unit was established within the Department of Education – the In-Career Development Unit (ICDU). Provision for an expanded and strengthened in-career development programme was made available through the National Development Plan, 1994–99. With the assistance of the European Social Fund a sum of £36 million was made available for this purpose for the plan's duration. The central function of the ICDU was to develop, manage and evaluate a national programme of teacher in-career development. Three senior inspectors were assigned to the unit from primary, post-primary and the psychological service. The first appointees were Emer Egan, Maura Clancy and Lee McCurtain. The Unit was supported by a high-powered internal policy committee of administrative and inspectoral staff chaired by the Chief Inspector. Two Advisory Committees, of a representative character (one for primary and one for post-primary), were also established, chaired by the Deputy Chief Inspector for each of the sectors. The ICDU brought a new coherence to the policy, provision, delivery and evaluation of in-career development. The much greater expansion of in-career development services for teachers occurred at an opportune time of significant curricular and pedagogic change in the school system. To a very large degree, the in-career programmes were operated by agencies outside the ICDU, who acted in accordance with criteria established by the Unit and who reported to it. This meant that the inspectorate's role shifted from a hands-on approach to a policy and advisory role for in-career teacher education. The consultative process allowed feedback to refine provision, over the years.

The Primary Education Review Body (1990), the OECD (1991) and the Green Paper (1992) had emphasised the need for greater co-ordination of educational research, particularly of policy-related research to help educational policy formulation. Early in 1992, the Research and Development Committee of the Department of Education was re-vitalised under the chairmanship of the Chief Inspector. In November 1992, this Committee organised an Education Research Forum. This was the first occasion on which the various educational research agencies were gathered together in a common forum with

43 *Annual Report for 1992–93,* p. 4.

Department of Education staff. The Forum emphasised the desirability of liaison and co-ordination between research agencies and the Department of Education. Over subsequent years, the Committee invited research proposals and tendered for research projects from interested parties. A number of dissemination conferences were held and a worthwhile tradition was nurtured of supportive relationships between the inspectorate and academic researchers.

Education for special needs children became an issue of increasing policy concern during the 1990s. When Ireland held the presidency of the EEC in 1990, it championed the idea of the integration of special needs children into mainstream schooling, as much as was possible. In September 1991, a Special Education Review Body was established, with wide-ranging terms of reference. Five members of the inspectorate/psychological service, with experience in special education were assigned to the Review Committee, two Divisional Inspectors on a full time basis. One of these, Micheál Ó Flannagáin, acted as secretary to the Committee and another Liam Ó h-Éigearta, largely drafted and edited the report.[44] Members of the inspectorate also completed a position paper for the Committee on educational provision for each of the fourteen categories of pupils with disabilities and special needs. The Committee published its report in September 1993. Chapter 2 of the Report highlighted many deficiencies in existing provision, and it went on to make a large number of recommendations for action. Among these were the restructuring of the Special Education Section within the Department, and it recommended that a greatly expanded school psychological service 'should be established on a countrywide basis without delay'.[45] It made many recommendations regarding support for pupils with specific learning disabilities.

A three year pilot phase of a psychological service to primary schools, focussing on the areas of West Tallaght/Clondalkin and South Tipperary, formally ended in the summer of 1993. At the end of 1993, the Minister decided to put the service on a permanent basis in these two areas, and to extend the scheme, on a gradual basis, to primary schools generally, beginning with the employment of ten additional psychologists for that purpose in 1994–95.[46] In subsequent years, greater resources were made available to the schools psychological service. Parental and public opinion became more vocal on inadequacies of educational provision for various categories of pupils with disabilities. This coincided with greater legislative provision for the rights of children. A number of high profile court cases were taken, which involved the input of evidence by inspectors and other Departmental staff, and which tended to take up an increasing amount of their time. A significant outcome of some cases was that the State was required to make better provision in this area, so the special education role of the Department expanded over the years. This included the provision of a new category of personnel in schools – the Special Needs Assistant.

44 *Annual Report for 1992–93*, p. 10.   45 *Report of the Special Education Review Body* (Dept of Education, 1993), p. 226.   46 *Annual Report for 1993–94*, p. 19.

Other categories of support teachers provided for the needs of children with special needs were remedial, resource and visiting teachers.

Greater equity in educational provision was also highlighted for socially and economically disadvantaged children. A range of schemes were initiated which sought to make inroads into such inequality. In 1990, a Home-School-Community-Liaison scheme (HSCL) was introduced for primary pupils in designated urban areas which experienced a high degree of disadvantage. One of its key targets was to engage parents more supportively in the education of their children. Following successful reportage from evaluators, the HSCL was extended as a mainstream resource in selected schools, in designated areas of disadvantage from the beginning of the school year 1993–94. In these years the scheme was managed centrally by an Assistant Chief Inspector, Colm Ó Maoláin, who chaired the Steering Committee on which three inspectors/psychologists sat.[47] The scheme was led by Dr Concepta Conaty and it has continued since and has encompassed post-primary as well as primary schools. Another example of an intervention project to alleviate educational disadvantage was the 'Early Start' Pre-School Project, initiated in June 1994. This was aimed at socio-economically deprived young children with a view to preparing them optimally for success in the early stages of formal schooling, and harnessing parental and community involvement. The design and management of the relatively small-scale project involved the input of five inspectors. Inspectors were also centrally involved in the increased provision of educational facilities for traveller children in the nineties. The primary inspectorate had been particularly involved with the various schemes such as preschool classes, the Special Additional Assistants for children of travellers, the mainstream primary integration, and the special schools. In 1993–94 thirty-one new posts of Special Teachers for Travellers were sanctioned bringing the total to 188 in 159 primary schools.[48] In 1992, the post of National Education Officer for Travellers was instituted and the inspectorate managed the Visiting Teacher Service for Travellers. During the nineties increased efforts were made for the enrolment of travellers in mainstream post-primary schools. A number of post-primary inspectors were involved in securing improvements in participation.

An educational initiative – Youthreach – for young people in the 15 to 18 year age group who left school without qualifications or vocational training was introduced in 1989. By 1993 it had 1600 participants in courses run by 28 VECs, in conjunction with FÁS. In 1993, eleven inspectors undertook a review of this scheme, visiting the 55 centres of operation. They furnished a report on each centre. In general, the inspectors found that the courses were delivered to a high standard by well-motivated staff, and they made recommendations to help improve programmes.[49]

47 Ibid.   48 Ibid., p. 10.   49 Ibid., p. 37.

Indeed, the whole area of pupil guidance received a good deal of attention in the early nineties, partly influenced by EU approaches to the free movement of goods, services and people throughout the single market. Under the auspices of the EU PETRA programme three Department psychologists participated in the 'Training of Guidance Counsellors' and 'Parents in Guidance Projects'. Three psychologists also participated in a representative committee which, in 1994, drew up a set of guidelines for guidance. Guidance counselling was further promoted by the establishment, in 1995, of the National Council for Guidance in Education (NCGE). This Centre was separate from the Department of Education, but operated in close liaison with the psychologists within the Department.

Work on the public examinations continued to dominate the time of the post-primary inspectorate. The annual report for 1990–91 stated that at 6% of the post-primary inspectorate's total activity, 'it is clear that the amount spent on school inspection has reached an unacceptably low level … and highlights the need for an appraisal of the diverse activities engaged in by the inspectors and to revise priorities'.[50] The Report for 1992–93 indicated that the situation had changed little, with just 9% of post-primary inspectors' time devoted to school inspection, though in a questionnaire survey the inspectors confirmed that they regarded it 'as the most important aspect of their work'.[51] Without a fundamental restructuring of the role and work of the inspectorate it was difficult to see how a re-balancing in favour of school inspection would occur.

The numbers of students taking the public examinations continued to increase and the logistical problems in ensuring that no faults occurred in the operation of the examinations were demanding. A useful initiative in this regard was the establishment of the Examinations Co-ordinating Committee in November 1993. The Committee co-ordinated the contribution of the Examinations Branch, the inspectorate, the Personnel Section, the Pupil Database Section and the Communications Office on a range of issues. This cross-sectoral team approach towards the management of the examinations was important for the Department. The inspectorate was represented by the Chief Inspector, Sean Mac Gleannáin, by Deputy Chief Inspectors Domhnall Ó Séaghdha (to 2004) and Cearbhall Ó Dálaigh (from 2004), and by Tomás Ó Conaill, Assistant Chief Inspector. Despite its best efforts, some problems did occur such as those relating to the Leaving Certificate Art Examination in 1995. This led to the calling in of a consultancy firm, Price Waterhouse, to conduct an investigation. As well as specific criticisms relating to the conduct of the art examinations, in their report (1996) the consultants focussed on 'systems failure', including the structure and staffing of the 'Examinations Branch of Education and the dual structure of Department of Education as it impacts on the examination process'. By dual structure it meant the administrative and professional divide. While recognising the work of the Co-ordinating Committee, the report considered that it did not go far enough. The report stated that the implementation of its recommendations would constitute a major change programme for the Examinations Branch and the inspectorate.[52] The implications of the Report may have prompted a re-think of the Green Paper (1992) proposal to set up a Curriculum and Assessment Agency responsible for the administration of the certificate examinations. This document had also proposed an Agency for the School Psychological Service and for Special Education, issues which would re-emerge later in policy formulation. The immediate impact of the 1996 report led to a number of reforms in the administration of the examinations, including much closer collaboration of the inspectorate with the administrative staff, which was to be the forerunner of new relationships between both sectors in policy and administrative matters. An Examination Management Group was established in 1997, which was jointly chaired by the newly appointed Chief Inspector, Eamon Stack, and Patrick Burke, Assistant Secretary. The group also included Cearbhall Ó Dálaigh, Deputy Chief Inspector, John McGinty, Assistant Chief Inspector and Martin Hanevy, Principal Officer of the Examinations Branch. The practice of publication of the Chief Examiner's Report, which had gone into abeyance, was restored. Marking schemes were also published. Appeal Commissioners were appointed, and techniques such as bar-coding were introduced to improve communication. A further major change was introduced in 1998 when the examination scripts were made available to schools by which students could re-visit their answers and the mode of correction was transparent. This initiative, which became known as the 'return of scripts' was introduced by the then Minister, Micheál Martin, arising from a proposal made to him by Chief Inspector Eamon Stack, following a study visit by the latter to New Zealand earlier in the year. The close teamwork and collaborative work engaged in by the administrative staff and the inspectorate at this time changed more traditional sub-cultural patterns and opened up new possibilities for joint policy-making. This was to prove to be a very important development in the way the Department of Education and Science operated in later years.

Cearbhall Ó Dálaigh, Senior Inspector, was seconded for a number of years from September 1991 to become Chief Executive of the newly-established National Council for Vocational Awards (NCVA). This body was set up by the Department as a certification body for the wide range of European Social Fund vocational training programmes. The NCVA also contributed to senior cycle initiatives such as the Revised Leaving Certificate Vocational Programme, the Transition Year Programme and to aspects of what was to become known as the Leaving Certificate Applied. Its initial work in relation

---

52 Price Waterhouse, *Report on the Investigations on the 1995 Leaving Certificate Art Examinations*, 14 June 1996, pp 53, 63.

to the lower levels of attainment contributed to the development of the lower levels of the National Qualifications Framework. The NCVA later became part of the Further Education and Training Awards Council (FETAC).

In September 1995 the Government established TEASTAS, the Irish National Certification Authority, on an interim basis. Chris Connolly, a Senior Inspector, was appointed as chief executive of the interim authority. TEASTAS prepared the way for a national qualifications authority and, in late 1999, Connolly resumed his role as a departmental inspector. The new tripartite qualifications structure of the National Qualifications Authority (NQAI), HETAC and FETAC was established by legislation in 2000, becoming operative in 2001.

The inspectorate was very involved in curricular policy issues through the nineties. The primary inspectorate was deeply engaged with the NCCA on the reform of the primary curriculum, but was also involved in schemes such as the development and training for SPHE, involving Social and Personal Education, Health Education and Sexuality Education. At post-primary level, inspectors contributed to the revision of many Junior Certificate and Senior Certificate syllabi. A committee was established on the Junior Certificate School Programme, chaired by the Deputy Chief Inspector, Cearbhall Ó Dálaigh, and with four inspectors/psychologists. It recommended to the NCCA that the programme be developed to meet the requirement of national certification. In association with the NCCA, inspectors devised a course for Civic Social and Political Education (CSPE), which, following the pilot scheme, became mandatory for all schools, at junior cycle level, from 1996–97. However, it was in the area of senior cycle education that the most significant changes were made in these years. The availability of a six-year post-primary cycle, coupled with the varying needs of a pupil clientele of whom 82% stayed on to the end of the Leaving Certificate course prompted new thinking on the appropriate curricular provision for them. A special policy committee, jointly chaired by the Chief Inspector and an Assistant Secretary, recommended, in 1993, that the Leaving Certificate should be envisaged, with three strands – the established Leaving Certificate; Leaving Certificate Vocational Programmes (LCVP) and Leaving Certificate Applied (LCA). There would also be a one year, non certified programme option, the Transition Year Programme as part of the senior cycle. The Leaving Certificate Vocational Programme had been devised by the ESF Steering Group in the Department and became operative, with EEC funding, in 1989. A Steering Committee was set up to revise the LCVP, which became more widely available to schools from September 1994. The Transition Year Programme had also had an earlier existence, but was now revamped, with a support group appointed to assist its implementation in schools from September 1994. A rationale and operational plan was developed for the LCA. A Senior Cycle Task Force, chaired by Eamon Stack, was set up within the Department, with five inspectors and one psychologist, and a number of administrative personnel, to monitor and facilitate the introduction of the senior cycle changes. There was also an external representative Monitoring Group established. A two-year development phase for the LCA began in September 1995, involving 53 schools. Three post-primary inspectors and two assistant chief inspectors were involved in the design and implementation of the LCA programme.[53] By September 1996, 132 schools offered the LCA to their students. In March 1995, the inspectorate undertook an evaluation of the Transition Year Programme in 146 schools and published an evaluation report in February 1996. The general result was satisfactory with 89% of the schools implementing the Departmental guidelines satisfactorily, and with good reactions from principals, teachers and pupils.[54] In May 1995 the new LCVP programme was monitored in 43% of participating schools by eighteen inspectors.[55]

Overall, the restructuring of the senior cycle was regarded as a successful policy achievement, to which the inspectors contributed greatly, together with the other partners, particularly the NCCA. In 1997, the launch of 'Schools IT 2000' was also a successful policy initiative to boost the use of ICT in schools. This project was an early example of close productive co-operation between the inspectorate and the administrative staff on a major multi-million policy initiative on ICT investment in education. The establishment of the National Council for Technology in Education (NCTE) in 1998 as a separate, but co-operating unit with the Department, gave vital leadership to this policy.

When the Green Paper, in 1992, announced that in future it was envisaged that inspection 'will be "whole school" inspection, using a team approach and related to overall school performance' it was laying down a significant challenge to the traditional modes of examining by the Irish inspectorates. While this method had been adopted in England and some European countries, it would require a culture change in Irish circumstances, although aspects of it had been in operation at primary level. To prepare for this change the Chief Inspector set up a working party of inspectors on Whole School Inspection (WSI). It prepared a series of documents which were discussed by the inspectorate at their annual conference in 1995. In his address to that conference the Chief Inspector, Seán Mac Gleannáin, referred to the longevity of the inspectorate, going back for over 160 years. He went on to state, 'much tradition and many practices have grown, some of which have now outlived their usefulness. We must continue to refine the way in which we execute our tasks and be prepared to discard parts of the old if they do not fit into the modern world'.[56] It was recognised that a historic change of procedure was afoot. The inspectors established their policy approach on WSI at that conference. On 13 March 1996 the Department presented its draft

53 *Annual Report for 1995–96*, p. 18.   **54** *Annual Report for 1994–95*, p. 16.   **55** *Annual Report for 1995–96*, pp 51–52.   **56** Opening Address by Chief Inspector to 1995 Annual Conference.

proposals on the purposes, procedures, and methods of WSI at a Consultative Conference with the education partners.[57] This was an example of a new approach of open dialogue with education partner interests on how inspection practice could be reformed from both a policy and an on-the-ground perspective. The consultative conference was chaired by Frank Murray, Executive Chairperson of the Commission on School Accommodation, and the Department's presenters were Margaret Condon, Post-Primary Inspector, Frank Kavanagh, Psychologist and Gearóid Ó Conluain, Senior Inspector. Arising from the conference the partners were invited to respond in writing to the Department's proposals and bilateral meetings took place with them on the issues. The aim was to secure agreement by December 1997 so that pilot exercises on WSI, later to be known as WSE, could take place in 1998.

The presentations and discussions which took place at the consultative conference in 1996, and at subsequent meetings, served a very useful purpose in deepening the understanding of the issues involved and, through consultative dialogue, nurturing support among the partners for the initiative, as part of a national educational reform strategy. The adoption of a gradualist approach and the policy of learning from pilot exercises also helped to create a favourable climate for the initiative. In the course of discussions the inspectorate stressed that WSI could only be accomplished with the co-operation and collaboration of the other partners in the school system. The overall process also helped to focus attention and cultivate awareness of the complex, professional work involved in core inspectorial work – the evaluation of the teaching, learning and administrative activity of schools. It was also recognised that qualitative staff development and resourcing would be required for the satisfactory implementation of a WSI system. Thus, the foundations were well laid for the implementation of the national policy on whole school inspection.

The White Paper was published in May 1995 and the Chief Inspector took a very pro-active stance in readying the inspectorate for the aspects of the White Paper which were likely to affect its work. In the same month, May 1995, he established sixteen 'meithealacha oibre', or working groups, involving a total of 127 inspectors, to report on the sixteen themes selected for review. This was a stimulus to the inspectorate to inform themselves thoroughly on these aspects of the White Paper and of their potential consequences. The final reports from each meitheal were submitted to the Chief Inspector by 31 March 1996.[58]

The White Paper reflected some of the work going on within the Department of Education in relation to the government's policies of 1994, the Strategic Management Initiative (SMI) and the Value for Money Initiative

---

57 S. McGuinness, 'Report on the WSI Consultative Conference', 21 March 1996 (Unpublished). 58 *Annual Report for 1995–96*, pp 40–41.

(VMI).[59] As part of that process the Chief Inspector issued a Working Document to the inspectorate on 23 November, 1994, which was discussed at the annual conference in December 1994. The document was prepared in conjunction with the two Deputy Chief Inspectors, Seán Ó Fiachra and Cearbhall Ó Dálaigh. It envisaged a fully integrated inspectorate which would 'facilitate a common approach to inspection of the various types of schools and also a clarification of the role of the inspectorate vis-à-vis the administrative sections'.[60] The document identified the following as the essential functions of the integrated inspectorate: an inspection function; an examination/assessment management function; a policy advisory function; monitoring of in-career development; special services to and on behalf of the Department. There would be an organisational structure of a Chief Inspector with overall responsibility. The two Deputy Chief Inspectors would have responsibility respectively for the Inspection function and the Examination/Assessment function. There would be ten Assistant Chief Inspectors each with responsibility for managing a regional and/or specialised function. Then, there could be clusters of Senior Inspectors and Inspectors. It was stated that the ultimate outcome of the work of the inspectorate would be the production of an independent annual report on the effectiveness of the system. This represented an interesting effort at putting in place an organisational framework on the inspectorate for contemporary circumstances, but one of the problems would be changing concepts of the future pattern of the inspectorate at national level. This was highlighted by the fact that while the Education bill of 1997 envisaged a central and a regional inspectorate, the Education bill (2) of 1997, and the Education Act of 1998 legislated only for a central inspectorate, located within the Department of Education.

As well as more traditional forms of staff development for the inspectorate, a special Management of Change programme operated over a three year period from 1993 to 1996. This involved residential courses for cohorts of inspectors, and they were facilitated by external consultants. Among the aims of the courses was 'to help participants to face change and cope with it positively'. At this period there was a good deal of confusion within the inspectorate as to their role and mode of operation, and not all fully supported the front-leadership style of the Chief Inspector. Nevertheless, it was wise to seek to get inspectors to reflect in some depth on the nature of the transitional context in which they worked during this time, and to be proactive with regard to change. When Sean Mac Gleannáin was succeeded as Chief Inspector by Eamon Stack in 1997, the agenda for accomplishing change was well advanced.

Over the period 1990 to 1998 a great deal of change was occurring in the policy perspective on the inspectorate and in the work of the inspectorate as

59 *White Paper*, op. cit., pp 192–93. 60 'Integration of the Inspectorate: Working Document', 23 November 1994, p. 2 (unpublished).

it responded to a fast-changing societal context and educational environment. One key aspect of that environment was the more consultative relationships which were fostered between the education partners. This was also a striking feature of the inspectorate at this time. Their engagement with the debates in the policy papers and in fora such as the National Education Convention (NEC) opened up opportunities for dialogue with other partners. The expressed respect for the role of the inspectorate by participants at the NEC was noteworthy, and supportive to it. New relationships were developed between the inspectorate and academics/researchers. Close links continued to exist between some inspectors and staff in the Educational Research Centre. The discussions relating to WSI facilitated much constructive dialogue between the inspectors and school stakeholders. The role of the ICDU involved closer links between the inspectors and other agencies and teachers involved in professional development activities. Relations between the inspectorate and the NCCA became more integrative as they engaged on major joint initiatives on curriculum reform. Within the Department of Education, from about 1996 onwards, one detects a new spirit of collegiality and co-operation between the leaders of the inspectorate and the senior administrative staff, which was to develop in subsequent years. Valuable linkages were also developed between the inspectorate and international agencies. An interesting example of that was the secondment of Gearóid Ó Conluain, Divisional Inspector, to the Education Department of the Scottish Office in 1994. His report on his experiences was a useful input to the debates going on at that time within the Irish inspectorate. Inspectors increasingly paid visits to other systems or attended conferences abroad. Engagement with research projects by international bodies such as the TIMSS studies, the EUA studies and the OECD studies was developmental. The OECD's *Education At A Glance* provided useful comparators on a range of educational issues. The inspectorate had an involvement with the increasing role being exercised by the EU in educational affairs. Ireland became a participant in a newly-formed European association, the Standing International Conference of Inspectors (SICI). In the mid nineties the Irish inspectorate participated in a major EU project, 'Transnational Co-operation on Assessing, Evaluating and Assuring Quality in Schools in the EU'. The Irish representative was Gearóid Ó Conluain, and the outcome of the project influenced the development of inspection models and practices in Ireland. The development of such professional relationships between the inspectors and cognate agencies at home and abroad during these years of transition for the inspectorate were to be highly beneficial for the period of restructuring which was to follow.

17

Restructuring the Inspectorate, 1998–2008

THE INSPECTORATE WITHIN A CHANGING EDUCATION DEPARTMENT

The decade 1998 to 2008 was a very eventful one for the inspectorate. Great changes were occurring in Irish society, in the Irish public service, within the Department of Education and Science, and in the education system generally. So, it was not surprising that the inspectorate would be subject to significant restructuring. As was seen in the previous chapter, change in the inspectorate was already underway prior to 1998, but the process experienced accelerated momentum subsequently. By 2008, it had eventually emerged as a remodelled organisation with a new framework, with newly defined roles and functions, with many traditional functions devolved, with a higher public profile, and with improved morale. The changes are too recent to allow for historical evaluation of their full significance. However, it is important to chart the key developments and to provide an interpretative framework within which to locate them. This chapter is devoted to this task, while recognising that a greater time period will need to elapse before adjudication on the success of the changes can be fully substantiated.

Developments within the inspectorate during this period need to be viewed in relation to changes taking place in the structure and role of the Department of Education and Science, of which the inspectorate was a part. As was the case with other government departments, the Department of Education and Science had to respond to legislation such as the Public Service Management Act of 1997, which provided the enabling legislation for the Strategic Management Initiative, and to the Freedom of Information Act of April 1998, which emphasised new openness and accountability in the public service. However, the Department of Education and Science itself took the initiative of commissioning consultants' reports on its internal structures, staffing and mode of operation, which provided recommendations for its future organisation and structure.

The most significant of these were the Deloitte and Touche Report, commissioned in July 1996, which reported in late 1999, and the Cromien Report, commissioned in May 2000, and which reported in October 2000. The Cromien team had the other reports available to it. These reports were to lead to significant changes within the Department of Education and Science and also signalled major changes for the inspectorate, as a section of the Department.

In its opening statement the Deloitte and Touche Report stated:

> Our interviews with all senior management of the Department reviewed a Department which was overworked, reactive, and subject to continuous changes without having time to indulge in a process of adjustment and self examination to ensure that structured evolution was logical and aim oriented.[1]

This indicates the awareness of the senior staff of the serious problems being faced by the Department. The report highlighted many weaknesses in the Department's mode of operation at that time such as lack of co-ordination, lacking a mechanism for planning and managing change, too much involvement in detail and operational activities, heavily centralised decision-making and administration, inadequate attention to research, analysis, and evaluation, inadequate staffing and poor staff development. Its recommendations for the Department, to be introduced in five phases, were focussed as follows:

(i)   To become more strategic in focus.
(ii) To ensure a continuum of integrated policies, planning and strategies across all levels of the system.
(iii) To delegate and ideally regularise the decision-making and to devolve responsibility to point of delivery where possible.
(iv) To outsource non-core and large operational activities.
(v)   To become process oriented in mode of operation.

It identified three core processes for the Department: Policy and Planning; Quality Assurance; Resourcing.

Section 5.8 of the Report was devoted to the inspectorate, which was regarded as linked to the Quality Assurance process of the Department. The Report listed sixty-six core functions being exercised by the then inspectorate.[2]

Among the recommendations for the inspectorate were, 'That the Inspectorate service needs to be augmented and the emergent multi-disciplinary approach needs to be strengthened and formalised'.[3] It urged reduction in its engagement with the public examinations. The report urged a development of the recently established Evaluation Support and Research Unit within the inspectorate.

The inspectorate was also to be affected by the Report's recommendations about the outsourcing of some of the Departmental functions to executive agencies, including examinations, buildings, transport, in-career education, teacher certificate examinations. The report also recommended the provision

1 Deloitte and Touche, *Organisational Review of the Department of Education and Science*, Nov. 1999, p. 1.   2 Ibid., pp 128, 129.   3 Ibid., p. 160.

of regional area-based networks for education services, involving the inspectorate. In summary, the Deloitte and Touche Report signalled the desirability of significant changes in the structure and organisation of the Department of Education and Science and of the inspectorate.

In May 2000, Mr John Dennehy, Secretary General of the Department of Education and Science, on behalf of Minister Michael Woods, TD, invited Mr Sean Cromien, to conduct a review of the Department's operations, systems and staffing needs, taking into account a number of reports such as that of Deloitte and Touche. Among the terms of reference were:

> To identify the deficiencies in existing organisational structures, systems and processes as highlighted in these reports and studies and to identify the immediate, short-term and long-term measures required to remedy these deficiencies.[4]

Mr Cromien was a retired Secretary General of the Department of Finance and had a good familiarity with the workings of government departments. He was assisted by a task force of two Principal Officers, Pat Dowling and Liam Kilroy, and an Assistant Chief Inspector, Torlach O'Connor, from the Department of Education and Science. This task force was a valuable link to staff within the Department and aided the credibility and sense of ownership of the report which was produced. Mr Cromien recorded that the Top Management Group (TMG) in the Department was very positive in its approach to the review. This was a further indication that the Department's senior staff were initiators of the reform process, and considered that they needed the leverage of authoritative analyses to make the case with the Department of Finance for the support and resources to carry through significant organisational change. Mr Cromien submitted his report in October 2000.

In his foreword to the report Mr Cromien stated, 'There is a feeling at every level that there is something seriously amiss with the structure of the Department.' He referred to the greatly increased volume of work being conducted by the Department over recent times and stated that in dealing with this 'management and staff are hampered by the antiquated structure of the Department which needs urgent reform.' In particular, he considered that 'the over-centralisation leads to endless pressures on the staff'. He remarked that top management had identified that, 'corporate governance should be improved and that this needs to be done at management levels throughout the Department'.[5]

In the course of his detailed analysis Cromien remarked that his review confirmed the conclusions expressed in the Deloitte and Touche study. Cromien stated, 'Many of the problems come from a lack of adequate plan-

4 Sean Cromien, *Review of the Department's Operations, Systems and Staffing Needs*, Department of Education and Science, 2000, Appendix 1, p. 70. 5 Ibid., pp i, ii.

ning. Policy evolves haphazardly'.[6] He noted that there was a unanimous view that the Department was swamped with unnecessarily detailed work which clogged up the administrative machinery. He stated:

> There is vagueness, caused by the absence of clear structures, about where in the Department policy is formulated and whose responsibility it is to formulate it.

He went on to state:

> We also examined the structures in the Department. We found them outdated and inefficient for a modern Department of Education and believe they contribute to its problems, particularly those of lack of coherence and overlapping of work.[7]

Among key proposals of the Cromien Report to remedy the identified deficiencies was the devolution of work outside the Department to specialised agencies which would report to the Department. It supported the view of the concurrent Planning Group on Special Education, that many aspects of special education should be devolved to such an external agency. The Report also urged greater devolution of aspects of vocational education from the Department to the Vocational Education Committees. As with the Deloitte and Touche Report, it supported the devolution of school transport and the conduct of the public examinations to external bodies. The Department was also urged to devolve many of the operational aspects of in-service education for teachers. The report recommended that operational work relating to the Institutes of Technology should be devolved to the Higher Education Authority and to the institutions themselves. Student grant schemes should also be devolved. Responsibility for minor capital works should be devolved to schools themselves, and other changes were proposed for the Building Unit. Another significant recommendation was that the Department 'should establish a number of local offices which will provide an integrated access to services for those in a particular area'. The report used the phrase of the Clive Hopes Report of 1991 when it stated, 'To the extent possible, the aim should be to have a 'one-stop shop' of educational services', at regional level.[8]

Thus, it is clear that the Cromien Report, reflecting a good deal of the thinking within the Department of Education and Science itself, was recommending fundamental changes in the structure, organisational framework, workload and operational procedures of the Department. Many of the proposals had implications for the work of the inspectorate, but the report also had a specific chapter devoted to the inspectorate, which it is important for this study to focus on. The report made the unambiguous statement:

6 Ibid., p. 2.   7 Ibid., p. 3.   8 Ibid., pp 8, 9.

> We consider that qualitative assurance constitutes the core function of the inspectorate. The core function comprises two aspects, evaluation of provision (e.g. inspection and Whole School Evaluation) and policy formulation. However, there is a general view that the inspectorate's capacity to focus on these core objectives is hampered by its involvement in a wide range of other activities. [9]

Cromien's other proposals for Departmental reform, and the inspectorate's own initiatives, already afoot, would result in the dropping of many of the multifaceted roles which the inspectorate had come to be involved with, allowing for a clearer focus on the core functions of evaluation and policy formulation. The report encouraged closer collaboration of the inspectorate with the administrative sector of the Department stating, 'We consider that particular efforts are required to ensure closer communication and co-operation between administrative and inspectorate staff',[10] and it referred to the example of the Examinations Management Group, established in 1997, and jointly chaired by the Chief Inspector and an Assistant Secretary, as a good model. The report also urged, that the inspectorate should be intimately involved with the Central Planning Group it proposed. The report recommended the WSE should include evaluation of all aspects of school life and the macro analyses of WSE reports and school plans should be conducted for policy purposes. While it welcomed the recently-established Evaluation Support and Research Unit within the inspectorate, the report urged that its role and mode of co-operation with the Central Planning Unit should be clarified. The report favoured the establishment of a separate public examinations agency and sought a reduction in the inspectorate's involvement with the examinations. Cromien also favoured the secondment of experienced teachers to the inspectorate for specific purposes, on a rotational basis, and so 'free inspectors for core tasks'. It also favoured the secondment of skilled staff to the inspectorate on a temporary basis to act as co-ordinators of schemes such as the Stay in School Programme, Youthreach etc. In recommending the local office network of 'one-stop shops' for educational services, the report was keen to ensure the maintenance of good communications between the centre and local offices and urged the mobility of local office staff. Overall, the general recommendations of the Cromien Report for reform of the Department of Education and Science's mode of operation and the specific recommendations regarding the inspectorate gave new emphasis to the reconceptualisation of the work of the inspectorate, as well as providing support for reforming initiatives already underway. The Minister for Education, Mr Michael Woods, remarked of the Cromien Report, 'At the core of these recommendations was the absolute need to shift my Department from its overwhelming

9 Ibid., p. 42. 10 Ibid., p. 43.

focus on operational matters to a situation where attention could be given to the vital areas of policy development, forward planning and evaluation.'[11]

Prior to the Cromien Report being produced, the Chief Inspector met the Department of Finance directly, in association with the senior administrative side of the Department of Education and Science and pressed the case for improved staffing and changed organisation of the inspectorate.[12] The publication of the Cromien Report, building on other consultative reports, gave the Department of Education and Science leverage in negotiating with the Department of Finance on a new deal for a restructured Department. Again, the Chief Inspector formed part of the team with senior administrative staff which negotiated with the Finance Department on reform plans for the Department of Education and Science. Following oral discussions, the Education Department team was invited to prepare a detailed written submission outlining what a restructured department would look like, setting out the rationale for reforms and how improved efficiencies or added value might accrue from the changes. A plan was drawn up which set out four major elements. These involved a strategic outsourcing dimension, for example, for public examinations and special education; the Regional office concept linking with other local agencies and bearing in mind spatial strategy considerations; setting up an appeal framework which would deal with such things as appeals on teacher deployment, school transport etc; and an internal re-organisation agenda in line with advice of the consultants, and including re-organisation of the inspectorate. Negotiations with the Department of Finance and contact with the Minister for Finance led to the approval of the plans and authority to employ 250 extra staff to operationalise the planned changes.[13] This was a landmark achievement.

The process engaged in fostered closer co-operation between the inspectorate and the administrative side and demonstrated the productive value of joint policy planning. The joint approach was also put into play in detailed negotiations and dialogue with unions and staff which took place over an eighteen-month period. Staff who would be devolved to the proposed agencies needed to be assured of civil service-type status, promotion rights and so on. Eventually, agreement was reached with all involved parties. A memorandum was prepared for government on the plans, with the support of the Department of Finance. The reform plans won general support. The developments built on the spirit of partnership committees which were part of the national social partnership agreements, and which were employed within the Strategic Management Initiative and the Performance Management and Development System (PMDS). These developments also coincided with buoyant national economic performance and awareness in government that

11 *Nuachtlitir do Chigirí*, no. 2, July 2001, p. 2.   12 Interview with the Chief Inspector, Mr Eamon Stack, 15 Oct. 2007.   13 Interview with Assistant Secretaries, Mr Pat Burke and Mr Martin Hanebry, 15 Oct. 2007.

investment in education was crucial to Ireland's future in the knowledge society. In line with the advice of the Cromien Report, the internal workings of the Department were re-organised. New areas of responsibility were established for the Assistant Secretaries. The TMG was renamed the Management Advisory Committee (MAC) and it set up standing committees of administrative staff and inspectors on thematic issues. Provision was also made for joint ad hoc groups to deal with issues which might arise such as the ASTI dispute on supervision and substitution. The concept of the policy advisory role of the inspectorate was altered from submitting formal papers to administrative staff to participative group engagement by staff of both sectors, reflecting and dialoguing collectively on policy issues. A team approach became the predominant way of working. Business plans and strategy statements emerged from collaborative teamwork, focused on corporate goals. A Senior Management Forum was set up at which all managers within the Department came together under the chairmanship of the Secretary General three or four times a year. Further cross-fertilisation occurred through the Chief Inspector addressing meetings of the Principal Officers, and Assistant Secretaries addressing inspectors on aspects of the work of the Department. In 1999, in line with the Public Service Management Act, the Department renewed the policy, abandoned in the 1960s, of issuing an Annual Report. To many commentators this almost forty year gap in publishing annual reports was a regrettable omission by the Department. The new reports commented on the Department's success in achieving the goals set out in its Strategy Statements. They were compiled by the inspectorate and administrative staff.

The work of the Department during recent years has been affected by the government's decentralisation plan, announced in December 2003. The headquarters of the Department were to be located in Mullingar with other sections located in Athlone and Tullamore. To date (2008) this has not been fully put into effect.

REORGANISATION WITHIN THE INSPECTORATE

Arising from the Public Service Management Act of 1997, internal reorganisation took place within the inspectorate, as a division within the Department of Education and Science. The Department issued its Strategy Statement on 1 May 1998. Partnership Committees were established in 1998, representative of management, unions and staff. The Business Planning process began from 1 January 1999. The inspectors began work on individual business plans or job profiles on 31 May 1999, in line with the Social Partnership Agreement. The Senior Management Group within the inspectorate comprised the Chief Inspector, two Deputy Chiefs and ten Assistant Chief Inspectors. They led the process for business planning for the inspectorate as a division, for the responsibilities of the Deputy Chiefs and Assistant Chiefs and for individual inspectors. This process took a lot of time and dialogue before it was fully operational. By spring 2001 a good deal of the framework was in place, and by 2002 all inspectors had role profiles completed. In July 2001 a Partnership Committee of the inspectorate and sub-committees were set up. Five days training were provided for each inspector regarding the Performance Management and Development System (PMDS). The mechanisms for full integration of the PMDS scheme with the HR policy and processes were agreed in June 2005 within the Department as a whole.[14] During these years the Civil Service Performance Verification Group reported favourably on staff performance in relation to benchmarking and the general pay round increases for staff. This re-organisation was assisted by greatly increased funding for training, from the year 2000.

As part of the Strategic Management Initiative a Divisional Business Plan for the inspectorate was agreed by December 1998. It set out a sequence of 'High Level Divisional Objectives', 'Supporting Divisional Objectives', and the inspectorial personnel responsible for implementation. The statement of objectives coupled with what were termed the 'Day to Day Objectives' and 'Related Outputs' bear testimony to the very wide range of activities with which the inspectorate were still engaged.[15] Business Plans prepared over subsequent years reflected a less disparate range of activities and a more focused approach.[16] This was linked to the greater clarity which emerged from the Education Act's specification of the functions of the inspectorate and from the gradual devolution of responsibilities to external agencies. The devising of the Business Plans and the allocation of responsibilities required considerable amount of consultation with staff, and communication and dialogue with the Impact trade union, representing inspectors. Improved mechanisms for such consultation and dialogue were put in place.

The Business Planning process was linked to the restructuring of the organisational framework of the inspectorate, which was already underway before 1998. By May 1999, it had evolved in the format of a Senior Management Group comprising the Chief Inspector, who had overall responsibility, two Deputy Chiefs who reported to the Chief, on their specific responsibilities. Five Assistant Chiefs reported to each of the Deputy Chiefs. Each of the ten Assistant Chiefs had specific inspectorial responsibilities allocated to them, while eight of them had responsibility for the management of a regional area. One Assistant Chief had responsibility for the psychological service, while another had responsibility for the recently established Evaluation Support and Research Unit. While the inspectorate was now regarded as an integrated one, the 22 Divisional and 44 District Inspectors at primary level reported to one of the Deputy Chiefs, while the 22 senior and 34 inspectors at post-primary

14 *Annual Report of the Department of Education and Science for 2005*, p. 38.   15 *Divisional Business Plan for the Inspectorate*, December 1998.   16 See for instance, *Business Plan for 2003*

level reported to the other Deputy Chief. The 13 senior psychologists and 38 psychologists reported to one of the Assistant Chiefs who had responsibility for psychological and guidance services. During this process of change in inspectorial affairs a useful mechanism was employed as a forum for communication and exchange of views. This was the institution of *Nuachtlitir* or Newsletter, for inspectors, first published in April 1998, and published periodically since. Subsequently, in 2001, the inspectorate benefited from the allocation of new accommodation in Block 3 of the newly refurbished Department buildings in Marlborough Street, and in nearby accommodation in Cathal Brugha Street. The Chief Inspector established his office in Block 1, adjacent to the other members of MAC. The quality of the new accommodation for inspectors was a major improvement from that which existed previously, often in the form of pre-fab buildings.

As might be expected, the organisational framework changed over subsequent years in the light of experience and changing responsibilities of the inspectorate. A great deal of effort was put in at macro staff level and with individual inspectors to seek to accommodate the concerns and abilities of staff with regard to task assignments.

By 2003, the organisational framework for the inspectorate had evolved to include two subdivisions – a Regional Subdivision and a Policy Support Subdivision. Each subdivision had five Business Units associated with it, which related to the Deputy Chief Inspector in charge. Table 17.1 sets out the overall framework in 2008.

The country was organised into five regions, each of which was termed a Business Unit. As mentioned earlier, these differed from the network of regional offices set up by the Department of Education and Science, although instances would occur where a school inspector of an inspectorial region would liaise with staff in the regional office when appropriate. As can be noted from the functions outlined for the Business Units of the Policy Support Directorate, the inspectorate has become more focused on its evaluation, research and policy advice role, and less diversified than it used to be.

One of the Policy Support Business Units, Unit 6 – Evaluation Support and Research Unit (ESRU) – played a major part in preparing the inspectorate to develop its new role in a highly professional way. Its remit was spelled out in the Chief Inspector's Report to the Annual Conference on 1 December 1998. It was to undertake research and give advice on best practice in evaluation, to prepare annual inspection plans, devise how best Whole School Evaluation could be conducted, analyse inspection reports, follow-up on issues arising, maintain a data base on all inspections, provide support for school planning and school self-review, provide professional input to the Department's Annual Report, and publish reports on aspects of the functioning of the education system.[17] The

17 Chief Inspector's Address to the Annual Conference of Inspectors 1998, pp 40–43.

Table 17.1 Overview of the inspectorate subdivisions and business units, 2008

Inspectorate Division Eamon Stack *Chief Inspector*	The Chief Inspector provides leadership and strategic direction to the work of the Inspectorate. He has overall responsibility for the preparation of the annual business plan for the Inspectorate and its implementation. The Chief Inspector is chair of the Senior Management Group (SMG) of the Inspectorate. This group includes the two deputy Chief Inspectors and the Assistant Chief Inspectors who together are responsible for the management of the Inspectorate Division. The Chief Inspector is also a member of the Department's Management Advisory Committee (MAC) – the body responsible for the overall management of the Department of Education and Science.	
Regional Subdivision Is responsible for the delivery and management of inspection/evaluative services and related advisory activities in school and centres for education in five regional business units covering the county Dr Cearbhall Ó Dálaigh *Deputy Chief Inspector*	**BUSINESS UNITS (BU)** **BU 1 – North & Dublin North Region** Doreen McMorris, *Assistant Chief Inspector* **BU 2 – South East & Dublin South Region** Lorcan Mac Conaonaigh, *Assistant Chief Inspector* **BU 3 – West & Mid-West Region** Hilde Bn Mhic Aoidh, *Assistant Chief Inspector* **BU 4 – South Region** Seán Ó Floinn, *Assistant Chief Inspector* **BU 5 – Midlands & Dublin West Region** Deirdre Mathews, *Assistant Chief Inspector*	Cavan, Donegal, Dublin (Fingal), Dublin (North), Leitrim, Louth, Meath, Monaghan, Sligo Carlow, Dublin South, Dun Laoghaire–Rathdown, Kildare (North), Kilkenny, Wexford, Wicklow Clare, Galway, Limerick, Mayo, Roscommon, Tipperary (North Riding) Cork, Kerry, Tipperary (South Riding) and Waterford Dublin (West and South West), Kildare (South), Laois, Longford, Offaly, Westmeath

Policy Support Subdivision
Is responsible for contributing to the development of Departmental policy across a wide range of areas, for supporting inspection/evaluative activity generally and for operational service for the Inspectorate

Gearóid Ó Conluain
Deputy Chief Inspector

BU 6 – Evaluation Support & Research Unit
Harold Hislop, *Assistant Chief Inspector*

Support of all inspection activities and involvement in research and development. Publishing thematic and programme reports

BU 7 – Teacher Education
Emer Egan, *Assistant Chief Inspector*

Involvement in policy advice/development in primary and post-primary initial teacher education, induction and in-career development; support programmes and initiatives

BU 8 – Qualifications, Curriculum & Assessment
Eamonn Murtagh, *Assistant Chief Inspector*

Involvement in policy advice/development in curriculum and assessment issues for primary and post-primary education.

BU 9 – Special Education and Early Childhood Education & Educational Research
Don Mahon, *Assistant Chief Inspector*

Involvement in policy advice/development in special education, educational research and early childhood education.

BU 10 – Inspectorate Services & International Links
Gary Ó Donnchadha, *Assistant Chief Inspector*

Management of operational services for the Inspectorate, business planning. Inspectorate CPD and involvement in international fora

Directorate of Regional Services (DRS)
DRS – Overall management of Inspectorate in Regional Offices
Pat McSitric, *Assistant Chief Inspector*

Contributing to the development and delivery of the services of the Department through he Departments network of regional offices

Assigned to other duties

Some inspectors are assigned to other sections within the Department of Education and Science including the Teacher Education Section and the Planning and Building Unit elaborate brief indicated that the ESRU was to be a key academic and research hub for the modernisation of the inspectorate. In terms of research, planning, analysis and reportage the ESRU's establishment indicated a felt need for an agency to provide authoritative guidance for new ways of operating within the inspectorate. From 1 September 1999 the ESRU was established with two full-time and two part-time inspectors, and with administrative support.[18] The first head of the ESRU was Gearóid Ó Conluain, then an Assistant Chief Inspector.

Coincident with this, was the Department's concern to establish regional offices in which a range of educational services would be locally available from a regional centre. A Directorate of Regional Services was established in 2003 within the Department of Education and Science which set up 10 regional offices on a phased basis throughout the country, equipped with appropriate ICT resources. The regional office network was a major initiative by the Department to provide more co-ordinated, joined-up services from a range of education and development agencies in regional areas. A main purpose was to increase accessibility of the public and of interest groups to information. Ian Murphy was the first assistant chief inspector to be assigned to the Directorate of Regional Services, and a senior or divisional inspector has been allocated to each of the regional offices. They operate in a different capacity to the general inspectorate who work from local offices and who perform their various functions with a focus on their specific areas of responsibility, mainly relating to schools and subject areas. Inspectors in the regional offices liaise with local development agencies, county development committees, early childhood and adult education groups, social inclusion groups, local health committees, area partnerships, drug task forces etc. Bodies such as the NEPS, NCSE, NEWB are expected to cooperate closely with the regional centres. The regional offices put a special focus on non-formal education and social inclusion measures. Among special tasks allocated to the regional offices are the managing of the visiting teacher services to Travellers and the visually and hearing impaired. They also examine local complaints regarding school boards, and they deal with appeals under Section 29 of the Education Act. Regional offices are also allocated specialist roles which other centres can utilise. There are five staff allocated to each regional office, and a job specification exists to guide the inspector on his/her role as a team member. Reports of meetings are forwarded to the Directorate of Regional Services, and reports containing information of relevance to any section of the Department are forwarded to that section.[19]

In 2004, Noel Dempsey TD, the Minister for Education and Science, launched his campaign, 'Your Education Service' (YES). This was a nationwide consultative process on the future development of the education system, with a particular emphasis on parents' viewpoints. The Chief Inspector, and

18 Ibid., for 1999 Conference. 19 *Nuachtlitir*, No. 12, April 2004, pp 5–7.

other members of the inspectorate, atended the meetings and noted the viewpoints being expressed.

New approaches were adopted for the induction of new recruits to the
inspectorate and for the continuing professional development of established
staff from 1998. Recruitment to the inspectorate was to be crucially important over these years, in the first instance because augmentation of a seriously
depleted inspectorate was over due, but also in the context of the State
Examinations Commission being established in 2003 to which a large number
of inspectors were assigned. As the inspectors' *Newsletter* commented, 'This
massive transfusion of new blood is the most important development in our
workforce for many years.'[20] In 1998 a set of principles was laid down upon
which the induction of new inspectors would be based. The process of induction would involve a week of formal training involving a variety of inputs,
including the use of videotapes of classes. Each inductee would be allocated a
mentor from the established inspectorate as a guide and confidant. There
would also be work-shadowing during the first year and the preparation of an
'induction task'. There would also be ICT training as required, as well as
study visits to the various sections within the Department.[21]

As was noted by the *Newsletter*, it was also realised that continuing professional development for the established inspectors was crucial:

> If as an inspectorate we were to become deskilled or lacking in up-to-
> date knowledge of the new developments happening all around us,
> the result would impact seriously on our work in schools. It would
> also have a bad effect on our individual and collective self-esteem.[22]

It was planned that the generic, human aspects of the development of the
inspectorate would be addressed in the context of regional teams. This was
supplemented by a range of other Continuing Professional Development
(CPD) inputs. Some of this was done from the inspectors' ranks themselves
and some from external specialist facilitators. Eamon Stack, Chief Inspector,
put forward the concept of the inspectorate as a 'learning organisation' and in
the era of lifelong learning staff development became an integral part of the
inspectors' operations. In the year 2000 for instance, £100,000 was made
available for inspectorial staff development. Over subsequent years staff development took many forms and related to a variety of purposes. Increasingly,
the annual conferences became organised as staff development occasions. For
instance, at the Annual Conference of 2008, as well as plenary sessions, there
were five strands of working groups with 15 sessions and several panel discussion groups. A significant number of inspectors have been supported in
undertaking post-graduate courses in universities. Inspectors engage in meetings and working sessions with their international peers. Then a host of spe-

20 *Nuachtlitir*, No. 2, July 1998, p. 4.   21 Nuachtlitir, No. 4, May 1999, p. 7.   22 Nuachtlitir,
No. 2, July 1998, p. 2.

cific CPD engagements occur on various thematic and generic issues. While CPD became a stronger feature of the life of the inspectorate a very notable aspect of the profile of the inspectorate was the proportion of recent recruits to the service. Of the 155 inspectors in service in 2007, 119 had been recruited since 1998.[23] While making demands on appropriate induction to the service, this represented a massive injection of new blood. There may have been a loss of experience and 'memoire collective', but these staff were highly qualified, well motivated and energetic. It provided a great opportunity for the Senior Management Group to orient them to the espirit de corps of the modernising inspectorate. The inspectorate now operated more on merit performance than seniority and new career development opportunities opened up for skilled, hard-working, enterprising staff, on whom older sub-cultures had little influence. Adaptability and flexible working practices were desired. Formal recognition was being given to the quality of this reorganised division of the Department, which liaised more interactively with the administrative side than had formerly been the case. At the inspectors' conference in 2006, Secretary General, Bridget McManus, referred to the inspectorate as 'a vibrant and dynamic organisation within the Department', which could be taken as a commendation on the reorganisation of the inspectorate which had taken place.

THE INSPECTORATE AND EXTERNAL AGENCIES AND SUPPORT TEAMS

A significant development in the structure of the Irish education system over recent years has been the establishment of a number of agencies and support teams to whom responsibilities for the provision of a variety of educational services has been devolved. Some of these are statutorily established agencies working at a remove from the Department of Education and Science while still under the control of the Minister. Others operate in close relationship with the Department in their functioning. A traditional feature of the education system had been its centralised mode of governance. Many analysts had concluded that such a centralised mode of operation led to clogging and dysfunction of the system. In the absence of regional education authorities who would undertake appropriate functions, the setting up of agencies and support groups was regarded as the best mode of relieving the over-burdened centre, and allowing for more efficient delivery of services. This policy was to have important consequences for the structure and mode of operation of the inspectorate.

As early as 1987 the National Council for Curriculum and Assessment (NCCA) had been established, which acted as an advisory body to the

23 Address of Chief Inspector to Annual Conference, 2007.

Minister and on whose council and sub-committees the inspectorate was represented. The National Council for Guidance in Education (NCGE) had been set up in 1995 and was linked to the psychologists within the inspectorate. From 1998, in the context of other changes within the Department the establishment of such agencies gathered pace. In 1998, the National Council for Technology in Education (NCTE) was set up. The planning for and incorporation of ICT in the system drew heavily on the work of the inspectorate. An ICT infrastructure for schools was put in place and training courses for teachers were conducted, with 9,000 teachers benefiting in 1998. The NCTE would carry the work forward in association with Department personnel. Inspectors were behind the launch of IT 2000 in November 1998, and assisted in the Planning of SCOILNET, which was launched on 28 September 1999. From 1998, inspectors were gradually supplied with IT equipment and training. Such training was continued over the years allied to the needs of individual inspectors. The availability of ICT technology such as mobile phones, e-mails, laptop computers had a huge influence on the work of the inspectorate. For instance, mobile phones meant ready communication among inspectors and quicker access to colleagues for all sorts of work reasons. ICT greatly reduced the aspect of isolation which had been a problem for the inspectorate in former times. The establishment of the NCTE and associated initiatives for ICT training and provision in the period 1998–2000 encouraged a new dimension in teaching and learning in Irish schools, which developed further over subsequent years.

When psychologists were recruited to the Department in the mid 1960s they were incorporated within the inspectorate. In the changing circumstances of the modern education system there was questioning if this was the best arrangement. In September 1997, the Minister for Education, Mr Martin, set up a planning group to investigate the best way forward. The group was chaired by Eamon Stack, Chief Inspector. It reported in September 1998 and recommended the establishment of a separate entity, which was to be known as the National Educational Psychological Service (NEPS). An implementation group was set up to prepare the way for such a development and to prepare a memorandum for government on the matter. Approval was forthcoming in February 1999 and NEPS was established, with an acting Director, in September 1999. A good deal of discussion was needed with staff and union to facilitate the setting up of NEPS. Once conditions of work were clarified most of the existing psychologists opted to go to NEPS, while a small minority remained as part of the inspectorial staff. Further recruitment was undertaken to ensure that NEPS had a complement of staff to allow it begin undertaking its new responsibilities. The separation of the psychologists from the inspectorate involved careful planning, and its success was not without its difficulties.

During the nineties the area of special education and education for people with disabilities became issues of wide public concern. In 1993, the Report of the Special Education Review Committee was published. It involved a wide-ranging review and made an extensive range of recommendations. Through the nineties many court cases were taken by parents who were dissatisfied with the special education provision being provided. Such cases often involved a large time input from inspectors and administrative staff. The same was true of a contemporary but different issue of public concern – the abuse of children which had taken place when in institutional care. In October 1999, Mícheál Martin, Minister for Education and Science, established a Planning Group under the chairmanship of Eamon Stack, Chief Inspector, to review special education provision. The Planning Group had the task of preparing the way for setting up a national council for special education as an external agency and the preparation of a memorandum for government on the issue. Work was also done on the rationalisation of the special education duties of the inspectorate and devising transitional aspects of the inspectorate's work practices in the area. In July 2001 the government agreed to set up a National Council for Special Education (NCSE). It was set up in 2002 by Ministerial Order. The Council was statutorily established in January 2004 under the Education for Persons with Special Educational Needs Act. Its functions include the provision of services at local and national level to meet the educational needs of children with disabilities, and to undertake research and give advice to the Minister on special education policy. The Council is assisted by a nationwide network of Special Educational Needs Organisers. The establishment of this specialist body relieved the inspectorate of much work in this area, while allowing professional linkages to continue. The inspectorate also assisted in the establishment of the National Education Welfare Board (NEWB), in 2002, in relation to school attendance-type issues and has maintained liaison with it, giving it both leadership and support.

Close involvement with the public examinations had been a cherished dimension of the secondary school inspectorate. Initiatives since the 1970s to remove the examinations from such direct engagement were not successful. However, a number of analyses including those of Deloitte and Touche (1999) and Cromien (2000) recommended that this should be done. The Secretary General, John Dennehy, established a committee to progress some of the reforms recommended by Cromien. This committee was chaired by Patrick Burke, Assistant Secretary, and included Chief Inspector Eamon Stack and Martin Hanevy, Assistant Secretary in its composition. This committee planned for the establishment of the State Examinations Commission and the regional office network. The SMG exercised great care in communication and consultation with the inspectors regarding the new development. Deputy Chief Inspector Cearbhall Ó Dálaigh held private and confidential discussion with each individual inspector, who had an involvement with the examinations. Efforts were made to elicit the type of inspectorial work preferred by each individual. In the event, about half of the post-primary inspectorate indicated that they would prefer the work on examinations. The State Examinations Commission was established on 1 January 2003, as a non-departmental civil service body with vesting day on 6 March 2003. Its core business is the assessment and certification of the post-primary school examinations, and of certain other trade and professional examinations. Thirty-five inspectors transferred to the Commission. The fact that the vast majority of inspectors were seen to be getting their choice of career option made for a smooth transition. This transfer of responsibility for examinations from the Department's inspectorate and administration to the Commission was, in the words of the Department's Annual Report for 2003, 'A historic move'. The inspectorate's *Newsletter* recorded, 'The transfer of almost 50% of the cohort of post-primary inspectors was a very significant experience for all concerned.'[24]

The move allowed the SMG to recruit a replacement cohort of inspectors who could be oriented to the new work practices which were being promoted, as well as facilitating the inspectorate to focus more on its evaluative and advisory functions. The inspectorate did retain its links with the Educational Research Centre with regard to international testing such as TIMSS and PISA.

Traditionally, the Department of Education and Science had an involvement in certifying the qualifications of teachers, particularly those seeking recognition of qualifications achieved abroad. Through the nineties a great deal of attention was given to the establishment of a Teaching Council. This was a policy included in the government's White Paper, *Charting Our Education Future* in 1995. On 4 November, 1997, Minister Mícheál Martin set up a Technical Working Group and a Steering Committee to report to him on the establishment of such a Council. The inspectorate was represented in the Technical Working Group by Assistant Chief Inspector, Maura Clancy. The report of the Steering Committee was presented in 1998. Legislation to establish the Council was passed in 2001, and the Council came into being in 2005. The Council includes representation from the Teacher Education Section of the Department of Education. The representative, Emer Egan, is an Assistant Chief Inspector. The Council has extensive powers over entry standards to the teaching profession, on accreditation of courses, ethics and disciplinary code, continuing professional development and research on teacher education issues. While being an independent body, the Council needs the approval of the Minister for major decisions, and the Council liaises closely with the Department of Education and Science. The Council's establishment has alleviated the workload of the Department of Education and Science.

Reflecting on the developments which had taken place over recent years, the Chief Inspector, Eamon Stack, stated at the Annual Conference in 2007:

> It is very evident that the restructuring and reorganisation within the Inspectorate, and in the wider Department over the last six years, has

24 *Nuachtlitir*, No. 10, July 2003, p.2.

had a very positive impact on our capacity to deliver. Most significantly we have been able to de-clutter and re-organise our service
around our core work of evaluation and advice.

He went on to give a long list of activities with which the inspectorate was no
longer involved, and concluded:

Just a short few years ago our work involved a very broad and disparate collection of activities that competed heavily for our time.
Now, thankfully, our work is directed in a very tangible way towards
school and system improvement.[25]

Thus, the strategy which had been taken was to adopt the recommendations
of a number of reports such as those of Hopes (1991), Deloitte Touche
(1999), Cromien (2000) and establish a clear purpose for the role of the
inspectorate while discarding accretory functions which had grown up, but
which distracted it from its core business. It was also significant that despite
the devolution of many time-consuming activities to the new entities, the
number of inspectors, grew from 121 in 1997 to 161 in 2008.

The inspectorate had traditionally taken a hands-on approach to the in-
service education of teachers, now more popularly termed continuing professional
development (CPD). However, a number of reports indicated that a more co-
ordinating, support and evaluative role, rather than a delivery role would be more
appropriate. In 1994, the In-Career Development Unit was established in the
Department to promote such an approach. While some delivery of in-service
work by inspectors continued, as, for instance, the work by science inspectors in
promoting science for girls, which led to a notable colloquium in September 1998
in Cork, the inspectorate's approach changed in this area. From the mid-nineties
the older Teacher Centres were improved and developed, and they became
known as Education Centres. The Department of Education and Science began
to draw more on these as loci for specific in-service programmes. A very
significant feature of the new approach was the appointment of support teams,
comprised of skilled experienced teachers or school leaders, to work closely with
school personnel on in-service education priorities.

National policy was that schools should be encouraged to prepare school
plans and to become self-evaluative of their work. To assist them in this
regard the School Development Planning Initiative (SDPI) was launched in
May 1999. The inspectorate drew up the Guidelines for School Development
Planning (SDP) for both primary and post-primary schools. At first, the support was focused on disadvantaged schools, and was later extended to all
schools. The inspectorate provided training for the facilitators, and seminars
for school principals. The primary inspectorate had experience in promoting

25 Chief Inspector's address to Annual Conference, 2007, p. 4.

school plans since the early 1980s. Drawing on such experience as well as new thinking on the issue, the inspectors generally had a major input through school planning on the life of modern Irish classrooms. A whole range of areas were covered such as behaviour code, bullying, child protection, enrolment policy, special needs provision, curricular planning. The support teams continue to assist schools in their planning activities. Another support group which was set up in July 1999 was the Primary Curriculum Support Programme (PCSP). As its name implies, this was designed to assist in the phased implementation of the new Primary School Curriculum, published in 1999. The inspectorate had a major input into the planning of the implementation of the primary curriculum, which was conducted in a highly sophisticated way. The PCSP continues to be a valued implementation support, with rotating cohorts of seconded teachers working with their peers on various aspects of the curriculum. Close liaison is maintained with the school inspectorate and the Teacher Education Section of the Department. From September 2008, the PCSP and the SDPS for primary level were merged under one title, Primary Professional Development Service (PPDS). At post-primary level, the Second Level Support Service (SLSS) is in operation supporting, particularly, curriculum reform initiatives at post-primary level. Another support programme for both primary and post-primary schools is the Leadership Development Support. This assists prospective and in-career school leaders to adopt best practice in an area whose importance is increasingly recognised. Other supports include the Special Education Support Service (SESS) and the National Behaviour Support Service (NBSS). Quite clearly such support services form as the Chief Inspector states, 'a critical part of our education system'. In 2007, there were more than 600 personnel engaged in the support services.[26] They operate under the general control of the Teacher Education Section of the Department. As such, they represent a massive extension of inspectorial influence, which could never be achieved by inspectors alone as a group. Over recent years, the inspectorate has also drawn on the services of retired inspectors to participate in some interview boards, to help with the probation of the largely increased numbers of primary teachers, and to sit on committees thus releasing the full-time inspectorate for other duties. John Byrne, a retired Assistant Chief Inspector, coordinated the involvement of retired inspectors in certain interview boards

NEW APPROACHES TO SCHOOL INSPECTION

For the first time ever the inspectorate and its functions were given statutory status in section 13 of the Education Act, 1998. Its functions were spelled out in great detail. As it happens, the Act had to be amended subsequently to

26 Ibid.

take account of new agencies and their responsibilities, such as the State Examinations Commissions and NEPS. The core statutory remit of the inspectorate under the Act can be summarised as follows:

- Programme of inspection in schools
- Promoting compliance with regulation and legislation
- Advisory role for schools and the Department
- Contribution to policy development.[27]

The remit could also be characterised as system evaluation, system development, and system support.

The pilot project on Whole School Evaluation (WSE) was completed in 1999 and involved 17 post primary schools and 18 primary schools throughout the country. A report on the pilot project was prepared by the ESRU and circulated to all schools in December 1999. The Department's Annual Report for 1999 remarked of it, 'The WSE pilot project experience in 1999 was a landmark in the development of a new model of school evaluation and a milestone in the preparation of the Inspectorate for its evolving role in school and system quality assurance'.[28] Subsequent to this pilot phase the inspectorate, particularly through the agency of the ESRU, did a good deal of further preparatory work before WSE was established as a national system. Further work was done on the evaluation criteria and these were published. The *Professional Code of Practice on Evaluation and Reporting* was published in November 2000. Circulars were issued to schools on WSE practices and procedures, which had been negotiated with the education partners. Consultation with the education partners and direct meetings by the Chief Inspector and senior staff with the Executive Committees of the teacher unions were crucial in securing the implementation of WSE. An appeal mechanism for school boards on the outcome of inspection was devised. Training programmes for inspectors, many of whom were new recruits, were undertaken. New inspection templates and schedules of visitation were prepared. The publication *Looking at Our Schools*, which focused on primary and post-primary schools, was published in 2003.

WSE became established in primary schools in the autumn of 2003 and in post-primary schools in spring 2004. WSE is conducted by teams of inspectors who work in a school over a period of days. The outcomes of a school's own self review, development and planning activities feed into the evaluation. This forms part of the pre-evaluation phase, which also involves discussion with school personnel – board members, parents and teaching staff. Efforts are made to establish contextual factors such as location, the socio-economic background

27 Eamon Stack, 'Inspection and Evaluation; A Strategic Perceptive', Address to the Principal Officer Network in the DES, 4 Oct. 2007.   28 *Annual Report of the Department of Education and Science, 1999*, p. 39.

of pupils, characteristics of pupil intake such as the extent of special educational needs, and prior attainment. The in-school evaluation phase evaluates five main areas, namely the quality of school management, school planning, curriculum provision, learning and teaching, and support for students. The post-evaluation phase involves the drawing up of a report by the inspectors, discussion of this with teaching staff and school board, and the correction of any factual errors. The school has the option of preparing a school response which is published simultaneously with the WSE report. Inspection reports were first published on the Department's website in June 2006. Minister Mary Hanafin TD remarked, 'This is the first time in the history of the inspectorate that reports on individual schools will have been made available to the general public.' She also praised 'the balanced and fair assessment of the work of schools' contained in these reports, in contrast to league table reports based solely on examination results.[29] By November 2008, a total of 2,430 individual school inspection reports had been published on the Department's website.

As well as WSE evaluation other forms of inspection were revised and renewed. At primary level there was a huge increase in the inspection of probationary teachers, from 453 in 1998 to 2,639 in 2008.[30] Quite clearly, work with such a huge number of probationary teachers makes great inroads on the inspectors' time. Senior inspectors would prefer the probationary role to be undertaken by school principals, but the very long and skilled experience of the inspectorate in evaluating probation is greatly valued by the system. In 2001 subject inspection was reintroduced to all post-primary schools, in line with new templates and procedures. The number of such inspections grew substantially: 81 such reports were issued to schools in 2001 yet by 2007, 758 of these inspections were undertaken.[31] Another form of evaluation undertaken by the inspectorate in these years was thematic evaluations. Examples of these were an evaluation of educational provision for children with autistic spectrum disorders, an evaluation of special classes for pupils with specific speech and language disorders, an evaluation of planning in thirty primary schools, mathematics achievement in Irish primary schools, Irish in primary schools, literacy and numeracy in disadvantaged schools, and ICT in schools. Inspectors developed inspection models to evaluate specific programmes in schools including the Junior Certificate schools Programme, Transition Year, the Leaving Certificate Applied programme and the Leaving Certificate Vocational Programme. Inspectors also undertook evaluations in the non-mainstream sector – Youth Encounter, Youthreach and Traveller Education.

The Inspectorate sought to make available information about trends and patterns that emerged from the inspection programme. *Fifty School Reports: What Inspectors Say*, which presented an analysis of whole-school evaluation

Nuachtlitir, No. 14, July 2006, p. 3.   **29** Eamon Stack, 'Inspection and Evaluation', op. cit., p. 8, and figures for 2008 supplied by Department.   **30** Ibid.   **31** *Chief Inspector's Report, 2008* (Department of Education and Science, 2009).

reports in primary schools was the first such composite report to be published in 2002. It was followed by *Inspection of Modern Languages: Observations and Issues* in 2004 and a series of publications analysing the outcomes of subject inspection reports in post-primary schools including publications on English, geography, history, Irish, home economics, materials technology (wood), music and Junior Cycle Science.

The *Chief Inspector's Report 2008* provides a valuable summary of the scale of the emphases now being placed on various forms of school inspection and includes focused comments on strengths and weaknesses of various aspects of the system.[32] The report also posits the directions in which developments need to go for the future. The following table gives an overview of the forms of inspection during the period 2005–08.

Table 17.2: Summary of types of inspection, 2005–8

	2005	2006	2007	2008	Total
Tuairisc scoile (*School Report*)	90				90
WSE Primary	163	228	244	245	880
WSE Post-primary	53	57	59	60	229
Subject inspections – stand alone	452	507	540	443	1,942
Subject inspections within WSE	224	223	218	225	890
Programme evaluations			23	42	65
Probation of teachers (Primary) (*numbers of teachers*)	1,611	2,080	2,362	2,639	8,692
Evaluations of courses in Irish colleges (*Coláistí Gaeilge*)	62	48	57	72	239
Centres for education (Youthreach, Youth Encounter, Senior Traveller Training Centres, Centre for European Schooling)		18	23	17	58
Thematic evaluations	67	28	9*	41*	145
Assessments of education in places other than recognised schools (conducted on behalf of NEWB)	9			3	12
Total inspections	2,731	3,189	3,535	3,787	13,242

Source: *Chief Inspector's Report, 2008*.
* Almost all thematic evaluations in 2007 and some in 2008 were conducted in the context of whole-school evaluations or subject inspections and are included under those categories. Nine further thematic evaluations were conducted in schools in 2007 and 41 in 2008.

32 *Annual Report of the Department of Education and Science for 2005*, p. 4.

The table clearly emphasises the extensive engagement by the contemporary inspectorate with the work of teachers, school communities, and provision outside the mainstream system. The agencies inspected receive reports on their individual activities. Reports are published, and in specific publications the inspectors comment on issues and trends of importance to the quality of the education system.

In specific chapters of the *Chief Inspector's Report for 2008* there is incisive, targeted comment on what is working well in the primary and post-primary schools, what needs to be improved in such schools, and what needs to be done for the future. Section two of the report is divided into five thematic chapters on the following themes: special education in mainstream and special schools; tackling disadvantage; teaching and learning in Irish; using ICT in our schools; improving the quality of teaching. The third section identifies and specifies areas that must be prioritised at both school and system levels in the immediate future. Overall, the Report is reflective of a significant shift in direction for much of the work of the inspectorate in which evaluation and monitoring of educational quality is centre stage, extensive feedback is given to practitioners, findings are interpreted, policy advice is collated and reflection occurs on emerging trends.

The theme of the 2007 Annual Conference was 'After Inspection: Ensuring that School Improvement Happens for Students'. This placed the focus on how best to ensure that schools and their management implemented improvements recommended during inspections and how the school support services could assist schools, where appropriate, in this work. It also led to the development of better systems within the Department to ensure that administrative officials and inspectors could co-operate more effectively in identifying the small number of schools where follow-up actions were required. Inspectors also reported on beginning teachers' performance in primary schools in the publication, *Learning to Teach*. The inspectors have also been involved with teacher education agencies on a pilot programme for the induction of newly-qualified teachers, 2002–08.

ENGAGEMENT WITH CURRICULUM

The NCCA has major responsibility for providing policy advice on curriculum and assessment issues and it also undertakes work on the development of curricula and syllabi for schools. The inspectorate relates very closely with it. An Assistant Chief Inspector represents the Department on the NCCA Council. An inspector also sits on each NCCA course committee. Thus, the inspectorate is closely integrated with the work of the NCCA and contributes continuously to its work. As was noted in the previous chapter, inspectors made major contributions to the formulation of the new primary curriculum and teacher guidelines which were published as 23 volumes in 1999. This was a landmark occasion for Irish primary education. The inspectorate was on the implementation committee for the curriculum. A major implementation mechanism was the setting up, in 1999, of the support group, the Primary Curriculum Support Programme (PCSP). This has continued to operate in close co-operation with the inspectorate, as has its sister agency the School Development Planning Service. These services are now merged as the Primary Professional Development Service (PPDS). The inspectorate has also been monitoring aspects of the implementation of the curriculum and has produced reports such as *An Evaluation of Curriculum Implementation in Primary Schools: English, Mathematics and Visual Arts* (2005) and *Literacy and Numeracy in Disadvantaged Schools* (2005).

The inspectorate also evaluated the implementation of major curricular initiatives at post-primary level – Transition Year, Leaving Certificate Vocational Programme, Leaving Certificate Applied and the Junior Certificate School Programme. Inspectors work on an-going basis on the updating of Syllabi for a range of subjects.

Under the National Development Plan 2000–06 the Department of Education and Science was provided with funding for a dedicated Gender Equality Unit. This Unit subsumed the Equality Committee which had already existed. An Assistant Chief Inspector, Hilde McHugh, was assigned overall responsibility for the promotion of gender equality by the inspectorate and Maureen Bohan, Senior Inspector, was assigned to the Department's Gender Equality Unit. A new resource pack, 'Equal Measures' for gender mainstreaming in primary schools was developed, which involved a manual, a DVD, parents' pack, lessons plans and resources. This resource was circulated to all primary schools in September 2006. A pack 'Exploring Masculinities' was made available to senior cycle post-primary schools in 2000. A further pack, similar to 'Equal Measures' to help gender mainstreaming in post primary schools, was prepared in 2007. Leadership training courses for female teachers to assume leadership positions in school were also developed. The inspectorate also participated in European Community Projects on gender equality in education.

Among other new areas of emphasis within the curriculum on which inspectors worked was the Social, Personal and Health Education (SPHE) programme. This was introduced in the year 2000 to post-primary schools, and was a shared initiative with the Department of Health. The implementation of the SPHE dimension of the new primary curriculum began in 2003. Another new area in which the inspectorate assisted was the introduction of Religious Education as a formal school subject, which could be taken for examination purposes.

A series of initiatives by the Social Inclusion Unit, set up in 1998 focused on alleviating problems of educational disadvantage also had curricular implications. Among such projects were the Early School Leaver Initiative (ESLI) and the 'Stay in School' Retention Initiative (SSRI), and Giving Children an Even Break. In 2005, inspectors assisted in the planning of Delivering Equality of Opportunity in Schools (DEIS). This aimed at greater co-ordination of initiatives to tackle educational disadvantage. Under the new plan children in schools serving the most disadvantaged communities would benefit from a range of extra supports, including smaller classes, school meals, homework clubs, improved funding for school books and better home-school liaison, as well as improved pre-school education. In June 2005, the Department established a Steering Committee, on which the inspectorate was represented, to co-ordinate the response to the educational needs of migrant pupils in Irish schools.[33] Inspectors were very involved in providing guidelines and supports for the integration of immigrant pupils from varied ethnic, religious and language backgrounds into the school system.

INTERNATIONAL LINKAGES

Following the Good Friday Agreement in Northern Ireland in 1998, the momentum of co-operation between the inspectorates in both parts of Ireland gathered apace. Mr Tom Shaw, Chief Inspector in Northern Ireland, was a special guest at the inspectors' annual conference in December 1998, where it was agreed that stronger links would be forged, with regular management meetings sharing ideas and promoting co-operation. The participation of inspectors at each others' annual conference became the norm. In 1999, a North/South Committee of Inspectors was set up to co-ordinate initiatives and act as a focus and forum for joint activities. The expectation was that 'In the medium to long term, the Committee will be an important instrument in formulating Department policy in relation to North/South co-operation in education and also in ensuring that a streamlined and coherent response to North/South issues will be readily available to the inspectorate'.[34] The inspectorate relates with the International Section of the Department on the management and monitoring of various North/South educational projects. This includes applications under the EU Special Support Programme for Peace and Reconciliation (SSPPR) in Northern Ireland and in the border counties. Among areas where discussions between the two inspectorates have yielded worthwhile developments were ICT in education, school development planning, educational disadvantage, education for pupils with disabilities and the professional development of inspectors. A seminar of joint training between the two inspectorates took place on 24 and 25 July 2000, of which the *Newsletter* commented: 'It proved to be a tremendous learning experience for all of us'.[35] Since 2000 there has been a strong working relationship

33 *Nuachtlitir*, No. 6, Nov. 1999, p. 15.   34 *Nuachtlitir*, No. 8, Nov. 2000, p. 4.   35 *Nuachtlitir*, No. 11, Dec. 2003, pp 4–6.

between both inspectorates, In 2008 a scheme was instituted for the short-term exchange of inspectors between Northern Ireland and the Republic.

The inspectorate continued its involvement with international testing projects such as those of PISA, conducted by the OECD. Inspectors liaised with staff in the Educational Research Centre in the planning and conduct of such tests, and in dissemination conferences on the outcomes of the tests. The inspectorate is represented in the education committee of the Centre for Education Innovations and Research (CERI), and maintains liaison with its various projects such as the 'What Works in Innovation in Education'? series. Inspectors were also involved in various ways with EU projects. For instance, on 7–9 May 1998 a large number of inspectors participated in a conference promoting the European dimension in education, and how Irish schools and teachers might engage to best effect under Comenius-linked programmes. Inspectors also participated on the Board of Inspectors for European Schools, both primary and post-primary, and engaged as members of inspection teams for such schools. This provided useful experience in working on inspection with international peers. The Irish inspectorate had the Presidency of the European Schools in 2002–03 with Eamon Stack as president of the Board of Governors. The presidency involved a significant workload for the Irish inspectorate, including preparing the way for the large extension of EU membership which was to take place in 2004.[36] The inspectorate ensured that the Centre for European Schooling in Dunshaughlin was recognised as a form of European schooling. The inspectorate also had an involvement in supporting educational activities as part of Ireland's Presidency of the EU in the first half of 2004.

The inspectorate kept up its involvement with the Standing Conference of Inspectorates (SICI). Representatives attended SICI conferences abroad. The inspectorate also participated in international projects on such aspects as School Self Evaluation and School Inspection.[37] By 2007, in conjunction with the European Network of Policy Makers for the Evaluation of Education Systems, the inspectorate had completed the Co-operative School Evaluation Project (CSEP) which developed international indicators for the evaluation of non–curricular school policies in a school development planning context.[38] The inspectorate also participated in Council of Europe projects such as the review of languages in 2007. The range of engagements of the inspectorate with international agencies and peer organisations helped to avoid insular perspectives and kept the inspectorate in contact with best international practice.

RESEARCH AND DEVELOPMENT, AND PUBLICATIONS

The Research and Development Committee (RDC) of the Department of Education and Science continued its role during the years under review of

---

36 *Nuachtlitir*, no. 11, Dec. 2003, pp 4–6.   37 Address of Chief Inspector to Annual Conference, 2002.   38 Address of Chief Inspector to Annual Conference, 2007.

Table 17.3: Number of publications issued by the inspectorate, 2002–08

Types of publication	Number
Thematic, composite and other evaluation reports	32
Guides on inspection, school self-evaluation and school planning, policy development and implementation	17
Evaluation and support materials for Scrúdú Cailíocht sa Ghaeilge	3
Editions of Oideas	4
Evaluation reports produced in conjunction with the Educational Research Centre, Drumcondra	5
Total	61

Source: Chief Inspector's Report 2001–2004; Chief Inspector's Report 2008.

allocating funding in respect of small-scale research and development projects focusing on first and second-level education. The RDC invites research proposals on given education research issues which are likely to be of policy significance to the Department. Some researchers submit unsolicited research proposals for approval by the RDC. The majority of successful applicants are drawn from staff in Education and Social Science Departments of universities. There are usually three inspectors of senior rank on the RDC to help in the review and adjudication of research proposals.

On 20 October 1999 a major Research Dissemination Conference was jointly convened in Malahide by the RDC and the recently established inspectorate body, the ESRU. The Conference proved to be a very successful event attracting researchers, policy makers, inspectors, curriculum development specialists, teacher educators, and teachers. Presentations were made on nine research projects which had been assisted by the RDC. In January 2002, the Department of Education and Science published a large compendium, 'Research and Development Projects, 1994–2000', which presented reports on the research projects which had been supported by the RDC. This coincided with an increased interest by the inspectorate in such research, choosing 'Educational Research and the Inspectorate' as the theme of its annual conference in 2002.

The establishment of the ESRU as a unit within the inspectorate in 1999, was to be a pivotal move in the modernisation of the inspectorate. Its work in staff training, on researching best inspectorate practice, on providing manuals, templates and codes of practice for new approaches to inspection were dealt with earlier in this chapter. While *Oideas* continued to be published, reaching its 50th edition in 2003, the publication output of the ESRU and the Inspectorate generally became very impressive over the years. The topics covered were extensive, ranging from school inspection reports, subject inspection reports, guides to evaluation, thematic studies and so on. In 2005, it published the significant *Chief Inspector's Report for 2001–04*, and, in 2009, the *Chief Inspector's Report 2008* was published. These provided valuable compendia of the work of the inspectorate during the years under review. The range of major publications can be illustrated by the table on p. 289.

Over sixty publications were issued between 2002 and 2008 and, in addition, a range of information leaflets and newsletters was produced. When this is contrasted with the previous paucity of published data, the change is very significant. Furthermore, the quality of the publications in terms of presentation and quality is impressive. Huge numbers of reports on inspections have been posted on the website. This approach reflects an attitude of greater transparency, accountability, partnership and professionalism. The material made available is of value to a range of interests including school authorities, parents, teachers and policy makers. In an address to the inspectorate in September 2008, the Minister for Education and Science, Batt O' Keeffe, TD highlighted the value of the publications stating, 'Through these publications the Inspectorate is playing a key role in advising the system about the challenges that are emerging today that may seriously affect the progress of learners in the future … These reports will help to equip the Department to make sound evidence-based policy decisions which can lead to improving the educational opportunities of Ireland's school-going population.'[39]

In 2005, the inspectorate commissioned MORI to carry out a customer attitude survey of the inspectorate. This was published in January 2006. The survey focused, in particular, on professional relationships in the context of school evaluation, evaluation procedures and reporting. A sample group of 150 principals and 539 teachers was surveyed. The survey found very high levels of satisfaction with the performance of the inspectorate. The survey findings highlighted many of the inspectorate's strengths: its professional expertise, objectivity, fairness, professionalism, courtesy, interpersonal skills and oral and written communication abilities. Despite the very strong positive endorsement areas for improvement were indicated, most notably in the administrative procedures.[40] The inspectorate undertook to address such matters. Overall, the outcome was a strong endorsement of the quality of the newly-structured inspectorate's work. It should also serve as a morale booster for the work ahead in a changing environment, which was outlined at the Conference in Spring 2008, under the theme, 'Towards 2020: The Future of Schooling for Learners.' The re-structured Irish school inspectorate would seem to be well equipped to cope with the emerging challenges of the future, and thus add to its long and distinguished contributions in the service of Irish education.

39 Address by Batt O'Keeffe TD, Minister for Education and Science, to the Inspectorate's Continuing Professional Development Conference, 2 September 2008, at IMI Sandyford (unpublished).   **40** MORI, *Customer Survey, on behalf of the Inspectorate* (Department of Education and Science, 2005, pp 34–36).

18

Overview

The state inspectorate of schools in Ireland is over 175 years in existence. Over that period the school system, building on deep foundational roots, has developed, expanded and diversified in an impressive way. In 2008, the national school system, in which children can be enrolled from the age of four and remain normally to the age of 12, caters for about 96% of all children. There are five types of post-primary school – secondary, vocational, community college, comprehensive and community school – at which about 82% of pupils complete the post-primary educational programme. Non-mainstream and further education programmes cater for about another 4% of the age cohort. Almost 65% of post-primary school leavers go on to participate in a diversified tertiary education sector. Many agencies have contributed to the shaping of this impressive modern education system. This book set out to identify and examine the role of the inspectorate in the process. Arising from the long story of the inspectorate as it related to different stages of the development of the school system, it seems appropriate to draw some general reflections on aspects of the evolution of the inspectorate to round off the study. This may also allow for lines of the inspectorate's development as a professional corps to be more clearly distinguished when less closely intertwined with the general educational context and the detailed treatment of inspectorial work engagement.

THE PRIMARY INSPECTORATE (1831–1990)

Early beginnings

The Stanley letter of 1831 instituted school inspection in the national schools of Ireland and this has had continuous existence to the present day. Among the distinctive foundations of the Westminster government in Ireland, the school inspection system at primary level of the Department of Education and Science is among the longest established inspection systems in the world. Founded as a key element of the government scheme to give state aid for primary schools, the inspection system developed and grew as a key adjunct to the national school administration in Marlborough Street in Dublin.

When Edward Stanley devised his new arrangement for grant aid for schools in 1831, inspectors were assigned a pivotal role at the very heart of the national school system. Stanley's injunctions for inspection were very significant and had long and enduring effect on the spirit and character of school inspection in primary education. At root, the critical aspect was that inspectors would visit and report on schools so that the Commissioners could be in possession of accurate and dependable reports and might be able to make decisions based on reliable information. Since the school system was intended to be national in the sense that it would embrace all of Ireland, rules and regulations that would be consistently applied were required. Thus, the Commissioners produced their *Rules and Regulations for National Schools* and these came to be an especially significant element of the state's limited but powerful control of primary education. Regularly updated and revised throughout the ninety-year existence of the National Board, the rules were a defining feature of the primary school system. The inspection system was the mechanism by which the Commissioners ensured that their rules were observed thus copper-fastening their control of the very large school system that evolved in time. .

Strongly supported by the ordinary people of Ireland, the national school system grew rapidly in size and importance more or less eliminating the hedge schools within a generation. Thus, state provision for primary education came early to Ireland, relatively speaking, and a remarkable feature was that, despite various problems, the national schools proved to be a great success in many ways. With the growth of the system, the number of inspectors increased, and their role and presence in the school system was of considerable significance and influence throughout the years. In its earliest manifestation, the inspection system bore the hallmark of its colonial origin with an avowed purpose of loyalty to the crown and seeking to foster appropriate deference to its authority in Ireland. Queen Victoria granted Royal Charters of Incorporation to the Commissioners in 1845 and 1861 though the national school system was never given a formal statutory basis under British rule. For all of ninety years, the inspectors operated under the authority of the Board and the crown in a system that came to command close to universal acceptance as the primary school system of the country.

The national school system was a state-aided one with an interesting balance of responsibilities and power between the centre and the local in the provision of schooling. In general, the centre held the power to determine curricula, sanction textbooks, regulate teacher employment, provide salary payments and grants, set out rules and regulations, and sanction aid for approved local applications. The power of school management at local level resided principally in the appointment and dismissal of teachers, in distributing teacher salaries, in monitoring the general work of the school, and in supporting the denominational ethos, in so far as this was possible. All denominations took a keen interest in the latter and the system was gradually shaped to be a de facto denominational one even though official policy had designed it as an inter-denominational system.

From the beginning, the inspectors were to be the major agents by which the centre sought to implement its policies and, to an extent, the inspectors also acted as conduits to report on local issues to the Commissioners. Acting in this capacity it was unambiguously established that the role of the inspectors was much wider than the evaluation of the work of the state-aided schools. The range of their duties became very extensive as they sought to be the eyes and ears of the Board as they 'read' local situations, investigated a variety of issues affecting applications for aid, examined proposed school buildings, assessed local conditions and interest in education, and so on. This was apart altogether from their more direct role of relating with teachers, evaluating teaching in relation to school conditions, examining pupil performance, checking on school apparatus, investigating attendance rolls and reporting on the quality of the education being provided. Thus, the national school inspectors can be viewed as system builders as well as monitors of schooling quality.

Inspection in Ireland under the national school system took on a character that was distinctive to Ireland. Mainly because it was the main agency of state supervision, inspection became a controlling influence within the school system linked very closely to the rules and regulations of the Commissioners. The position of inspector was accorded a high social status in contrast to the somewhat lowly position given to the teachers for a long period. The inspectors were well remunerated and high expectations were set for them in terms of the work they were expected to accomplish while travelling extensively in the course of their work at all times of the year and in all weathers. Detailed instructions governed the work of the inspectors and the system of circular letters was availed of regularly to update or alter the instructions. The most comprehensive set of instructions to inspectors was issued in 1855 and these formed the core framework of procedure for inspection for many years. The instructions were very elaborate and reflected a 'top-down', bureaucratic approach. The tradition was also established of very detailed and prompt reportage by the inspectors to the National Education Office in Dublin. Their itineraries were subject to official approval and their expenses were closely scrutinised. There were also limitations on personal lifestyle. Their salaries and social status were conceived to be on a different level to teachers. While advised to be courteous to teachers, particularly in front of pupils, the power they exercised and the investigatory character of their work fostered tensions in inspector-teacher relationships, which became engrained in the system particularly when inspectors' reports were linked to teacher emoluments. From 1860, inspectors were recruited through competitive entry under the aegis of the Civil Service Commissioners.

The national school system grew to be a vast system of provision for education. Within fifty years of its foundation, it had 7,648 national schools, 30 model schools, 94 agricultural schools, with more than a million pupils on roll. Many thousands of individuals worked as teachers, as monitors, as pupil teachers, as workmistresses, supported by a significant staff at the Office in Dublin as well as some 72 inspectors. Throughout the years the National Board produced a prodigious amount of published information about the system. This included annual reports with extensive appendices giving statistical accounts and data about every aspect of its functioning. This material included the published reports of inspectors printed for the purpose of public accountability. A striking feature of the national school provision was the enormous systematisation of every aspect of its operations. Its highly regarded and internationally sought after school textbooks, its arrangement for roll books and registers, the lists of school requisites, the elaborate statistical tables, the listings of schools all over Ireland, all bore testimony to an extraordinary degree of systematic organisation and exactitude.

Payment by results, 1872–1901

The introduction of payment by results in 1872–73 represented a major change in national policy. This arose from the accountability and utilitarian ideology of the time when officialdom raised questions as to whether sufficient value was being obtained for the expenditure incurred in primary education. It was also linked to the drive to achieve high levels of basic literacy and numeracy amongst the mass of the population. This was the beginning of a new and distinctive era in the work of the inspectors. The fact that the policy as implemented in Ireland was designed by the Chief of Inspection, Patrick Keenan, gave it a legitimacy for many inspectors. However, its practical operation was to cause much difficulty and proved very burdensome and laborious. The new system called for the individual examination, in a range of subjects, by the inspector of all children each year in every school. The annual results examination was to be the arbiter of each school's efficacy and the determinant of about one-third of the emolument of each teacher every year. The notes governing the operation of the system were labyrinthine. For some time the detailed reportage involved the inspectors in calculating and tabulating the money value of the results examinations and transferring data from marking sheets to examination rolls. The fact that the results examinations affected teacher income added to the pressure for all concerned. Problems arose regarding uniformity of inspectorial practice which the senior inspectors sought to address. A significant increase in staff in the Office in Dublin was necessitated by the introduction of the payment by results system.

While the inspectors performed their duties under the new system with diligence, an outcome of the process was that it led to something of a distortion of their educational role. So much time had to be devoted to the investigation of rolls and the examination of individual pupils, that no time was available for the broader role of inspection of teacher methods, or demonstrating improved technique. The quality of teachers' work was being assessed indirectly through pupil performance on a given day on a range of tests, regardless of other relevant circumstances. This tended to give an aura of inquisitor to the role of the inspector rather than that of evaluator and advisor on teaching method.

Whereas the payment by results policy did give a notable stimulus to the national school system in general and particularly to the implementation of the programme of instruction and the promotion of children through the class grades, the policy had many notable ill effects on the overall operation of the school system. Essentially, the policy continued in operation with far too great an intensity for much too long. It was to be 1901 before the policy was finally abandoned. For children and teachers, there were deep constraints on learning and teaching but for the inspectors, payment by results produced baneful and lasting effects on their efficacy and contribution to the school system. Though the inspectors voiced many and varied criticisms of the policy and its manifestations in schools in their annual reports, the administration in Marlborough Street did not pay real attention to what had become a serious flaw in the operation and work of the national schools. Notably absent in the inspection corps was a unified view and policy stance about important aspects of their work in the schools.

The Revised Programme of 1900

Finally and belatedly, it was the initiative of the Belmore Commission that identified the need to reconsider the results system as it took stock of the need to introduce new areas of study into the national schools. This did eventually transpire under the command of Dr W.J.M. Starkie whose inexperience of the national school system allied to fast-changing and complex circumstances in the National Education Office, precipitated a number of significant difficulties within the administration. Most importantly for inspectors, major reorganisation of their role and functioning took effect in 1900–01 and fundamental realignment of their linkages within the Office occurred. The scale and import of some of the changes introduced with this major reorganisation created extraordinary tensions that were to have lasting effects. For a considerable period after 1900, some of the inspectors in leadership positions remained disaffected and this, combined with significant problems over teachers' salaries and other difficulties, precipitated serious troubles for the administration of the national school system.

The publication of the Revised Programme in 1900 heralded the beginning of a remarkable new phase in the national school system. A radical shift in curricular policy and the abolition of payment by results were the main features of the new approach. A broad and child-centred curriculum with new teaching methodologies brought a sudden change affecting many features of the system including teachers' salary arrangements. Whereas inspectors had not made a large contribution to either the programme itself or the detailed arrangements governing its introduction, they were an important part of the administrative infrastructure charged with its implementation. A particular element that had deep significance for the future was the involvement of the inspectors with teachers' promotions and increments of salary dependent on annual evaluation of work in schools.

New approaches to inspection were devised in line with the principles of the Revised Programme involving observation of teaching methodology and the oral examination of pupils on a class basis. Circulars were issued to inspectors on the type of inspection required and quality rather than quantity of work was emphasised. Although there were various difficulties hindering the implementation of the Revised Programme, significant progress was made in the schools in implementing certain aspects of the programme. School life became much more interesting and pleasant for school children, particularly for younger pupils. While it took time for some inspectors to adjust to new procedures, and while the burden placed on them regarding teachers' increments and promotions was invidious, there is evidence that the inspectors and the in-career organisers did much to help promote good curricular and teaching practice in the schools during that era. Although there was notable progress in terms of the work in schools, tensions between the teachers and the National Board reached breaking point in 1912. The Dill Committee of Inquiry was established to investigate the problems but only minor changes resulted from this. A strong residual antipathy against inspectors and against Starkie's administration remained, however.

After independence

With the foundation of the Irish Free State in 1922, primary education in Ireland was set on a new course with a radical new approach towards cultural and nationalist aspects. The attempt to Gaelicise the schools and to revive the Irish language was a major undertaking that had profound effect on all elements of the primary school sector for well over forty years. Because the state exercised considerable control over the primary schools by means of inspection, inspectors were placed at the forefront of the drive to reshape primary education. Under native government, inspectors in national schools came to be identified very much with the Irish language. This period lent a distinct aura of Irishness and nationality to the corps of inspectors while education issues of a more general character tended to be subordinated to the quest for Gaelicisation by means of the schools.

Inspired by the ideology of cultural nationalism the national schools were regarded as major agencies for a cultural revival, with a particular focus on restoring Irish as a general vernacular language. The new programme evolved from the first National Programme Conference in 1921–22, in which inspectors took no part. However, some inspectors did have an input to the two other stages of its evolution, the Second Programme Conference 1925–26, and the Revised Programme of 1934. On the partition settlement inspectors had the option of going to the Northern Ireland administration, or retirement, or staying in position in Dublin. However, it became clear that proficiency in Irish and a zeal for its promotion in the schools became very desirable characteristics under the new regime in Dublin. On the appointment of twelve new inspectors in 1923 particular emphasis was placed on competence in Irish and the ability to provide courses in Irish. The twelve appointed were referred to as 'the twelve apostles of the revival'. As had happened in 1872 and 1900, the inspectors were faced with a very different approach to education and they had to adjust to the new priorities, and to a context in which the Irish language was the preferred medium of discourse.

Now under the control of native government, the inspection corps was reorganised once more as a part of the Department of Education from 1924. In remarkably short time, the inspectors took on the mantle of the new state as regards Irish language requirements. Primary inspectors were arranged territorially in districts and divisions. The range of their activity was very varied. In relation to the evaluation of work within the schools, the inspectors' evaluations were again linked to a rating system for teachers upon which increments and promotion prospects depended. The rating system categorised teachers as highly efficient, efficient and non-efficient. After a few years, proficiency in the teaching of Irish became a pre-requisite for the grades of efficient and highly efficient. By means of the rating system, the inspection corps exercised a huge influence on classroom practice. A report on the inspectorate in 1927 led to a few changes in general practice, including an appeal mechanism against inspectors' reports.

National teachers came under considerable pressure to become proficient in Irish and high expectations were set for the primary schools as part of the Gaelicisation ambitions of the fledgling state. The Irish language elements of school work added a new challenge for all connected with primary education. Relations between the teachers and the inspectors remained cool and formal in many respects. As might be expected, in the circumstances of the primary schools, relations between teachers and inspectors were often tense and unfriendly. Teacher lore frequently included reference to authoritarian or oppressive treatment at the hands of some inspectors. In the course of its *A Plan for Education*, published in 1947, the INTO included a strong critique of inspectorial practice and urged a significant change of direction in the process of inspection. In 1949 the rating system was altered, with the highly efficient rating dropped. Furthermore, once a teacher was regarded as 'satisfactory' following his/her probation period, inspection had no longer a direct connection with teacher emoluments. A new circular on inspection was issued in 1959, reflective of a less investigative and more advisory role for the inspector, which led to more cordial inspector-teacher relationships.

The Primary School Curriculum, 1971

During the 1960s Irish society underwent major socio-economic and cultural change. A re-appraisal of all aspects of educational policy was undertaken. A notable instance of this was a move towards a major reform of the primary school curriculum. For the first time ever, it was the inspectors who were the initiators and the formulators of what became known as the 'New Curriculum', published in 1971. This curriculum was a radical change from that which had existed for almost fifty years, and reflected many aspects of the Revised Programme of 1900. It was a very broad, child-centred curriculum which encouraged discovery-type methods and which saw the school as a life-enhancing environment for children. The curriculum was warmly welcomed. Inspectors took leading roles in the provision of in-service training for teachers in relation to its implementation. Due to a variety of circumstantial problems, the aspirations of the curriculum authors were never fully realised, but much progress was made and the character of Irish primary school life was greatly altered for the better.

The inspectorate also became very involved in new emphases which were emerging in Irish education policy. These included much greater and more sophisticated provision for children with special educational needs, as well as those experiencing disabilities such as visual and hearing impairment. The primary inspectorate was also very much to the fore in the provision of better education for travellers. The educational problems experienced by children with serious socio-economic disadvantage were receiving greater political attention and primary inspectors participated in a range of projects and initiatives to improve their position. In association with their colleagues, the psychologists and inspectors of guidance services, they devised new forms of educational attainment tests for children. The primary inspectorate was also to the fore in harnessing new technologies for language teaching and distinctively new lesson series were developed for use in schools from the mid 1960s. The role of the inspectorate was also important in the rationalisation of small schools policy, initiated in 1966.

Reflecting both a sense of self-confidence and a desire for future planning, the primary inspectorate engaged in a significant analysis of its work and role and, in 1981 produced a notable document known as the Collins Report. This report made a number of important recommendations that crystallised strategic thinking within the service at that time. Among the outcomes of the report were the preparation of annual reports by the primary inspectorate, criteria for the evaluation of teachers' work, and a more structured time pattern for school reports. Despite experiencing an embargo on recruitment from 1981 to 1992, the primary inspectorate continued to be effectively and efficiently active on many fronts, including participation in the Review Body on the Primary Curriculum (1987) and the Primary Education Review Body (1988), which paved the way for new developments in primary education into the future.

Under native government from 1922, very few female inspectors were recruited to the service. Remarkably, throughout almost the entire twentieth century, despite the fact that there were many thousands of female teachers working in primary schools, only a few women were taken on to discharge the role of inspector. However, this was to change significantly in the period after 1998.

THE SECONDARY INSPECTORATE, 1901–90

In the nineteenth century secondary education was regarded as much more a matter of private concern than a state concern. The secondary schools were established by private organisations (many of them religious groups) and by individuals. When pressure was applied for state support for these institutions the owners wished to delimit, as far as possible, the influence which the state might exert in return for such subvention. The Intermediate Education Act of 1878 confined the state's involvement to payments on the results of pupils' performance in the examinations set by the Commissioners, without an inspection process. When, twenty years later, the Palles Commission came to examine the system inspection became a disputatious issue within the Commission. Some members wished to replace the results examinations with an inspection system, but a majority favoured the existing procedure. Even though the Intermediate Education Act of 1900 gave the right to the Board to appoint inspectors subject to the sanction of the lord lieutenant and the approval of the Treasury, it did not make clear whether these could be in addition to, or as a replacement for the results examinations.

In 1901, the Board appointed six Englishmen as 'temporary' inspectors. These were the first secondary school inspectors. The inspectors had a wide brief to report on – teaching, condition of schools, timetable, qualifications of staff and equipment for teaching practical subjects. Their reports for the school years 1901–02 and 1902–03 were published in five volumes. When the Board urged the chief secretary to approve the appointment of a permanent inspectorate he refused because the Board did not propose to reduce the expenditure for examinations by a sum equivalent to the cost of inspection. A stalemate ensued on the issue. The temporary inspectors were dropped and the issue of inspection fell into abeyance. Despite the recommendation of the Dale and Stephens Report of 1905 that payment by results examinations be abolished and replaced by an inspection system, with comprehensive powers, no action was taken on the matter at that time.

This outline of the background to the secondary inspectorate indicates what a contentious issue it was involving political, religious, economic and cultural concerns. Eventually, following a threat of resignation by the Intermediate Board on the matter in 1908, Chief Secretary Birrell agreed that six inspectors could be appointed on a permanent basis. The six appointed were all Irishmen with experience of secondary education. The regulations for the inspectorate were approved by Lord Lieutenant Aberdeen, and were very extensive in scope. This again raised the hackles of the private school managements who resented such powers and, to a degree, succeeded in delimiting them. Thus, when the new secondary inspectorate began to operate in October 1909 it was in a much more sensitive arena than had existed for the national school inspectorate.

Apart from the Preparatory Grade Examination, which was dropped in 1913, the traditional results examinations continued to operate, in conjunction with the inspectorate. Nevertheless, the inspectors carried out their work according to an elaborate reportage template, covering many features of school life. The inspectorate worked hard and conscientiously and in their first school year, 1909–10, they recorded reports on 368 schools. Their reports were independent-minded, professional, well-focussed and frank. The reports gave an intimate and fascinating insight into the conditions of schools and the quality of teaching and learning at the time.

The secondary inspectors had their headquarters in 1 Hume Street, where the Secretary of the Department of Education was also located up to the late 1930s. The fact that from 1924 to 1968 the Secretary had been a secondary inspector, gave a certain niche to this branch. The inspectors were well-educated and scholarly men and their small number facilitated the development of a good esprit de corps. The secondary inspectors were not at all as tightly bound by regulations as the national school inspectors. Neither did they have an influence on the remuneration or career prospects of the teachers they inspected, unlike the national school inspectorate. Overall, their impact on the secondary school system was limited. Yet this first group of secondary inspectors performed their work to high professional standards and were diplomatic in the delicate political context in which they found themselves.

Following the establishment of the new state in 1922, the Department of Education was quick to state formally the limited role which the state exercised, or intended to exercise, regarding secondary schooling. There was full acceptance of the private character of the secondary schools. The mode of state subvention for secondary schooling was, however, changed. The results examinations were abolished and a capitation system installed based on the 'recognised' status of schools as verified by a system of school inspection. Two certificate examinations replaced the three results examinations. Regulations were laid down regarding teacher qualifications and salary payments. Approved courses of study were laid down for secondary schools. The state's main interest was in the curriculum and assessment process, and its concern for the promotion of the Irish language was very clear from the regulations devised.

As was the case with the national school inspectorate, the secondary inspectorate was to play a central role in the implementation of the state's mechanisms of influence. However, even in the new regime their authority in the schools was not as strongly established as that of the national school inspectorate. The schools were careful to emphasise their private character, with the inspectors cast somewhat as guests in the schools, sometimes benefiting from hospitality provided. The numbers of inspectors remained small, even as late as 1950 there were only fourteen secondary school inspectors in total. The country was divided into three inspectorial divisions, with normally three inspectors in each division. Inspectors had to apply considerable ingenuity in planning their inspectorial visits and travelling expenses were closely scrutinised. Subjects were organised in groups to which inspectors were assigned, sometimes covering subjects which had not formed part of their degree studies. When visiting schools inspectors were expected to advise teachers on teaching methods, textbooks, and suchlike. While inspectors could alert school managers to inadequate teaching performance among staff, they could take no direct action on incompetence. Thus, in general, secondary school inspection was of a light-touch model.

Where the secondary inspectorate became very involved was in the preparation of the public examination papers, in the administration of the examinations, and in correcting, or monitoring the correction of scripts. They participated in Standardising Committees and in adjustments to examination course arrangements. The inspectors' reports on the work of schools in the Department's annual reports tended to be desultory and bland. A notable feature of the staffing of secondary schools was the high proportion of unregistered teachers, amounting almost to 50% in 1933–34, but there is no record available as to whether the inspectorate expressed a view on this serious matter.

It was noteworthy that it was Mr de Valera, as President of the Executive Council, later as Taoiseach, who took the initiative on changing the open course model of 1924–25 to the prescribed courses of his preference for secondary education, from 1939–40. The political role proved more influential than the professional one of the inspectorate. No significant changes were made in the secondary education system for more than two decades later, by which time, in 1961, there were 80,400 pupils attending 542 secondary schools, but with no corresponding increase in the secondary inspectorate.

Unlike previous decades, the Department of Education took a pro-active approach to post-primary educational policy development in the 1960s. It was noteworthy that a committee of inspectors produced a report in 1962 which involved radical thinking on the future of post-primary schooling. It remained unpublished, but it was influential. The expansion and development of post-primary education formed a central core of the new policy. It was timely then, in 1962, that seven new appointments were made to the secondary inspectorate. Curriculum reform, the expansion of the public examinations and post-primary school re-organisation became very central concerns of the inspectorate from the early sixties. The secondary inspectors also became very involved in organising and providing in-service education for teachers in relation to the syllabi reforms. The 'free' secondary education scheme of 1967 greatly augmented the growing trends of pupil enrolment. The secondary schools were no longer to be the sole providers of secondary education as the vocational schools were permitted to offer the full secondary course of studies, as were the newly-established comprehensive and community schools. The Department of Education sought to establish an integrated post-primary inspectorate for the changing circumstances, but with little success.

To help re-structure post-primary school provision, school rationalisation meetings took place at which the secondary inspectorate contributed. Work on curricular issues and the public examinations, for which the number of candidates had greatly increased, continued to dominate the work of the secondary inspectorate. The impact of these pressures was that visiting schools and evaluating their work became more marginalised. Even at that, difficulties arose when the ASTI adopted a policy which stated inspectorial observation of teachers' teaching could only be done when the teachers volunteered for it.

When the Curriculum and Examinations Board (CEB) was established in 1984, the secondary inspectorate had some concerns that this was an intrusion on their professional arena. But they co-operated with it as they did with its successor, the NCCA. The reaction was somewhat similar when ministers appointed special advisers from outside the Department, but the inspectorate came to see that these personnel did not infringe on their work, but could, on occasion, be partners with them.

Perhaps the biggest problem which faced the secondary inspectorate occurred during the 1980s. The dilemma included a number of factors. One was that they experienced a depletion of staff at a time when the post-primary system was greatly expanding. Even the Curriculum Unit, which was established with high hopes, was very under-staffed and under-resourced. A further issue related to a lack of clear focus on what the inspectors' key role was. A multitude of duties had grown up incrementally, but there was a lack of clear rationale or prioritisation of function. Work on the public examinations dominated their involvement, but there was an underlying unease that their credibility as inspectors was being eroded as they became more distanced from classroom practice. Furthermore, there was a lack of clarity in relation to the line of authority to which senior inspectors related. They also resented what they saw as their marginalisation from the policy arena, which they regarded as being monopolised by the senior administrative staff in the Department. To their credit some senior secondary inspectors identified and analysed the problems they faced. However, they were not successful in achieving redress of the difficulties they encountered at the time. Neither were they as pro-active as the other branches in shaping their own way forward. The secondary inspectorate, however, sustained its commitment to maintaining the standards and status of the curricula and the public examinations.

The vocational inspectorate came into being in association with the Department of Agriculture and Technical Instruction which began operating on the first year of the new century, 1900. The inspectorate, part of the Technical Instruction Branch (TIB), shared both the optimistic hopes of the DATI for a new form of practical and technical education and its generous support for all agencies promoting the cause of such education at the time. One of the first significant achievements of this inspectorate was to work in partnership with the Intermediate Board to greatly improve the teaching of science and drawing in the existing secondary schools. By 1904 they had provided and equipped 243 science laboratories in schools. While, in 1899, only 705 pupils sat the science examinations, by 1903, 5,950 students were taking science and earning grants from the DATI on the basis of its inspection system. By 1919–20, £36,000 was being paid to secondary schools in relation to 16,077 students studying experimental science and drawing. The TIB inspectorate was accepted much more easily in secondary schools than the secondary inspectors, as their remit was limited to the teaching of these subjects and the facilities available for this purpose. The teacher training courses organised and, to some extent, delivered by the DATI inspectors were of high standard and very popular with teachers. The inspectors made occasional visits to secondary schools during the school year and engaged in more formal inspections in April and May. Most of this inspection was through oral and practical work. The reports of the inspectors were detailed and informative. The career framework of the inspectorate evolved into Senior Inspector, Inspector and Junior Inspector, and they reported for various districts such as, 'The Southern District'.

The other side of the inspectorate's work was to help lay the groundwork for local schemes of technical education, working with the newly established local technical instruction committees. By 1902–03, 57 such schemes were in operation. The work went on apace so that by 1907–08 every county and nearly every urban authority had technical instruction schemes in operation. The contribution of the inspectorate to establishing the first nationwide scheme of technical instruction was enormous and took much time, expertise, diplomatic skill and perseverance. By 1909–10, £49,110 was being paid in attendance grants for 42,909 students in technical schools and classes. In 1913, the inspectors designed Ireland's own scheme of Technical School Examinations. The TIB inspectors saw themselves as system builders in these early formative years of technical education.

The First World War caused difficulties for the work of the DATI and its inspectors, but there was no diminution of student attendance, except in the Belfast region. On the partition settlement, responsibility for technical education was transferred to the Northern Ireland parliament on 1 January 1922, and some of the DATI inspectors transferred to that jurisdiction. Technical education in the South came under the control of the Department of Education on its establishment in 1924.

It was significant that very early on in the new regime the senior technical inspectors advised that it was desirable that a thorough investigation should be carried out on industrial and commercial training in relation to the needs of the new state. When the Commission on Technical Education was set up in 1926, it was placed under the chairmanship of Mr John Ingram, Senior Inspector of Technical Education. The Ingram Report (1927) provided the blueprint for the Vocational Education Act of 1930, which was a historic landmark for vocational and technical education. The 38 new Vocational Education Committees, set up by the Act, got down to work quickly. In doing this they got valuable advice and assistance from the inspectorate, who worked closely with the newly-appointed CEOs. The inspectors prepared an explanatory memorandum in 1931, prepared new regulations, and provided needed official documentation. From the beginning, it was established that the inspectorate would have a close and intimate relationship with the vocational schools and the educational schemes. The inspectors held courses for teachers and issued teaching notes to guide them. In 1936 the inspectorate devised a new scheme of Technical School Examinations which became highly successful and was in operation up to the early years of this century. The amount of work carried out by the Technical Instruction Branch, as it was called, was very impressive, but even by 1938 there were only 16 inspectors in total.

In the wake of the new Constitution of 1937, the vocational school system came under some criticism from Catholic Church spokesmen, in that it did not reflect a denominational ethos, and other critics commented that the Irish language did not feature prominently enough. Stung by such criticisms, the Department prepared Memo V40, in 1942, which was largely authored by J.P. Hackett, a senior TIB inspector. While this gave a new emphasis to the work of the vocational schools giving it a more religious and Irish language character, it did not silence other agencies from criticising the system during the Second World War years. However, despite some difficulties, the system emerged unscathed. A new Group Certificate Examination was devised by the inspectorate which became operational from 1947. During the 1950s the inspectorate continued to work co-operatively with the VECs and the system expanded. By 1959 there were 272 vocational schools, with about 27,000 full-time pupils and 12,000 part-time, with over 86,000 attending evening classes. The inspectorate also related with the technical education classes provided by VECs for post 16-year-old students.

One of the *leitmotifs* of educational policy in the 1960s was the promotion and development of vocational and technical education. The status of the vocational schools was raised and the scope of their studies expanded. A new institution, the Regional Technical College (RTC), was planned, with the first five of them opening in 1969. Teacher education for teachers of practical and applied subjects was greatly altered and became localised in the new Thomond College in Limerick. Technical education under VECs such as Dublin, Cork and Limerick was greatly expanded, modernised and well equipped. Vocational inspectors regarded themselves as pro-active agents in supporting all these developments. They took a very hands-on role in ensuring the successful implementation of such new policies. It could be said that the vocational inspectors again saw themselves as system builders and drew inspiration from the tradition of the DATI at the period of their formation. As well as helping in course content and improved methodology, they also assisted in the design of buildings, laboratories, advised on equipment, participated in staff selection and exercised responsibility for the Technical Examinations which had become extensive. With the expansion of the RTCs and the development of tertiary colleges such as those of CDVEC, reorganised as the Dublin Institute of Technology (DIT) in 1978, the work of the vocational inspectorate took on a greater tertiary education dimension, which further differentiated it from the primary and secondary branches. This was also evident in vocational inspectors' involvement with the National Council for Educational Awards (NCEA), set up in 1972.

The vocational inspectorate also took an active role in a variety of curriculum development initiatives during the seventies and eighties, and liaised with a number of curriculum units established by VECs. They also took a leading role on a range of curriculum innovations supported by European regional and structured funds such as pre-employment courses and vocational preparation and training programmes. Both the secondary and the vocational inspectors liaised constructively with the new category of inspectors – the inspectors of school guidance services – who were first recruited in the mid-sixties. The greatly expanded pupil clientele in post-primary schools highlighted the need for the personal, educational and career guidance of pupils, and the new category of personnel was a major asset in this regard.

THE COMBINED INSPECTORATE

Up to the 1990s, the three branches of the inspectorate, which had originated in very different circumstances, developed largely as compartmentalised units, each with a clear sense of its own identity related to its work environment. Common salary scales were devised in the early seventies, but it was only in the early nineties that separate union branches were amalgamated and that gradually annual conferences encompassed the combined inspectorate.

The developments were contemporary with some studies and policy developments which focussed on the inspectorate at this time. Notable among these was the Clive Hopes Report of 1991, which included a detailed critique of the structure and operation of the inspectorate. The OECD report of 1991 also called for significant policy changes for the inspectorate. Some of those points fed into the policy proposals of the Green Paper in 1992. Policy on the inspectorate was also an issue for focussed discussion at the National Education Convention of 1993. Its Report called for significant changes, but also recorded the strong expressions of support for the inspectorate, as an institution, put forward by stakeholders at the Convention. The White Paper of 1995 set out a new policy framework for the inspectorate which was included in the Education bill (1) of 1997. However, a change of government led to significant changes on the planned inspectorial framework. Part III, Section 13 of the Education Act of 1998, for the first time, gave statutory status to the inspectorate and clearly set out the functions of the inspectorate for modern educational purposes.

While such deliberations on the inspectorate were taking place in the general policy arena, from the early nineties the inspectorate itself was engaging in its own re-structuring. Appointment to senior positions became opened to merit, rather than seniority. This also helped to break an older hierarchical tradition within the sub-culture of the inspectorate whereby junior staff were expected to be deferential to their superiors, and were discouraged from expressing questioning viewpoints. Another important change was that senior appointments came from across the inspectorate, rather than from a particular branch. Seán Mac Gleannáin was appointed as Chief Inspector in 1991 and he set out to ensure that the position would be one of substantial leadership. He favoured closer integration of the inspectorate and, in 1991, both primary and post-primary inspectors came together for the first time at an Annual Conference. From October 1991 he began preparing annual reports which would be reflective of the work of the whole inspectorate, and involve cross-sectoral themes. He drew attention to the erosion of time spent on inspection in schools and deprecated this pattern. Nine new inspectors were recruited in 1992, which was an important augury that the tide was turning from the enervating effects of the staff recruitment embargo introduced in 1981.

The induction and professional development programmes for the inspectorate were improved and henceforth were to be devised on a cross-sectoral basis. The composition of new inspectorial committees, which were established for particular purposes, were now also cross-sectoral. The hands-on involvement by inspectors in the delivery of in-service courses for teachers and the delivery of courses in remedial education was terminated. Arising from legislation in 1992, inspectors would no longer be involved in the administration of the RTCs and the DIT. Such changes helped to bring more rationalisation to the work of the inspectorate and helped to focus its professional work profile. Sub-committees of the combined inspectorate were also set up to plan for the future in the light of the policy trends which were emerging in the government's policy papers, during these years. These developments indicate that the inspectorate was seeking to position itself as a more combined, focussed agency at a period of significant educational change.

While the inspectorate concerned itself with such structural and organisational issues it continued, of course, to interface with the educational system in its day-to-day development. Curricular issues in particular loomed very large. One of the most important of these was the detailed engagement of the primary inspectorate, with the NCCA, throughout the nineties in planning the revised Primary School Curriculum, published in 1999. At post-primary level, one of the great curricular achievements was a new design for the senior cycle of post-primary education. Again, in association with the NCCA, the inspectorate re-configured the senior cycle to include a Transition Year Programme, the Leaving Certificate Vocational Programme, the Leaving Certificate Applied Programme and reforms to the syllabi of the traditional Leaving Certificate Programme. Other areas of major inspectorial engagement in these years related to special education and the education of children with specific learning disabilities. The moves towards the mainstreaming of special education required much skill and expertise. The promotion of gender equality in schooling was also an area which got greater attention. Furthermore, the educational needs of socially and economically-deprived children, including traveller children, assumed a higher policy priority, necessitating a variety of intervention programmes led by the inspectorate.

Drawing on international trends, the inspectorate also engaged in intensive planning for a new form of inspection, Whole School Evaluation (WSE). The public examinations continued to loom large on the inspectorial work agenda. A useful initiative to help the central co-ordination of this work was the establishment of the Examinations Co-ordinating Committee in 1993, on a cross-sectoral basis between professional and administrative staff. During these years the inspectorate also established better relationships with external stakeholders, researchers and academics. A partnership approach to the formulation of educational policy was adopted at national level in the 1990s. A greater transparency about the inspectorate's work facilitated constructive dialogue with the variety of associations which now represented stakeholders in a society with a mature and sophisticated interest in educational developments. The greater preparedness of inspectors to deliver papers at conferences and symposia helped the partnership approach.

The Education Act of 1998 was the first comprehensive education act in the history of the state. The senior inspectorate ensured that the inspectorate as an agency would form a specific section of the Act. The fact that it had already shaped itself into a more cohesive professional corps probably helped in achieving this. The Act also gave a greater sense of assurance and confidence to the inspectorate in relation to its future development. In 1997, Eamon Stack had taken over as Chief Inspector and demonstrated that he intended to sustain the momentum for change and to foster the inspectorate as a combined force.

In this regard, the inspectorate was part of a broader reform movement within the Department of Education and Science in recent years. A number of consultants' reports were commissioned, most notably those of Deloitte and Touche (1999) and of Cromien (2000). These pointed to serious problems in the structure and functions of the Department and made many recommendations for change. Among these was closer liaison between the professional and administrative sides of the Department, a process which was already afoot. This process gave the inspectorate a more intimate role in policy formulation, but it also opened access to negotiations directly with the Department of Finance. One of the key directions for the reform of the Department of Education and Science was to de-clutter it from the vast range of duties which were over-absorbing it, to the detriment of strategic policy. The chosen way forward was to establish a number of bodies and support teams which would undertake responsibility for specific functions. Among the entities set up were NCTE (1998), NEPS (1999), NEWB (2002), NCSE (2004) and the State Examinations Commission (2003). Such agencies, most particularly in the case of the State Examinations Commission, relieved the inspectorate of many responsibilities which it had hitherto exercised. This allowed the Chief Inspector and his senior staff to tighten the focus of the inspectorate's professional work towards evaluation and advice, as well as school and system improvement. It was interesting that in a survey of the attitudes of post-primary inspectors in the mid-nineties they regarded their hands-on involvement with the in-service education of teachers and with the public examinations as being central to their *raison d'etre*. Yet, when these roles were removed within a decade it did not impair the profile of the inspectorate at all but, arguably, strengthened its true inspectorial image.

To position itself for its changed role the inspectorate re-structured its organisational framework. By 2003, a Senior Management Group (SMG) was established comprising of the Chief Inspector, two Deputy Chiefs and ten Assistant Chief Inspectors. The country was divided into five regions, each under the direct responsibility of an Assistant Chief, who reported to one of the Deputy Chief Inspectors. The other Deputy Chief oversaw the work of the other five Assistant Chiefs, each of which was allocated a Business Unit with a specific policy support function. Another Assistant Chief was to manage the inspectorate's engagement with the new framework of Department's regional education offices. Much new recruitment occurred, particularly following the departure of a large number of inspectors to the State Examinations Commission. An improved form of induction for new recruits was devised, and sophisticated forms of staff development were introduced.

The incorporation of the new technologies into the work of the contemporary inspectorate greatly improved communication, reportage and data collection. The establishment of the Evaluation, Support and Research Unit within the inspectorate has proved to be of great benefit to its professional performance. The fact that the inspectorate's headquarters became located in improved accommodation in Marlborough Street and its precincts facilitated co-operative relationships and joint working within the combined inspectorate.

The inspectorate's work was also assisted by the establishment of support teams of experienced teachers to work with their peers on curricular implementation, school development planning, and school leadership. These support groups liaised closely with the inspectorate and greatly increased the manpower available to improve the operation of schools.

One of the areas where a good deal of emphasis on staff development was placed was in the preparation of the inspectorate for the implementation of the Whole School Evaluation policy. The system became established in primary schools in 2003 and in post-primary schools in spring 2004. This was a landmark change in the mode of school inspection, which has continued to be refined since that time. For the first time ever, the inspectorate published its inspection reports in June 2006 and by November 2008 a total of 2,430 such reports had appeared on the Department's website. Other forms of inspection are also being implemented such as subject inspections, programme evaluations, probation of primary teachers, evaluation of Irish colleges, evaluation of non-mainstream educational centres, and thematic evaluations. This work emphasises how much the inspectorate has re-directed its activities into the schools and to relating with teachers in the classrooms of the country.

The close involvement of the inspectorate with the life of schools has given great credibility to its commentary on the quality of the school system and to its advice at policy level. Another notable feature of the modern inspectorate is the range and quality of its publications on many aspects of the system. Between 2002 and 2008 the inspectorate issued over sixty major publications with much valuable material for policy makers, school authorities, teachers, parents, and other stakeholders.

The developments within the combined inspectorate have also brought a new dimension to the inspectorate's contribution to educational policy formulation. The relationship of the inspectorate with the administrators of the education system is an interesting sub-theme throughout the history of the inspectorate, which should be outlined.

Among the functions set out for the inspectorate in section 13 of the Education Act (1998) are 'to provide support in the formulation of policy by the Minister' and 'to advise the Minister on any matter relating to education policy and provision'. This specifies a statutory role for the inspectorate in assisting in the formulations of educational policy.

In the long history of the inspectorate there existed some ambiguity about this role. While their work of school inspection and evaluating standards could be seen as indirectly contributing considerations for policy, the inspectorate's direct engagement in formulating policy was not always in evidence, nor did their career structure within the Department facilitate it. While it is true that individual inspectors were promoted to posts as Secretary or Assistant Secretary, and in personal capacities were then in positions of policy influence, the senior inspectorate per se was not part of the inner circle of policy–decision making. It was only in 1991 that the Chief Inspector became a member of the Top Management Group, with whom the Minister directly related on policy issues.

During the early decades of the primary inspectorate, while they were very involved in many aspects of the building up of the national school system, the Commissioners of National Education viewed them as very much implementers of their policies. The rules and regulations governing the operation of the system were of a 'top-down' variety. While the inspectors and particularly former Chief of Inspection, Patrick Keenan, devised the school programme to be followed from 1872 for the payment by results policy, this was to implement the policy approach already decided by the Commissioners. The work of the inspectors during this era very much involved them as implementers of system involving detailed investigations and reportage. By the 1890s they had lost faith in the system, but it was not they who instigated the reform measures. The Belmore Commission was instigated by the Commissioners and it led to a radically changed programme. The new Resident Commissioner, Dr Starkie, had no confidence in the Chiefs of Inspection and greatly altered their roles. This gave rise to a number of difficulties, including the temporary suspension of the two Chiefs of Inspection. Source material from that period clearly indicates that the inspectorate was not regarded as part of the policy-making arm of the administration.

The context in which the permanent secondary inspectorate came into operation in 1909 was one where power relations were already established between the private owners of the schools and the Intermediate Commissioners who subvented the schools on the basis of the pupils' success in their public examinations. While Lord Lieutenant Aberdeen envisaged significant investigative powers for the inspectorate these were not always operable. The inspectors reported on the standards of teaching and general facilities but, operating as an addition to the results examinations, they exercised only limited influence on the schools and had no role in the policy for secondary education, which the Commissioners themselves described in 1920 as 'toppling to destruction'.

When the DATI inspectorate was introduced in 1900, it was part of a new state system, involving a partnership between central authority and local authorities. The inspectorate was influential in the shaping of policy in conjunction with the Technical Instruction Board. Inspectors set out to improve the teaching of Science and Drawing in the secondary schools and assisted the local technical instruction committees in devising technical instruction programmes for the country. When Senior Inspector George Fletcher was promoted to Assistant Secretary of the DATI in 1904 he maintained close links with the inspectorate corps, which gave them an influence on on-going policy issues.

When the Department of Education was established in 1924 all three branches of the inspectorate came under its remit. The main thrust of the new governments' policy was inspired by the curricular ideology of cultural nationalism, with little emphasis on change in the administration of the school system. The primary and secondary inspectorates were not significant influences on the educational policy, but they became very committed to the curricular goals of government. Even though the four secretaries of the Department of Education, from 1924 to 1968, had all been secondary inspectors, it is not clear if they sought to introduce change initiatives on policy. Once the initial changes were made in primary and secondary schooling by the new regime continuity rather than change was the policy pattern for several decades. When in the late thirties, curricular changes were introduced for secondary schools, these were initiated by politicians rather than inspectors or civil servants.

A difference occurred in the vocational school sector. As was pointed out above, there the senior inspectors took the initiative in advising the authorities of the need for improvements in industrial and technical training for the needs of the new state. In 1926 Senior Inspector, John Ingram, was appointed chairman of the Commission on Technical Education. While its report in 1927, urged some radical changes for all aspects of the education system, it was its recommendations on vocational and technical education which were adopted. These were highly influential in shaping the Vocational Education Act of 1930, which proved to be a flexible and adaptable piece of legislation, which still provides part of the legislative framework for vocational education.

One area of national education policy which was backed by all branches of the inspectorate following independence was the policy of promoting the Irish language. Many of the inspectorial leaders were committed to the Irish language revival and were impatient or dismissive of any questioning of the policy. It was generally accepted by the inspectors that one of the great tasks of the post-independent era was the promotion and extension of usage of the Irish language. They considered that, as key representatives of the Department of Education at local level, they had a particular responsibility to be exemplars and encouragers in this significant task of cultural change. Many of the inspectors were fine scholars of the language and their competence in Irish was relevant to promotion within the inspectorate. Irish became the normal language of discourse within the inspectorate and, to some extent, contributed to a sense of cultural elitism among the most proficient in the language. While this tradition did not disappear, it became less evident within the changed educational policy approaches of the 1960s, which became more diverse.

The 1960s was a period of major re-appraisal of the educational system and of policy development and reform. While reports such as the Investment in Education report were a central element in the rethinking which took place, inspectors contributed in a variety of ways to the policy developments. At primary level, the inspectors were the authors of the radical new curriculum which was published in 1971. They also contributed to the new developments in educational equipment, educational building and the rationalisation of primary schools. Inspectors were also to the fore in curricular changes for post-primary schools and assisted in the evolution of thinking on the new types of school – comprehensive and community schools. There was a good deal of interchange of administrative and professional staff on planning and public consultation relating to new post-primary school provision and on the new school building unit. Inspectors were very engaged in the planning and equipping of the new regional technical colleges.

Yet this type of momentum was not sustained. In the early seventies common salary scales were agreed for the three branches of the inspectorate, but efforts to integrate the secondary and vocational inspectorate were not successful. The office of an overall Chief Inspector was established but, crucially, his role in the policy-making process was never clearly defined nor satisfactorily established. There was no formal pattern whereby ministers met and consulted with the inspectorate. As procedures evolved it was relatively unusual for a minister to have direct contact with the senior inspectorate in the deliberation of policy. Mr John Harris, who acted as a special adviser to three different Ministers for Education, John Boland, Gemma Hussey and Paddy Cooney, describes the situation which existed in the 1980s as follows:

> Their (the inspectors') influence on decision-making in many areas of educational administration is relatively small, regrettably too small. There is an unfortunate gulf at times between inspectors as professional educators on the one hand and administrators as professional civil servants on the other. On many issues of policy, including those in which the minister takes a direct interest, the views of inspectors may or may not be sought, and even if they are they may be edited or amended by administrative officials. Generally speaking the inspectorates' views are channelled to the minister through the administrative side of the Department, unless the Minister specifically arranges otherwise.[1]

1 John Harris, 'The Policy-Making Role of the Department of Education' in D.G. Mulcahy and Denis O'Sullivan (eds), *Irish Educational Policy: Process and Substance* (Dublin: IPA, 1989), pp 7–26, p. 1.

The attitudes of individual Secretaries of the Department on the involvement of the inspectorate within the policy arena was also an influence on the situation. As was noted in Chapter 13 of this study the marginalisation from the policy arena was resented, at least, by the secondary inspectorate during the 1980s. When coupled with the decline in inspectorial staff in the context of a greatly expanding school system, this position did not enhance staff morale.

During the 1990s both the inspectorate as a Departmental division, and the Department of Education and Science came under scrutiny with a view to their reform. From the early nineties the inspectorate itself initiated steps towards its own re-organisation. In 1991 the Chief Inspector became a member of the TMG. He set afoot moves towards greater unification of the inspectorate. From the mid-nineties closer structural liaison was established between the inspectorate and the administrative side in relation to the conduct of the public examinations. This proved to be a harbinger for a new tradition of joint decision-making on many policy issues. The re-organisation of the inspectorate into the Senior Management Group, involving the Chief Inspector, two Deputy Chiefs and ten Assistant Chiefs, and incorporating ten business units, gave an improved co-ordination framework to the inspectorate. This positioned it better to avail of new opportunities such as were provided by the Education Act, 1998, and by reforms in the working of the Department.

It is arguable that the inspectorate could not fully re-structure itself unless a concomitant re-structuring took place within the Department. Reviewing some of the projected changes for the Department of Education in the early nineties, the *Report on the National Education Convention* (1994) stated:

> These (changes) would include a significant departure from long-established, inherited procedures within the Department of Education, the genuine devolution of some responsibilities from the Department, fostering an orientation towards policy-making within the Department, improving communication networks, continuing the improvement of statistical procedures, and harnessing research towards policy formulation ... The changes outlined above, and other envisaged changes, would involve the most significant re-organisation of the Department since its establishment.[2]

It was only after the Cromien Report of 2000 that substantial progress was made in re-structuring the Department with the devolution of responsibilities to a range of special agencies, the establishment of a network of regional offices, and the setting up of the State Examinations Commission. Such

2 John Coolahan (ed.), *Report on the National Education Convention* (National Education Convention Secretariat, 1994), p. 10 and p. 15.

development changed the organisational environment and created the space for the inspectorate to continue the re-focussing of its role primarily on the evaluation of the quality of the education system and providing advice for policy formulation. In the process, the inspectorate has both become much closer to the work of schools and at the same time, closer to educational policy formulation.

Looking back to the Stanley letter of 1831, with its directive that government funds should be supplied to pay inspectors 'for visiting and reporting upon schools' one can see its long-term effect on the evolution of education in Ireland. In every sense, the provision of reports based on visitation, and reliant on insightful and informed judgment, is still at the heart of the work of school inspection in Ireland. Its raison d'etre is to provide for government and people, or whomsoever, a balanced and fair assessment of how education is being provided. Based mainly on direct observation of, and encounter with, the teacher and the pupil or student in school or college, the work of inspection is an important feature of a modern education system. Because it is children and vulnerable young people who are the recipients of education in the first instance, and their parents in a sense the customers of schools, there is need for checks and balances to help to protect the interests of all concerned. The public and social interests of the country are also notable factors to bear in mind in this regard. Throughout its history, the inspectorate of the Department of Education and Science has acted as an important mechanism to assist the process of checks and balances in Irish education. The inspectorate has had a profound role in and influence over education development throughout the period of state involvement with education in Ireland. It has contributed notably to the evolution and refinement of an education system that is held in high regard in the world today.

The inspectors of today are heirs to a very long and committed tradition of service to education. That tradition has been closely involved with all stages of the development of the modern Irish education system. Their statutory position and high-profile involvement in contemporary education allow them to be key agents in the promotion of education quality. As was evident at the National Education Convention and in the 2006 MORI survey, there is evidence that the Irish public has a high regard for the work of the inspectorate. In an increasingly global world the inspectorate has been pro-active in maintaining contact with inspectorates in many countries, and has established particularly close links with the inspectorate in Northern Ireland. Its involvement with the European Schools and with various EU and OECD committees has kept it in touch with international trends and developments. Thus, despite the vicissitudes of fortune over a very long time period, the Irish school inspectorate is well positioned to build on its long, distinctive traditions in contributing to the betterment of Irish education into the future.

Primary, Secondary, Vocational and Post-Primary Inspectors, 1832–2008

The following is a list of people who served as primary, secondary, vocational or post-primary inspectors since 1832. Appendix II lists separately the inspectors of guidance services and psychologists who were or had been in the Department of Education and Science prior to the establishment of NEPS. While every effort has been made to check the accuracy of the list, the authors cannot accept responsibility for any inadvertent omissions or other errors.

Surname	First Name	Surname	First Name
Adair	Samuel	Beatty	H.M.
Aherne	Siobhán	Beveridge	Catherine Elisabeth
Ainsworth	J.F.	Birmingham	Edward W.
Alexander	T.J.	Bithrey	John William
Allman	S.	Black	Daniel
Anderson	Emily	Blakely	D.L.
Anderson	Thomas	Bole	W.
Appleyard	Albie	Bolger	William
Atkinson	George	Bonfil	Maire A.
Baker	Kathleen S.	Bourke	Margaret Mary
Baker	Michael	Boyle	William
Baldwin	Thomas	Bradford	John
Bambury	Noreen	Bradley	Walter
Bamford	W.	Bradshaw	J.M.
Bannan	Edward Timothy	Brady	Dolores
Barnes	Paraic	Breathnach	Bernaidin
Barrett	Ernest Priestley	Breathnach	Mícheál
Barrett	John	Breathnach	Mícheál S.
Bartley	Charles	Breathnach	Nioclás
Bartley	W.	Breathnach	Seán
Bastabal	Nora	Broderick	Siobhán
Bateman	C.W.	Brogan	Michael
Bateman	Godfrey	Brown	John
Beamish	Frank	Brown	S.
Bearnais	Colm	Browne	John

Browne	Samuel	Corcoran	Frank
Browne	W.J.	Corcoran	John
Browne	William Alcock	Corcoran	Liam
Bryan	Martin	Corcoran	Sylvia
Burke	Andrew	Cotter	Ursula
Burke	J.F.	Coughlan	Richard
Burns	Mary	Cowley	A.S.
Butler	Edward	Cox	H.
Butler	James R.	Coyle	Michael
Byrne	Annie	Coyne	James A.
Caffrey	Paul	Craig	Isaac
Caomhánach	Séamus	Craig	J.
Cahalane	Declan	Cregan	Colm
Carlisle	John	Cremer	Seán
Carroll	Thomas	Cromie	Edward Stuart
Carter	Alfred Ernest	Crowley	Michael
Cashman	J.	Cúc	Mícheál
Chambers	Joseph	Culhane	Mary
Childs	Edward	Curran	John
Clancy	Maura	Currie	R.S.
Clarke	L.S.	Currivan	Eugene
Clarke	Henry P.	Curtis	Bernard F.
Clavin	Edward	Cussen	Joseph Stephen
Cleary	Michael	Dale	Edward
Clements	W.T.	Dalton	John Patrick
Close	Leo Joseph	Daly	Louis S.
Codrington	A.J.	D'Andún	M.
Codyre	Martin Joseph	D'Arcy	Henry L.
Coffey	Patrick	Dardis	Christopher Patrick
Colclough	Agnes	Darmody	Michael
Cole	James Alex	Davidson	William C.
Coleman	Thomas Joseph	Davitt	Arthur
Colgan	Thomas	de Bhál	Dolores
Collins	Elaine	de Bhál	Séamus
Conachy	Gráinne	de Bhaldraithe	Pádraic
Condon	Margaret	de Brún	G.
Conneely	Suzanne	de Buitléir	Séamus
Connellan	Peter	de Búrca	Dominic
Connelly	W.R.P.	de Búrca	Mícheál
Connolly	James	de Búrca	Oilibhéir
Connolly	Peter J.	de Búrca	Pádraig S.
Conwell	Eugene A.	de Búrca	Séan C.
Corcoran	Alexander Martin	de Ceannt	Eibhlín

de Gras	Fionnghuala	Fenton	James
de Lása	Liam	Field	George
de Nais	Diarmuid P.	Finn	Thomas
de Paor	Brendán	Fiorentini	Noreen
de Paor	Séamus	Fitzgerald	John
de Paor	Siobhán	Fitzgerald	Michael
Dee	John	Fitzgerald	Patrick John
Delea	Patrick	Fitzgerald	David Paul
Dennehy	John	Fitzgerald	J.G.
Desmond	Margaret Mary	Fitzpatrick	Patrick
Desmond	Tim	Fleming	Domnall
Dewar	E.P.	Fleming	John G.
Dick	James Taylor	Fletcher	George
Dickie	John	Franklin	Michael
Dillon	Suzanne	Frawley	Raymond
Dixon	W.V.	Freamhain	Riobard
Doheney	James	Friel	Nora
Doherty	Michael	Funge	Paul
Dolan	John Blake	Gannon	Don
Donavan	Catherine	Geary	Amanda
Donnelly	Thomas Noel	Gilbride	Mary
Donoghue	Carmel	Gillic	Joseph
Donoghue	Thomas	Gloster	Arthur Bird
Donovan	Henry A.	Goodman	Peter
Doody	Brendan	Gordon	J.
Doody	James Joseph	Graham	Christopher
Dowling	Joseph Hughes	Greer	J.
Downing	Edmund	Griffin	Clare
Duffy	E.	Hackett	J.B.
Duffy	Geraldine	Hagan	J.F.
Dugan	Charles	Haicéid	Diarmuid
Dullaghan	Diarmuid	Hamill	Hugh
Dundon	Michael	Hamilton	A.
Dunlop	William Wallace	Hanlon	John
Dunne	Alan	Hanrahan	Joan
Dunne	Mary	Harkin	L.
Dunne	Timonthy P.	Harney	Catherine
Dunning	Margaret	Harrison	Gabriel
Eardley	Francis	Harrison	Joe
Egan	Emer	Hartnett	Cecelia
Falconer	William	Harvey	Patrick
Fee	Gerard	Hayes	Michael
Feerick	Anne	Hayes	James

Headen	James Joseph	Kelly	
Headen	W.P.	(Ní Annracháin)	Jennifer
Heller	William Mayhew	Kennedy	Cuthbert
Henderson	John Francis	Kennedy	W.
Heron	Richard Cobden	Kinsella	Maurice
Hickey	Michael	Kirk	Pádraig
Hickey		Kirk	Treasa
McDonagh	Sheelagh	Kirkpatrick	Robert
Hislop	Harold	Kirkpatrick	Samuel
Hogan	James Francis	Kirkpatrick	Thomas
Hollins	Frederick Merrick	Kirwan	Joseph
Holohan	Frank	Knox	Séamus
Holton	Karina	Kyle	John Andrew
Honan	P.J.	Kyle	William
Horan	Patrick Joseph	Lally	Martin
Horgan	Miriam	Lane	J.C.
Hughes	Robert Wood	Lavelle	Francis B.
Hughes	Michael	Lawler	M.
Hunter	William A.	Layton	Colum
Huston	Nollaig	Lehane	Daniel
Hynes	J.J.	Leonard	Jerome
Ingram	John	Lindsay	William
Irvine	R.	Little	Robert James
Isdell	Liam P.	Lorigan	Maria
Jordan	Mags	Lough	Margaret
Kane	Wilfred Bernard	Loughnan	J.M.
Kavanagh	James W.	Lowry	Isaac A.
Kavanagh	Noreen	Luibhéad	Séamus
Kealy	James	Lyddy	Deirdre
Kearns	P.J.	Lynam	J.P.D.
Keating	Yvonne	Mac an Tánaiste	Seán
Keenan	M.	Mac Anna	T.F.
Keenan	Patrick Joseph	Mac Aodha	Lughaidh
Keith	J.	Mac Aodha	M.
Kelly	Anthony	Mac Aonghusa	Eamonn
Kelly	Brian Albert	Mac Canna	Peadar
Kelly	Edward	Mac Canna	Somhairle
Kelly	Miriam Roche	Mac Cárthaigh	Seán S.
Kelly	Niall	Mac Cionnaith	Peadar
Kelly	Patrick Joseph	Mac Cionnaith	Séamus
Kelly	Seamus	Mac Coitir	Eamon
Kelly	Una	Mac Coluim	Fionán
Kelly	William Joseph	Mac Conaonaigh	Lorcán

Mac Conchradha	Seán S.	Mac Spealáin	Prionsias Gearóid
Mac Conghalaigh	Seán F.	Mac Suibhne	Mícheál C.
Mac Conmara	Seán C.	Mac Suibhne	Proinnisias
Mac Cormaic	Macartan	Mac Suibhne	Risteárd
Mac Creanor	E.	Mac Tighearnáin	Seán S.
Mac Cumhghaill	Brian	Mac Uait	S.
Mac Curtáin	Seán	Mac William	W.
Mac Dermott	William	Macaulay	P.T.
Mac Domhnaill	Mícheál	Maguire	Elias
Mac Domhnaill	U.	Mahon	Don
Mac Donncha	Páraic A.	Mahon	John Stewart
Mac Donnchadha	Caoimhín	Mahony	C.
Mac Donnchadha	Liam Breandán	Mangan	Denis
Mac Donnchadha	Maitiú	Marchant	T.F.
Mac Donnell	J.	Marshall	Eva S.
Mac Duibhir	Séamus P.	Martin	Gabriel
Mac Eachmharcaigh	Mícheál	Martin	Thomas
Mac Eamuinn	Pádraig	Mathews	Deirdre
Mac Eoin	Peadar Pól	Mc Alister	J.
Mac Fheorais	Mathúin	McCallum	J.
Mac Fhlannchadha	Pádraig	McCarthy	Kevin
Mac Gabhann	Seán	McCarthy	Maria
Mac Gearailt	Tomás	McClean	Kevin
Mac Geehin	Mary F.	McClintock	W.J.
Mac Giolla Eoin	Seán	McCreedy	William
Mac Giolla		McElwaine	A.J.
Phádraig	Brian	McElwee	C.B.
Mac Giontaigh	Seán P.T.	McEnery	Daniel Thomas
Mac Gleannáin	Seán S.	McEvoy	Aidan
Mac Liam	Seán Seosamh	McEvoy	T.A.
Mac Loingsigh	Liam	McGlade	Patrick Joseph
Mac Millan (Jr)	W.	McGrath	Maria
Mac Namara	Joseph C.	McGrath	Seán
Mac Namara	Thaddeus	McGuill	Gerard
Mac Niocaill	Seoirse	McHugh	Nora
Mac Niocláis	Seán	McIntyre	Helen
Mac Pháidín	Seán A.	McIlroy	Thomas
Mac Riocaird	S.T.	McKell	R.C.
Mac Riodán	Tomás Seosaimh	McKenna	James
Mac Ruairc	Gerry	McLochlin	James
Mac Seáin	Pádraig	McMahon	Joseph Aloysius
Mac Sheehy	Brian	McManus	Hugh
Mac Sitric	Pádraig	McManus	John Doran

McMorris	Doreen	Ní Aingleis	Áine Bernadette
McMorrow	Noreen	Ní Bhraonáin	Caitlín
McNeill	John	Ní Bhroin	Deirdre
McSorley	Teresa	Ní Bhroite	Máire
McSweeney	John	Ní Chatháin	Helen
Meagher	Brigit	Ní Cheallaigh	Máire F.
Meaney	Edel	Ní Chinnéide	Máire F.
Meaney	Mary	Ní Chléirigh	Caithlin
Meeke	M.	Ní Chochláin	Mairéad
Mernagh	Niamh	Ní Chonaill	Máire T.
Mescal	John	Ní Chuidithe	Aingeal Úna
Mhic Aoidh	Hilde Bn.	Ní Dhálaigh	Brigid
Mitchell	John J.	Ní Dhálaigh	Suin P.
Molloy	John	Ní Dhubhshláinghe	Máiréad
Molloy	William R.	Ní Dhuibhir	Máire T.
Mongey	Alan	Ní Dhuighbhir	Máire T.
Moore	Columba M.	Ní Dhúill	Áine M.
Moran	J.	Ní Eilighe	Máire B.
Moran	James Francis	Ní Eirmhin	Eibhlín M.
Morell	James	Ní Fhearghusa	Jacqueline
Morgan	A.P.	Ní Ghallchobhair	Antoinette
Morris	Henry	Ní Ghiolla	
Morrison	Majella	Phádraig	Máiréad
Muckley	Nicola	Ní Ghógáin	Máire
Mulcahy	Ann	Ní Ghuidhin	Eibhlín
Mullally	M.	Ní Ghuidir	Eibhlín
Mullany	J.J.	Ní hIcí	F.
Murdoch	W.	Ní Lochlainn	Eibhlín M
Murnane	Terry	Ní Luadhagáin	Eibhlín
Murphy	Ian R.	Ní Luain	Máire
Murphy	John	Ní Mháirtín	Máire
Murphy	W.R.E.	Ní Mhaloid	Nóra B.
Murphy	J.J.	Ní Mhaoilchiaráin	Máire S.
Murray	John Fisher	Ní Mhaolthuille	Máire
Murray	Niamh	Ní Mhathghamhna	Siobhán
Murtagh	Éamonn	Ní Mhóráin	Muireann
Nash	David	Ní Mhurchadha	Bríd
Nesbitt	R.	Ní Mhurchú	Siobhán
Newell	F.W.	Ní Nualláin	Cristíne
Newell	P.	Ní Nualláin	Máire
Newell	W. O'B.	Ní Réagáin	Áine
Newell	William H.	Ní Ríordáin	Helen M.
Ní Aicéid	Pádraigín	Ní Ruadhagáin	Eibhlín

Ní Ruairc	Bernadette	Ó Cearnaigh	Gearóid
Ní Scannláin	Eibhlín	Ó Ciarba	Seán
Ní Seasnáin	Máiréad	Ó Ciardha	Eamonn
Ní Shiomóin	Seasamhain M.	Ó Cillín	Peadar S.
Ní Suibhne	Siobhán	Ó Cillín	Ruairi L.
Ní Súilleabháin	Caitríona	Ó Cléireacháin	Séamus
Ní Threasaigh	Marina	Ó Cléirigh	Pádraig S.
Nic Amhlaoibh	Mairéad	Ó Cléirigh	Seosamh B.
Nic Aodháin	Máire F.	Ó Coileáin	Domhnal S.
Nic Con Iomaire	Nuala	Ó Coinghéallaigh	Diarmuid B.
Nic Gabhann	Síle	Ó Colla	Tomás S.
Nicholls	W.	Ó Colmáin	Tomás
Nixon	John	Ó Conaill	Domhnall
Ó Baoghaill	Eoghan	Ó Conaill	Tomas P.
Ó Beagáin	Gearóid P.	Ó Conaire	Proinnsias
Ó Beoláin	Colm	Ó Conchubhair	Pádraig
Ó Beoláin	Pádraig S.	Ó Conghaile	Caoimhín Míchéal
Ó Breacháin	Eamonn	Ó Conghaile	Criostóir
Ó Breasláin	Seán S.	Ó Conghaile	Mícheál
Ó Briain	Seán	Ó Conghaile	Pádraig
Ó Bric	Breandán	Ó Conluain	Gearóid P.
Ó Broin	Risteárd	Ó Cróinín	Breandán
Ó Broin	Seán	Ó Cuilleanáin	Tomás A.
Ó Broin	Seán P.	Ó Cuinn	M.S.
Ó Broin	Seoirse	Ó Dálaigh	Cearbhall
Ó Brolcháin	Donnchadh	Ó Dálaigh	Mícheál Tomás
Ó Brolcháin	U.	Ó Dálaigh	Seán F.
Ó Bruin	Gearóid D.	Ó Diomasaigh	Seán
Ó Buachalla	Séamus	Ó Dochartaigh	Cathal
Ó Buachalla	Seán P.	Ó Dochartaigh	Eamon
Ó Caoimh	Conchúir C.	Ó Dóláin	S.
Ó Caoindealbhain	Tomás	Ó Domhnaill	Pádraig
Ó Casaide	Seán S.	Ó Domhnaill	Peadar
Ó Catháin	Gearóid S.	Ó Domhnalláin	Tomás
Ó Catháin	Stiophán	Ó Donnabháin	Seán S.
Ó Ceallacháin	Colm	Ó Donnabháin	Pádraig P.
Ó Ceallacháin	D.F.	Ó Donnabháin	Peadar S.
Ó Ceallacháin	Pádraig	Ó Donnagáin	Conal G.
Ó Ceallaigh	Pádraic	Ó Donnchadha	Aodán
Ó Ceallaigh	Proinnsias A.	Ó Donnchadha	Gary
Ó Ceallaigh	Proinnsias	Ó Donnchadha	Proinnsias
Ó Ceallaigh	Proinsias	Ó Donnchadha	Tomás
Ó Cearbhaill	Seán G.	Ó Donnghusa	Seán

Ó Dubhagáin	Muiris	Ó hOistín	Liam
Ó Dubháin	Conchubháir	Ó hUallacháin	Pádraig
Ó Dubháin	Seán	Ó hUallacháin	Séamus
Ó Dubhda	S.	Ó hUallacháin	Domhnall
Ó Dubhgáin	Amhlaoibh	Ó Láimhín	Pádraig S.
Ó Dubhghaill	Brian	Ó Laoghaire	Donncadh
Ó Dubhthaigh	Bearnárd	Ó Laoi	Tomás C.
Ó Dubhthaigh	Proinnsias	Ó Laoire	Seán S.
Ó Dughaill	Proinnsias	Ó Leathlobhair	Liam P.
Ó Duinneacha	Séamus F.	Ó Lionáin	M.
Ó Duinnín	Pádraig	Ó Lionáird	Mícheál
Ó Duinnshléibhe	Seán S.	Ó Lionáird	Seán M.
Ó Dunadaighe	Domhnall	Ó Lochlainn	Gearóid
Ó Fallamháin	Séamus	Ó Loingsigh	Mícheál A.
Ó Fiacháin	Tomás A.	Ó Loingsigh	Pádraig M.
Ó Fiachra	Seán M.	Ó Longáin	Máirtín
Ó Fionnghalaigh	Pádraig S.	Ó Longáin	Seán P.
Ó Flannagáin	Mícheál S.	Ó Luanaigh	T.
Ó Flannagáin	Mícheál	Ó Madagáin	Breandán A.
Ó Floinn	Seán	Ó Máille	Pádraig P.
Ó Floinn	Tomás	Ó Máille	Peader G.
Ó Foghlú	Risteard	Ó Mainnín	Liam P.
Ó Fuaráin	Eamonn	Ó Maoláin	P.C.
Ó Gadhra	Mícheál S.	Ó Maolalaidh	Criostóir S.
Ó Gallchobhair	Pádraig	Ó Maolchatha	Liam
Ó Gara	Anne	Ó Maoldia	Breandán
Ó Geallabháin	Mícheál	Ó Maolmhichíl	Liam
Ó Gláimhín	Tadhg	Ó Maolmhuaidh	Proinsias P.
Ó Gormáin	Tony	Ó Maonaigh	Mícheál S.
Ó Greidhm	Risteard	Ó Mathghamhna	Eibhear P.
Ó hAodha	Muiris	Ó Mathúna	Mícheál
Ó hAodha	Séamus	Ó Modhráin	Séamus F.
Ó hÉalaithe	Denis	Ó Mórdha	Mícheál
Ó hEdhrain	Mícheál	Ó Muircheartaigh	Eighneachán
Ó hEidhin	Mícheál	Ó Muircheartaigh	Tomás
Ó hEidhin	Oilibhéir	Ó Muireadhaigh	Labhrás Seosamh
Ó hEidhin	Pádraig	Ó Muirghis	Tomás G.
Ó hEigceartaigh	Diarmuid	Ó Muirí	Silvester
Ó hÉigearta	Liam A.	Ó Murchú	Conchubhar B.
Ó hEigeartaigh	Seán	Ó Murchú	Fionnbarra
Ó hEilí	Séamus	Ó Murchú	Seán Pádraig
Ó hOdhráin	M.B.	Ó Murchú	Breandán E.
Ó hOdhráin	Mícheál S.	Ó Náirigh	Pádraig

Ó Néill	Pádraig S.	O'Connell	Jeremiah Ambrose
Ó Nualláin	Mícheál	O'Connell	P.
Ó Nualláin	Pádraig	O'Connor	D.J.
Ó Raithbheartaigh		O'Connor	Geraldine
	Toirdhealbhach	O'Connor	Jeremiah Joseph
Ó Ríordáin	S.B.	O'Connor	Orlaith
Ó Rodaigh	Mícheál	O'Connor	Thomas P.
Ó Séadaigh	Diarmaid	O'Connor	Tom
Ó Seaghdha	Domhnall C.	O'Connor	Torlach
Ó Seasnáin	Donnchadh P.	O'Doherty	Carmel
Ó Seitheacháin	C.	O'Donoghue	J.
Ó Siaghail	Tomás P.C.	O'Donovan	Lily
Ó Sibhéir	Annraoi S.	O'Donovan	Kevin
Ó Siocfhradha	Tadhg	O'Driscoll	D.F.
Ó Síocháin	Tadhg	O'Flynn	John
Ó Siochrú	Ciarán E.	O'Galligan	George R.
Ó Siochrú	Mícheál	O'Gorman	Anthony
Ó Sionnaigh	Pádraig S.	O'Hara	T.
Ó Sioradáin	Mícheál	O'Keeffe	Micheal John
Ó Síothcháin	Diarmuid P.	O'Loughlin	T.
Ó Súilleabháin	Conchubhair	O'Neill	Ann Marie Clare
	Séamus	O'Neill	Liz
Ó Súilleabháin	Eoghan	O'Neill	Joseph James
Ó Súilleabháin	Eoin	O'Neill	Patrick
Ó Súilleabháin	Gearóid A.	O'Neill	Robert H.
Ó Súilleabháin	Mícheál	O'Neill	G.F.
Ó Súilleabháin	P.E.	O'Regan	Brendan
Ó Súilleabháin	Párthalán	O'Reilly	L.
Ó Súilleabháin	Séamus L.	O'Riordan	Jeremiah
Ó Súilleabháin	Proinnsias S.	O'Riordan	Helen
Ó Súilleabháin	Seán	Osborne	A.T.
Ó Súilleabháin	Tomás	O'Shea	Mary
Ó Tighearnaigh	Proinnsias	O'Sullivan	Anne
Ó Tiodhgáin	Liam	O'Sullivan	Daniel
Ó Tuama	Fionnbarra	O'Sullivan	Eileen
Ó Tuama	Tadhg	O'Sullivan	James Luke
O'Brien	Catherine	O'Sullivan	M.
O'Callaghan	Andrew	O'Sullivan	Máirín
O'Carroll	Catherine	O'Sullivan	Patrick
O'Carroll	P.F.	O'Sullivan	Thomas
O'Carroll	Kate	O'Tierney	F.
O'Connell	Thomas Francis	O'Toole	Lynda
O'Connell	Donal	Patten	James

Patterson	James	Seantan	Mairéad
Pedlow	W.	Semple	John
Perry	John	Seymour	M.S.
Perry	William Millar	Shannon	Charles Patrick
Piogóid	Siobhán	Shannon	P.
Pleamonn	Pádraig Seosamh	Sheehy	E.
Porter	D.C.	Sheehy	Morgan M.
Porter	George	Sheridan	Elaine
Potterton	R.	Sheridan	John E.
Power	Ger	Sheridan	Robert Nicholas
Prendergast	M.	Sherwin	Mary
Proctor	Moira	Simpson	Alexander J.
Purser	Alfred	Skeffington	J.B.
Pye	Mary Bell	Skelly	Gerardine
Quigley	Mary	Smith	Christopher
Quinlan	Patrick	Smyth	John
Quirke	Gerard	Smyth	Sheila
Ralph	Joseph	Stack	Eamon
Ramsbottom	Linda	Stapleton	Hazel
Réamonn	Seosamh	Starrit	S.
Richards	Ruth	Steede	J.
Ring	Emer	Steele	J.
Riordan	Eugene K.	Stokes	Isaiah Joseph
Rís	Nioclás C.	Strong	T.K.
Roantree	D.J.	Stronge	Samuel E.
Robertson	Thomas Jaffray	Sullivan	M.
Robertson	W.	Sullivan	Robert
Robinson	John	Sutton	Joan
Robinson	Robert	Sweeney	Thomas
Robinson	W.	Teegan	William Thomas
Rodgers	H.W.M.	Terry	Seán A.
Rodgers	John W	Thompson	Archibald
Rogers	John Croston	Tibbs	John Harding
Rooney	J.F.	Tóibín	Tomás
Ross	James	Toolan	Eugene
Rowan	William Henry	Topping	John
Ryan	Desmond	Travers	Michael
Ryan	P.F.	Turnbull	Robert
Savage	William	Twomey	Timothy
Sayles	Howard Alan	Tynan	Fionnuala
Scanlon	Siobhan	Tyner	Thomas
Scott	Audrey	Ua Grianáin	Tomás P.
Scott	Samuel	Ua Loinghsigh	Eoghan

Uí Bhreasláin	Clár	Waters	Charles J.
Uí Chathasaigh	Fionnghuala	Watson	George Hugh
Uí Chongaile	Máire	Weatherup	Samuel
Uí Dhuinnshléibhe	Bríd	Weir	Tony
Uí Ghrianna	Catríona	Weir	W.M.
Uí Ríordáin	Bríd	Welply	William Henry
Uí Shé	Máire	White	John
Varilly	Mary B.T.	White	William
Walsh	Michael	Whyte	Martin
Walsh	Thomas	Williams	Joan
Walsh	Annie	Wilson	D.M.
Walsh	E.	Wilson	James
Walsh	Liam	Wingfield	E.J.M.
Walsh-Bohan	Maureen	Worsley	H.
Walshe	James Anthony	Wyse	Andrew N. Bonaparte
Warner	J. McK.	Yates	J.
Warnock	William Herbert	Young	E.

Inspectors of Guidance Services and Psychologists, 1965–99

The following is a list of Inspectors of Guidance Services and Psychologists who were or had been employed in the Department before the establishment of the National Educational Psychological Service (NEPS) in 1999.

Blain, Sidney
Bradley, John
Burke, Kieran
Carson, Rita
Connolly, Brendan
Corcoran, Rory
Cotter, Breda
Coyle, Mary
Crowley, Peadar
Culbert, John
Donoghue, Tom*
Gordon, Mary
Greene, Gabrielle
Grogan, Margaret
Heavey, Bernadette
Hennessy, Colette
Kavanagh, Frank
Keating, Anne
King, Denis
Leahy, Máire
MacCurtain, Lee
McDonald, Nuala
Moran, Lily
Moran, Therese
Morris, Dermot
Morrow, Ruby

Mulholland, Ann
Mulrooney, Vincent
Ó Casaide, Feargus
Ó Dúill, Pádraig
Ó Gormáin, Tony*
Ó hOdhráin, Tom
O'Connor, Torlach*
O'Dowd, Therese
O'Dwyer, Paddy
O'Leary, John
O'Neill, Feargal
O'Shaughnessy, Noel
O'Sullivan, Ann
Poynton, Audrey
Rogers, Colin
Sheehan, Ann Marie
Sheehan, Michael
Tyrrell, Trish
Vaughan, Austin
Walshe, Joan
Walsh, Valerie
Walsh-Bohan, Maureen*
Wright, Pam

* did not transfer to NEPS

Chief Inspectors and Deputy Chief Inspectors, 1922–2008

1922–71

Chief Inspectors Primary Branch	Chief Inspectors Secondary Branch	Chief Inspectors Vocational Branch
T.P. O'Connor	S. Mac Niocaill	W.V. Dixon
M. Franklin	T. Ó Raithbheartáigh	R. Turnbull
P.S. Ó Tighearnaigh	L. Close	J. Ingram
J.A. Kyle	M. Ó Siochrú	P.E. Ó Suilleabháin
M. Kinsella	T. Ó Floinn	M.M. Sheehy
S. Ó Súilleabháin	R. Ó Foghlú	M. Ó Flannagáin
D.F. ÓhUallacháin		
G. Ó Suilleabháin		

1972–90

Chief Inspectors	Deputy Chief Inspectors Primary Branch	Deputy Chief Inspectors Secondary Branch	Deputy Chief Inspectors Vocational Branch
M. Ó Flannagáin	G. Ó Suilleabháin	R. Ó Foghlú	M. Mac Eachmharcaigh
G. Ó Súilleabháin	T. Ó Cuilleanáin	S. Ó Laoire	T. Ua Grianán
D.F. Ó Ceallacháin	S.B. Ó Cléirigh	P. Ó Nualláin	D.F. Ó Ceallacháin
P. Ó Nualláin	C. Ó Suilleabháin	S. Mac Carthaigh	L. Ó Maolchatha
L. Ó Maolchatha	M. Ó Mórdha	D. Ó Seaghdha	P. Ó Náirigh
P. Ó Nualláin	D. Ó Coileáin		M. Ó Longáin
	M. Ó Sioradáin		
	S. de Buitléir		
	S. Mac Gleannáin		

1991–2002

Chief Inspectors	Deputy Chief Inspectors Primary Branch	Deputy Chief Inspectors Post-Primary Branch
S. Mac Gleannáin	S. Ó Fiachra	D. Ó Seaghdha
E. Stack	G. Ó Conluain	C. Ó Dálaigh

2003–08

Chief Inspector	Deputy Chief Inspector *Policy Support Subdivision**	Deputy Chief Inspector *Regional Subdivision**
E. Stack	G. Ó Conluain	C. Ó Dálaigh

*As part of the restructuring of the inspectorate in 2003, the role of both deputy chief inspectors changed to Head of Policy Support sub-division and Head of Regional sub-division.

Index